INSTRUMENTS OF THE ORCHESTRA

THE BASSOON
AND CONTRABASSOON

THE BASSOON
AND
CONTRABASSOON

LYNDESAY G. LANGWILL

LONDON · ERNEST BENN LIMITED

NEW YORK · W W NORTON & COMPANY INC

First published by Ernest Benn Limited 1965
Bouverie House · Fleet Street · London · EC4
and W. W. Norton & Company
55 Fifth Avenue · New York 3

Published in Canada by
General Publishing Company Limited · Toronto

© *Lyndesay G. Langwill 1965*

Printed in Great Britain

ISBN 13: 978-0-393-33662-7

Foreword

by PROFESSOR SIDNEY NEWMAN

M.A. (OXON.), HON.D.MUS. (DUNELM.), F.R.S.E., F.R.C.O., F.T.C.L.

I BELIEVE this to be the first full-scale book in any language devoted to the bassoon—a history of its emergence and development and of its orchestral employment, a study of its physical properties, a conspectus of its teaching apparatus ('methods' and 'tutors') and of its own music outside the orchestral field in solo and chamber music, a biographical survey of a large selection of notable performers of the last two centuries, and throughout a full documentation of all relevant sources. It is a special pleasure for me to be privileged to be the first to welcome its appearance, for in the course of some two dozen years of close acquaintance with the author in Edinburgh (during which time I have as a conductor been indebted on innumerable occasions to him for his fundamental contributions as orchestral performer) I have watched with admiration the steady pressure of research and the flow of expert published articles on special studies within this field which he has maintained in pursuance of a lifetime's study commenced many years earlier. It had become increasingly clear, especially having regard to the fruitful climate of interest and the high standard of critical researches in the history of musical instruments promoted and inspired by the collaborative activities of the Galpin Society in these last twenty years (a Society of which Mr. Langwill was one of the seven founder-members), that there was a book that ultimately ought to be and must be written. How it comes about that an authoritative work on so specialist and yet ultimately so large a field of musicological study should be written by a busy practising Chartered Accountant the author himself explains in his Preface. What he could not in modesty add it is my pleasure to record—namely, that some fifteen years ago Mr. Langwill was elected an Honorary Fellow of Trinity College of Music in recognition of his musicological studies, and that in 1964 the University of Edinburgh conferred upon him the degree of M.A. *honoris causa.*

This book supplies the bass line to the growing ensemble of a distinguished series of publications devoted to 'the Instruments of the

Orchestra'. The author has occasion somewhere to hint his suspicion that composers in general have been inclined to take the bassoon for granted to the effect that they keep it inordinately busy. It may well be that the general public—devotees of orchestral music—are likewise inclined to take the bassoon for granted except in moments of expressive solo or of acrobatic dexterity. That is not a mistake that any conductor or any single member of the wind ensemble will make, for they recognise the second bassoonist to play a role of cardinal responsibility for the whole ensemble. But to what extent do players themselves take their modern (or comparatively modern) instruments for granted? Anyone, whether he be professional or amateur, who once begins to be historically inquisitive will I think find here either the answers to his questions or direction to the further reading that will satisfy him as to what is known. Some, like myself, will find age-old pretty etymological romances exploded; some will be fascinated (as I) to find that attempts at fully rational mechanical perfection of the instrument have always been confronted with the fact that preservation of the true character of the tone sets a limit to such aspirations. Some may find that such a wealth of detailed information whilst satisfying their immediate interests yet goes far beyond these. That indeed is as it should be, for this is both a study and history of the instrument and an authoritative source book, and as it is the fruit of unremitting scholarly research and a lifetime's experience I hope it may itself prove the stimulus to further discoveries and studies in the years to come wherever its influence may fall.

June 1965   SIDNEY NEWMAN
                                          Reid Professor of Music
                                         University of Edinburgh

Preface

THE present volume marks the culmination of half a century of interest in music and in the bassoon in particular. As a schoolboy I became fascinated by the strange appearance of the long dark instrument always played, in those days pre-1914, in the left corner of the theatre band-pit.

The old player, though certainly far from proficient, was my hero whose every note was listened to and even his fingering was studied from the lofty heights of the gallery. My parents, however, would not hear of my acquiring a bassoon so I chose the 'cello which enabled me to take part in orchestras which never included a bassoon until professionals attended the concerts twice a year. After ten years, however, I was enabled to purchase a bassoon from my teacher who had been an army bandsman but played with taste and skill in the Reid Orchestra under Sir Donald Tovey.

A Christmas gift of Canon Galpin's classic *Old English Instruments of Music* inspired me to read all I could about my instrument in books of reference in libraries and the copious extracts then made were to serve as a basis of research in many branches of musical history.

The subject of Waits attracted me as the bassoon was a frequent component of those small groups. The old west gallery minstrels of the English churches from 1640–1840 likewise aroused my interest, for a bassoonist was a regular member of these groups which were often composed of Waits.

The monotonous repetition of a few dubious statements about the origin of the bassoon prompted me to write a succession of articles and soon I was invited to read papers before The Royal Musical Association, The Society of Antiquaries, The Incorporated Society of Musicians, music clubs and schools. The publication of Heckel's *Der Fagott* in 1931 made me decide I must learn German, which I did, so as to translate the book into English. The presentation of a copy of the translation to Herr Heckel led to a visit to Biebrich and a friendship which lasted until his death in 1952.

A knowledge of German had proved essential to the study of instrumental history and enabled me to widen my reading while I built up a small specialist library from the limited resources available to the musicologist. Chief among these were the now rare catalogues of the instrumental collections in Berlin, Vienna, Boston, Brussels, Paris and New York. The acquisition of a large number of catalogues of lesser collections led me to compile a card-index of bassoon-makers—soon extended to makers of all wind instruments. When in 1960 the index cards numbered 3,000, I decided to publish it privately and the first edition was exhausted in a year. Many additions were received from readers throughout the world and in 1962 I published an enlarged illustrated second edition of which 800 copies have been sent all over the world.

The information acquired from correspondents, museum curators and private collectors, enlarged my knowledge of the bassoon which I continued to play, as well as a contrabassoon which Edinburgh University owned without a player.

An invitation from the late Eric Blom to contribute to the Fifth Edition of Grove's *Dictionary* fresh articles on the bassoon, the contra and Waits, and a score of other smaller articles enabled me to place on permanent record the results of my research. The subsequent invitation to write the present volume followed in 1963 and I must confess that the assignment filled me with trepidation as I considered it could be undertaken only in my retirement. Nothing daunted, however, I have completed it with the generous help of many fellow-members of the Galpin Society of which I became a founder-member in 1946. Others too have helped me greatly and have permitted me to quote from the writings of themselves or deceased relatives. To the following then I acknowledge my indebtedness: Messrs. A. C. Baines, P. A. T. Bate, Dr. A. Bouhuys, Mr. G. A. S. Dibley, Mrs. V. F. Carse (on behalf of the late Professor Adam Carse), Dipl. Ing. Franz Groffy, Mr. Will Jansen, Dr. H. Lowery, Mrs. Alan Mackay (on behalf of the late Professor Bernard Hague), Messrs. G. Melville-Mason (for his valuable appendix of Music and Discography, and for help with proof-reading); Maurice M. Porter, L.D.S., R.C.S., and in particular to Mr. Richard Newton and Mr. R. Morley-Pegge for invaluable assistance in reading the text and offering suggestions for its improvement.

The writing of this book has been carried out during a busy professional life not of a musician but of an accountant. If, therefore, it falls short of the requirements of the learned musical historian, it will, I trust, appeal to the amateur musician to whom the study of instrumental history may be, as to me, a parergon—a pursuit to sweeten leisure.

Contents

Illustrations

PLATE I

Joints of the bassoon and cross-section of the instrument as shown in
La Borde's *Essai sur la Musique* (1780).

Fig. 1. A. The bell.
B. The long- or bass-joint.
C. The butt or double-joint. (*Left:* back. *Right:* front.)
D. The wing- or tenor-joint. ((*a*) back; (*b*) front.)
Ee. The crook.
fg. The reed.
Holes 1–6 for L.1, 2, 3 and R.1, 2, 3; 7 and 8 covered by keys for R.4;
9 for RT; and 12 for LT; 10, 11 and 13 covered by keys for LT.

Fig. 2. Cross-section.
L. The U-bend in the bore.
[*Vide* Chapter 1, pp. 2–3, and Chapter 3, pp. 36–37.]

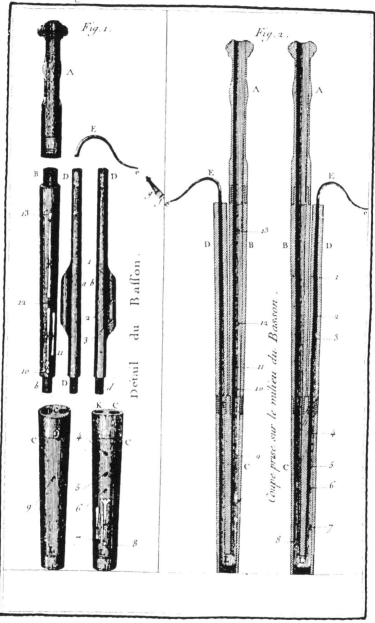

Fig. 1.

Fig. 2.

Détail du Basson.

Coupe prise sur le milieu du Basson.

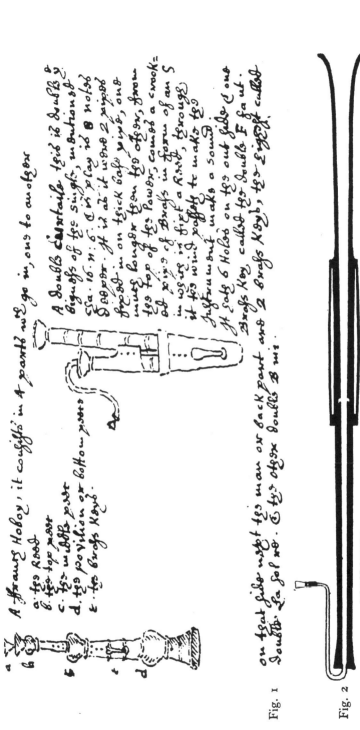

A France Hoboy, it consists in 4 parts not go in, one to another

a. the Reed
b. the top part
c. the midolt part
d. the pavilion or bottom part
e. the brass keys.

A double Curtaile it is 8 & 23 &
Bignessess of the single instrument
ca. 16. n. 6. & it play it 8 notes
Lower. If it is woodd 2 pipes
fixed in on thick base pipe, one
much longer than the other, from
the top of the power, comes a crook=
of pine of brass in form of an S
it goes in & fret a Reede, through
it the wind passes to make the
Instrument make a sound.
It hath 6 holes on the out side (one
brass key called the double F fa ut.

on the out side next the man or back part and 2 brass keys, the Eight called
double La sol re. & the other double B mi.

Fig. I

Fig. 2

BASSPOMMER

3

PLATE 2

Fig. 1 Drawing and description of a double curtaile by Randle Holme, c. 1688. Front view showing 6 holes and the F-key. On the back would be the B♭, and D keys (and two thumb-holes for C and E—not specified in the MS.). [*Vide* Chapter 1, p. 10.]

Fig. 2 'Bass-Pommer: cross-section for comparison with Dulzian and Fagott in Plate 3.

PLATE 3

Nikol Rosenkron, Nürnberg (1679), with a Gross-Bass-Pommer. [*Vide* Chapter 2, pp. 21–22.]

Dulzian and Fagott: cross-section. Note the Fagott has a bell extension and a narrower bore.

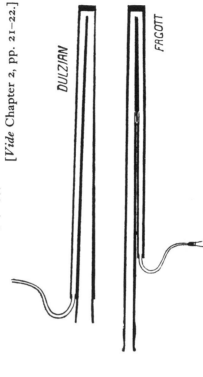

4

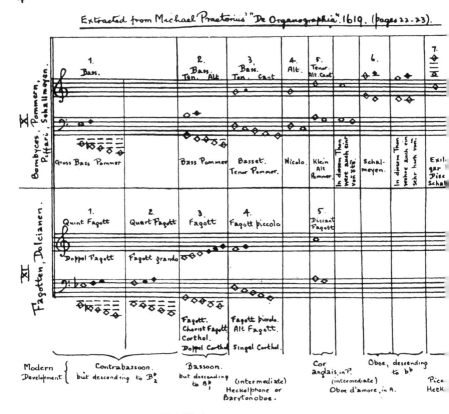

Extracted from Michael Praetorius' "De Organographia". 1619. (pages 22-23).

PLATE 4

In 1619 the Pommers were still in use beside the Fagotten. The table shows the compass of the respective members of both families, and below, the modern survivals which have evolved from those above.

[*Vide* Chapter 2, pp. 20 and 22–23.]

PLATE 5 [*opposite*]

Praetorius' Plate XI showing the two sizes of Shawm and three sizes of Pommer. The presence of a 'pirouette' in the cases of all but the Bass-Pommer should be noted. The Gross-Bass-Pommer appears on another plate (VI) and is not shown here.

[*Vide* Chapter 2, pp. 22–23.]

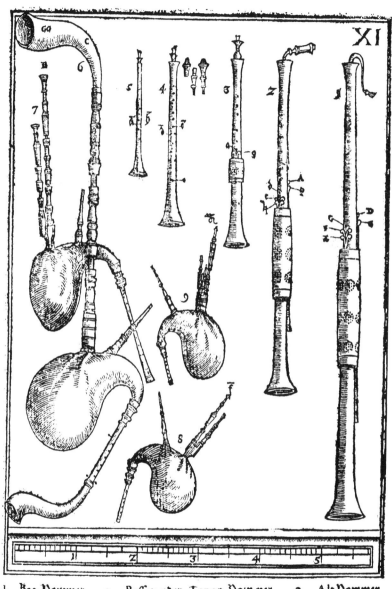

XI

1. Bas Pommer   2. Baſſet oder Tenor-Poinmer.   3. Alt Pommer.
4. Diſcant Schalmey.   5. Klein Schalmey.   6. Groſſer Bock.
7. Schaper Pfeiff.   8. Hümmelchen.   9. Dudey.

B ij

6

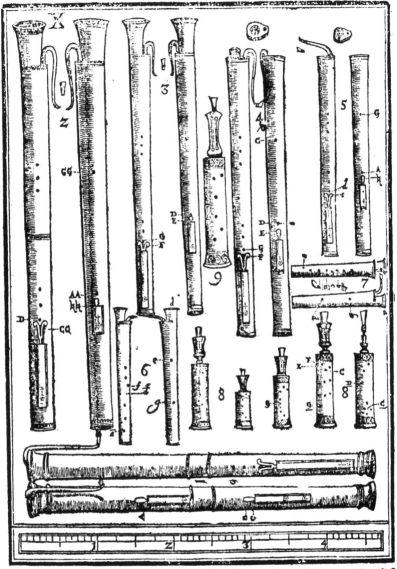

1. Sorduen-Bas auff beyden Seiten. GG. 2. Doppel-Fagott bis ins GG. 3. Essen Chorist-Fagott C. 4. Gedact Chorist-Fagott. C. 5. Singu Kortholt. Baser oder Tenor zum Chorist-
Fagott. G. 6. Alt. d. 7. Discant oder Exilent zum Chor: Fagott. a. 8. Stimm erst Racketten,
9. Groß-Rackett/ so tieff als der gar Grosse Bas-Bombard, CC, Uff 16 · Fuß Thon.

NB Buden 1. 2. 3. 4. 5. stehen die Buchstaben des Clavis beym Loch/ do es zugemacht wird.
Im 6. 7. 8. 8. aber stehen die Buchstaben des Clavis, do das Loch offen bleibt.

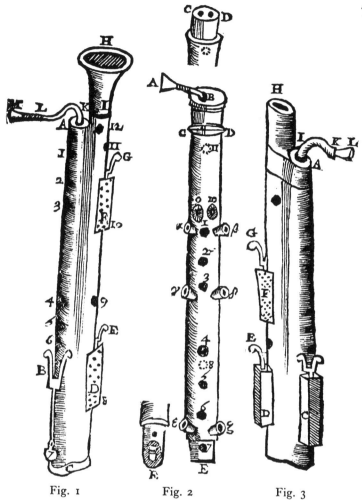

Fig. 1   Fig. 2   Fig. 3

PLATE 7

Mersenne (1636) shows (Figs. 1 and 3) two 'Fagots' and (Fig. 2) a Courtaut. Note the key cover-plates on the Fagots and the 'tetines', small wooden tubes protruding from the Courtaut—another obsolete cylindrically-bored instrument. [*Vide* Chap. 2, pp. 25–26.]

PLATE 6 [*opposite*]

Praetorius' Plate X showing the five sizes of Fagott. The type instrument the Chorist-Fagott is of two kinds, No. 3 unmuted and No. 4 muted. No. 1 is a Bass-Sordun, an obsolete type of cylindrically-bored, wood-wind, double-reed instrument. Nos. 8 and 9: a set (Stimmwerck) of Racketts, another obsolete type. *Vide* Chapter 2, pp. 27–28.   [*Vide* Chapter 2, p. 23.]

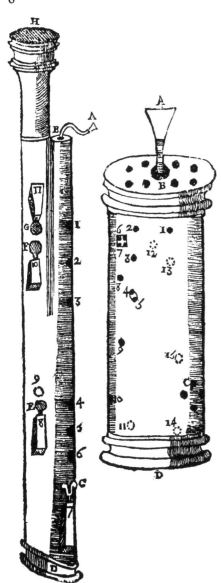

Fig. 4   Fig. 5

PLATE 8

Mersenne's 'Basson' (Fig. 4) and 'Cervelat' (Fig. 5). The crude drawings are reproduced from the originals. The Cervelat (*aliter* Rackett, Wurst-Fagott) is shown here *without* a 'pirouette'. *Cf.* Plate 6.   [*Vide* Chapter 2, pp. 26–28.]

PLATE 9 [*opposite*]

Fig. 1   Portrait of a mid-seventeenth-century bassoon-player. One of a series depicting 'The Senses', but whether this represents 'Hearing' or 'Smelling' (as the player is taking a pinch of snuff) is not certain. The picture is in the Art Museum of Aachen and is reproduced by kind permission of the Director.   [*Vide* Chapter 2, p. 28.]

Fig. 2   A unique drawing of a wood-wind maker, *c.* 1698. It is specially noteworthy that both Dulzians and an early Bassoon are portrayed.   [*Vide* Chapter 2, pp. 28–29.]

9

Fig. 2

Fig. 1

10

This detail from a very large painting of a procession in Antwerp in 1616
provides valuable evidence of the employment of the Dulzian as
bass. Note that it is played at the left side with hands reversed.

[*Vide* Chapter 2, p. 30.]

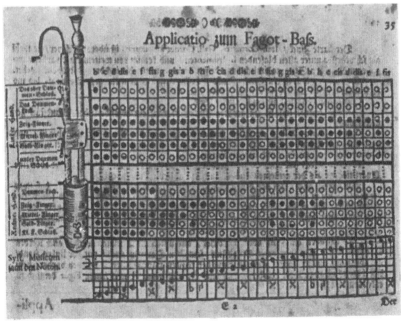

Majer's fingering-chart of 1732. The drawing of the 3-keyed bassoon is
very inaccurate. [*Vide* Chapter 3, p. 35.]

PLATE 10

11

Num. VIII.

Figur zu dem BASSON,
Wird p. 101. gebunden.

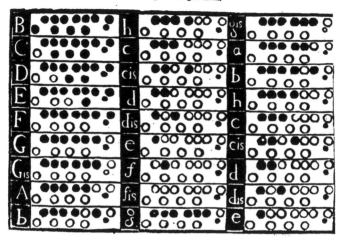

Num. IX.

Figur zu dem Teutschen BASSON.
Wird p. 104. beygebunden.

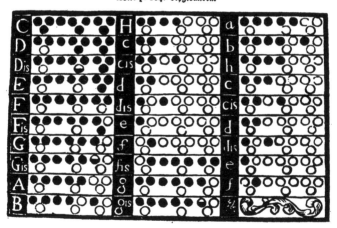

PLATE 11

Eisel's fingering-charts of 1738.

Above: For a 4-keyed bassoon. *Below:* For a 2-keyed dulzian which he terms 'Teutsche Basson' or 'Bombardo'.

This is the earliest foreign chart for a 4-keyed bassoon. Walsh in London, however, had published one in 1730. (*Vide* p. 166.)

[*Vide* Chapter 3, p. 35.]

12

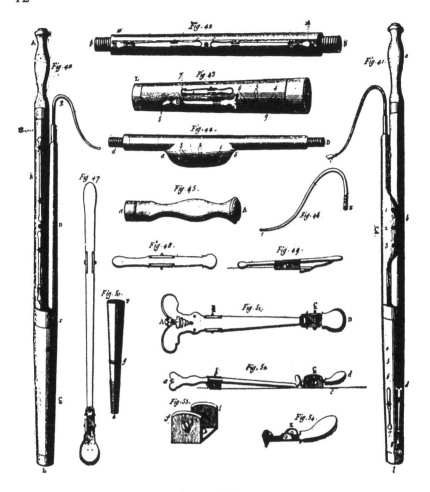

PLATE 12

Plate IX in the section *Lutherie* in Diderot and D'Alembert's *Encyclo-pédie* (1751–65). The various parts of a 4-keyed bassoon are shown in detail. At that period keys were mounted in saddles (Fig. 53) and the key-heads were padded with flat leather. The long reed (Fig. 50) is noteworthy.   [*Vide* Chapter 3, pp. 35–36.]

PLATE 13 [*opposite*]

This engraving of 1780 from La Borde's *Essai sur la Musique* shows a 4-keyed bassoon being played to the accompaniment of a 'clavecin vertical'.   [*Vide* Chapter 3, p. 36.]

Clavecin Vertical   *Basson.*

14

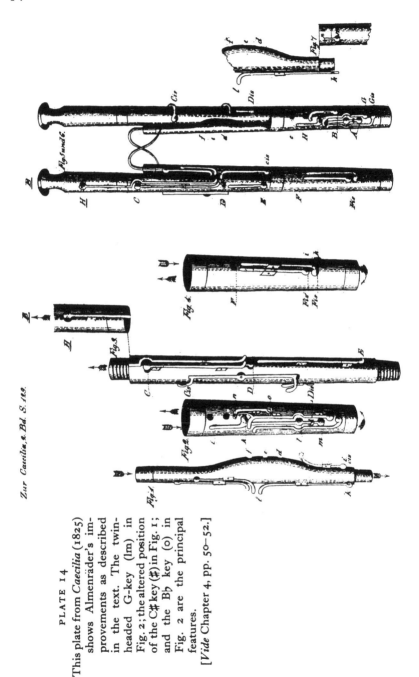

PLATE 14

This plate from *Caecilia* (1825) shows Almenräder's improvements as described in the text. The twin-headed G-key (lm) in Fig. 2; the altered position of the C♯ key (♯) in Fig. 1; and the B♭ key (o) in Fig. 2 are the principal features.

[*Vide* Chapter 4, pp. 50–52.]

15

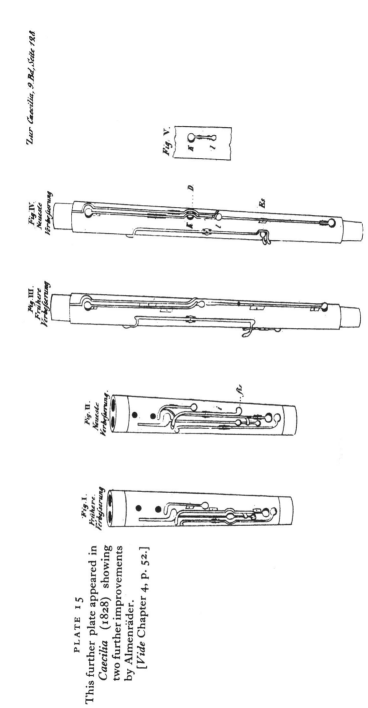

Zur Caecilia, 9.Bd.Seite 248.

Fig. IV.
Neueste
Verbesserung

Fig. III.
Frühere
Verbesserung

Fig. V.

Fig. II.
Neueste
Verbesserung

Fig. I.
Frühere
Verbesserung

PLATE 15
This further plate appeared in
Caecilia (1828) showing
two further improvements
by Almenräder.
[*Vide* Chapter 4, p. 52.]

Fagotte nach dieser neuesten Verbesserung werden verfertigt bey B.Schott's Söhnen in Mainx.

16

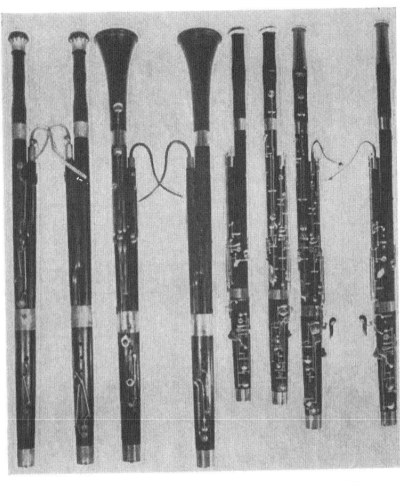

Fig. 1   Fig. 2   Fig. 3   Fig. 4

PLATE 16

Fig. 1 (*Back and Front*). Bassoon by Winnen, Paris, *c.* 1840. 7 keys—one engraved 'Inventé par Félix, mécanicien à Paris'. The curious lie of the keys is unique. Height, 1,270 mm.

Fig. 2 (*Back and Front*). Bassonore by Winnen, Paris, *c.* 1844. Though claimed to have four times the power of a bassoon, the instrument was a failure.   [*Vide* Chap. 4, pp. 58–59.]

Fig. 3 (*Back and Front*). Modern Heckel Bassoon.

Fig. 4 (*Back and Front*). Another type of Heckel Bassoon. The hand-rest or crutch is clearly shown.   [*Vide* Chap. 1, p. 3 and Chap. 4, pp. 54–55.]

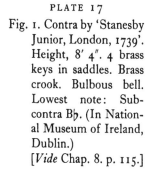

17

Fig. 1. Contra by 'Stanesby Junior, London, 1739'. Height, 8′ 4″. 4 brass keys in saddles. Brass crook. Bulbous bell. Lowest note: Subcontra B♭. (In National Museum of Ireland, Dublin.) [*Vide* Chap. 8. p. 115.]

Fig. 2. Contra by 'Stehle, vormals Küss, Wien', *c.* 1840. Height originally 6′ 6″ but now 8′ 4″. Originally 8 brass keys and brass bell giving Contra C. The Rev. Canon Galpin owned this instrument formerly and had the bell extended and a 9th key added to give Sub-contra B♭. (In Museum of Fine Arts, Boston, US.A.). [*Vide* Chapter 8, *passim.*]

Fig. 1   Fig. 2

18

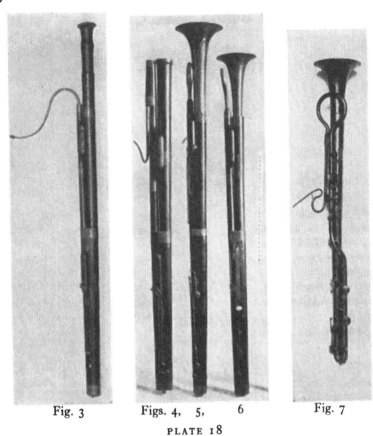

Fig. 3   Figs. 4, 5,   6   Fig. 7

PLATE 18

Fig. 3. Contra by Doke, Linz. Late eighteenth century. Height, 5′ 8″. 6 brass keys. Large crook. Lowest note: Contra C.

Fig. 4. Contra by W. Horák, Prague, c. 1830. Height, 5′ 1″. 5 brass keys. Double butt. Entirely of wood. Lowest note: Contra C.

Fig. 5. Contra by unknown Austrian maker, mid-nineteenth century. Height, 5′ 6″. 10 brass keys.

Fig. 6. Contra by Schöllnast, Pressburg. Early nineteenth century. Height, 5′ 2″. 6 brass keys.   [*Vide* Chapter 8, p. 119.]

Both Figs. 5 and 6 have a coiled brass crook, flared brass bell, and lowest note Contra C.

Fig. 7. Brass Contra by Johann Stehle, Vienna, c. 1850. Height, 5′ 6″. 15 keys. Ophicleide shape. Heyer-Leipzig Coll., No. 1404.
          [*Vide* Chapter 8, p. 122.]

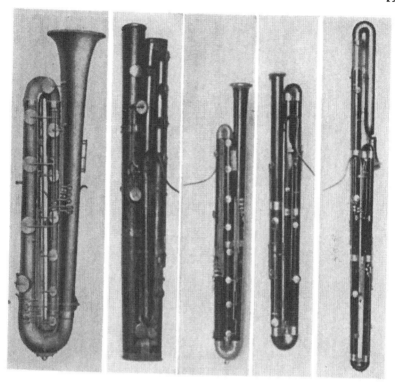

Fig. 8   Fig. 9   Fig. 10   Fig. 11   Fig. 12

PLATE 19

Fig. 8. Contrebasse-à-anche as designed by Mahillon, Brussels, in 1868. 17 keys. Lowest note D,. Entirely of brass. [*Vide* Chap. 8, p. 124.]

Fig. 9. Contrabassophon by H. J. Haseneier, Coblenz, *c.* 1849. Height, 4′ 8″. 19 brass keys. Wide bore and large holes. Lowest note: Contra C. (Heyer-Leipzig Coll., No. 1403.)
[*Vide* Chap. 8, pp. 126 and 128–129.]

Fig. 10. Contra by W. Bradka, Vienna, 1888. Height, 4′ 5″. Fourfold coil. 22 keys. Lowest note: Contra C.   [*Vide* Chap. 8, p. 127.]

Fig. 11. Contrabassoon by Heckel, Biebrich, *c.* 1877. Height 4′. Stritter System: played right hand above left, but usual fingering. Lowest note: Contra C. (Heyer-Leipzig Coll., No. 1406.)
[*Vide* Chap. 8, pp. 129–130.]

Fig. 12. Contra by Heckel, Biebrich, *c.* 1909. Height, 6′ 4″. Wood with inverted metal bell. Five-coil model descending to Sub-contra B♭. (Heyer-Leipzig Coll., No. 1408.)   [*Vide* Chap. 8, p. 133.]

20

Klaviaturkontrafagott von C.W. Moritz
in Berlin.

Fig. 13 Fig. 14

PLATE 20

Fig. 13. Contrabass Sarrusophone in E♭ by C. G. Conn, Elkhart,
Ind., U.S.A. Height, 3′ 9″. Lowest note: Contra D♭. Orchestral
model in C descends to Sub-contra B♭.

[*Vide* Chapter 8, pp. 131–32.]

Fig. 14. Klaviaturkontrafagott by C. W. Moritz, 1845. 15 keys were
actuated by a keyboard, resembling the modern piano-accordion.
Although the instrument was patented in 1856, no surviving specimen is known. [*Vide* Chapter 8, pp. 122–23.]

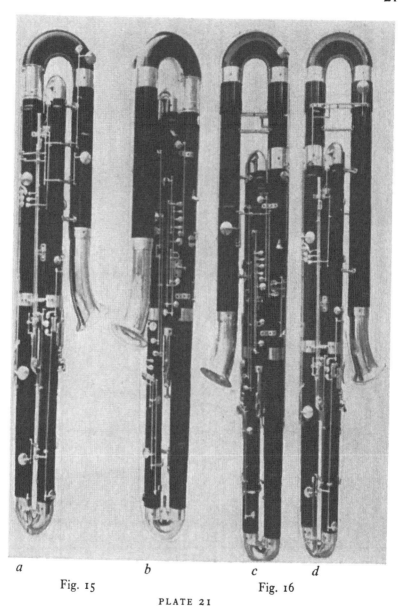

a   b   c   d

Fig. 15   Fig. 16

PLATE 21

Fig. 15. Heckel Contra descending to B♮‚‚: (*a*) back; (*b*) front.

Fig. 16. Heckel Contra descending to A‚‚: (*c*) front; (*d*) back.

(Photographs by courtesy of Herr Groffy, proprietor of Wilhelm Heckel, Biebrich-am-Rhein, Wiesbaden.) [*Vide* Chap. 8, p. 133.]

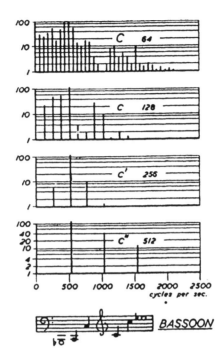

Fig. 1

BASSOON

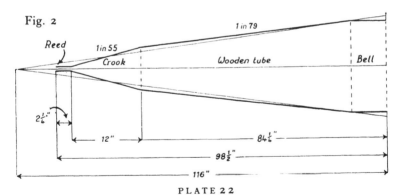

Fig. 2

PLATE 22

Fig. 1. Tonal spectra of the bassoon fundamental C and three octaves above. Reproduced from Meyer & Buchmann, *Die Klangspektren der Musikinstrumente* (1931).   [*Vide* Chapter 9, pp. 148–49.]

Fig. 2. Diagrammatic section of the cone of the bassoon (not to scale). Owing to its irregular conical course, the tube behaves as though it were a single true cone of greater length.

[*Vide* Chapter 9, p. 150.]

PLATE 23

Mr. Wm. Waterhouse playing his Heckel bassoon fitted with a straightened crook and adjustable spike. The spike has been in use in the
U.S.A. for some years, but is now being marketed by Schreiber
of Nauheim to the order of Mr. Waterhouse.

[*Vide* Chap. 11, p. 162.]

Introductory Notes

Notation. For convenience, the following method has been adopted

16^{ft} 8^{ve}	8^{ft} 8^{ve}	4^{ft} 8^{ve}	2^{ft} 8^{ve}	1^{ft} 8^{ve}
C, to B,	C to B	c to b	c' to b'	c'' to b''

References. The following is the conventional means of referring to parts of the instrument:

The top or upper end: the end nearest to the reed or blowing end.

The lower end: in the bassoon this is, paradoxically, the bell or highest part.

Right and left are defined from the viewpoint of the player.

Front is the side away from the player and *back* is that nearest him while playing.

Keys are of two varieties, open-standing and closed. *Open keys* are named from the note they produce on closure. *Closed keys* are given the name of the note produced on opening them.

Holes. On the analogy of holes closed by keys, those closed by the fingers and thumbs take their name from the noted produced on opening them. Holes are numbered from the top downwards, and the fingers and thumbs are denoted:

Left: L1, L2, L3, L4, LT (Thumb), and *Right:* R1, R2, R3, R4, RT.

Parts of the Bassoon

English	German	French	Italian	Spanish
Bell	Stürze, Haube, Schallstück or Kopfstück	Bonnet or Pavillon	Campana or Padiglione	Campana or Pabellón
Long-joint or bass-joint	Bass-röhre, Mittel-stück or Stange	Grande branche	Pezzo lungo	Cuerpo centrico
Butt or double-joint	Stiefelstück or Doppelloch	Culasse	Sacco	Culata or cuerpo inferior
Wing or tenor joint	Flügel	Petite branche	Piccolo tubo	Tudelere
Crook	S-Rohr	Bocal	Esse	Tudel
Reed	Rohr	Anche	Ancia	Cãna
Key	Klappe	Clef or Clé	Chiave	Llave

CHAPTER I

Introductory Description, Etymology and Origins

UNTIL the advent of radio it is not too much to say that the bassoon was little known apart from such references as Tennyson's lines from 'In Memoriam':

> 'All night have the roses heard
> The flute, violin, bassoon'. . .

Ella Wheeler Wilcox in 'The Beautiful Blue Danube' writes:

> 'If the great bassoons that mutter
> If the clarionets [*sic*] that blow
> Were given a voice to utter
> The secret things they know.'

Much earlier John Clare (1793–1864) had written in his 'Summer Images':

> 'There bees go courting every flower that's ripe,
> And droning dragon-fly on rude bassoon
> Attempts to give God thanks
> In no discordant tune.'

Again Charles L. Graves in his 'Ode to Discord', set to music by Stanford, writes:

> 'Let the loud bassoon
> Bay like a blood-hound at
>   the full-orbed moon' . . .

Coleridge's lines from 'The Ancient Mariner' are the best-known reference:

> 'The Wedding-guest here beat his breast
> For he heard the loud bassoon'

It is perhaps due to an unhappy assonance that the bassoon has been dubbed buffoon and Professor E. Prout reinforced this by terming it 'the clown of the orchestra'.

Wordsworth wrote:

'O blithe new-comer! I have heard,
I hear thee and rejoice:
Fagotto! Shall I call thee bird,
or but a wandering Voice?'

As might be expected, Browning's reference is cryptic:

'The rest may reason and welcome:
'tis we bassoonists know.'

The popular 'Floral Dance', the song by Kate Moss, is well known, though the inclusion of the bassoon is a mistake for a bassoonist does not and could not participate in the brass band which parades on foot in Helston on 8 May annually:

'Fiddle, 'cello, big bass drum,
Bassoon, flute, euphonium.'

The bassoon as we know it today has altered little in outward appearance for two hundred years. The name appears first in 1706 in Edward Phillips' *New World of Words*,[1] a dictionary which appeared in six editions between 1658 and 1706. Until then and indeed until about 1750 the instrument was known as the curtall (or double curtall), which will be described later in this chapter.

The bassoon consists of a wooden tube of cylindro-conical bore about 100 inches in length. For convenience, this is doubled back in U-shape and is divided into sections (Plate 1):[2] A. the *bell-joint*, B. the *long- or bass-joint*, C. the *butt, boot, or double joint*, D, the *wing or tenor joint*, and E. the *crook* or metal S-shaped tube to which the *double reed* (g) is affixed. The double-joint is the feature peculiar to the bassoon as it consists of twin channels—C a narrow bore enlarging downwards, turning at the foot and increasing as it continues to K the top of the parallel bore. The upper end of each bore is provided with a metal-lined socket into which the long-joint and tenor-joint are inserted. These two sections each have a tenon b and d in which cork is inlaid to provide an air-tight joint. The top of the long-joint has a second tenon B at its upper extremity to which is fitted A the *bell*, a rather misleading term borrowed from brass instruments. It does not flare to any extent (though Austrian bassoons of the early nineteenth century had flared bells usually of metal). The wing- or tenor-joint is so named from the shape of the wood which in old bassoons was even more pronouncedly wing-shaped and lay overlapping the long-joint to which in some cases since mid-nineteenth century it is attached by a small vertical sliding bolt. Finally, the crook, E, which has a cork-lined tenon, is inserted into a metal-lined socket D at the top of the tenor-joint and when a double-reed g is fitted on to the crook, the instrument is complete.

OTHER FEATURES

A ring shown on the metal mount at the top of the butt, enables a hook or swivel of the neck- or shoulder-sling to be affixed in playing. A sling is necessary to relieve the player of the weight of the instrument which, since *c.* 1700, has been held inclined to the left, with the butt at the right thigh. On German bassoons and bassoons with German-type key-mechanism, a hand-rest or crutch is screwed into the butt and lies between the thumb and fingers during play. For military and other use on the march, a small spring clip, termed a 'lyre', is screwed to the top of the long-joint to hold the music which in such cases is printed on a small card.

Mute. Examples are given in Chapter 2 of 'offen' and 'gedackt' dulzians of the seventeenth century. The muting was then achieved by a perforated cap over the bell-mouth This device was not continued on the bassoon and, to this day, it is very rare for a mute to be used on the instrument. According to Baines, a muted bassoon was demanded by Keiser in 'Otto'. In the article 'Mute' in Grove's *Dictionary*, 5th edit., Baines cites the low D for the 3rd bassoon at the opening of Debussy's *Pelléas et Mélisande*. French players place a handkerchief in the bell and this proves effective for notes other than B♭, which must then necessarily be unplayable and B♮, which is unsteady. In Germany a mute is used which consists of a narrow brass cylinder 3 inches long, lapped with soft wrapping sufficient to hold the cylinder lightly in place, half inside the bell. The outer end may be covered with wire gauze. This mute is said to soften the lowest fifth without endangering the attack or altering the quality.

The twin bores in the double-joint are carried through in manufacture and, to form a continuous channel at the foot, L., a plug is inserted. In old bassoons this was a simple oval cork which later gave place to a metal lined plug suitably curved to provide continuity of the bore. In German bassoons it takes the form of a metal U-tube which can be withdrawn as a water-outlet and for cleaning, but it is seldom used. In French instruments the plug is screwed in and covered by a metal casing or 'shoe'.

It will be obvious that with a tube of some 8 feet in length, the intervals between even the primary six holes are too great for the first three fingers of each hand to cover the holes. This is overcome by boring the holes obliquely ╱ and ╲, an expedient which was adopted

in the earliest types of bassoon and still continues. It is to this peculiarity that the bassoon's tone is largely due. The finger-holes are relatively small and the passage of the air from the bore continues through
a measurable thickness of the wood as shown in the cross-section
(Fig. 1). This does not occur in any other modern wind instrument.
It would, of course, be quite possible to place the finger-holes at their
rational position allowing the air to emerge freely and closing the holes
by a system of keys and rods as used for the other notes on the instrument. This was, in fact, carried out by C. J. Sax (père) in 1825, by C.
Ward of London in 1853 and again by Triébert of Paris in 1855 when
attempts were made to apply rational acoustic principles to the bassoon.
(*Vide* Chapter 6.) All resulted in failure. Much the same principles were
applied to the sarrusophone—a family of metal double-reed instruments invented by a French bandmaster Sarrus in 1856. The contrabass sarrusophone alone has survived and mainly in the U.S.A., but the
vibrant, full, 'open' timbre is the very antithesis of the rather veiled
husky quality of the bassoon as we know it.

References have been made above to the German and French types
of bassoon which differ mainly in the key mechanism although the bore
differs also. These differences will be described in Chapter 6.

The compass of the modern bassoon extends from B♭, to f″ though
Heckel's fingering chart extends to a♭″.* For ordinary orchestral purposes, the compass is three octaves ending on b♭′ or c″ and the increasing tendency to write above this is to be regretted. Not only is the
production of the higher notes a strain—both nervous and physical—
for the performer, but the quality of the notes is foreign to the nature
of the instrument. The compass may be divided thus:

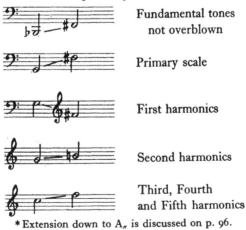

Fundamental tones
not overblown

Primary scale

First harmonics

Second harmonics

Third, Fourth
and Fifth harmonics

* Extension down to Aͮ is discussed on p. 96.

The primary scale of the bassoon has been variously denoted as that of C (Sachs); F (Forsyth); and G (Prout),[3] the latter being the six-hole scale of the simple flute. On the other hand, C is historically the basic scale of the primitive bassoon and the fact that it requires the use of keys for B♭, D and F is incidental to such a long tube where both thumbs and seven fingers are employed.

Against F it may be argued that, starting by the use of one key (for R4), the scale involves B♭ which requires a key on the German type, though a very satisfactory note can still be obtained by 'cross-fingering' (*Fr.* doigté-fourché: *Ger.* gabel-griff) on the French type. Cross-fingering is older than the bassoon, indeed as old as the Middle Ages. (*Vide* Grove's *Dictionary*, 5th edit., *s.v.* Fingering.)

In addition to the normal bassoon which can be described as in C, *i.e.* non-transposing, there is now only the contrabassoon, an octave lower. As recently as 1889, however, at the International Exhibition in Paris, Evette and Schaeffer showed smaller bassoons, a semitone, a minor third, a fourth and a fifth above the normal bassoon.[4] References to these and earlier exceptional use of small bassoons will be made in Chapter 7.

ETYMOLOGY

The word bassoon first occurs in an English dictionary of 1706 as stated above and is unquestionably derived from Latin *bassus*: French *bas*: Italian *basso*: Spanish *basco* (archaic) and *bajo* in the sense of deep-sounding, with the augmentative suffix *-oon*. In English borrowings from Anglo-French or later Parisian French down to *c.* 1650, French words were thoroughly naturalised in English and, sooner or later, were made to conform to the rules of English pronunciation and accent; while in later borrowings an attempt is generally made to pronounce these in French fashion. In English the tendency is to stress the first syllable and this is reflected in words adopted pre-1650, *e.g.* baron, button, mutton, while in subsequent borrowings from French words ending on *-on*, the accent is thrown forward, *e.g.* bassoon, buffoon, cartoon, balloon.[5]

Mersenne in 1636[6] appears to be the first to use the word *basson* as an equivalent for *fagotto*:

> Proposition XXXII, p. 298, 'Expliquer la figure, la grandeur, l'estendü et el'usage des Bassons, Fagots, Courtaux & Cervelats de Musique.'

p. 229. '. . . encore an autre Fagot ou Basson.'
Proposition XXXIII, p. 303. '. . . Quant au Fagot, ou au Basson.'

It is clear that the word bassoon came into the English language from French but it is not known in which of the Romance languages it first arose.

Mention must be made of a curious error in a quotation from Mersenne first made by Antoine Furetière in his *Dictionaire* [*sic*] *universel*[7] *s.v.* Basson. 'Il se brise en deux parties pour être porté plus commodément et alors on l'appelle *fagot*, parce qu'il ressemble à deux morceaux de bois liez et fagottez ensemble. Sa patte a presque neuf pouces *de diamètre* et on bouche ses trous avec des boëstes et des clefs, comme aux autres grandes flûtes. Quelques-uns appellent cet instrument *tarot*.' This was copied by Trévoux,[8] by Littré,[9] and again in translation by Grassineau,[10] by Hoyle[11] as late as the Edition of 1828 and by Dr. Johnson in his *English Dictionary*. What Mersenne stated was 'Cette pate a quasi 9 pouces . . .' meaning 'the bell measures about nine inches in length'. This is an example of careless repetition by lexicographers who have misled even musical historians not versed in organology.

An alternative derivation propounded by Littré, *viz. bas-son*, deep sound, may be dismissed as etymologically unsound.

Michel Tornatoris was appointed serpentist and bassoonist to the Church of Notre-Dame des Doms, Avignon in 1602. (*Musical Times*, 1 July 1927.) This is probably the earliest reference to a bassoonist in France.

SPAIN

In Spain, the earliest recorded reference to *bajon* is found at Madrid in the list of members of the Royal Band[12] which in 1588 included: 'Un bajon, Melchior de Camargo' who is mentioned again in 1633 and 1637[13]—certainly a long-service musician.

The lists for 1633 and 1637 also include Francisco de Valdez, *baxoncillo* or *bajoncillo*, denoting a small bassoon (fagottino), specimens of which from the Barbieri Collection, Madrid, preserved in the Collection of the Brussels Conservatoire, are described in Chapter 2.

At Valladolid in 1601, the boys of the church choir were encouraged, during their change of voice, to learn to play 'bajón' among other wind and stringed instruments.[14]

ITALY

In Italy the earliest record of the word *fagotto* is in 1546 at Verona where on '9 Maggio furono comperati da Alvise soldata un Fagotto ed una Dolzana'.[15]

In 1562 the Inventory of the Verona Accademia Filarmonica lists: 'Un Fagoto, con le sue canelle' and 'una cassa biancha de pezzo per le cornamute et fagoto . . .'.[16]

In 1569 the Inventory still included a fagoto and by 1585 there were fagotti.[17]

In 1589 at the wedding, in Florence, of Duke Ferdinand I of Medici and Christina of Lorena, an interlude for voices in seven parts was accompanied by 'Tromboni, cornetti, dolzaine et fagotti'.[18]

In 1600, 1612 and 1617 Inventories of the Este Collection of Instruments included fagotti.[19] Reference will be made later to Zacconi's account of the Fagotto Chorista in Venice in 1592. In 1620, Giovanni Battista Riccio published at Venice 'I. terzo libro delle divine lodi musicali . . .' which included a 'canzon La Grimaneta con il Tremolo a 2 Flautin à Fagoto'.[20]

GERMANY

The operas and ballets of Lully[21] and the achievements of French instrument-makers exerted considerable influence upon German music in the seventeenth century. This adoption of French taste extended to the names of instruments: *Flöte* became *Flûte traversière Schalmei* became *Hautbois*, and *Fagott* became *Basson*. Quantz, in 1752, alludes to this: 'Nachdem aber die Französen, nach ihrem angenehmen tiefern Töne, die deutsche Querpfeife in die Flöte traversière, die Schallmey in den Hoboe und den Bombart in den Basson verwandelt hatten.'[22]

It is a curious circumstance that the name fagott should have been superseded in Germany for over a century—in fact, from *c.* 1690 until 1800—by which time the French 'basson' was finally discarded and the German 'fagott' restored. 'Bassons' are recorded in the places listed in Appendix V, which also gives the relevant dates and sources.

THE PHAGOTUM

The origin of the bassoon is still shrouded in mystery. Even the country of its origin is uncertain. No such instrumental type is mentioned by Virdung,[23] Agricola[24] or Luscinius.[25] It is probable that the device of two parallel channels connected in U-shape can be attributed to Canon Afranio of Ferrara (1480–*c.* 1565) who before 1521 was experimenting with an instrument he named *Phagotum* embodying a pair of such U-tubes. The Canon was able to play a solo on 'il suo fagoto' at a banquet at Mantua in 1532 but posterity would have remained in ignorance of the Phagotum had it not been for an illustrated description by Teseo Albonesi, a nephew of Afranio, in a most unlikely book, *Introductio in Chaldaicam Linguam,*[26] printed in Pavia in 1539. A second contemporary item is a sheet of Instructions for playing the Phagotum dated 1565 and discovered in 1893 by Count Luigi Valdrighi in the archives of the State of Modena.[27] We are indebted to Canon Francis W. Galpin, our great English musicologist, for a full account of Afranio's invention in *The Romance of the Phagotum,*[28] where he gives a translation of Albonesi's Latin text and reproduces not only the front and back views of the phagotum but also the fingering chart of 1565.

The Italian name for the bassoon has been fagotto since the late sixteenth century. The word may well have been derived from phagotum but this has led to great confusion and to the belief that the bassoon is descended from the phagotum. Every reference book for centuries has credited Afranio with 'the invention of the bassoon'. Marin Mersenne[29] described the phagotum as 'une espèce de Fagot', a term under which he groups all double-tube bass instruments. Fétis[30] refers to Albonesi's description and illustrations as 'du basson, dont il attribue l'invention à ce chanoine'. Lavignac[31] adds to the misconception by boldly stating that Afranio 'créa le premier basson'. We may dispose of the fallacy by contrasting the features of the two instruments:

Phagotum	*Bassoon*
Bellows-blown.	Mouth-blown.
Single metal reeds.	Double cane-reed.
Twin U-tubes, *c.* 22 in. high.	Single U-tube, 4 ft. high.
Cylindrical bore.	Conical bore.

It is remarkable that there is no record of any attempt to reconstruct a phagotum until 1959. William A. Cocks, the leading British authority on the Bagpipe, successfully constructed a working instrument though 'the task proved to be one of extreme difficulty'.[32]

There is a further misconception associated with the name fagotto. Again, works of reference repeat with irritating persistence that the name arose from the resemblance of the instrument to 'a faggot or bundle of sticks'. The absurdity of this has escaped many musical writers. While the small phagotum *may* have resembled a bundle of wood, it was not until well into the seventeenth century that the bassoon was constructed in sections. The similarity in the phagotum may have suggested what is a nickname, *un nombre satirico*, according to Pedrell.[33] As Canon Galpin has remarked: 'On the Instructions sheet of 1565 each of the larger pillars (twin-bored U-tubes) is separately called a *fagoto*. From this narrower and somewhat incorrect use of the word, the name appears to have passed to any bass instrument bored with parallel tubes such as the deep-toned *Sordoni* or to the later dulzians with their conical tubes in one block.'

E. van der Straeten records[34] that two 'contrabass instruments called *fagotes* in two cylindrical cases' are listed in the Spanish inventory of 1559 of the Flemish Band of Marie, widowed Queen of Hungary, on her departure from Flanders for Spain. They are distinguished from two contrabass shawms (chirimias) which were in two pieces, each instrument being in 'a great case'. A 'fagot contra alt' is also mentioned.

It is Zacconi[35] who first refers to the bassoon proper—the *Fagotto Chorista* with a compass of two octaves less a tone from C. The name shows the use to which the primitive instrument was put for supporting the voices in church praise—a use which survived in English churches until the late nineteenth century.

THE CURTALL

On its introduction to England the early bassoon or dulzian was known as the curtall in various spellings, curtail, curtoll, etc., from the Romanic root *cur*, shortened. The word first occurs in the Household Accounts of Sir Thomas Kytson of Hengrave Hall, Suffolk:[36]

'1574 Dec. For an instrument called a curtall XXXs.'

The wording suggests that the instrument was not well known, but in 1603, after Sir Thomas's death, the Inventory specified *inter alia* 'Three hoeboys with a curtall'.

In 1575 a double curtall was included in the Waits Band of Exeter[37] and c. 1582 Stephen Batman in his translation of Bartholomaeus's *De Proprietatibus Rerum*[38] writes: 'The common bleting musicke is the drone, hobuis and curtoll' (*i.e.* bagpipe, shawm and bassoon). One further reference occurs before the close of the sixteenth century in the accounts of the Corporation of the City of London.[39] In 1597 we read: 'The Chamberlain shall presently buy and provide the several instruments called a double saggbutt, a single saggbutt and a curtal for the musicians at the charge of the city.'

There is no English description of the curtal until *c.* 1688 in the MS. of the third Randle Holme (died 1707), preserved in the British Museum[40] and reproduced here (Plate 2). The text runs:

'A double curtaile. This is double the bignesse of the single, mentioned Chap. XVI, n.6' (the MS. begins at Chap. XVII of Book 3) 'and is played eight notes deeper. It is as it were two pipes fixed in one thick bass pipe, one much longer than the other, from the top of the lower comes a crooked pipe of brass in form of an S in which is fixt a Reed, through it the wind passeth to make the instrument make a sound. It hath six holes on the outside and one brass key called the double F fa ut: on that side next the man or back part are two brass keys, the highest called double La' (error for D) 'sol re and the other double B mi.'

This transcription is given in full in view of certain errors and omissions in the transcription in the late Kathleen Schlesinger's article on Bassoon in *Encyclopaedia Britannica* (11th edit.).

This provides conclusive evidence that the curtall in its evolution from the one-piece dulzian during the seventeenth century acquired a separate bell-joint, a bass-joint, a wing joint and an extra key. The three keys, named according to the Gamut are D and F of the dulzian and contra B flat. Holme curiously overlooks the two thumb-holes on the back of the curtall.

During the seventeenth century English references to the curtal become more frequent.

At a service in St. George's Chapel, Windsor, on 17 April 1661, by order of the Sovereign and the Knights of the Garter[41] 'two double sackbuts and two double courtals' were 'placed . . . among the . . . choirs, to the end that all might distinctly hear'.

The Lord Chamberlain's Records[42] state:

1662 Aug. 30. 'Order that Robert Strong and Edward Strong are to attend with their double curtolls in His Majesty's Chappell Royall at Whitehall . . . every Sunday and Holyday. . . .'

1663 June 20. 'Warrant to pay Edward Strong, musician, the sum of £50 for three good curtalls, by him bought and delivered for his Majesty's service.'

1669 Nov. 30. 'Warrant to pay the sum of £52 to Robert Strong, one of his Majesty's musicians in ordinary, for two double curtolls bought and delivered for their Majesties' service, and given to Segnior Francisco for the service of the Queene's Majesty.'

At Coventry in 1678 the Common Council appointed four Town Waits and after prescribing their salary, livery and duties mentions their instruments, 'two treables, one tenor and a double curtall, all of them to be tunable'.[43] The quaint proviso was probably inserted as a result of sad experience of the waits' intonation in the past!

The Sackbut, as the trombone was then called, and the double curtal figured in the procession at the Coronation of James II on 23 April 1685.[44] The choir of Westminster was followed by three of the King's Musicians each in a scarlet mantle—Edmond Flower and Theophilus Fittz each playing a sackbut and, between them, Henry Gregory 'playing on a Double Courtal'. It is amusing to observe that the engraver in the illustrations appended to Francis Sandford's History of the Coronation portrays these three musicians with two large trumpets and a tenor cornetto!

Hawkins[45] states that the 'courtal' figures again in 1714 at the Coronation of George I.

In Scotland, a single reference occurs in the Records of Edinburgh Town Council.[46]

On 17 April 1696 the Council replaced the instruments used by the five waits, viz. 'schalmes, howboyes and siclyk' (such like), by appointing players on 'the French hautboyes and double curtle', instruments considered far more proper than those hitherto in use—a reference no doubt to the cornetti then going out of fashion.

Three interesting entries of this period occur in The Diary of a Country Physician by Claver Morris (1684–1726).[47] At his Music Club at Wells he played the harpsichord, organ, violin, double bass, bassoon or curtill, hoboy and flute (1700–25).

On another occasion 'Mr. Dingleton assisted our consort with his bassoon, trumpet or hautboy'.

The diarist's accounts for 1688 record the payment of '£2 10s.—for a Bassoon or Curtill'.

Edward Ward in Hudibras Redivivus (1707)[48] used the expression 'With voice as hoarse as double curtal' and in The London Spy, 1698–1700, Part V, he refers to 'the Image of a Bear . . . upon a Sign-Post, perk'd up . . . with a great Faggot-Bat in his claws, that he looked like one of the City-Waits playing upon the Double-Curtel'. The reference was to a Cheapside shop.

A contemporary broadside[49] describing the York Waits in a doggerel rhyme mentions:

'Cortal with deep hum hum
Cries out, "We come, we come" '

At Exeter in 1737—160 years after the first reference to the curtall
there—an account of Christmas customs runs as follows:[50]

'The Waits may now, in blackest month go through
Ev'n the suspicious Close of Bartho'mew
Nor by that Calvary hear dismal groan
But dismal from that snuffling Courtal blown.'

The military bands then coming into existence readily adopted the
curtall. Thus, on 7 June 1722[51] 'one hautboy and one courtal' were
added to the Grenadiers' Music (of the H.A.C.) and, on 11 October
1731, 'the Grenadiers' Music was ordered to consist of one curtail,
three hautboys and no more'. By 1783, the word 'curtail' was dropped
and the band consisted of four clarinets, two horns, one trumpet, two
'bassoons'.

An unique instance of the two names in association occurs in a
manuscript[52] of Dr. Robert Creighton dated 1727:

'I hear a thunder rolling here beneath,
Where Curtals and Bassoons their murmurs breathe.'

Handel, with the notable exception in 'Saul', normally used the
bassoon to double the bass, designating it 'fagotto'. A British Museum
MS.[53] (not later than 1732), states that Handel's pastoral 'Acis' needed
a double curtal for the accompaniment of some of the songs.

Grassineau's *Musical Dictionary* (1740) contains almost the last
reference to the curtal:

'Curtail double, a musical wind instrument like the Bassoon,
which plays the bass to the Hautboy. See Bassoon and Hautboy.'

It is amusing to observe how the final references to the curtal add
to the reader's confusion.

Bailey in the 2nd edition of his *Dictionary* (1736) plays for safety:

'Double Curtail—a musical instrument that plays the bass.
Bassoon—a musical instrument, a Hautboy.'

Tans'ur in his *Musical Grammar* (c. 1770) defines the Curtail as a
double bassoon. The bassoon is 'a Reed Instrument, being Bass to
Hautboys &c., stopped like a Flute and more grand in Psalmody than
Tin Pipes, 9 feet long'.

John Hoyle in his *Dictionary* of 1770 completes the confusion thus:
'Fagottino, a single curtail . . . something like a small bassoon.
Fagotto, the double Curtail, or, in reality a double bassoon as
big again as the Fagottino.'

The fagotto was indeed twice the size of the fagottino, but the double
bassoon was twice the size of the fagotto! Hoyle can be excused for his
ignorance of the true double bassoon which was not in use in England
in 1770.

Thus, after two centuries during which the instrument was doubtless
in far wider use than recorded instances of its name would appear to
indicate, the word curtall dropped out of the language.

Before leaving the curtal, it seems appropriate to correct a misapprehension by Pulver in his *Dictionary of Old English Music*[54] where
he states: 'There can be no doubt that the curtal was, for some time,
used side by side with the bassoon which was soon to displace it.' This
would imply that the two were separate and distinct. As has been shown
above, curtal was no more than a name for the bassoon during its
evolution from the sixteenth to the eighteenth centuries, after which
the French 'basson' was adopted and anglicised. Pulver has repeated[55]
an error of Carl Engel who referred to[56] a rare specimen of a 'courtaut'
'. . . dating from the fifteenth century' in the Museum of the Conservatoire of Music, Paris. Engel should have written 'cervelat' (*vide*
Chouquet's Catalogue No. 497), an admittedly rare specimen of the
strange squat 'Sausage Bassoon' (*Ger.* Wurstfagott or Rackett from
ranke = crooked) in this case by Rozet, a Paris maker, *c.* 1692, hardly
fifteenth century! Pulver, moreover, adds to the confusion by quoting
from De Félice's *Encyclopédie* of 1772 a description of the 'courtaut',
an instrument bearing no relation to the curtall (unless it be that both
were characterised by a U-tube). The tube of the curtall was conical
while that of the courtaut was cylindrical. It is remarkable that no
original specimen of the true courtaut has survived in this country or
even on the continent.

A very remarkable discovery was brought to light about 1947 when
Robert Donington drew the attention of Anthony Baines, then Editor
of the *Galpin Society Journal*, to Music MS. 1187 in Christ Church
Library, Oxford. One of a few personal papers of Henry Aldrich, Dean
of Christ Church from 1689 to 1711, it consists of particulars of various
instruments, supplied by well-known London players, *e.g.* John Shore,
Finger and Paisible. The information was gathered by James Talbot

who became a Fellow of Trinity College, Cambridge, in 1689 and was Regius Professor of Hebrew from 1689 to 1704. The date of the MS. must be between 1695 and 1701. We are indebted to Anthony Baines for a transcription of Talbot's fragmentary jottings on wind instruments, published in *Galpin Society Journal.*[57]

In certain cases, dimensions are given in feet, inches and eighth parts of an inch. These are sometimes followed by tablatures and tunings, and general observations.

There are two sections, entitled 'Basson' and 'Double Courtaut'.

Basson. This is a three-keyed instrument and precise measurements are given for the diameter of the eleven holes, their distance apart, the joints and tenons, the crook and the reed. The dimensions of the reed are given as: Length 1 $\frac{13}{16}$ inches: Width $\frac{1}{2}$ inch. An incomplete tablature covers only the lowest octave—B♭, to B—but below it is written:

'Pedal or Double Basson.   Mr. Finger.
FFF
Fagot & Double Courtaut.   Tenor & Treble courtaut.
CC
Note that the fingering of the Basson, Pedal & Double Courtaut & Fagot is the same with that of the Flute.
Pedal or Double Basson, FFF, touch as Basson.
Double Courtaut, CC, touch same with Basson: there are treble and tenor courtauts.
Fagot disused: touch same with Basson: CC same with Double Courtaut.
Not used in Consort.
Basson has 4 Joynts, Fagot entire.
Best reeds from Marshes of Spain and Provence.'

Baines has observed that 'if the "Double Basson" was a jointed instrument like the Basson (as opposed to the one-piece Quart-fagot of Praetorius) this is the earliest known record of a true bassoon deeper than the ordinary'. A unique example of an English eight-keyed Quart-bassoon in low G by J. Samme, London, *c.* 1853, is in the R.C.M. Collection, London. Like Talbot's 'Double Basson', it also descends to F,.

Double Courtaut. From the dimensions, in which an obvious error has occurred, we can establish that this is a one-piece two-keyed dulzian or choristfagott, descending to C. It is important to note that this double-courtaut is not the same as the jointed three-keyed bassoon, termed double curtaile, in Randle Holme's MS. of *c.* 1688. In Talbot, the French form of the name denotes a dulzian and under 'Basson' above, he mentions the 'Fagot' as 'entire' and 'disused'. No tablature or observations are added.

An illustrated article 'The Curtal (1550–1750), a Chapter in the Evolution of the Bassoon' by the present author appeared in *Musical Times*, April 1937.

REFERENCES

[1] Phillips, E.: *The New World of Words* 6th edit. (London, 1706).

[2] de Laborde, J. B.: *Essai sur la Musique* (Paris, 1780). Fig. 1 is taken from Vol. I, p. 325.

[3] Langwill, L. G.: 'Some Notes on the Bassoon with Particular Reference to its Fundamental Scale', *Musical Progress & Mail* (London, August 1933).

[4] Pierre, C.: *La Facture Instrumentale* (Paris, 1890), pp. 25–29.

[5] Smith, L. Pearsall: *The English Language* (London, 1912), pp. 36–37.

[6] Mersenne, Père Marin: *Harmonie Universelle* (Paris, 1636).

[7] Furetière, Antoine: *Dictionaire [sic] universel* (Rotterdam, 1690).

[8] Trévoux: *Dictionnaire universel français et latin* (Paris, six editions between 1704 and 1771).

[9] Littré: *Dictionnaire de la langue française* (Paris, 1863–72).

[10] Grassineau, James: *A Musical Dictionary* (London, 1740). Largely based on Brossard's *Dictionnaire de Musique* (Paris, 1703).

[11] Hoyle, John: *Dictionary or Treasury of Music* (London, 1770 and 1790). A mere abridgment of Grassineau's Dictionary.

[12] van der Straeten, E.: *Histoire de la Musique aux Pays-Bas avant le XIX Siècle* (Brussels, 1867–88), Vol. VIII, p. 183.

[13] ——: *ibid.*, Vol. VIII, pp. 424 and 428 *et seq.*

[14] ——: *ibid.*, Vol. VIII, pp. 189–90.

[15] Turini, Guiseppe, *L'Accademia Filarmonica di Verona dall fondazione . . . (Maggio 1543) al 1600 . . .* (Verona, 1941), p. 41.

[16] *Ibid.*, p. 88.

[17] *Ibid.*, pp. 180 and 188.

[18] Tommasseo, N. and Bellini, B.: *Dizionario della Lingua Italiana* (Turin, 1865–79).

[19] Valdrighi, L. F.: *Capelle, Concerti et Musiche di Casa d'Este dal sec. XV al XVIII* (Modena, 1884), pp. 59 *et seq.*

[20] Sartori, C.: *Bibliografia della musica strumentale stampata in Italia fino al 1700* (Florence, 1952), p. 262.

[21] Hass, Robert: *Die Musik des Barock* (Wildpark–Potsdam, 1929).

[22] Quantz, J. J.: *Versuch einer Anweisung die Flöte traversière zu spielen . . .* (Berlin, 1752). (Breslau, 1789, p. 241.)

[23] Virdung, S.: *Musica getutscht . . .* (Basel, 1511; facsimile 1931).

[24] Agricola, Martin: *Musica instrumentalis deudsch* (Wittemberg, 1529 and 1545; new edit. Leipzig, 1896).

[25] Luscinius, O.: *Musurgia seu Praxis musical . . .* (Strasburg, 1536).

[26] Albonesi, Teseo: *Introductio in Chaldaicam Linguam . . .* (Pavia, 1539).

[27] *Musurgiana*, Series I, No. 4 and II, No. 2 (Modena, 1895).

[28] *Proceedings of the Musical Association*, Session LXVII (London, 1940–1).

[29] Mersenne, Père Marin: *Harmonie Universelle* (Paris, 1636), Book V, Chap. XXXII.

[30] Fétis, F.-J.: *Biographie Universelle des Musiciens*. 2nd edit. (Paris, 1860–5)

[31] Lavignac, Laurencie: *Encyclopédie de la Musique* (Paris, 1927). The section dealing with Bassoon is by Letellier and E. Flament.

[32] Article in *Galpin Society Journal*, XII (May 1959), pp. 57–59 and illustration.

[33] Pedrell, F.: *Emporio . . . de Organografia musical antigua española* (Barcelona, 1901).

[34] Van der Straeten, E.: *Histoire de la Musique aux Pays-Bas*, Vol. VII, pp. 433, 436 and 448. The date of the inventory is given in error as 1555.

[35] Zacconi, L.: *Prattica di Musica* (Venice, 1596), Book IV, p. 218.

[36] Gage, J.: *History and Antiquities of Hengrave in Suffolk* (London, 1822), p. 204.

[37] Vowell, John, alias Hoker: *Description of Exeter* (Devon and Cornwall Record Society, 1919) and H. Lloyd Parry, *History of Exeter Guildhall* (Exeter, 1936), p. 159.

[38] Batman, Stephen: *Upon Bartholome*, being a translation of Bartholomaeus' treatise, *De Proprietatibus Rerum*, 423/1 margin).

[39] Quoted by Hadland, F. A.: 'The Waits', in *Musical News*, 7 August 1915.

[40] British Museum, Harl. 2034f. 207b.

[41] Ashmole, E.: *Institution, Laws, etc., of the Order of the Garter* (London, 1672), p. 576.

[42] de Lafontaine, H. C.: *The King's Musick* (London, 1909), pp. 147, 158 and 220.

[43] Sharp, T.: *Dissertation on Pageants . . . at Coventry* (Coventry, 1825), p. 210.

[44] Sandford, F.: *History of the Coronation of James II* (London, 1687), p. 70.

[45] Hawkins, J.: *History of Music* (London, 1776), Book XVII, Chap. CLIX, footnote.

[46] Edinburgh Town Council MS. Records, Vol. 35, folio 249, 17 April 1696.

[47] Morris, Claver: *The Diary of a Country Physician* (1684–1726) (London? 1934).

[48] Ward, Edward: *Hudibras Redivivus* (3rd edit., London, 1715), Vol. II, p. 24.

[49] Proclamations, Broadsides, etc., in Cheetham Library, Manchester, No. 1524. 'York Waits', quoted in *Notes and Queries*, 3rd Series, Vol. VII, p. 380.

[50] Brice, A.: *The Mobiad: or the Battle of the Voice . . .* (Exeter, 1770), cited in *Notes and Queries*, 2nd Series, Vol. X, p. 464.

[51] Raikes, G. A.: *History of the H.A.C.* (London, 1878), Vol. I, p. 270: Vol. II, p. 93.

[52] British Museum, Addtl. MS. 37074.

[53] —— Addtl. MS. 36710.

[54] Pulver, J.: *A Dictionary of Old English Music and Musical Instruments* (London, 1923), p. 68.

[55] —— *loc. cit. ante*, p. 66.

[56] Catalogue of the Special Exhibition of Ancient Musical Instruments, South Kensington Museum, London, 1872, Introduction, p. ix.

[57] *Galpin Society Journal*, I, March 1948, pp. 9–26.

CHAPTER 2

Precursors of the Bassoon in Praetorius and Mersenne and Surviving Specimens

It is very fortunate that at the period when the dulzian or two-keyed fagott was still in use with the bombards or pommers, Michael Praetorius (1571–1621) compiled his monumental works *De Organographia* (1619) and *Theatrum Instrumentorum* or *Sciagraphia* (1620).

The following is a translation of the chapters relating to the Shawms/Pommers and the Fagotten in *De Organographia*.

CHAPTER X

Pommers/Bombarts/Bombardoni; Schalmeyen Illustrations, Plate XI

Long pipes, which were also called by the Greeks *Bombyces* or *Bombi*, were blown with difficulty and with great pressure of breath and give out a fairly coarse sound.

Pommers (Italian *bombardo*, or *bombardone*: the French call them *hautbois*, the English *hoboys*) derive their name, without any doubt, from *bombo*, on account of the humming and buzzing; and are all—the small as well as the large—called by the name bombart or pommer. In Italian the gross bass pommer is called *bombardone*: and the true bass, *bombardo*. The tenor has four keys by means of which, if necessary, a bass can be played because, with the keys, it descends to G in the bass. On that account it is called bassett. Following this is the nicolo, which is of the same size and pitch as the bassett, except that it has only one key, and on that account cannot go any deeper than the C in the tenor. The altpommer—which is almost of the same size as the schalmey, except that it has one key, and is a fifth deeper, is called *bombardo piccolo*. Only the highest *discant*, which has no brass key, is called schalmey (Italian, *piffaro*; Latin, *gingrina*, from the cackling, so it would appear, like a goose, the characteristic of which is to cackle).

In pitch most of the schalmeys are about a tone higher than the cornetts and trombones (*i.e.* 'cammerton', a tone higher than 'chorton').

But it must be remarked here that from olden times up till this very day all wind instruments, like flutes, pommers, schalmeys, krummhorns, etc., have, for the most part, been fashioned and pitched in groups (Accorten) or registers, always differing one from the other by a fifth:

so that, at all times one can use three and three together: the first as a kind of bass, the second as tenor and alto (for these two pitches (tenor and alto) can be played always on concordant and similar groups and instruments), the third, however, can be used for the melody. When, however, the four are to be taken, then the composition must be arranged for that purpose, and not transposed a fifth (lower) from c′ major into f major, but as in the Hypoionian mode a fourth lower into g major and than a *cantus fictus* made out of that. Or, if a melody is found already set in f major, one must transpose the piece about a tone (or a second, as many people say) higher: in this way it is produced quite clearly and really distinctly on the pommers and schalmeys. When, however, one wants to use a fifth instrument in the low or high ranges, then it is very troublesome to make them harmonise: then the uppermost instrument is separated from the lowest (as may be seen in the table) by way of five fifths, *i.e.* being separated by a seventeenth (like a Ditone or major third), and that is very difficult to piece together. Despite this, when the air is specially arranged in that manner, and care is diligently taken over it, even this is made possible. So nevertheless one is justified in advising an instrument-maker to work always with the correct treble and tenor pipes, and also with one about a tone lower, so that, accordingly, the latter may be sounded not a fifth, but only a fourth higher than the instrument immediately preceding (*i.e.* bass pommer). Then one can with such and similar instruments combine and harmonise, one with the other, the highest and lowest, even of five kinds clearly and well. However popular this grouping may have been then, at present it is in use to probably only a small extent. The gross bass pommer is 10 feet 1 inch long,* as may be seen in the Illustrations, Plate VI, 3, and can be measured easily from that.

EXPLANATORY NOTES

1. What Praetorius means to say is that there are five groups of fifths from the highest to the lowest instrument. He states that in olden days the different sizes of instrument in each family differed from each other by a fifth—a very awkward form of scaling, as he says later. But between the uppermost instrument and the fifth of the lowest, there is a seventeenth, *i.e. four* fifths.

Thus:

* The measurements are all given in Brunswick feet and inches and plates drawn to that scale. 1 Brunswick foot was equivalent to 11·235 English inches or 285·36 mm.

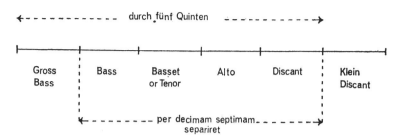

2. In the Middle Ages the word 'Hypo' was added to the original names of the seven modes to denote the same mode transposed a fourth *lower*. Hence by old writers it was used to denote such an interval reckoned *downwards* instead of upwards. Hence the transposition was not to be a fifth from c,

i.e. c′ to f

but a fourth, c′ to g

3. The schalmeien were used in secular music and were therefore in the pitch of Cammer-Ton. The cornetti and trombones were employed in church music, often with the organ, and were, therefore, in Chor-Ton, a note lower. They must have transposed if they played with the flutes and reeds, but on referring to Praetorius' compass tables we find that for the higher-pitched flutes and reeds, he gives alternative compasses a whole tone lower—so probably the players had double sets of instruments—one for Cammer-Ton, the other for Chor-Ton. This is confirmed by old instruments owned by Canon Galpin: his cornettino (1418) was in d. Praetorius gives e as the lowest note but in Chapter IV, p. 19, he states that all his compass scales are shown in Cammer-Ton (*i.e.* a tone higher). Canon Galpin's sackbut (1557) was in B1 (Chor-Ton). The shawm (*c.* 1650) was a whole tone below the usual discant (*i.e.* Chor-Ton).

How the basses and contrabasses managed we do not know, but no doubt their parts were probably somewhat simple and could be transposed.

4. Referring to the pitch of the tenor pommer, Praetorius suggests that, in combination, the instrument should be made a tone lower in pitch so that the pitch would be only a *fourth* above the instrument immediately preceding it (*i.e.* the bass pommer), instead of the usual fifth. In Canon Galpin's set of recorders, the bass was in F and the tenor in B♭ instead of the more usual C, and it worked well in combination.

c

CHAPTER XI

Fagotten-Dolcians
Illustrations Plate X

Fagotten and dolcians (Italian, *fagotto* and *dolcesuono*) are so called indiscriminately, but some think that those which the English call single curtail (zingel korthol) are the genuine dolcians: and in depth of pitch as well as in tone they are like the bassett of the pommers, only that the dolcians, like the fagotten also, are quieter and softer in tone than the pommers. Hence it is perhaps because of their sweetness that they are named dolcians, or dolcisonantes. This arises from the fact that, while the bodies of the pommers have equal length in a straight line and are quite open at the bell, in the case of fagotten the length of the body is doubled back so that the hole from which the sound issues is at the top and in some cases (not in all, for it is sometimes 'open') covered and 'vented' with little holes (as in some stops in the organ mentioned in Part IV). Hence the tone is necessarily not so strong, but somewhat softer and sweeter. In the same way as in the organ, the principal and trombone registers having their correct length and diameter throughout, sound much stronger and brighter than the 'stopped' ones and other 'stopped' reed registers; and this for the reason explained above.

C is the lowest note of the *chorist fagott*, F, of the *doppel fagott*, though it is to be noted in passing that the *doppel fagott* is of two kinds: the first is so pitched that one can obtain low F, as on the *gross bass pommer* and is called *quint-fagott*: the other, however, is the *quart fagott*, which can be employed only down to G,. The latter can be used most suitably in the natural key, the former, on the other hand, in flat keys: and it is very convenient, when the instrumentarium includes both these kinds; for the semitones cannot be so well produced from the holes covered by keys as through those which are fingered.

Now the Meister[1] who made the octave trombone is said to be at work on a large *fagot-contra* which will sound the C of the sixteen-foot octave a fourth below the *doppel-fagott*, and thus an octave below the *chorist-fagott*. If he succeeds it will be a splendid instrument, the like of which has never before been seen, and will really be something to marvel at; organ builders have up to now experienced great difficulty in producing clearly and well the lowest two notes D or C in the sixteen-foot octave of the large trombone register. Time will show.

These Chapters X and XI are supplemented by compass tables from which those referring to the shawm-pommer group and the fagott-dulzians are collated here in Plate 4. For purposes of comparison the corresponding members of each family are set underneath one another and below are the modern instruments which may be regarded as having evolved from them. The type instrument is No. 3 the *chorist-fagott* or *doppel-corthol* (*Eng.* double curtal).

As the terms 'double' and 'single' have often puzzled musicians, reference may be made to the author's article in Grove's *Dictionary of Music*, 5th edit. *s.v.* double and single. Briefly, it may be stated that in sixteenth-century England the recognised musical scale, based on the Guidonian septenaries, embraced a chromatic compass from G to f″. Playford (1661) states that the compass employed at the close of the Elizabethan era was confined within these limits, but adds 'those below Gamut in the Bassus are called double notes. I have, therefore, expressed them with double letters.' Praetorius affords conclusive corroboration, for he states that in England the fagott piccolo (Pl. XI, No. 4), descending to G was called 'singel corthol' and No. 3, descending to C (old style CC) was the 'doppel corthol'. He also explains that the largest pommer (Pl. X, No. 1), a fifth below the bass pommer (Pl. X, No. 2), (C–c′) was termed gross doppel quint pommer (F,–f). The lowest fagotts, the quart (Pl. XI, No. 1) and quint-fagott (Pl. XI, No. 2)—a fourth and a fifth respectively below the Choristfagott (C–g′)—were collectively termed 'doppelfagott'.

It may be noted that Randle Holme's 'double curtaile' was described as being an octave below the 'single curtaile'. From Praetorius' chart it will be observed that the 'doppel corthol' was only a fifth below the 'singel corthol'.

We will now consider *Theatrum Instrumentorum* of 1620. Plate VI shows the deepest member of the shawm-pommer family, the gross-doppel-quint-pommer, 4 keys, compass (F,–e (f)), approximate length 2·94 m. This giant instrument can never have been commonly in use, but at least one engraving of *c.* 1679 survives showing Nikol Rosenkron holding such a pommer.[2] Its name refers to the fact that its lowest note was F, a fifth below C, the lowest note of the bass-pommer. Both instruments had six finger-holes, those for the first and third fingers of each hand being bored obliquely to bring them within reach and four primitive long brass open-standing keys. These keys were arranged in pairs—one pair on the front of the instrument giving B♭, and A, to be played by the little finger of whichever hand was held lowermost, and the other pair, behind, giving G, and F, to be played by the thumb of the lowermost hand. So that the four keys, normally open, could be closed by one finger and a thumb, the pairs were ingeniously overlaid so that pressure on the 'touch' of a lower key automatically closed the key higher, which latter (in the case of both pairs) could, however, be operated separately. (A survival of this device exists on the long-joint of the French bassoon to this day where B♭, key closes C and D keys and C closes D.) A further peculiarity of the 'touches' of keys operated by the little finger is found on all such keys from the sixteenth to the eighteenth centuries and persisting even into the nineteenth century. This is a swallow-tailed or bifurcated 'touch' to suit players holding either the left or right hand lowermost. The 'touches' of the thumb-keys of the Bass- and Gross-Bass-Pommer were of course, simple in form, no bifurcation being necessary, whichever thumb was used.

In the engraving of Rosenkron (Plate 3) the curious perforated protuberance on the instrument is the engraver's rather unsuccessful attempt to portray another characteristic feature of early keyed woodwind instruments. The open-standing brass keys with their long rods and leaf-springs were very susceptible to damage so protection was afforded by a barrel-shaped wooden sleeve (*Ger.* Schütz-Kapsel) with a brass ring or mount at each end to prevent splitting. This barrel-cap was perforated in a number of concentric circles or other conventional designs to allow the air to escape from the open holes below. As it was not long enough to cover the longer of the two thumb-keys, a small brass box was nailed over the portion which projected below the wooden barrel-cap.

Surviving original gross-bass-pommers are exceedingly rare. Not one is to be found in Britain and only reproductions in U.S.A. and in several continental countries. One original from Danzig Marienkirche is now in Berlin.[3] Another original was in Salzburg.[4] Two further specimens survive respectively in the Museum at Poznan, Poland[5] and in the Franz Liszt Museum at Sopron, Hungary.[6] The source of the word pommer is interesting. The onomatopoeic Greek: βόμβος, Latin: *bombus*, humming or buzzing, gave rise to Italian *bombardo*, Spanish, *bombarda*, French *bombarde* and became in Old German, *bomhart*, *bumhart*, *bombardt*, *pumhart* and in New High German, *pommer*. The buzzing of the powerful double-reeds intensified by the pronounced wide conical bore led to the pommers being also designated in Germany, '*brummers*'.

Plate XI of *Theatrum Instrumentorum* (Plate 5) shows the other members of the Shawm-Pommer family:

1. Bass pommer, four keys, compass C–b♭ (c). Length 1·82 m. The key-mechanism has been explained under the gross-doppel-quint-pommer above. The six-hole scale commenced at G and

two pairs of keys, on front and back respectively, extended the
compass F E D and C.

2. Tenor or bassett pommer was of two kinds: with a single key,
   compass c–g′ (a′) or, with four keys, compass G–g′ (a′); length
   1·33 m.

3. Alt-pommer also of two kinds: the 'klein' (small) had one key:
   compass g–d″: length 0·77 m. The 'gross' (large) type had four
   keys with downward compass reaching d. This type is repre-
   sented by the modern cor anglais.

4. Discant schalmey or treble shawm which is the precursor of the
   modern oboe. Compass d′–b♭″ or c′–g″ (a″). Length 0·66 m.

5. Klein discant schalmey or small treble shawm which Praetorius
   states was rarely used. Compass b♭′–b♭‴, length 0·44 m.

Nos. 2, 3, 4 and 5 were all played with a 'pirouette' into which the
reed was fitted and the lips were pressed against the pirouette.[7]
In Plate X (Plate 6) we find the five sizes of Fagott including an Alt-
Fagott (lowest note d) which does not appear in Praetorius' compass
table. Conversely in Plate XIII he shows a 'Nicolo', a one-keyed
instrument having the double-reed covered by a cap. It is, therefore,
of the crumhorn family and should not have been included in the
compass table of the shawms.

No. 2 in Plate X is a doppel-fagott and it was of two kinds: a
quart-fagott (as depicted) with two keys; compass G,–f (a) and
a *quint-fagott* with two keys; compass F,–e♭ (g).

Nos. 3 and 4 are the *chorist-fagott*, corthol or doppel corthol, the
type instrument, with two keys, compass C–d′ (g′). No. 3 is
'offen' (unmuted) while No. 4 is 'gedackt' (muted).

No. 5 *Singel corthol.* Basset or tenor to the chorist-fagott, but also
termed fagott piccolo or alt fagott in the compass table. Two
keys. Compass G–f′ (g′).

No. 6 *Alt-fagott* (not included in the compass table), keyless;
compass d–?

No. 7 *Discant fagott* or *exilent* to the chorist-fagott, an octave
above No. 5. Keyless. Compass (g) a–c″.

Notes

1. In Plate X Praetorius states that the letters in the cases of
   Nos. 1–5 denote the notes produced by *closing* the holes: in the

cases of Nos. 6 and 7 the letters denote the notes produced by *opening* the holes.

2. In the Compass table, in the case of No. 3 (chorist-fagott) the upper limit is d′ but black notes are indicated for e′, f′ and g′. The explanation is that the instrument would overblow freely to d′ but less so thereafter. This arose from the shortness of the remaining effective length of the tube and the proximity of the upper holes to the reed.

3. Praetorius informs us that there were in the seventeenth century '*Accort*' and '*Sorten*' of instruments. An *Accort* was a complete group (eighty-six wind instruments) comprising set numbers of each type of instrument from the deepest member to the smallest discant of each. *Sorten*, on the other hand, referred to one particular type from among the nine families comprising an accort. The sorten of shawm-pommers and of fagotten were composed as follows:

Fagott		*Shawm-Pommers*	
Discant	1	Gar Klein Schalmey	1
Fagott Piccolo	2	Schalmey	2
Chorist Fagott	3	Klein Alt-Pommer	3
Doppel Fagott:—		Gross Alt-Pommer	2
Quart Fagott	1	Basset or Tenor Pommer	2
Quint Fagott	1	Bass Pommer	2
		Gross Bass Pommer	1
	—		—
	8		13
	—		—

We have no record of a performance by an accort but it would have to be heard to be believed when one considers that the other sorten were: 8 transverse flutes, 21 recorders, 8 trombones and the following obsolete types, 6 bassanelli, 7 rackets, 9 crumhorns and 6 corna-musen.

THE BASSOON IN MERSENNE'S HARMONIE UNIVERSELLE
(1636)

Following Praetorius' exposition in 1619 in Germany, we have the comprehensive treatise of Marin Mersenne (1588–1648). (Paris 1636.) In Book 5 he deals with wind instruments in twenty-five 'Propositions' or chapters. Chapter XXXII is entitled: 'Expliquer la figure, la grandeur, l'étendue et l'usage des Bassons, Fagots, Courtaux et Cervelats de Musique.'

As no translation of Mersenne is readily accessible to the student, the following version will be of interest:

'I have dealt with these kinds of bass instruments because they can join in concert with oboes and because they are somewhat different from the preceding bass oboe (Chapter XXXI) in that they are in two parts to enable them to be carried and handled more conveniently. That is why they are called "fagots", since they resemble two pieces of wood which are attached and "fagotés" together. Now the first fagot, on the left of Plate 7, Figure 1, commences at the letter A, where we see the crook LK fixed to carry the wind into the tube ABEI. The wind issues at the bell (pate) H which is removable at the point I. As regards the interval between the holes, there are, to begin with, 4 inches from the crook-socket, *i.e.* from the top of A, to the first hole: and $4\frac{1}{2}$ inches from the third to the fourth hole: there are sixteen lines from the sixth to the seventh; 5 inches from the seventh to the eighth; $6\frac{1}{4}$ inches from the eighth to the 9th; $2\frac{1}{3}$ inches from the ninth to the tenth, etc. From eleventh to twelfth $7\frac{1}{2}$ inches and from there to the top of the fagot which is concealed under the bell HI is $5\frac{1}{2}$ inches. This bell measures about 9 inches from I–H, but the other holes are distant only $1\frac{1}{4}$ inches one from another. It must be noted that the crook (porte-vent) and consequently the socket A into which one puts it, is six lines in diameter; that the end of the fagot concealed under IH has a $1\frac{1}{4}$-inch opening; that the diameter of the twelfth hole which is not stopped is six lines and that the diameter of each of the first six holes is only three lines.

'The letter M shows the reed on the crook (*canal*) LK which is termed *cuivret* because it usually is made of brass (*cuivre*), but it may be of glass, of wood, of gold or silver, etc.

'This bassoon has three keys of which the first B which closes the seventh hole is unprotected, while the second key, E, and the third, G, are protected by cover-plates (*poches*) D and F. C is the mount, or shoe, of brass or other metal which binds together the two branches of this instrument when the latter is not made in a single piece. The bore-ends in these two sections of the bassoon are closed with two plugs which on the one hand prevent leakage and on the other ensure internal continuity of the two tubes so that the wind which enters by the reed M issues only by the twelfth hole and by the bell, H, when all eleven holes are closed.

'What I have just said about these two plugs will be quite readily understood from the butt R, which I have shown separately, where the hole above it is the seventh of the bassoon although it serves to represent the butt E of the *Courtaut* BE which I shall explain later.

'Figure 3 at the right [of Plate 7] shows yet another fagot or bassoon with three keys and eleven holes, but it has no bell to cover the end H, which shows the end hidden under the bell IH in Figure 1. There is no need to explain the keys G, E, B nor the position of the holes which they close, *viz.* F, D, C; nor the crook IK, with its reed L, as all that has already been stated in the explanation of the other bassoon (Fig. 1).

'It remains only to add that bassoons and fagots are not all of the same size. There are those which descend a third or a fourth lower than others. Some people call this kind of instrument *Tarot*[8] but it matters little how one calls them provided one understands their construction and use which is to serve as bass in consorts of *Musettes* and voices, and they play all kinds of music within their compass of a tenth or an eleventh.

'It is unnecessary to explain the method of producing the notes on this instrument as one need only uncover the holes one after the other as on the flute. That is why I now come to explain the middle Figure 2 which is called *Courtaut* although it is nothing other than a shortened fagot or basson which also serves as bass to musettes. It is made of a single cylindrical piece of wood and resembles a thick walking-stick; hence it comes about that some people make large drones out of them like those of the Pilgrims of St. James. But it is sufficient to represent it by the figure BE which has eleven holes marked, of which the seven first are shown open on the front side and the 8, 9, 10 and 11 are marked in white with little points to indicate that these holes are at the back of the instrument which is pierced throughout with two bores C, D which show the end of the courtaut hidden under the cap BCD. This has an opening at the point B to admit the crook and reed AB. The seventh hole shows the place where the two bores C and D emerge to be linked. That is why it is covered by another cap similar to BCD to preclude loss of wind which must be carried from the reed to the eleventh hole where it issues. The wind thus traverses the bore, descending and ascending again.

'There are six more holes in this instrument, *viz.* three at the right side for those who play right-handed and three at the left for left-handed players. They are marked a, γ and ϵ and by β, δ and σ, but one must close the one set or the other with wax when using the holes of the other side which are stopped by the fleshy part of the same fingers which close the proximate holes in the middle of the instrument.

'Moreover, small tubes of wood, called "*tetines*", are inserted in the body of the courtaut to pierce the second channel at the back. As regards the order to be followed with these holes to play through the full range of this instrument, observe that the two below 9 and 10 produce the highest note of all and that one is for right-handed players, the other for left-handed players. The six holes shown and numbered 1, 2, 3, 4, 5 and 6 follow next so that the hole marked 6 produces the seventh note. The tenth hole is called the thumb-hold because it is closed by the thumb and, like the six holes which follow, communicates with the first channel which traverses the entire instrument. The seventh is not a tone-hole but serves purely to make continuous the air in the two channels which meet and unite at this seventh hole. The tetines ϵ, γ, a or σ, δ and β enter only the rear channel which explains why they produce the eighth, ninth and tenth notes so that a and β are the final holes of the courtaut. Hole 11 serves only for the passage of the wind which issues only by this eleventh hole when all the others are closed.

'Explanation must now be given of other figures which also serve as the bass in all kinds of consorts, *viz.* [Plate 8, Fig. 4] the "basson"

BDH which is at the left and the "cervelat" BD. As for the bassoon which consists of a single shaft of wood, it is simple to understand its construction and accessories from what we have written about the preceding fagots. We need only add that this bassoon has four keys because it goes lower and the same thumb which opens the key G opens likewise the key F. The thumb which opens the ninth hole, which is at the back of the instrument, also opens the eighth hole by means of the key E. As for the first key C, it is opened by the little finger of the right hand.

'The last instrument [Plate 8, Fig. 5] is called "*cervelat*" and is none other than a courtaut or a fagot so shortened and so small that it can be concealed in the hand because it is only 5 inches long. But before dealing with the arrangement of the holes and its compass, we must explain the dimensions of the preceding bassoon which goes down a fourth below the ordinary bassoon. Firstly, then, it would extend to $5\frac{1}{2}$ feet if it were deployed, *i.e.* if the two channels BD and DH were continuous in a straight line. It is $2\frac{3}{4}$ feet from B to D and from B to H, indicating the height of the bell, is 8 inches. In the second place, it is $9\frac{1}{2}$ inches from B to the first hole; 8 inches from the third to the fourth hole; and only $1\frac{1}{2}$ inches between the other holes as far as the sixth. In the third place, there are 7 inches from the sixth to the seventh; from the seventh to the eighth which is behind, 4 inches: from the eighth to the ninth it is 7 inches; from the ninth to the tenth only $5\frac{1}{2}$ inches. Finally, there are 10 inches from the tenth to the eleventh and from this eleventh hole to the bell-mouth, *i.e.* to B is 3 inches. The diameter of the bell is 3 inches, but it must be noted that the bore of the bassoon, *i.e.* its channel, is narrow at its commencement and widens to its other end. This occurs similarly with the oboe and cornetts, rendering their notes stronger than those of instruments which are bored to the same diameter from beginning to end.

'There remains only to explain the *cervelat*, the upper surface of which has eight holes of equal diameter and these are the termination of channels which traverse the length of the instrument. The base also has thus eight holes which nevertheless form a single continuous channel so that the harmonic cervelat descends as low as an instrument eight times as long, *i.e.* $3\frac{1}{2}$ feet long approximately. This explains why the holes must be placed on this cylinder as shown here, so as to penetrate the bore at the appropriate points to produce the notes of this instrument. The reed A is in the middle of the eight holes already mentioned which are covered by a metal plate or cap as shown at D. They are also plugged with small pieces of parchment or wood or any other material preferred, so as to be continuous and form a single channel.

'As regards the position of the holes, this is marked by the fourteen numbers above the holes—1 denotes the first hole, 2 the second and so on with the others, to the fourteenth. But observe that those which are white and starred are behind and cannot be seen at the same time as those which are black and are in front, *viz.* 1, 2, 3, 4 and 5. These are near each other on the outside only because inside the bore they are separated as much as the others, being pierced obliquely—one upwards, the other downwards to 6 and 7 which have each four holes yet giving but two notes because the upper two meet at the same point in the concavity of the channel as likewise do the lower two and finally 8, 9 and 10. But 11, 12, 13 and 14 are on the other side and 15 gives the lowest note of all when closed and all the others are kept closed. Opening the first gives the highest note so this cervelat has a compass of a fifteenth of which every note is produced by closing all the holes one after the other. This can be done the more easily since they are very near each other and one can close two, three or four with the same finger. The wind issues by the four unnumbered holes c lower down at the right and by another hole which is in the base-plate.'

It is not possible to state precisely when in the seventeenth century the one-piece two-keyed dulzian gave place to the jointed three-keyed bassoon. The change entailed separation of the long-joint and tenor-joint, connected through the U-shaped butt-joint, and the addition of a bell-joint prolonging the bore to enable the production of B♭, which remains to this day the lowest note of the bassoon. As already mentioned Praetorius (1619) did not know the jointed bassoon and though Mersenne (1636) shows several types and vaguely refers to the tubes of one being 'fagotées ou liées', all appear to be of dulzian formation. A. Kircher (1601–80)[9] mentions the '*Dulcinum* or Fagotto', but merely copies Mersenne. Cerone (1560–1625)[10] largely copied Zacconi and so adds nothing to our knowledge of the bassoon. It is at this stage, however, that pictorial examples can be of assistance.

In the Art Museum of Aachen there is a half-portrait (Plate 9) 'Der Fagottspieler' said to be by Harmen Hals, son of the famous Frans Hals. If this painting of the Dutch School is correctly attributed to Harmen Hals (1611–69) it shows that the bassoon had developed considerably since Praetorius and Mersenne. Although only the bell-joint, the crook, the reed and the upper parts of the long and tenor joints are visible, it is enough to identify it with (1) Randle Holme's 'Double curtaile' of *c.* 1688 (see Plate 2, Fig. 1); (2) the bassoon shown in Rijkel's Trade-card, and (3) as made by Denner.

Perhaps the most conclusive evidence is that of a German woodcut and engraving of drawings by Johann Christoff Weigel, Nuremberg (1661–1726). The woodcut (Plate 9) is from a very comprehensive work of 1698: *Abbildung der Gemein-Nützlichen Haupt-Stände* and shows a bassoon-maker at work at his bench boring the finger-holes of a dulzian, while on the floor beside him lies a second dulzian. Leaning against his bench, however, is a three-keyed bassoon of transitional form with elaborate mouldings turned on the lathe. It is precisely such a bassoon that Weigel shows in one of a large number of partly-coloured illustrations of instrumentalists included in his *Musikalisches Theatrum*.[11] This undated work may be attributed to the period 1715–35 and at least twenty-three of the drawings are closely connected with the same number of paragraphs in Mattheson's *Neu Eröffnete Orchestre* of 1713. Of the twenty-three drawings, No. 9 is of a left-handed bassoon-player whose instrument is identical with the type of instrument leaning against the bench in the woodcut of 1698. Beneath the engraving is the following verse:

Fagott

Wo Orgel und Regal auch Clavizijmbel fehlen,
  und selbst der Violon, in Suma Fundament,
da kan man meine Stim zum besten Grund erwehlen
  der starck getriebene Hauch und aufgeweckte Händ
erzwingen solche Thön, darob man sich verwundert
  und die sonst schaffe Seel zur Fröhlichkeit ermuntert.

'When the organ, the regal, and the harpsichord are inadequate, and even the lowest notes of the double bass, then for the best reasons my preference is for the bassoon; such notes are produced from it, by steadily expelled breath and deft hand, that they rouse the listener to wonder and instil joy in his spirit, hitherto unmoved.'

It is important to remember that so long as the bassoon had only three keys (two for the thumbs and one for L or R 4) it could be played at the left-thigh as in Weigel's drawing or at the right-thigh as it is today. The addition of the fourth key (G♯) stabilised the manner of holding the bassoon as the G♯ key lies beside the F-key and is played with the same finger, but it could not be reached if the hands were reversed. In the case of the oboe it was for long the practice to duplicate the d♯ key to accommodate players who preferred to play left-hand above the right or vice versa. Among many hundreds of bassoons known to the author, only one has a duplicate G♯ key. This is a unique fagottino by Scherer, c. 1750, in the Hug Collection, Zurich, with four keys, of which two are duplicate G♯ keys mounted in wooden 'blocks'.

In the Kunsthistorisches Museum, Vienna,[12] among the unique sixteenth- and seventeenth-century instruments from the Ambras Collection are three dulzians of presumed Italian origin and of special significance for our present purpose:

No. 195   A two-keyed dulzian in C, of one piece (no maker's mark), held in normal fashion. Length of twin bores 98 + 86 cm.

No. 199   A two-keyed dulzian or doppel-fagott in low A (marked 'HIER.S.') and held right hand above left—reverse of normal. Possibly made in two pieces and glued under the ornamental band. Length of twin bores 131·7 + 116·7 cm.

No. 201   A two-keyed dulzian in C of unique transitional form (no maker's mark), held in normal fashion. The instrument is in three joints—tenor-joint, bass-joint and butt. (The D key is missing.) No other such specimen has survived. Length of twin bores 105 + 101 cm.

There are five other dulzians in this wonderful collection and three of them are for playing right hand above left.

It is very interesting that four paintings of a group of six wind musicians of *c.* 1616 have survived. The first, reproduced here (Plate 10) is a detail from a painting by Denis van Alsloot dated 1616, preserved in the National Museum, Madrid. It portrays 'The Procession of the Religious Orders of the Town of Antwerp on the day of the Fête de la Vierge du Rosaire'. The six musicians are painted with great precision and from right to left the instruments are: trombone, alto pommer, discant schalmey, cornetto, a second alto pommer and a dulzian played at the left thigh with right hand uppermost. It is noteworthy that the wood-wind bass is here supplied by a dulzian and not by a bass pommer.

Mahillon[13] has drawn attention to the curious fact that the same musicians with identical instruments appear in two pictures by Antoine Sallaert in the Musée royal de Peinture de Bruxelles. One of these represents 'La Procession des Pucelles du Sablon', the other 'L'Infante Isabelle abattant l'oiseau au tir du grand Serment'. The question arises, did the Antwerp musicians take part in the Brussels festivities or did Sallaert merely borrow his ideas from van Alsloot whose pupil he may have been?

Dr. Karl Geiringer has reproduced[14] a similar group (three pommers, trombone and dulzian) from a painting by Antoine Sallaert in the Turin Art Gallery. He is in error, however, in ascribing the painting to the sixteenth century. Sallaert was born in Brussels *c.* 1590, inscribed as pupil-painter in 1606 and master-painter in 1613. His paintings must, therefore, be of the seventeenth century and most probably subsequent to Alsloot's painting of 1616. These authentic representations of a continental wind-band of *c.* 1616 deserve greater attention than they have as yet received.

As dated wood-wind instruments are comparatively rare, it is fortunate that a typical two-keyed dulzian survives at Frankfurt-am-Main[15] engraved above the finger-holes with the Frankfurt eagle and the date '1605'. The collection includes two other contemporary dulzians and bass-dulzian or quart-fagott unique in being covered with gold embossed leather. Other collections possessing dulzians are: Hamburg;[16] Heyer-Lepizig[17]—a pair, one of which is by J. C. Denner of Nürnberg. It is 'gedackt' (*i.e.* muted) illustrating a seventeenth-century custom in Germany where dulzians were termed 'offen' or 'gedackt' depending on the absence or presence of a perforated capsule placed over the mouth of the bell. Berlin[18] has seven dulzians, five of which came from St. Wenzels-kirche in Naumburg. The German National Museum, Nürnberg, has three dulzians including two by J. C. Denner.[19] Vienna Kunsthistorisches Museum has acquired from the 'Gesellschaft der Musikfreunde in Wien'[20] a unique form of dulzian with four open keys. The second and third keys are interlocked so that closing the second closes the third but allows the third to function independently. This device is the embryo of many improvements subsequently effected in wood-wind keys. The original bears the marks: CK–AAL–S.F.S. and on a metal bell-rim is the following quaint verse:

'Der. Dulcin, bin. ich. genant.
Nit. einem, iedem. wol. pekat.
Der. mich. wil. recht. pfeifen.
Der. mus. mich. wol. lerne. greifen.'

'The Dulzian am I called,
Not well known to everyone.
Whosoever will play me correctly,
Must learn well how to finger me.'

Salzburg has five dulzians (Nos. 196–200),[21] Linz has five,[22] Prague and Paris[23] each have one but both are defective. Brussels has a Collection[24] of seven originals and four facsimiles. The seven comprise three from the Correr Collection, Venice (Nos. 988–990) and a unique group of four Spanish 'bajoncillos' (fagottini):

No. 2327 Fagott piccolo in G (Height 0·645 m.)
No. 2328 Alt fagott in c (Height 0·505 m.)
No. 2329 Alt fagott in d (Height 0·430 m.)
No. 2330 Discant fagott in g (Height 0·342 m.)

The first three are marked in relief 'Melchor, R.S.' surmounted by a crown. Beyond the fact that these instruments came from the Barbieri Collection, Madrid, nothing more is known. It may be noted that the seventeenth-century reed group to support the voices in churches in Spain included chirimia (*i.e.* discant schalmey), bajoncillo (*i.e.* fagott-piccolo) and bajon (*i.e.* chorist fagott). Brunswick[25] has two dulzians and New York[26] Metropolitan Museum has three curious and apparently incomplete specimens.

Cecil Forsyth[27] remarks that 'most museums possess well-preserved examples of these instruments and there are many in the hands of private collectors'. The author does not know of a single dulzian in Britain—not even a facsimile—in public *or* private ownership. Exact copies of baroque wood-wind are, however, now being successfully made in Berlin by Otto Steinkopf, a bassoon-player, who uses one of his own instruments in concerted work.

REFERENCES

[1] According to Sachs, *Handbuch der Musikinstrumentenkunde* (Leipzig, 1920), p. 323, Schreiber was an Electoral Chamber-musician at Berlin.

[2] 'A 17th-century wood-wind curiosity' by L. G. Langwill in *Musical Times* (August, 1938).

[3] Sammlung Alter Musikinstrumente bei der Staatlichen Hochschule für Musik. Catalogue by Curt Sachs (Berlin, 1922), No. 289 and Plate 27. Length, 271½ cm., Lowest note A♭,.

[4] Alte Musik-Instrumente in Museum Carolino Augusteum, Salzburg by Karl Geiringer (Leipzig, 1932), No. 187 and Pl. III. Length, 244 cm., Lowest note B♭,.

[5] Museum Wielkopolskie. Katalog. (Poznan, 1949.) No. 165 and Illustration.

[6] Kindly communicated by Otto Oromszegi, Budapest. It is noteworthy that the Sopron Gross-Bass-Pommer is marked 'C.K.' a monogram which appears also on a Viennese F-Contra-bassoon in Poznan No. 182.

[7] Baines, A. C.: *Wood-wind Instruments and their History* (London, 1957). Plate XXXI, an excellent illustration of a sixteenth–seventeenth century pirouette.

[8] The word *tarot* is not defined in any musical sense in modern French dictionaries. La Grande Encyclopédie française (1750) defines Tarot: Instrument à anche et à vent qui a onze trous et qui sert de basse aux concerts de musettes. Littré and Larousse both give Tarot: ancien nom du basson.

[9] Kircher, A.: *Musurgia Universalis* (Rome, 1650), Book VI, p. 500 and Pl. facing.

[10] Cerone, P.: *El Melopeo* (Naples, 1613).

[11] A facsimile Volume of Weigel's *Musikalisches Theatrum*, edited by Dr. Alfred Berner, Berlin, has been published (Kassel, 1961).

[12] *Die Sammlung alter Musikinstrumente*, Kunsthistorisches Museum in Wien; Katalog von J. Schlosser (Vienna, 1920), pp. 82 and 83. Pl. XXXVIII.

[13] Catalogue du Museé instrumentale de Bruxelles by V. Mahillon (Ghent, 1909), Vol. II, p. 25.

[14] *Musical Instruments* by Karl Geiringer (London, 1943), Pl. XXVI.

[15] Katalog der Musikinstrumente im historischen Museum der Stadt Frankfurt am Main by Peter Epstein (Frankfurt a/M., 1927), p. 27. No. 138 and Pl. 2.

[16] Verzeichnis der Sammlung alter Musikinstrumente by Hans Schröder (Hamburg, 1930), No. 1928, 389, p. 71 and Pl. 18, c.

[17] Musikhistorisches Museum von Wilhelm Heyer in Cöln: Kleiner Katalog by Georg Kinsky (Cologne, 1913), pp. 159–60 and Pl. 27, Nos. 1360 and 1361.

[18] *Vide* reference No. 3 *supra*.

[19] Germ. Nat. Museum, Nürnberg: Nos. MI 125, height 0·95 m., and MI 124, height 0·67 m. Kindly communicated by Dr. J. van der Meer.

[20] Zusatz-Band zur Geschichte der K. K. Gesellschaft der Musikfreunde in Wien by E. Mandyczewski (Vienna, 1912), pp. 166–7, No. 117. A facsimile is No. 994 in the Brussels Collection. *Vide* Mahillon, Catal. II (2nd edit.), pp. 266–7. This facsimile was lent to the Royal Military Exhib., London, 1890, and is described in the Catalogue by Capt. Day under No. 149.

[21] *Vide* reference No. 4 *supra*.

[22] Die Musikinstrumenten-Sammlung des Oberösterreichischen Landesmuseum by O. Wessely (Linz, 1952), p. 37.

[23] Supplément au Catalogue du Musée du Conservatoire national de Musique by L. Pillaut (Paris, 1894), No. 1119, pp. 28–9.

[24] *Vide* reference No. 13 *supra*. Vol. IV, pp. 197–9.

[25] Verzeichnis der Sammlung alter Musikinstrumente im Städtischen Museum, Braunschweig, by Hans Schröder (Brunswick, 1928), Nos. 94 and 95 on p. 31 and Illust., p. 30.

[26] Catalogue of the Crosby Brown Collection (New York, 1902), p. 147, Nos. 1350, 1674 and 2036.

[27] *Orchestration* by Cecil Forsyth (London, 2nd edit., 1935), p. 231.

CHAPTER 3

The Bassoon in Other Reference Books
from the Late Seventeenth Century Onwards

COMMENCING at the close of the seventeenth century, we have a
valuable work of 1687 by Daniel Speer,[1] *Grund-richtiger, kurz, leicht
und nöthiger jetzt wol-vermehrter Unterricht der musicalischen Kunst*,
Part III is entitled: *Allerhand Instrumenta greiffen und blasen lernen.*
Speer poses the question: 'How many holes has a Bass-Fagott and
how is such an instrument fingered?' He then states: 'It has, including
the key, seven holes above and, including the key, three holes below.
It is fingered in the following manner, but it must be understood that
the left hand must be kept above opposite the mouth. This must likewise be kept in mind when following the Chart No. II.' The fingering
chart is that of a two-keyed Dulzian with open-keys for E and F and
the compass is C–f'. Speer adds a note: 'Should, however, anyone use
the right hand uppermost, opposite the mouth, it must be understood
that what is stated in the fingering for the left hand then applies to the
right hand and the following two Sonatas will show the nature and
manipulation of a Fagott and can be played with two or three Fagotts.'
We now come to a very different work in Mattheson's *Das neu-
eröffnete Orchestre* (1713).[2] 'Von den musicalischen Instrumenten' deals
with the bassoon:

'The stately Bassoon, Basse de Chormorne [*sic*], *It.* Fagotto, *vulgo*
Dulcian, is the usual bass, the foundation or accompaniment of
the Hautbois. It should, of course, be easier to play than the oboe
because it does not require the same finesse or manipulation. . . .
He who would distinguish himself on the bassoon will find that
elegance and speed especially in the high register tax his powers
to the full. Especially with bassoons and oboes one must be
supplied with good reeds and the best players take care to make
them themselves to suit their mouth "because a good reed is half
the battle". The compass of the bassoon extends over three and
a half octaves from C to f' or g'. Occasionally it produces contra

B flat and A in addition. The "Bombardi", of which use was formerly made in place of Bassoons, are no longer in fashion.' Mattheson was still familiar with the two-keyed dulzian (lowest note C) as well as the newer fagott (lowest note B♭, or even A,). The bombardi were the straight-tubed pommers—bass to the schalmeys.

We find a curious distinction drawn by Niedt in his *Musicalische Handleitung*[3] (1721) in a list of definitions where he describes:

'Dulcian: ein teutscher Fagott
Fagotto: . . . frantzösisch Basson. . . .'

Walther's *Lexikon*[4] (1732) adds nothing fresh to our knowledge as the definitions are almost verbatim those of Mattheson (*vide supra*). On the other hand, Majer's *Music-Saal*[5] (1732) while textually in the main repetitive of Mattheson and Walther, includes a fingering chart for a three-keyed 'Fagot-Bass' with compass B♭, to f♯'. Unfortunately, the sketch beside the chart is absurdly drawn as the keys and hole for LT are shown on the wing instead of on the long-joint! (Plate 10)

The next reference work is Zedler's *Lexikon*[6] of 1733 containing a mere repetition of Walther, but in 1738 Eisel published under the pseudonym '*Musicus autodidactus*', a valuable treatise[7] in the form of question and answer on contemporary instruments. He distinguishes the 'Basson', a four-keyed type, with compass B♭, to e' from the 'Teutsche Basson', a two-keyed dulzian with compass C to f' and gives fingering-charts for both (Plate 11). The following is Eisel's quaint allusion to the dulzian:

'The Teutschen Bassons, Fagotte or Bombardi, as used by our German ancestors before Music had become clothed in Italian and French fashion, are no longer in use and accordingly it is unnecessary to waste paper with a description of them. He who is a connoisseur of antiques can inform himself about them from the accompanying chart.'

It may be remarked that Eisel's chart for the Dulzian agrees with that of Speer, already mentioned, but the chart for the four-keyed 'Basson' is the first to show a G♯ key. Eisel ends his chapter on the bassoon by specifying the five requirements in a player: '1. A good reed (the best are made in Berlin). 2. A quick tongue. 3. Adroit fingers. 4. Daily practice. 5. Inborn natural disposition and a good pair of lungs.'

Diderot and D'Alembert's *Encyclopédie*[8] (1751–65) includes a long chapter dealing with Plate IX of the section *Lutherie* (Plate 12). The fingering chart covers the compass A, to a' and is for a four-keyed

D

bassoon. The production of A,, B♭, and B♮, is 'sans déboucher aucun trou, par la seule manière de pousser le vent dans l'instrument' (*i.e.* without uncovering any hole, but solely by the manner in which the instrument is blown). The notes were, in fact, 'lipped'.

It has been repeatedly stated that the fourth key G♯ (R4) was added in 1751 but, as has been shown, Eisel records it in 1738[*] and there survive two dated bassoons having this fourth key: (i) Bassoon by Stanesby Junior (1747) formerly owned by Canon Galpin;[9] (ii) Bassoon bearing what is presumed to be an owner's name 'G. de Bruijn 1730' in Brussels.[10] Pictorial evidence is afforded by the Dutch Trade-card of Coenraad Rijkel[11] *c.* 1705, master flute-maker, born in Amsterdam in 1667 and apprenticed in 1679 to his uncle Richard Haka whose partner he became till Haka's death *c.* 1705. Adam Carse has remarked[12] that G♯ 'the first chromatic key in the primary scale of the bassoon, was already well known on the contemporary flute and oboe; both of these had their D sharp key before the end of the seventeenth century, so there was ample precedent for the new bassoon key'.

In 1756 there appeared *Apollo's Cabinet* or *The Muses' Delight*.[13] 'The Gamut or Scale of the Bassoon' is for a four-keyed instrument with compass B♭, to g'. The notes for f♯ upwards are designated, 'These are pincht Notes'.

Adlung's *Anleitung zur musikalischen Gelehrheit*[14] (1758) defines 'Basson' as 'der Fagott' and 'Fagott ist mit Basson einerlei'.

It is still for the four-keyed basson that Tans'ur[15] in 1772 includes a fingering-chart and the same chart appeared in the 7th edit. of 1829!

A very rare Tutor, *Principe de Basson* by Abrahame[16] (1764–*c.* 1805), a Paris clarinettist at the Opera and composer for his instrument, includes a fingering-chart the importance of which lies in the appearance of a fifth key, E♭ (for LT) on the long-joint. It is difficult to assign a precise date for Abrahame's Tutor, but it must date from the period 1780–1800. The compass shown is B♭' to a'. Another Méthode possibly of earlier date is a reprint of Hotteterre le Romain, *Méthode . . . de la Flûte traversière, de la Flûte-à-bec et du Hautbois* (1707).[17] Reissued by Antoine Bailleux 'Marchand de Musique' in Paris *c.* 1765 it has, added to the original text, tablatures for clarinet and bassoon. The scale is for a five-keyed bassoon (B♭,, D, E♭, F, G♯) with compass B♭,–a'.

The *Essai sur la Musique . . .* of La Borde[18] (1780) provides a very important record for historical purposes as the section dealing with the Bassoon is the work of Pierre Cugnier, a pupil of Capelle and player of

[*] Walsh in 1730 published a similar chart. *Vide* p. 166.

distinction, born in Paris in 1740. He was appointed a Bassoonist at the Opera in 1764 and was one of the four bassoonists at the Concert Spirituel in 1774. La Borde informs us that Cugnier would never play a solo in public, considering that the effort of preparation of a solo harmed the equality of tone necessary for accompaniment, but his Tutor, on account of its authoritative nature, was included by La Borde in his *Essai*. The chart here again is for a five-keyed bassoon, including E♭ (for LT) and the compass B♭, to f'. Referring to the upper register, Cugnier remarks 'ces derniers tons ne sont point usités, surtout Ut, Re, Mi, Fa, mais cependant ils ne sont pas infesables, on verra cy après pour quoy on les a placés icy' (*i.e.* these last notes are not used, especially c, d, e and f, but they are not actually unplayable: it will be seen in due course why they are included here).

The addition of the fifth and sixth closed keys (E flat and F sharp) was almost contemporaneous. From the foregoing it is probable that E♭ (LT on French and English bassoons and L4 on German bassoons) was the earlier of the two keys. In the author's collection of photographs of some 500 bassoons in public and private collections throughout the world, there is only one instance of a five-keyed bassoon with F♯ as the fifth key and it is clearly a later addition. It is remarkable to reflect that Mozart's Bassoon Concerto would be performed on a four-keyed instrument and it was not till nearly the close of the century that the six-keyed bassoon became standard.

Mahillon was the first to draw attention to a rare Dutch dictionary, *Muzijkaal Kunst-Woordenboek* by J. Verschuere Reynvaan,[19] (1795). In this the author completed letters A–M but was prevented from further publication by the invasion of Holland by the French in 1795. Further misfortune befell the greater part of the bound copies through fire, with the result that the book is very rare. The plates are of special interest as they depict fingering-charts for bassoons with four keys (compass B♭,–c''): with six keys B♭,, D, E♭, F, G♯ and a harmonic key opened for f' upwards (compass B♭,–g' or c''): and a curious chart for 'Bombardo or Bassoon with two keys', *i.e.* a dulzian (compass C–f'), but the instrument drawn at the left of the chart is a *bassoon* with only the F and G♯ keys! It is clear, however, from the fingering that they are intended to represent the E and F keys of a *dulzian*. In the text, p. 72, after referring to the four-keyed bassoon, Reynvaan states that bassoons can have one or even two more keys, but similarly there are those with only three keys, termed *vulgo* dulcian; also those with only two keys, termed bombardo: 'now, these for the greater part, have gone out of use'. It seems extraordinary that it should have been considered worth while in 1795 to deal with the two- or three-keyed dulzian. The text, however, contains (*s.v.* Fagotto) a very early reference to a *crook-key* 'for going up to a high g'. Under Ambitus (compass) we read: 'The lowest note of the bassoon is Contra B♭ and it can be blown quite easily enough to e′ and can actually reach c″.'

A manuscript sheet of the compass of wood-wind and brass in the hand of Samuel Wesley (1766–1837) is in the British Museum.[20] For Fagotto, he shows B♭,, C and every half note up to b♭′.

Koch's *Lexikon*[21] (1802) describes a seven-keyed bassoon (B♭,, D, E♭, F, G♯, a′, c″), the last two keys 'die man nur an neuern Fagotten findet', (*i.e.* which are found only on modern bassoons). The compass was B♭, to b♭′ but 'many play even up to d″'. Besides the normal bassoon, there was the quartfagott, a fourth lower and the contrafagott, an octave lower. It may be noted that Koch uses the masculine gender for bassoon—Der Fagott—in which he was followed by Heckel in his brochure of 1899.

A very strange article on the bassoon was written by C. F. D. Schubart (1743–91) and published in Vienna in 1806.[22] He considered that the bassoon was of French origin but remarks that it was made with great perfection in Nürnberg though the Parisians had bassoons of noteworthy excellence. Schubart concludes with a surprising exaggerated eulogy:

'It demands the fullest breath and such a sound and masculine embouchure that only few people are fit physically to play it in a masterly manner. Although the French invented it, the Germans have produced the greatest masters of it. For a long time, it was used only for accompaniment but the Germans were the first to wrest a solo from it, and, in fact, with such happy result that now the bassoon belongs to the first solo-instruments of the world. The tone of the instrument is so companionable, so delightfully talkative, so attuned for every pure soul, that until the Day of Judgment the bassoon can never be dispensed with. It assumes all roles: it accompanies martial music with manly dignity; it is heard majestically in church; it sustains the opera: it reasons with wisdom in the concert hall, gives a swing to the dance and fulfils every requirement.'

The bassoon's most loyal admirer today could hardly endorse such an overstatement! In the only practical reference to the instrument,

Schubart gives its compass as B♭, to a′, adding that 'skill produces still lower notes' and 'B♮, is obtained by pinching'.

One must exercise discretion in consulting *The Cyclopaedia* of Rees[23] (1810–24). Publication of the thirty-nine volumes was so delayed that much of the matter was quite out of date. Even allowing for this, Volume III containing the article 'Bassoon' describes a three-keyed instrument! The compass is stated as A, to a′ the tones and semitones being as complete as on any other keyed instrument. It is admitted that not every performer could produce a lower note than B♭, or a higher one than g′. The Plates for Vol. III, however, include a fingering chart for an eight-keyed bassoon with an excellent engraving of the instrument. Compass: B♭, to b♭′ (with no B♮, or C♯). The engraving is dated 1807 though the plates for Vol. III were published in 1820. The text refers to performers thus:

> 'In the last age, Miller was the favourite performer on the bassoon in England at all public places; but we have at present Mr. Holmes, a superior performer, at least in point of tone, to any that we have heard elsewhere. The two Bezozzis of Turin rendered these kindred instruments, the hautbois and bassoon, famous in Italy during the middle of last century.'

Carl Bärmann (1782–1842), 1st Bassoon in the Royal Prussian Orchestra, contributed in 1820 an article[24] of some technical merit entitled 'Concerning the nature and peculiarities of the Bassoon and its use as a Solo and Orchestral Instrument'. Bärmann was a pupil of Georg Wenzel Ritter (1748–1808). He stresses the importance of a player making his own reeds and recommends soft cane as opposed to the hard cane required for oboe and clarinet. As the bassoon plays a tenor part in music, all study must accordingly aim at imitating a fine tenor voice and at contesting for rank with a talented tenor singer. Noble impressiveness, *cantabile* and *sostenuto*, is admittedly very difficult to produce but this lies in the nature of the bassoon and is its true and most beautiful characteristic. Later, in his long article, he remarks on the difficulty of trills and f′ and g′ which are bad. He gives the compass as B♭, to b♮′ adding that one can descend to A, and rise to e♭″, e″ and even to f″ but he did not consider that these notes lay within the nature of the instrument and could be produced only by forcing them unnaturally to the detriment of the instrument and to the embouchure.

During a short stay in Switzerland in 1807 he met an amateur who had such a number of keys on his instrument that sometimes he did not know how to obtain certain notes. When Bärmann asked the purpose of all the extra keys he was told that they gave extra notes, but when asked to let him hear them, the player could only produce sounds resembling a cowhorn rather than a bassoon. The amateur was subsequently given a short lesson and shown how to play more moderately. After dealing with the orchestral use of the instrument, he stresses that as it comes nearest to the human voice, it is capable of expressing every feeling. To cultivate this quality, Bärmann, when in Naples for six months in 1807, took lessons from the singing-master, Mosca, who rehearsed with Bärmann very difficult recitatives and arias on the bassoon, accompanying them on the piano. Following the instruction he acquired, Bärmann sought in his playing to emulate this masterly singer and was then (1820) about to publish some original compositions for the bassoon as well as arrangements with piano accompaniment.

The condition of the bassoon in Austria in 1824 is disclosed in *Darstellung des Fabriks . . .* by von Keess.[25] Three types of bassoon were then being produced in Vienna. 1. The ordinary bassoon which by then had twelve instead of five keys. (He does not state the keys.) 2. The tenor bassoon pitched between the cor anglais and the ordinary bassoon. (Again he gives no details.) 3. The contrabassoon descending to $B\flat_{,,}$ and might be as much as six feet in height.

The name of Iwan Müller (1786–1854), a virtuoso clarinet-player of Russian extraction, is closely associated with a number of important improvements in his instrument in the first quarter of the nineteenth century. In 1825 Gambaro published Müller's *Méthode pour la nouvelle Clarinette*, dedicated to George IV, and about the same time Hofmeister published Müller's *Anweisung zu der neuen Clarinette*. On page 3 of the Introduction the following occurs:

'So that wind music may be performed to advantage according to my principles, it is indispensable to remedy in the bassoon, as made at present, inherent faults which often render very difficult the performance of a composition. I have succeeded in improving the instrument by adding three new keys. One gives the low notes, unobtainable until now, B♮, and C♯. The second is for b♭ and b♭' and the third is for c♯/d♭ and e♭/d♯. These new keys are also useful for many high, medium and low notes.'

As will be learned in Chapter 6, Simiot of Lyons had added keys for low B♮, and C as early as 1808 and Almenräder, *c.* 1820, gave credit to

Grenser for having added the middle c♯ key while he himself added the b♭ key for R3.

Müller's claim of c. 1825, to have been first to add these keys, would, therefore, appear to be unfounded.

Lichtenthal[26] (1826) is often cited but describes a four-keyed bassoon —in 1826!—adding that on recent bassoons there were keys for a' and c".

Castil-Blaze's *Dictionary*[27] (1833–51) is no more informative than Lichtenthal's but the following extract from the article 'Basson' is worthy of quotation:

> 'As the tone of the bassoon has little penetration, it is not always distinguishable in the full orchestra, but the effect it creates, the harmony it introduces there, exist none the less and it is due more credit than is sometimes given to other instruments. It is like the violet, hidden in the grass, perfuming the meadow, but does not reveal itself among the flowers which beautify the surroundings.'

Wilhelm Schneider [28] in 1834 dealt with the history, construction and compass of every instrument; their inventors, improvers, virtuosi and tutors, etc.

In the section on the bassoon (pp. 23–25) as usual, Gerber's *Lexikon* is cited as authority for Afranio's 'invention' and Schnitzer's skill as a sixteenth-century *bassoon*-maker—both erroneous attributions.

He informs us that in wind-music, military music in particular, the lower quartfagott and contrafagott were in use. The bassoon described was ten-keyed (B♭‚, D, E♭, F♯, G♯, F, b♭, c♯, a' and c") with a compass B♭‚–e♭" and he adds that 'recently bassoons are made with more keys but these, on account of their high price, are not in general use'. After referring to Almenräder's improvements, he describes the sling for hanging the instrument from a coat-button 'according to the height of the player'. In describing the crook he mentions 'a small hole, like a pin-hole in the side, to allow free passage of excess air'. It will be noted that there is no reference to a crook-key which was at that time being fitted by Savary to work independently or in conjunction with the high a' and c" keys. Curiously, the scale on Pl. IV is for a four-keyed bassoon—outmoded fifty years before—compass B♭‚–g♯'. By comparison, the other scales are for a seven-keyed clarinet and for Sellner's nine-keyed oboe.

Schilling[29] in 1835 repeats almost verbatim the article by Schneider, above. A ten-keyed bassoon is described but for orchestral purposes, the compass is given as D–a′ or b♭′. B♭, and C and notes above b♭′ are difficult and B♮, and C♯ are lacking. Schilling mentions the tenor bassoon, a fifth above the bassoon.

Between 1836 and 1838 there appeared in Paris a manual[30] in three volumes, left incomplete by A. E. Choron at his death and completed by J. A. de Lafage. In Chapter V, 'Observations on various instruments' . . . Section III is devoted to the bassoon. The only point of interest is the statement that the compass was A,–a′ but A, B♭, and B♮, were all obtained with all holes closed. Their intonation depended on lip control, 'ce qui n'est pas facile, en sorte que peu y réussissent'. This seems an understatement! Vol. I, Part III, pp. 268–71, describes the bassoon and states that formerly it had at most six or seven keys whereas modern bassoons (1839) had ten. Plate III depicts a crudely engraved bassoon with keys B♭,, D, E♭, c♯,, a′ and c″ for LT and in addition F, F♯, G♯ and b♭. A very interesting list of makers and addresses follows, twenty-five wood-wind makers, fourteen reed-makers and eighteen brass makers. The list formed the subject of an article by the author entitled 'Instrument-making in Paris in 1839'.[31] It is remarked that bassoons were not made in large numbers in France because they were little played by amateurs.

In 1855 H. Welcker von Gontershausen published his *Magazin*,[32] a somewhat rare work containing a wealth of detail not to be found elsewhere:

Part   I. A conspectus of musical instruments in antiquity and history of music down to 1855.

Part II. Description of gut-strung instruments: steel-strung instruments including keyboard instruments: wood-wind, brass wind: percussion, etc.

Part III. Rules of construction of stringed instruments, strings, etc., pianos and their mechanism and maintenance.

Part IV. Construction and preservation of the bassoon and reeds (pp. 374–86) followed by other wood-wind, brass, percussion, etc.

The historical account of the bassoon in Part II (pp. 137–8) is very inaccurate even to the spelling of names, but a list is given of keys on current bassoons—ten in number—B♭,, D, E♭, c♯,, a′ and c″ for LT—F♯ for RT—F, G♯ for R4—b♭ for R3. The crook-hole is still mentioned but no reference to a crook-key.

In an account of the Munich Industrie-Ausstellung 1854, special mention is made of a bassoon with twenty keys by Jacob Helwert, Stuttgart. At the Great Exhibition in London in 1851 Helwert had gained a Prize Medal for his new bassoon with nineteen keys. Unfortunately no specimen of Helwert's bassoon is known.

In Part IV, von Gontershausen gives the fullest account known to the author of the construction, etc., of the bassoon. After mentioning the contrabassoon, and three other smaller types rarely used, he describes Almenräder's improvements and a sixteen-keyed bassoon, adding that there was then no definite number of keys.

Attempts were being made to increase the number as, for example, Helwert's twenty-keyed instrument mentioned above. After describing key-mounting and choice of wood (to which Chapter X is devoted), Gontershausen gives a list of Almenräder's recommendations for remedying a number of defects of intonation, e.g. untrue octaves c/c', d/d', G/g and stresses the importance of B♭,, B♮,, C, D, E and F being accurately tuned first. The pin-hole (in the crook) 'almost always present in new bassoons' must always be made with a very fine borer. If the hole is too large, some high and low notes will give trouble, e.g. B♭, b', c'', d'', f'', E♭, D, C. The hole could be narrowed by a burnisher but if a greater reduction is necessary it can be remedied only by soldering-pewter. The very interesting chapter ends with directions for the care and maintenance of the bassoon: dry out the bore; clear the finger-holes with a feather; leave the joints apart for a time before placing them in the case; oil the bassoon at least once in every three months. The oils to be avoided are Bergamot, Almond, Walnut and Baumöl. All these easily form on the wall of the bore a crust which cannot be removed without difficulty and do more harm than good. The best oil is purified rape-seed oil. A bottle of this placed in warm sunshine to 'settle', allows impurities to form a sediment, after which the clear liquid may be poured off. After oiling the bore, the bassoon should not be blown for two or three days during which the oil will have become thoroughly absorbed by the wood. Finally, careful cleaning of the key-work, removing dust, etc., with a feather, is very important as is a good dust-proof case lined with soft material.

In 1865 Arrey von Dommer published his *Lexikon*[33] based largely upon Koch's work of 1802. According to von Dommer the bassoon had sixteen keys (including B♮, and C♯ lacking on old instruments): B♭,, B♮,, C, C♯, D, E♭, F, F♯, G, G♯, b♭, c♯, e♭, a', c'' and d''. Compass B♭,–e♭''.

Mendel's *Lexikon*[34] of 1870 has an excellent article describing Almenräder's sixteen-key bassoon and proceeds:

> 'The fingering of the bassoon is much simpler than that of the clarinet and can easily be learnt by self-study with the help of a fingering chart. . . . The lowest notes from B♭, to D are powerful but rather rough and like the notes above g' to c" or higher are not employed even by virtuosi. . . . The bassoon is seldom used in passages alone as its tone is too weak. Only passages which are also played by the 'cello, or else a stronger sounding instrument to add strength, should be given to the bassoon . . . for this reason orchestras were recently employing two or three bassoons for better balance in the wood-wind section.'

It may be noted that in Mendel's *Lexikon* the quartfagott is a fourth *lower* as usual, but the quintfagott is a fifth *higher*. The lack of consistency in nomenclature is very confusing.

Jacquot's *Dictionary*[35] (1886) is a very inaccurate work. The brief article *Basson* contains the remark that unfortunately the bassoon had been replaced in French military bands by the saxophone.

The appearance of Grove's *Dictionary of Music* in 1878[36] afforded the first good English account of the bassoon and this was from the pen of Dr. W. H. Stone, a Doctor of Medicine and, throughout his life, a devoted amateur player of bassoon, tenoroon and double-bassoon. Though the article is marred by several inaccurate historical statements, one must remember that the specialised study of the history of instruments has arisen only in the present century, due in large measure to the pioneer work of such enthusiasts as Arnold Dolmetsch and Canon F. W. Galpin. Stone praises the French bassoons of Savary and the English copies by Samme but makes only passing reference to Almenräder and to Ward's unsuccessful new bassoon of 1851. Stone, writing from long experience, states that 'the scale of the bassoon is complicated and capricious, . . . variable in different patterns so that even a fine player cannot play upon an unfamiliar instrument. Each has to be learned independently and although the theoretical imperfection of such a course is obvious, it has a certain compensation in the fact that a bassoon-player must necessarily rely upon his ear alone for correct intonation and that he thus more nearly approximates to the manipulation of stringed instruments than any member of the orchestra except the trombones.'

The article was only slightly revised in the 2nd, 3rd and 4th editions but for the 5th edition the author was invited by the then Editor, the late Eric Blom, to write fresh articles on both bassoon and double bassoon, in which necessary corrections were made of statements in earlier editions.

Concurrently with the publication of the German Bassoon *Method* (see Chapter 11) of Julius Weissenborn (1st Bassoon of the Gewandhaus, Leipzig and Professor at the Conservatorium there) in 1887, the German bassoon reached practically the state in which it is today.

Though Weissenborn's historical details are at times a little dubious, he gives a full description of bassoons with ten, nineteen and twenty-two keys (including two duplicate keys).

Italian writings on the bassoon are not numerous and apart from the Treatise by Tamplini (see Chapter 6) the following are the only two to which the author has had access.

Appunti intorni al Fagotto compiled for use in the School of the Royal Institute of Music, Florence, by Cav. Prof. Riccardo Gandolfi (1887) (7 pp.). The historical matter is very inaccurate, obviously copied from earlier accounts: *e.g.* the spelling of Schnitzer as 'Scheltzer' is found repeatedly where writers have not troubled to consult sources. Grenser and Almenräder are justly given credit for improvements on the German bassoon: Adler and Simiot on the French instrument. The usual number of keys was sixteen, but all bassoons did not have as many. He stresses the importance of reeds, praising those from Fréjus (France): gives the compass as B♭,–b♭' though soloists reached a fourth higher: and mentions the contrafagotto (for some unknown reason, the instrument in Italian is spelt controfagotto), compass B♭,,–f. He describes the fagottino as being a fifth above the bassoon. The closing section mentions noted performers: F. Reiner, G. Besozzi, E. Ozi (whose Méthode was used in Florence), F. R. Gebauer (author of a Méthode) and Lorenzo Lasagna.

Il Fagotto e gli strumenti congeneri by Armando Vittorioso (Naples 1913) (13 pp.). The historical matter is even more inaccurate than Gandolfi's. Afranio is credited with transforming the bass pommer into the fagotto in 1535!—doing so with the co-operation of Giambattista Raviglio of Ferrara. Again 'Scheltzer' [*sic*] is credited with having made excellent bassoons in 1569! The failure of Triébert's application of Boehm's principles to the bassoon is recorded. Professor Luigi Caccavaio 'celebrated Neapolitan bassoonist' is said to have given a great impulse to the perfecting of the bassoon, but the improved instrument, known only in the Neapolitan province, was destined to disappear, as its lack of response in the higher register failed to fill the requirements of the modern orchestra. The author has been unable to trace any details of the improvements of Caccavaio. After mentioning the sixteen-keyed bassoon, he lists the following:

> System Jancourt, as made by Maino e Orsi, Milan (with twenty-two keys),
> System Boogaerts, as made by Mahillon, Brussels (twenty keys),
> System Caccavaio, as made by Giosué Esposito, Naples (twenty-four keys).

The compass is then given as B♭,–f″. A warning is given against writing the upper five semitones for orchestral purposes. A paragraph is devoted to argument on the tonality of the bassoon, *i.e.* whether the natural scale is that of G or C. Vittorioso rightly regards C as correct and he considers the instrument sounds best in keys with not more than three sharps or four flats. He states that the fagottino (a fifth higher) is rarely used in the orchestra. One wonders if and when it was ever used in the orchestra in Italy. The contra is given the compass C,–f and although Evette and Schaeffer of Paris had made a contra giving B♭,, this note 'was better avoided as its intonation was not secure'. This is a strange statement to have been made as recently as 1913. The B♭,, on the Buffet-Crampon Contra (made by Evette and Schaeffer) is quite steady, but must be used with discretion. Italian bassoonists mentioned are: Lorenzo Lasagna; Torriani of Milan; and Luigi Caccavaio of Naples 'who, besides being an innovator, was the greatest fagottist of the nineteenth century'. The library of the Conservatorium of Naples contains many concerti of his and several transcriptions for the bassoon. Eduardo Buccini succeeded Caccavaio as teacher at the Conservatorium of S. Pietro a Maiella. *Storia del Fagotto* by A. Orefice (Turin 1926) is cited in *Musik in Geschichte und Gegenwart, s.v.* Fagott, but the author has been unable to obtain a copy of Orefice's work.

A useful list of bassoon-players and composers for the instrument is given in Chapter XXXVII of R. Profeta's *Storia e Letteratura degli Strumenti musicali* (Florence, 1942). The principal names are included in their appropriate chapters in the present volume.

REFERENCES

[1] Speer, Daniel: *Grundrichtiger . . . Unterricht der musicalischen Kunst.* (Ulm, 1st edit., 1687; 2nd edit., 1697), p. 241.
[2] Mattheson, Johann: *Das neu-eröffnete Orchestre* (Hamburg, 1713), Pt. III, para. 9.

[3] Niedt, Friedrich Erhard: *Musicalische Handleitung* (Hamburg, 1721).

[4] Walther, J. G.: *Musikalisches Lexikon* (Leipzig, 1732).

[5] Majer, J. F. B. C.: *Music-Saal* (Nürnberg, 1st edit., 1732; 2nd edit., 1741).

[6] Zedler, J. H.: *Universal Lexikon* (Halle and Leipzig, 1733).

[7] Eisel, J. P.: *Musicus autodidactus* (Erfurt, 1738), p. 104.

[8] Diderot and D'Alembert: *Encyclopédie* (Paris, 1751–65), Vol. 2.

[9] Galpin, F. W.: *Old English Instruments of Music* (London, 1910), Pl. XXXIV, 8.

[10] Mahillon, V.: *Catal. of Brussels Conservatoire Musée*, Vol. II, No. 997.

[11] Reproduced as frontispiece to A. Carse, *Musical Wind Instruments* and L. G. Langwill in *Index of Wind Instrument Makers* (2nd ed., 1962), Pl. facing p. 129.

[12] Carse, A.: *loc. cit. ante*, p. 188.

[13] *Apollo's Cabinet or The Muses' Delight* (Sadler, Liverpool, 1756), No. 188 in the Glen Collection presented in 1927 to National Library of Scotland, p. 45.

[14] Adlung, Jacob: *Anleitung zur musikalischen Gelehrheit* (Erfurt, 1st edit., 1758; Leipzig, 2nd edit., 1783).

[15] Tans'ur, Wm.: *The Elements of Musick display'd* (London, 1772), Book III.

[16] Abrahame: *Principe de Basson* (Schott, Antwerp, *c.* 1780).

[17] Hotteterre le Romain: *Méthode ... de la Flûte traversière ...* (Paris, 1707). Many later editions. *Vide* D. C. Miller, *Bibliography of the Flute* (Cleveland, 1935), pp. 57–8.

[18] De la Borde, J. B. and Roussier, P. J.: *Essai sur la Musique ancienne et moderne* (Paris, 1780), pp. 313–43.

[19] Verschuere Reynvaan, J.: *Muzijkaal Kunst-Woordenboek*, 618 pp., 40 plates (Amsterdam, 1795).

[20] British Museum, Addtl. MS. 35011, f. 166.

[21] Koch, H. C.: *Musikalisches Lexikon* (Frankfurt a/M, 1802).

[22] Schubart, C. F. D.: *Ideen zu einer Aesthetik der Tonkunst* (Vienna, 1806).

[23] *The Cyclopaedia or Universal Dictionary of the Arts*, by Abraham Rees, (London, 1810–24). The musical articles were written by Dr. Burney.

[24] *Allgemeine Musikalische Zeitung*, No. 36 of 6th September 1820.

[25] von Keess, Stephan Edlem: *Darstellung des Fabriks- und Gewerbewesens in seinen gegenwartigen Zustande* (Vienna, 1824).

[26] Lichtenthal, P.: *Dizionario e Biografia della Musica* (Milan, 1826).

[27] Castil-Blaze, F. H. J.: *Dictionnaire de la Conversation et de la Lecture* (Paris, 1833–51).

[28] Schneider, Wilhelm: *Technische Beschreibung der Musicalischen Instrumente* (Leipzig, 1834).

[29] Schilling, G.: *Universal Lexikon* (Stuttgart, 1835).

[30] Choron and Lafage: *Manuel complet de Musique vocale et instrumentale* (Paris, 1836–8).

[31] *Music and Letters* (April 1958).

[32] von Gontershausen, H. Welcker: *Neu eröffnetes Magazin musikalischer Tonwerkzeuge* (Frankfurt a/Main, 1855).

[33] von Dommer, Arrey: *Musikalisches Lexikon* (Heidelberg, 1865).

[34] Mendel, H.: *Conversations-Lexikon*, *s.v.* Fagott. The article is by Musik-director C. Billert (Berlin, 1870–83).

[35] Jacquot, A.: *Dictionnaire des Instruments de Musique* (Paris, 1886), *s.v.* Basson.

[36] Grove, G.: *Dictionary of Music and Musicians* (London, 1st edit., 1878–89), *s.v.* Bassoon.

CHAPTER 4

The Development of the Bassoon after 1750

As we have seen, the bassoon gained its fifth and sixth keys in the last quarter of the eighteenth century and such was the instrument when Beethoven's first symphony was performed in 1800. Almost at this very moment, makers in France and Germany began to add a seventh key, a 'wing-key' operated by the thumb and assisting the production of a' (as a twelfth of d in the fundamental scale), bb' and b♮'. Ozi's *Méthode de Basson* of 1803 shows such a seven-keyed bassoon. A second wing-key was soon added to aid the production of c", c♯" and d". Koch's *Lexikon* of 1802 specifies seven keys without low F♯ and adds that the two wing-keys are to be found 'only on modern bassoons, on which many performers played even up to d'. In some cases a third wing-key was added and further additional keys carried the compass up to f". English bassoons of c. 1800 were beginning to have eight keys, the normal six and two wing-keys. The bassoon c. 1800 was customarily carried in a green baize bag, the mouth of which was drawn shut by a cord. Another feature at that time was the custom of supporting the bassoon by a short loop of ribbon which the player hung on one of the buttons of the long coats then worn. The author has a bassoon of the period with the ribbon loop still tied to the ring on the butt. The crook of that time was a heavy brass tube, wider than a modern crook and without a crook-key hole. The author has a four-keyed bassoon of Cahusac, London, dated 1769, complete with a crook of this type.

A very interesting illustrated article[1] 'The Evolution of the Bassoon in England, 1750–1800' by Eric Halfpenny shows that special features of the late eighteenth- and early nineteenth-century bells were the 'baluster' external appearance and the inverted conical bore which acted as a 'choke' and modified the power of the lowest notes. The finger-hole (L1) on the wing-joint was sometimes lined with a brass tube and even protruding into the bore as a precaution against the decay of the wood at this first hole, inclined as it is so that water from condensation of the breath runs through it.

In the early nineteenth century, excellent bassoons were being made in Germany, *e.g.* by K. A. Grenser (1720–1807), by his nephew and successor J. H. Grenser (1764–1813) and by J. F. Grundmann (1727–1800) all of Dresden and pupils of J. Poerschmann of Leipzig. In France equally fine bassoons were being made by Savary père (active *c.* 1775–1827) and his son and successor J. N. Savary fils (born 1786, died *c.* 1850), Porthaux and other Paris makers. In England, Milhouse, Cahusac, Wood, and Bilton were among the best makers of the time.

GERMANY

Heckel[2] has remarked that though the Dresden bassoons excelled in their beautiful soft tone, they were adequate only so long as the instruments were used for accompaniment and then only in the keys of F, B♭, C and G major and in G and C minor. When smooth technique was required in other keys, *e.g.* A and E major, and short phrases and solos were demanded, the inequality of the individual notes became apparent. Although key after key was added to provide a remedy, the defects were not eliminated because notes produced with the aid of keys sounded even and clear while other notes sounded muffled and uneven. It was finally realised that the body of the bassoon was at fault and required radical change.

This task was undertaken by Carl Almenräder (1786–1843) a bandmaster, bassoon-player and later Chamber Musician at the Court of the Duke of Nassau in Biebrich and Wiesbaden.[3] He was afforded expert guidance by Gottfried Weber (1779–1839) celebrated as a musical theorist and acoustician as well as founder and editor of *Caecilia.*

In 1817 Almenräder experimented in Schott's factory at Mainz and published his findings, *c.* 1820, in a treatise[4] describing a fifteen-keyed bassoon. This and subsequent improvements upon it were described and illustrated by Gottfried Weber in *Caecilia.*[5]

In the Introduction to his *Traité* (which is printed in German with a very inaccurate French translation in parallel columns) Almenräder praises the good qualities of Grenser bassoons but remarks that the principal defects in purity of certain notes could be remedied only by the use of various complicated fingerings. These caused difficulties, however, which militated against a flowing execution and often embarrassed even the most skilful artists especially in little-used keys. Ozi, in his *Méthode de Basson* (1st edit., 1788) advised composers to avoid certain passages (which he cited on pp. 37 and 38) but such occurred in compositions prior to Ozi's tutor and similar or even more difficult passages appeared in contemporary works. As it was impossible for every composer to understand sufficiently the technical difficulties of each instrument, the only solution for the bassoon, as for other wind instruments, was to render it capable of smooth performance of the most difficult passages by perfecting its construction. Almenräder, himself a bassoonist, had, during his long career, so often keenly felt this necessity that he had made a special study of the correct means of bringing to perfection the bassoon as made by Grenser in the latter years of his life. Almenräder's experiments after certain modifications realised more and more the desired result—a bassoon, as shown in the plates included in the *Traité*, of eminent utility.

The greatest improvement, apart from extended compass, was the increased purity, uniformity and sweetness of the notes and many passages, involving almost insurmountable difficulties, could now be played with ease and enjoyment.

Almenräder then proceeded to describe in three parts (I) the alterations in the construction of the bassoon; (II) the use of different fingerings; and (III) the fingering of trills.

PART I (Plate 14)

Almenräder gives Grenser the credit of 'inventing' the key for c♯ and c♯' which he placed on the wing to be fingered by L4. This key, which also gave d♯ and d♯', could fulfil its function, but the position given to the hole by Grenser (Fig. 1 (c♯)) had the basic defect of allowing water to enter and form bubbles thus blocking the hole. Almenräder remedied this defect by transferring the hole and key to the other side of the wing (Fig. 1 (k)) where it could be operated by LT, free from any risk of water entering. As the notes produced by this key lacked clearness, Almenräder reduced the length of the butt somewhat and correspondingly lengthened the bass-joint and wing. By this means he was able to make the key-hole at a suitable place and by enlarging it to remedy the lack of clarity.

Next, he dealt with the A hole for R3 on the butt. Till then this hole had to be made narrower than it ought to be so that it could be fingered conveniently when R1, 2 and 3 covered the uncovered holes on the butt. The sound suffered in consequence. He, therefore, placed the hole lower between the rods of the F and G♯ keys and changed it into two holes, one of which (Fig. 2 (m)) opened into the narrow bore, the other (Fig. 2 (l)) into the wide bore, this latter hole serving at the same time to give 'vent' (*Ger.* Schalloch: *Fr.* Ouverture de résonnance).

These two holes were provided with an open key which passed under the upper part of the F-key and could be closed by R3 (near Fig. 2 (k)). By this means Almenräder obtained not only a pure octave A/a but also perfect equality of tone from A to a—an advantage almost always absent in ordinary bassoons. Moreover, in difficult keys AEB, etc., a great advantage was a true e obtained by closing the highest hole with L1. (In the French bassoon till this day, the addition of R2 and R3 is needed to give a clear e.)

Next, for Bb/bb he added, on the butt, a key for R3, an essential key for trills or cadences with A and Bb (Fig. 2 (o)).

On the back of the butt, he added beside the F♯ key (Fig. 4 (i)), an extra key (k) which was opened simultaneously with the former and produced with the ordinary fingering of G, a pure G♯. This gave the advantage of enabling the notes F♯/G♯ or G♯/F♯ to be slurred. This had not until then been possible.

To obtain low C♯, lacking on ordinary bassoons at that time, he added a key to the bass joint (Plate 14, Fig. 3) with articulated rods enabling the key to be operated by L4 near D♯. He also provided for low B♮ (likewise missing on the bassoons of his time) by using the Bb key which he transferred to the bell-joint (Plate 14, Fig. 3) where the hole (H) normally open served both as a 'vent' as well as having the important advantage of improving and strengthening the low notes from C to F.

Finally, to facilitate the closure of the Bb, B♮ and D keys with the intervening C hole, for all of which LT must serve, he added a short 'open-standing' key with a semi-spherical touch-piece which enabled the left thumb to work more easily and allowed the slurring of these low notes as well as the closure of two or more simultaneously. Anyone who has attempted on an old four- or six-keyed bassoon to close the C hole and the Bb and D keys lying above and below it, will appreciate the discomfort and difficulty of ensuring complete closure of the C hole. Almenräder's short key remedied this inconvenience and it exists to this day on French bassoons as well.

Almenräder ends the first part of his Treatise by describing the key-pads he was using in place of the old flat leather pads which did not ensure air-tight closure of the keys. Though he states that the improved pads had been known for several years, he does not mention what Gottfried Weber informs us in his article in *Caecilia*[6] that to his (Weber's) knowledge the new pads were first introduced by Iwan Müller (1786–1854). Almenräder gives the following instructions for making the improved pads:

E

'Cut the gut (*Ger.* Darmhaut), obtainable prepared for the purpose from B. Schott's Söhne, Mainz, or from the author at
Biebrich, to the shape of the keys, making it, to begin with, a third
larger. By taking in and sewing the edges back, we give them the
shape of pads which must be filled with good clean wool and by
contraction, we make them like flat coat-buttons. They are fixed
under the keys with sealing-wax. It will be easily seen that the
round and concave shape of the keys is the most adaptable for this
arrangement.'

He adds that keys thus fitted, function perfectly and silently and the
pads have the further advantage of sustaining no damage from oil or
water, remaining soft and pliable for several years as proved by his own
experience.

PART II

Almenräder devotes pp. 5–10 to the fingering of difficult passages
earlier cited by Ozi in his *Méthode*, including phrases from Mozart's
'Don Juan' Act II and Cherubini's Overture 'Deux Journées'.

PART III

The advantages of Almenräder's extra keys for low F♯, middle c♯
and b♭ are described as facilitating or actually making possible trills
earlier noted by Ozi as very difficult or impossible. The recommended
fingering is shown in Plate II for a fourteen-keyed bassoon with
compass B♭,–g″.

Three years later, in 1828, G. Weber published in *Caecilia*[7] an
account of Almenräder's further improvements with a plate (Plate 15).
Figures I and III, Improved Butt and long-joint as described in his
Traité and in *Caecilia* of 1825: and Figures II and IV, Butt and long-
joint as *further* improved between 1825–8.

The new features were:

1. An extra key for low F♯ on the front of the butt for R3 overlying
   the F-key touch. Fig. II (i).
2. The holes for C and for the E♭ key were moved more into their
   proper position making it possible to have them the size requisite
   for the production of a full sound. Fig. IV. The open-standing
   C-key touch (l) closes the key at K to give C as shown in detail in
   Fig. V.

G. Weber concludes by pointing out that notwithstanding the
removal of several tone-holes to often widely separated positions on

the bassoon, the key-work has been so devised that the fingers of the performer, now as before, could control these same holes from the positions hitherto normal. The bassoon had now acquired a complete chromatic compass from B♭, to a♭″, *i.e.* four octaves less a tone.

The subsequent history of the German bassoon is intimately associated with the world-renowned firm of Heckel established at Biebrich-am-Rhein, near Wiesbaden. Much information was given in a booklet *Der Fagott* by Wilhelm Heckel in 1899 and in a revised version by his son Wilhelm Hermann Heckel, published on the occasion of the centenary of the firm on 11 March 1931. The author of the present book enjoyed the friendship of Herr W. H. Heckel throughout many years, following an English translation he made and presented to Herr Heckel in 1933. A visit to the Heckel home and factory followed in August of that year when author and translator revised the translation, an abridged version of which, by Dr. Douglas Waples, appeared in the American Journal of Musicology.

It was in the year 1829 that Johann Adam Heckel (1812–77) set out from his native Adorf in Vogtland where he had learned his craft of instrument-maker. Arriving in Mainz, he obtained employment with B. Schott and met Carl Almenräder, then a man of forty-three years, busily engaged on his bassoon-improvements. Almenräder, recognising that the young Heckel was a skilled craftsman, induced him to join in founding a business at Biebrich on 11 March 1831. Until Almenräder's death in 1843 they made bassoons for Schott and the steel die-stamp is preserved, reading 'B. Schott fils, Mayence'.

The Heckel-Almenräder bassoon was progressively developed and an illustration and description of an Almenräder sixteen-key bassoon (of *c.* 1825–8) stamped 'Schott fils, Mayence', appears in Carse's *Musical Wind Instruments*.[9] Before Almenräder died in 1843 the middle B♭ hole was moved to the back of the butt and the key was provided with dual control, *i.e.* by RT and, by a lever passing through the butt, by R3 as normally—whichever might be more convenient. It was also found necessary to alter the position of the RT hole and enlarge it. To enable the hole to be covered satisfactorily an open key—the so-called E-plate for RT—was added. These among other mechanical devices remain essential features of the Heckel bassoon today. Before the mid-century Heckel discarded flat keys mounted on saddles in favour of cupped keys mounted on pillars and the adoption of rod-axles greatly improved the efficiency of the key mechanism. A Heckel bassoon of *c.* 1870 is also illustrated by Carse.[10]

On the death of Johann Adam Heckel in 1877 his son and successor Wilhelm (1856–1909) undertook a radical change in the bore, arguing that an even tone demanded an even course of the bore throughout. With the aid of a micrometer he regulated the course of the cone down to minute measurements. He established the principle that in the bassoon three lateral holes act as the guiding factor, *viz.* those giving F, G and A. Just as the A hole had been moved, he changed the F and G holes further downwards and widened the bore evenly to the bottom to suit the increased wind supply. W. H. Heckel claims that his father at this time established the correct position of the hole for L1. Thereafter, it was unnecessary to place the holes in their correct acoustical position because, in consequence of the correct cone, the egress of the wind could proceed evenly. He abandoned the twin-headed G-key for R3, moved the hole to a distinctly lower and more rational position and fitted a single large key. His reasons were threefold. In the position accorded to the A-hole by Almenräder it was liable to fill with water: the twin-headed key was difficult to 'pad' so as to ensure a good 'cover': a tube projecting into the interior of the bore, to prevent water running out of the hole, interfered with thorough cleaning of the bore and the tone suffered likewise.

Heckel accords a date *c.* 1870 for the introduction of the F♯/G♯ shake-key and *c.* 1880 for the C♯/D♯. The former had at first a shank-key (running in a lengthwise direction) and later assumed the oblique form working transversely as it is today. The C♯/D♯ shake was originally nothing more than an interlocking of the ring-mechanism with the C♯ key in such a way that by concurrently depressing the ring and the C♯ key, the D♯ auxiliary key opened. Soon afterwards, it occurred to Heckel that high b♮′ and c″ would be easier to take if the D♯ auxiliary hole remained open, and he formed the coupling in such a way that the hole in question is also automatically opened on pressing the high C-key. Thus arose the C♯/D♯ shake mechanism which is found on German bassoons of many makers.

In 1901 Heckel brought out his 'through-bored' G-key for R3 with a shank (like the F♯/G♯ shake) running through the wall of the butt.

In 1902 the self-operating ring-mechanism for the high g was introduced.

Over the years, different kinds of mechanism have been tried to close the vent-hole in the crook, but none was successful until, in 1905, the present mechanism was introduced. Operated by RT it leads from the low E-plate on the butt out, over the wing-joint, to the small vent-hole in the crook and has been copied by other bassoon-makers. This mechanism is made with a variety of supplementary devices for RT or LT.

One further device introduced by Wilhelm Heckel Senior is referred to in *Der Fagott* (1st edit.). The bassoon originally had a cork plug to close the base of the butt and allow the air to pass round in U-fashion. This cork was troublesome to remove for cleaning purposes and even more difficult to make air-tight on replacement. The Heckel-Almenräder bassoon was fitted with a brass tube bent in a semicircle and soldered to a plate which could be pushed in or out as a slide at the lower end of the butt. This device was later abandoned in favour of a broad plate fitted with cork as packing and held in place by springs. The modern device has a specially hard rubber packing and is made fast with ingeniously contrived screws.

A German Patent 162092 of 1904 was granted to Franz Fischer of Strasbourg for an improved water-outlet for the bassoon.

A departure from Heckel's open key for B♮ on the bell is found on bassoons by Schaufler of Stuttgart[11] who made what was termed Neukirchner's Model *c.* 1845. (Specimens in Heckel Museum and Carse Collection No. 54 in Horniman Museum, London.)[12] Wenzel Neukirchner (1805–89), a Bohemian virtuoso, became 1st Bassoon in the Royal Orchestra at Stuttgart in 1831 where no doubt he met Schaufler and employed him to make certain alterations, chief of which was that the low B♮ hole was covered by a closed key (as on French bassoons) instead of an open key. The Neukirchner Model did not survive its inventor.

An interesting side-light on the contemporary improvements being carried out by Adler in Paris is afforded by a letter from Neukirchner.[13] Adler's improvements on the bassoon had been described in the *Leipziger Algem. Ztg.*[14] and Neukirchner contemptuously terms Adler's work a bad imitation of a Neukirchner discovery as carried out by Schaufler. During his stay in Paris in 1839, Neukirchner had sold such an instrument through a third party to Adler who then gave out Neukirchner's improvements as his own discoveries. The real improvements are then detailed:

1. Omitting the pin-hole in the crook, already tried in 1814 by Schaufler and others. There are, however, altered proportions for the crook.

2. U-channel at the butt instead of twin plugs.
3. Broader bell. The Parisians have understood how to imitate only this bell, but this bell is effective only when the whole instrument is given new proportions.
4. Two more keys on the wing-joint.

Mr. R. Morley-Pegge, who owns an Adler (Paris) bassoon, kindly informs me that a crook-key is fitted both on an ordinary wing-joint and on a rack-work wing-joint. On the crook, which he believes is original, the pin-hole is just under the curve, facing the player, and not on the side, as normally. The crook-keys are so constructed to cover the hole in this unusual position.

Heckel realised the importance of having the wall of the bore as smooth and impervious to moisture as possible. Hence the need to oil the bore from time to time. If the bore of a wood-wind instrument is not smooth and shining, there form, as a result of moisture, very minute wood fibres which ultimately cover the bore like a velvety brush. The air in its passage has to meet this resistance and overcome it, but if a material be used which can be brought to a permanently fine polish, a brightness of tone and readiness of response will be assured. Wilhelm Heckel met this requirement in 1889 when he patented the vulcanised rubber lining (*Ger.* Ausfütterung).[15] It consists of a lining or sleeve for the bore of the wing and of the narrow bore of the butt— for in the bassoon only these parts are attacked by moisture. Heckel claimed that the instrument becomes no heavier by reason of this lining, the interior wood does not decay nor split and the conical course of the bore remains unchanged. For the correct fitting of the lining, a special secret process is employed. Nevertheless, the vulcanite lining is commonly found on bassoons of other makers and it may be remarked that a catalogue of *c.* 1870 of Lafleur, London, mentions that such a lining was then being fitted by Morton[16] of London who thus appears to have forestalled Heckel.

On the death of Wilhelm Heckel in 1909 he was succeeded by his two sons Wilhelm Hermann Heckel (1879–1952) and August Heckel (1880–1914) who had been his assistants for fifteen years. Generations of bassoon-players have the pleasantest recollections of the geniality and friendliness of Wilhelm H. Heckel who directed the firm for forty-three years. The present author wishes to place on record his own appreciation of Herr Heckel's courtesy and helpfulness throughout twenty years, interrupted only by the period 1939–45. Herr Heckel's only child married Franz Groffy, an engineer of Boppard-am-Rhein, who assisted his father-in-law from 1924, taking control in 1952. He, in turn, is now assisted by his son-in-law Adolf W. Gebhard and his daughter Edith, one of the few women bassoon-makers in the world.

FRANCE

The development of the bassoon in France has been recorded by Constant Pierre, a bassoon-player and Commis principal au Secrétariat du Conservatoire National de Musique, Paris. His books[17] *Les Facteurs* . . . (1893) and *La Facture* . . . (1890) contain a wealth of information, not to be found elsewhere.

We learn from a judgement of 1752[18] that there were then in Paris only five master-makers of wood-wind instruments: Charles Bizey, Thomas Lot, Paul Villars, Jacques Lusse (or Delusse) and Denis Vincent.

Specimens survive only in the case of Delusse, but whether by Jacques Delusse who was at quai Pelletier in 1769 or by Christophe Delusse who was at the same address in 1783–9 we cannot say. A small bassoon in Paris (No. 499) is wrongly described as a 'basson soprano en fa' by Pierre[19] and in Lavignac.[20] The author is indebted to Mr. R. Morley-Pegge for photographs of back and front of the instrument which is in fact an octave-bassoon or fagottino. All seven keys (B♭, D, E♭, F, F♯, G♯ and a') are not original and the key-mounting for E♭, F♯ and a' suggests that these have been later additions.

Delusse made a 'contrebasse de hautbois' which was announced in the *Almanach Musical* for 1781. It was played by Le Marchand, bassoon-player at the Opera, during six months with 'beaucoup d'effet dans un grand orchestre'. The Catalogue of the Musée errs in describing it (No. 459) as a 'contrebasse de bombarde' (an instrument obsolete a century before) and of 1760 instead of 1781.

The author is again indebted to Mr. Morley-Pegge for photographs showing the instrument 2·15 metres in length, with a bassoon crook and nine keys of which five are later additions.

Two octave-bassoons, c. 1780, by Martin Lot survive. Two makers named Lot, without an initial, occur in the *Tablettes de Renommée* for 1785. One fagottino has three keys (Donaldson Collection, R.C.M., London) and the other has five keys (Bate Collection, London).

In 1769 there appeared the *Essai sur l'almanach général d'indications, d'adresses*, etc., and a new wood-wind maker appears, PRUDENT

THIERRIOT of rue Dauphine, who acquired repute as a maker of oboes, clarinets and specially bassoons. He is better known as PRUDENT, with which name alone he marked his instruments. As both Prudent père and fils used the same mark, it is not possible to distinguish their workmanship. A five-keyed bassoon marked 'Prudent à Paris' in Paris Conservatoire is No. 503. A six-keyed bassoon by Prudent with an interchangeable wing-joint is No. 1121 in the same Museum.

Another noted Paris bassoon-maker active from 1782 was DOMINIQUE PORTHAUX 'facteur ordinaire de la musique du roi et des musiques militaires' at rue des Cordeliers in 1785. Pierre[21] remarks that the Porthaux bassoon in Paris (No. 1398) was the only one he then knew of (1890). Today we know of six with five–seven keys. Porthaux's bassoons have a narrow bore and are surprisingly light. The keys are slim and flat, in light saddles screwed into the wood. Porthaux gained some notoriety in 1808 when he brought an accusation[22] against the celebrated Savary for copying Porthaux's invention of a crook of wood instead of metal. Porthaux had invented an instrument which he named 'Tenore' and finding wood preferable to metal for the crook, he decided to do likwise in the case of the bassoon. Poor Porthaux! His inventiveness availed him nothing. Both his wooden crook and his Tenore passed into oblivion. His name appeared in almanacs until 1824, but latterly merely as a dealer in music and instruments.

MICHEL AMLINGUE, rue du Chantre, Paris, from 1785 until 1826, supplied flutes, oboes, boxwood five-keyed clarinets and bassoons with 5–8 keys for the French Guards and for the military bands formed after 1790.

WINNEN PÈRE (c. 1788–c. 1834) appears at rue de la Monnoie in the *Calendrier musical* for 1788 and is remembered partly on account of his employment of Triébert père and partly through the activity of 'Vinnen Cadet', one of his sons, thought to be Jean (1795–1867). Father and son invented the 'Bassonore' (Paris, No. 511) (Plate 16, Fig. 2), a bassoon with wide bore and bell for military use, and thirteen brass keys giving a compass, according to Chouquet's catalogue, of three octaves and a third ($B\flat$,–d''). According to Fétis,[23] Winnen's first model had a compass of three octaves from C, but $B\natural$, had been reached and $B\flat$, would be added. Fétis claimed for the bassonore a tone almost four times as powerful as the bassoon. Winnen cadet showed a 'basson à pavillon' at the Paris Exhibitions of 1834 and 1839 gaining a bronze medal on each occasion, but it was only in 1844 having perfected it and named it bassonore he showed it again, gaining a bronze medal. Pontécoulant indicates that Winnen took out a French patent for the bassonore in 1844 but no such patent has been traced. A beautifully made seven-keyed bassoon of Winnen is in the Collection G. Thibault, Paris. A key is engraved 'Inventé par Felix, mécanicien à Paris' and the keys are all of the rod-type with the touch and key-head on opposite sides. This system was combined with an oblique placing of the keys for Eb, F, F♯ and G♯ in a unique manner. (Plate 16, Fig. 1.)

In the nineteenth century wood-wind makers increased and tended to specialise. Some of the eighteenth-century makers continued active in the early nineteenth century. Others who contributed to the development of the French bassoon are the following:

PEZÉ, Paris (c. 1800–c. 1830), 6 keys.

BAUMANN, Paris (c. 1790–c. 1830), advertised contrabassoons in 1825, but no specimen is known. X. Lefèvre in his *Méthode de Clarinette* credits Baumann with being the first to add Lefèvre's sixth key (C♯/F♯) to that instrument (c. 1790). Two seven-keyed bassoons are recorded.

SAVARY. This name, more than any other, deserves to be remembered in connection with the French bassoon. Two generations contributed their skill and inventiveness. Savary père worked in Paris from c. 1788 until 1826 but has left strangely few examples of his craftsmanship. Only one bassoon clearly marked 'Savary père' is known (Brussels, No. 3120), of maplewood with nine brass keys including two wing-keys for a' and c'. The addition of 'père' to his stamp would appear to indicate that his son had by then commenced to make bassoons.

Jean-Nicolas Savary (Savary jeune), born 1786, devoted his life to the bassoon. Gaining 1st prize at the Conservatoire in 1808, he became solo bassoon at the Théatre des Italiens and was accordingly in a position to realise the imperfections of the instrument and to remedy them. In 1823 he founded a separate workshop from that of his father and in *Bottin* for 1823 he announced certain modifications in bassoon construction, in particular, a tuning-slide on the wing-joint controlled by a rack-mechanism (*Fr.* crémaillère) and a 'tip-up' butt (*Fr.* culasse à bascule), the precise form of which is not known. By this time (1823) he was 'fournisseur de la Maison du Roi, de l'Académie et de l'École royale'. Savary bassoons bear dates ranging from 1824 to 1842, but his name disappears from Paris directories in 1840. His death c. 1850 has not been recorded. His bassoons were very popular in England where they were highly esteemed by many of the principal players. Indeed, Savary bassoons were passed down from one generation to the next and some were still in use and very reluctantly discarded when orchestral sharp pitch began to be lowered in 1895, followed by military pitch in 1929.

Savary took no part in the recurrent Exhibitions in Paris and he is not included in Fétis' *Biographie Universelle*, 1st or 2nd editions.

Savary's business was bought by Galander (1834–55) who gave his name to a B♭ military bassoon he invented in 1853—the *Galandronome*. A single surviving specimen with flared metal bell is preserved in New York (No. 1675). The invention was never developed.

In 1854 the combined business of Savary-Galander was bought by Georges Schubert, who had succeeded Adler in the same year, but on Schubert's death in 1857 his stock was sold off.

FRÉDÉRIC GUILLAUME ADLER was established in rue Mandar, Paris, a little before 1809 in which year he brought out certain improvements to the bassoon. In 1827 he showed a bassoon (with Almenräder's fifteen keys) for which he received a mention and in 1834 he showed again his fifteen-keyed bassoons but with rollers.*

He also incorporated the tuning-slide and rack-work on the wing-joint invented by Winnen some years before. Fétis remarks[23] that though Adler's bassoons were of skilled workmanship, many defects of intonation and equality were noticeable. By 1839 the report of the Paris Exhibition judges stated that Adler's bassoon was longer than normal; the bell was small; two new keys produced high d″ and e″; though a little different in timbre from that of the ordinary bassoon it appeared to excel in accuracy, purity and evenness. As the fingering was unchanged several of the best-known players hastened to change over. Adler was awarded the bronze medal and in 1844 he gained a like award for an orchestral bassoon, a contrabassoon and a bassoon of new design with a metal bell resulting in a more powerful tone. In 1849 Adler received a new bronze medal for his bassoon placed in the first class. Pierre remarks[24] that he had seen a ten-keyed bassoon of Adler with no low B♮ nor any keys for the four fingers of the left-hand, and yet displaying innovations which others had introduced in the meantime; crook pin-hole, two harmonic keys on the wing for LT and a key on the butt with its touchpiece between R1 and R2 to give the

---

* Rollers (*Ger.* walzen, *Fr.* rouleaux) invented by César Janssen *c.* 1823 and soon used by all makers to facilitate movement from one key to another.

shake B/C♯, C/C♯, C♯/D♯, D/E♭ in the middle register and g/a and a/b♭ in the high register.

Eug. Jancourt (1815–1900), bassoon-soloist and teacher at the Paris Conservatoire (1875–91), published his *Méthode de Basson* in 1847 and in 1876 *Étude de basson perfectionné* as a supplement. Jancourt deals with new keys in a note prefaced to his twenty-four *Exercices melodiques*, op. 98. The sequence of progressive alterations in the French key-mechanism is difficult to follow as no fingering-chart is ever dated. It would appear, however, that *c.* 1845 Jancourt obtained the collaboration of Buffet-Crampon, the noted Paris makers, to carry out certain modifications:

1. The substitution of key-rods and pillars for the former key saddles.
2. Addition of a crook-key for L4 to close the pin-hole in the crook. Where such a hole existed formerly, there was no means of closing it and this made the lower notes unsafe. The crook-key, therefore, enabled the lower notes to be played much more piano.

A chart for this 'Basson ordinaire a 17 clefs' was included in Jancourt's *Méthode* of 1847 and with it a second chart for a 'Basson perfectionné à 16 clefs'. In his Preface, Jancourt states:

'Several skilful makers in our time have contributed to its improvement; in the first rank, we cite Messiers Savary, Adler and Frédéric Triébert. The last-named, though still young, is destined to develop further these improvements. The care he devotes to the making of keys renders performance easier.'

On p. 17 he adds a note:

'Triébert's bassoon has a real advantage over the old bassoons as regards evenness of tone and ease of fingering. Almost without changing the ordinary fingering, changes are confined to 3 notes in a compass of almost 4 octaves:
   '1. Middle *a* which can be taken with firmness without any fear that it will "fly", whereas on the old bassoon one had to add the right thumb.
   '2. e′ is excellent with L1 and opening the G♯ key with R4.
   '3. a♭′ or g♯′ can be played with L2 and L3. The f′ can be taken "all open", like f below.'

The middle register of Triébert's bassoon gained greater fulness without change of fingering. It had, moreover, an extra high note e″ produced by a key placed above L1 and, in rising, opened as well the key for e♭″. Finally, slurs to g′ which were difficult from lower notes on the old bassoon, required no effort of embouchure from any lower notes on the new bassoon.

In 1850 Jancourt and Triébert decided to move the A hole (which Almenräder had done in Germany thirty years previously). They fitted a plate for R3 giving the note greater steadiness and accuracy without any undue stretch between L2 and L3. Triébert was also altering the bore, widening the cone to give the lower notes more fulness, and fitting a metal tube in place of the base-plug. This too had long been carried out with the German bassoon. He also altered the bore of the crook to give perfect uniformity of both low and high notes. In a later chart about 1875 we find nineteen keys and a ring—the extra being a small vent-key B♮ (inclined to be flat) closed by R2. This stage is shown in a *Method* by Jancourt and Bordogni (Lafleur & Son, London: n.d.). A later addition was half-hole plate for L1 held down by a ring for L2. The rings were later abandoned and, when Jancourt became bassoon professor at the Conservatoire in 1875, he issued a final chart which shows the Conservatoire Model with twenty-two keys which became more or less standardised. These keys include two shake-keys on the butt, one, for R2 giving a number of different shakes but specially g′/a′: the other for low F♯/G♯. This last is an ingenious device of Buffet but of doubtful utility—doubtful because, for a century and more, F♯/G♯ had always been described as impossible on the bassoon. As a result, composers avoided it and the special key-work is left idle. Some players go so far as to dismantle it. It consists of an extra touch brought round the butt for RT and pressure on this (as well as on the F♯ key) closes the normally open F key. This releases R4 to operate the touch of the G♯ key which, on rising, has a projecting 'clutch' to open the F key with it.

Jancourt's *Méthode* of 1847 first shows rollers on the F and G♯ keys for R4, despite their invention *c.* 1823.

P. Goumas et Cie, Paris, wood-wind makers, published Jancourt's final chart, and by 1885 were succeeded by Evette and Schaeffer, trading as Buffet-Crampon et Cie, today the leading French bassoon-makers. Jancourt induced Evette and Schaeffer to continue the improvement of the bassoon. Rollers were fitted to the G and B♭ keys on the butt as had earlier been done in the case of the F and G♯ keys there.

L. Letellier (professor at the Paris Conservatoire 1922–33) designed a new crook (marked 'L') making it easier to ascend and descend and with greater accuracy.[25] With the former crook he maintained that normal fingering for b♮ (2nd octave) gave C♮ while c♮ (2nd octave) gave C♯. An ebonite lining was introduced for the wing-joint, as it had already been in England since *c.* 1875 and in Germany since 1889. Letellier claimed that the lining gave greater sonority throughout the compass but specially to the highest register a' to d".

Finally mention must be made of JACQUES FRANÇOIS SIMIOT of Lyons.[26] Before 1808 he added to the wing-joint a tuning-slide and a wing-key to assist in producing a' also keys for LT for low B♭ and C♯. In 1817 he replaced the butt-plug of cork by a metal U-tube: he added 'coulisses d'accord' (whether more than the tuning-slide added in 1808 is not clear): lastly, he gave the bell an oval shape with a view to increase the volume of the lower register.[27] At the Paris Exhibition of 1823 he gained a silver medal and the jury highly praised his bassoons. Bassoons by Simiot are very rare but one in the Musée des Arts et Métiers, Paris, embodying his improvements has nine keys, including two harmonic keys (for LT). Simiot continued in business till *c.* 1835.

BELGIUM

The efforts in Belgium to improve the bassoon must not be over-looked. CHARLES JOSEPH SAX (1791–1865) of Brussels was the first, *c.* 1820, to design a bassoon with covered holes and this he exhibited at Haarlem in 1825. After further experiment, *c.* 1840, he constructed a metal bassoon on this system for which he took out a Belgian patent in 1842.[28] It was doubtless this idea which led ADOLPHE (ANTOINE JOSEPH) SAX in Paris to produce in 1851 his twenty-three-keyed metal bassoon (Paris, No. 1401). Pontécoulant[29] relates that in 1851 Sax resumed his experiments on the design of 1842 and carried out a total reconstruction of the instrument and changed its proportions. By using finger-plates, he was enabled to place the holes at their correct intervals. Further, being of opinion that the material of which the instrument was made had no influence on the character of the sound, he made the bassoon tube of brass. At the Great Exhibition of 1851 in London it was demonstrated by Baumann, then a noted London player, and caused such a sensation that after the Exhibition Boehm, passing through Paris, called on Sax at rue Saint-Georges to see the bassoon and examine it, warmly complimenting the maker. Sax showed it again at the London Exhibition of 1862 but the instrument was not demonstrated and was never put into production.

J. B. J. Willent-Bordogni (1809–52),[30] while bassoon professor at the Brussels Conservatoire, published in 1844 a *Méthode* and obtained the help of George Chrétien Bachmann and Charles Mahillon to effect improvements on the bassoon but these do not appear to have materialised.

BOEHM'S SYSTEM

It was Triébert in Paris who persevered to improve the ordinary French bassoon and to evolve a bassoon according to Boehm's principles as applied to the flute and the oboe. First, Triébert gave the bassoon greater accuracy of intonation and fulness and, without greatly changing the fingering, extended the compass to e″. An illustration of the bassoon is in the 1st edition of Jancourt's *Méthode* of 1847. As to the Boehm system, Jancourt had tried, with the help of Buffet, to apply it to the bassoon, but had to renounce the attempt since it denaturalised the timbre.

In 1850 Boehm reported[31], that he had by then completed a bassoon tube with all lateral holes and it met all expectations. The 'attack' of all notes was easy and certain, the tone was full, very strong and accurate in intonation. The production of a new practicable fingering system was then his difficult task. In 1854 he enlisted the help of Triébert. Lavoix relates that he found easily the proportions of the bore and Triébert made an accurate instrument; but the system of rods and rings was difficult to apply to the bassoon since the long rods made a disagreeable clicking. Moreover, on account of their length, the metal rods, with rings and keys attached, needed frequent adjustment. Lavoix concluded that the bassoon had not then (1878) arrived at perfection but the skilful Triébert was continuing his efforts and would doubtless be able to achieve definite results. His model was still incomplete at the date of the Paris 1855 Exhibition and it was not till the 1862 Exhibition in London that the Triébert-Boehm bassoon could be judged. The key-mechanism was faultless, the tone accurate and more homogeneous than that of the ordinary bassoon but it had the disadvantage of differing a little too much from the other in respect of timbre and fulness. The high cost, 1200 frs., militated against its adoption. Nevertheless, Triébert was awarded the Prize Medal. Pierre[32] states that only three such instruments were made. The following are those which have been traced:

1. Stamped F. Triébert. Paris Conservatoire Museum. No. 510.
2. Stamped Breveté. Triébert à Paris. Brussels Conserv. Mus. No. 3119.
3. Stamped A. Marzoli à Paris. Breveté. Boston Mus. of Fine Arts. No. 151.
4. Stamped Marzoli à Paris. W. R. Waterhouse, London.

It may be mentioned that No. 3 once belonged to a band of the 60th Rifles and was acquired by the late Canon F. W. Galpin who showed it at the Royal Military Exhibition 1890.[33] The bassoon consists of two separate conical tubes of rosewood, connected at the lower ends by a U-tube of German silver, fastened by a spring. The instrument passed to the Fine Arts Museum, Boston.[34] No. 4 was acquired in Paris by Mr. R. Morley-Pegge who lent it to the author for a time before disposing of it to Mr. W. R. Waterhouse, the London bassoonist, who hopes to have the bassoon repaired and made playable. It will be observed that two of the four instruments bear the name of Marzoli who was bassoonist at the Théâtre Italien, and worked for some time with Triébert. Pierre states[35] that Marzoli played the Boehm-system bassoon in the theatre, and also made excellent bassoons and contrabassoons. Very few instruments stamped 'Marzoli' are known but G. Tamplini, the Italian bassoonist, to whom reference is made later, showed at the International Inventions Exhibition in London (1885), a tenoroon by 'Marzoli' and a contrabassoon, 6 ft. 2 ins. in height, by 'Marzoli and Triébert'. An F tenoroon bearing the monogram 'TMB' (Triébert, Marzoli, Boehm) is in the possession of W. R. Waterhouse, London, and an E♭ tenoroon by 'Marzoli' was owned by Dr. W. H. Stone.[36] We may assume, therefore, that Triébert and Marzoli were for a time associated and that Marzoli, before or after that, worked independently. A fingering chart by A. Marzoli and an illustrated sale-list published by Triébert et Cie, are both dated 1855.

Charles-Louis Triébert, the elder brother, died in 1867, aged fifty seven, leaving his brother Frédéric to continue the family business. It was to the latter, therefore, that the Gold Medal was awarded at the 1867 Paris Exhibition and, strangely, it was the last distinction he gained, for he died in 1878. In 1872 he had patented certain improvements to the oboe and bassoon and these were taken over with the firm 'mark' by Gautrot in 1881. It should be noted, therefore, that instruments bearing the 'Triébert' mark need not be of his making.

In Germany an attempt to produce a Boehm-system bassoon was

made by Heinrich J. Haseneier (1835–1921), a bassoon-maker in Coblenz, known better as inventor and maker of the contrabassophon (see under 'Contrabassoon'). His successful attempt might have remained unknown but for an article by R. Allison[37] describing a Boehm-system bassoon by H. J. Haseneier. The instrument was kindly lent to the author for examination and photographing for his article[38] 'The "Boehm" Bassoon: a retrospect'. Fully four inches shorter than a modern Buffet bassoon, the Haseneier has a wide and squat bell: the butt is very short and the bass joint and wing are unusually long. With a crook (which is not original), the pitch is almost a semitone above modern pitch. The instrument blows very freely with a harder more open tone than the French bassoon. There are twenty-one keys, chromatic on the bass-joint and then including finger-plates for G, A, B, (R3, 2 and 1) and c, d, e (L3, 2 and 1). L1 by itself gives e♭, L2 by itself gives e♮. Similarly R1, alone, gives B♭ and R2, alone, gives B♮. These four unique fingerings are very convenient and give notes of good and even quality, obviating any need for humouring necessary on many bassoons. The remaining keys are for middle c♯ (L4) and three small keys for LT controlling (i) the crook-key (missing); (ii) a' plus the crook-key; and (iii) c" plus the crook-key. This German type of bassoon might well have become general but the Heckel bassoon swept all before it in Germany, as it has since in most other countries except France and Spain.

The mid-nineteenth century was a period of great activity on the part of bassoon-makers and in England it was due to an Italian that efforts were made to design a bassoon on Boehm's system. Giuseppe Tamplini (1817–88) of Bologna came to London in 1847 from La Scala, Milan, and became 1st bassoon at Her Majesty's Theatre under Costa. Tamplini stayed for a time in 1847 in Marylebone with his friend Cornelius Ward, an inventive flute-maker and clever craftsman. Under Tamplini's guidance, Ward made a model bassoon with twenty-three covered holes and showed it at the Great Exhibition of 1851, patenting it in 1853.[39] In 1855 Tamplini took one of the new bassoons to Paris and showed it to Frédéric Triébert, but was disappointed to learn that Boehm had already visited Triébert (then in partnership with Marzoli, as mentioned above), and had promised to design a bassoon according to his (Boehm's) system. Tamplini, after serving as bandmaster of the Honourable Artillery Company, and editor of *The Bandsman* in which he published a fingering chart for Ward's bassoon, retired to his native Bologna in 1888. Before his death in that year he showed Ward's bassoon at an International Exhibition held at Bologna. Inquiries by the author have failed to locate either that bassoon or the others owned by Tamplini and previously exhibited by him at the International Inventions Exhibition, London, 1885.

Such then is the record of a century-old series of attempts to improve the fingering of the bassoon by applying rational acoustical principles. Their failure may in part be due to the impracticability of applying these principles while retaining the characteristic tone-quality of the bassoon. Failure can also be attributed to the traditional conservatism of makers, players and teachers—a circumstance which Tamplini deplored in his Italian treatise of 1888.[40]

Mention must be made of one other attempt to improve the bassoon—this time again by making it of metal. Lecomte et Cie., of Paris, constructed a bassoon of 'maillechort' (German silver). Sax in 1851 had not attempted to reproduce the oblique deep finger-holes of the wooden bassoon, but Lecomte added small tubes, called 'porte-vent', protruding from the wall of the tube for the same distance as finger-holes traverse the wood of the wing and butt. These tubes terminated in plates fixed to the instrument where it was held, thus simulating the exterior of the wooden bassoon. Pierre[41] explains that despite the theory of the negative influence of material on the timbre of instruments, Lecomte decided to use metal to give greater sonority to the bassoon. This was stressed in Lecomte's French and British patents,[42] in which 'extraordinary sonority and absolutely correct intonation' were claimed. Pierre justly claims that increased sonority was all that could result from a German-silver bassoon which differed in no other respect either in the bore or mechanism. Metal alone could not influence accuracy of intonation and Lecomte could therefore only expect greater volume when the metal bassoon was played in the open air or in a very large hall. Pierre informs us that in this respect the metal bassoon fulfilled expectations but the timbre was somewhat denaturalised. It was not unpleasant but differed from the wooden bassoon. The low notes were excellent, the middle register differed slightly from that of the normal bassoon and from the beginning of the third octave the notes had that metallic quality which characterises the saxophone at the top. It 'spoke' easily, and as a result of increased sonority, it was less tiring for the performer who could more easily play for longer. Pierre, as a bassoonist, adds a significant and perceptive observation. 'By virtue of its arbitrary construction, the bassoon, like the natural horn, affords a mixture of notes, some dull, veiled or bright to excess, which a skilled artist

F

compels himself to equalise; the German-silver bassoon of Lecomte et Cie., having greater general sonority, naturally exaggerates this defect which cannot be attributed solely to the metal.'

A seventeen-keyed specimen of Lecomte's metal bassoon is in Stearns' Collection, Ann Arbor (No. 682).

Pierre was unable to decide the cause of the altered volume and timbre. Was it due to the use of metal or to alterations in the proportions of the tube? The metal bassoon weighed 2 kilogrammes or 250 grammes less than a bassoon of maple with a wing of palisander (rosewood). Lecomte's metal bassoon had been completed on the eve of the Paris 1889 Exhibition. Pierre considered that it could be improved, for a first attempt could rarely achieve perfection and the inventor deserved credit. Experience would certainly reveal the necessary modifications.

No more was heard of Lecomte's metal bassoon, but in 1933 when the author visited the Heckel factory he was shown a metal bassoon made by Heckel, as an experiment. It was on precisely the lines of Lecomte's model.

A German visitor had also seen the instrument and wrote an article[43] having concluded that it was Heckel's intention to introduce metal for making bassoons. This brought forth a strongly worded rejoinder from the late W. H. Heckel.[44] In the course of this, he agreed that for half a century the opinion of acousticians was that the length and shape of the air-column alone conditioned the character of the sound produced. Helmholtz, however, and, recently, Dayton Miller, had established that wood, in consequence of its fibrous structure, came directly into resonant vibration and thus favourably influenced the composition of upper partials and, accordingly, the tone-colour. Metal, from its strong resistance, could not follow the vibrations of the air-column. Again, on account of the key-work, the whole body of the experimental instrument was soldered with plates and the tube was strengthened at the lateral holes since these were pressed out of the body metal or soldered which is equivalent to a strengthening. The case was quite other with instruments of the trumpet variety where each note runs through the entire instrument and where the free-moving thin-walled bell could probably exert a quivering and blaring influence upon the notes. Heckel pointed out that metal wood-wind instruments were no intellectual discovery of our time. He had in his Museum a double-walled brass E♭ clarinet by Streitwolf of c. 1825 and a metal B♭ clarinet by Heckel's grandfather of 1845. The article constitutes a powerful argument in favour of wood rather than metal for wood-wind.

The question is often asked why the German type of bassoon has all but ousted the French type since the 1930's everywhere but in France and Spain and to some extent in Italy. A comparison of the two types by a professional player intimately acquainted with both is given by Anthony Baines in his *Woodwind Instruments and their History* (pp. 154–63). He considers that the fingerings of the two types 'differ without giving either a decisive advantage'. He claims that, *e.g.* the Heckel tone is uniformly effective throughout the compass and from *p* to *f*. Moreover, an average reed of good quality will produce clear telling tone-quality, neither forced nor nasal. The French bassoon, *e.g.* the Buffet, is more sensitive to the reed, making it possible but much more difficult to produce corresponding results. This, in Mr. Baines' opinion, partly accounts for the success of the Heckel outside France and Spain. As he expresses it: 'It makes life easier for the orchestral player.' He agrees, however, that the French tone-quality is more subtle, vocal, and never without interest.

Recordings of such French artists as Dhérin and Oubradous disclose a dry rather reedy tone with a measure of vibrato. In England, players of the French bassoon prefer a rounder more mellow tone-quality to which German-type reeds contribute and vibrato is not favoured.

From time to time in the past thirty years heated argument has appeared in the musical and even in the national press as to the relative merits of the French and German bassoon. The supporters of the former described the German bassoon as a 'wooden horn' while its supporters accuse the French instrument of sounding like the buzzing of angry bees. The truth, of course, is that there are great artists on each type and it is a matter of the personal choice of the listener.

The history of the introduction of the German bassoon to Britain dates from Hans Richter's conductorship of the Hallé Orchestra, *i.e.* 1899–1912. On his arrival there were three bassoons and no contra and he decided to bring over two players from Vienna. Otto Schieder took up duty in October 1903 followed by Wichtl a year later. At the same time (1904) Richter gave two five-year Bassoon Scholarships to the Royal Manchester College of Music of which Schieder had become professor. The scholarships were awarded to Archie Camden and Maurice Whittaker who in turn succeeded Schieder 1914–33 and 1933–41 respectively. It happened that Archie Camden's father was associated with the firm of Higham, brass instrument-makers in Manchester, and he imported several German bassoons from Oskar Adler of Markneukirchen. Archie Camden decided to play one of them and he has adhered to the Adler ever since. His early recording of the Mozart concerto with the Hallé as well as orchestral recordings from Berlin, Vienna and Philadelphia (in which Heckels were used), were quickly followed by the visit of the New York Philharmonic Orchestra under Toscanini. The clear and apparently effortless tone of the bassoons induced many players to change from French to German bassoons and the B.B.C. at that time exerted pressure in favour of the move. It is noteworthy, however, that a number of British players, including several of the finest, still adhere to the Buffet, *e.g.* Cecil James, E. Wilson, Jos. Castaldini. There are old players too who speak with affection of the French instruments they formerly played.

There are still many French bassoons in Britain, often in schools, but the difficulty arises that the younger generations of teachers are likely to be unfamiliar with the French fingering. New Heckel bassoons are prohibitive in price as a result of Import Duty and Purchase Tax but other continental makes are being imported at a more reasonable figure. Students should beware, however, of so-called cheap bassoons from the Orient which are rarely musically or structurally sound.

REFERENCES

[1] *Galpin Society Journal*, X, May 1957, pp. 30–37.

[2] Heckel, W.: *Der Fagott* (1931), p. 13.

[3] Grove's *Dictionary* (5th edit.), *s.v.* Almenräder.

[4] *Traité sur le perfectionnement du basson avec deux tableaux* (Mainz, *c.* 1820).

[5] *Caecilia*, Band 2, No. 6 (1825), and Band 9, No. 34 (1828).

[6] *Ibid.*, Band 2, No. 6, p. 138.

[7] *Ibid.*, Band 9, No. 34, pp. 128–30.

[8] *American Journal of Musicology*, Vol. 2, No. 2 (Sept. 1940).

[9] Carse, A.: *Musical Wind Instruments*, pp. 196–8 and Pl. XIII K and XIV K.

[10] Carse, A.: *op. cit. ante*, Pl. XIII, N and XIV, N.

[11] Schaufler, Carl August (born 1792, died 1877): An active wood-wind maker in Stuttgart.

[12] Illustrations in Carse, *Musical Wind Instruments*, Pl. XIII L and XIV L, and pp. 199–200.

[13] *Jahrbücher des deutschen Nationalvereins* (Karlsruhe, 1839), pp. 32 and 55.

[14] *Leipziger Algem. Ztg.* XLI, 258.

[15] German Patent: 48160 of 30 January 1889.

[16] Morton, Alfred (born 1827, died 1898): A noted London wood-wind maker.

[17] Pierre, C.: *Les Facteurs d'Instruments de Musique* (Paris, 1893), and *La Facture instrumentale à l'Exposition de 1889* (Paris, 1890).

[18] Pierre, C.: *Les Facteurs*, pp. 40–46.

[19] Pierre, C.: *op. cit.*, p. 101.

[20] Lavignac: *Encyclopaedia*, *s.v.* Basson, p. 1557.

[21] Pierre, C.: *La Facture, loc. cit.*, p. 282.

[22] Pierre, C.: *Les Facteurs, loc. cit.*, pp. 148–9.

[23] *Gazette musicale de la Belgique*, 15 May 1834.
[24] Pierre, C.: *Les Facteurs, loc. cit.*, pp. 300–1.
[25] Lavignac, *Encyclopaedia, loc. cit.*, p. 1558.
[26] Pierre, C.: *Les Facteurs, loc. cit.*, pp. 303–4.
[27] *Rapport a l'Academie des Beaux-Arts*, 22 November 1817: and *Le Moniteur universel*, p. 236.
[28] Belgian Patent. Brevet 1634/1415 of 7 July 1842.
[29] Pontécoulant, A. de: *Douze jours à Londres* (Paris, 1862), p. 241.
[30] Lavoix, H.: *Histoire de l'Instrumentation, loc. cit.*, pp. 113–15.
[31] *Neuen Zeitschrift für Musik*, Jhg 1850, p. 183.
[32] Pierre, C.: *Les Facteurs, loc. cit.*, p. 319.
[33] Day, C. R.: Catal. of Royal Military Exhib. (London, 1891), No. 166.
[34] Bessaraboff: Catal. of Fine Arts Museum, Boston, Mass. (1941), No. 151.
[35] Pierre, C.: *Les Facteurs, loc. cit.*, p. 322.
[36] Grove's *Dictionary*, 1st edit., *s.v.* Oboe da caccia.
[37] *Woodwind*, October 1953.
[38] *Galpin Society Journal*, XII, May 1959, with two illustrations. Pl. IV.
[39] British Patent No. 140 of 1853.
[40] Tamplini, G.: *Brevi cenni sul sistema Boehm e della sua applicazione al Fagotto* (Bologna, 1888). Unpublished English translation by L. G. Langwill, Edinburgh.
[41] Pierre, C.: *La Facture, loc. cit.*, pp. 172–4.
[42] French Patent No. 199272 of 29 June 1889. British Patent No. 17259 of 31 October 1889.
[43] *Zeitschrift für Instrumentenbau*, 53 Jhg, No. 16.
[44] *Ibid.*, 53 Jhg, No. 18, 15 June 1933.

CHAPTER 5

The Employment of the Bassoon in the Seventeenth and Eighteenth Centuries

(i) PERIOD 1600–1750

THE evolution of the bassoon may be said to coincide with the evolution of the orchestra. It is customary to regard the orchestra as having arisen when modal vocal polyphony reached its culmination in the sixteenth century. Musicians then felt a desire to compose specifically for stringed, wind and keyboard instruments in combination. Thus the early forms of opera, oratorio and ballet were accompanied by primitive and unorganised orchestras and composition became more and more devoted to the new forms in place of church and secular vocal music. The evolution of the orchestra may be divided broadly into two periods, the first ending about the mid-eighteenth century with the death of Bach and Handel. The second commenced with the inception of modern orchestration by Haydn and Mozart.

As we have seen, the bassoon remained virtually unaltered from c. 1550 throughout the seventeenth and eighteenth centuries since the dulzian and the three-keyed bassoon possessed much the same musical capabilities. It was natural, therefore, that it should be accorded an unobtrusive bass role throughout the period of *basso-continuo* which continued until the time of Haydn and Mozart.

We may now consider the extent to which the bassoon was employed in the Baroque Era. Bukofzer[1] defines this as covering the period from the younger Gabrieli and Monteverdi to Bach and Handel. Suzanne Clercx[2] subdivides this into:

Early: the last third of the sixteenth century.
High: the whole of the seventeenth century.
Late: the first half of the eighteenth century.

The only change in the bassoon in the baroque era was the addition of a fourth key (G♯) in the late period and this decided finally the manner of holding the instrument as it is held today.

MICHAEL PRAETORIUS (1571-1621), to whom we owe our knowledge of the state of all the instruments of his time, employed the bassoon in his voluminous compositions, *e.g.* 'Herr Christ der einig Gottes Sohn' from Polyhymnia caduceatrix (1619) but does not give it a distinctive part.

G. B. FONTANA (?-1630) left his compositions to the Chiesa delle Grazie at Venice for publication which took place in 1641. The bassoon is accorded a distinctive part in his 'Sonate a 1, 2, 3 per il violino, o cornetto, fagotto, chitarone, violincino o simile altro Istromento'.

M. A. FERRO (*c.* 1649) employs the bassoon in his *Sonate a 2, 3 e 4 stromenti* (Venice, 1649). Sonatas 7 and 8 are for four instruments and continuo and specify viola da gamba or fagotto.

The compositions of GIOVANNI GABRIELI (1557-1612) and in particular his Symphoniae Sacrae, which survive in the form of printed part-books, serve as a link between the vocal polyphony of the sixteenth century and the instrumental part-writing of the seventeenth century. He wrote for two, three or four choirs with independent parts for cornetti, violins, trombones and bassoons. Unfortunately, it is not possible to fix the exact date of his Symphoniae, some of which were printed in 1597 while others appeared collectively in 1615, two years after his death. The 'Jubilate Deo' (1615) calls for a bassoon.

HEINRICH SCHÜTZ (1585-1672), a pupil of Gabrieli, introduced the same style and the same instrumental combinations into Germany. Amongst his many uses of fagotto, the following are specially noteworthy. References are to his *Sammtliche Werke*, Vols. I–XVIII.[3]

In 1619 Psalm 25, 'Zion spricht, der Herr hat mich verlassen'. One fagotto (G to a): also III 13; XIV 13; V 3; V 19.

In 1619 a Psalm (Vol. III, No. IV) is for 2 fagotti with 4 cornetti, 1 recorder, 3 violini and 4 tromboni.

In 1621 Syncharma Musicum (Vol. XV). 3 fagotti of which the lowest descends to B♭, three times.

In 1629 Symphoniae Sacrae (Part I, Vol. V, No. XVI). One of the first group, to the text 'In Lectulo per noctis', is accompanied by 3 fagotti. They play three different 'sinfonie' in 3-part canons. The highest part rises to g'; the lowest descends to C.

In 1619 Psalm 24 (Vol. XIII, No. I). Schütz employs 5 fagotti with 2 cornetti, 2 violini and 4 tromboni. The fagotti play as a group. The highest often rises to a'. The lowest descends to A, once.

JOHANN H. SCHEIN (1586–1630) mentions fagotto only in such cases as 'Basso, trombone o fagotto'. 'Hosianna, dem Sohne David' (1623)[4] includes three 'Bombardon'. Two are in tenor clef (range d to d'); the third is in bass clef (range D to g). These parts are for Basset and Bass Pommer and a significant feature of the parts is the quick repetition of one note which indicates that the instruments cannot have been played with 'pirouettes'. Similarly in sixteenth-century German town marches for discant and alto schalmeys[5] repeated notes occur and this is even stranger, for 'pirouettes' appear on the higher shawms in Praetorius' plates.

SIGMUND STADEN (1607–55), a stadtpfeifer and later organist and composer at Nuremberg, is chiefly known as composer of the first German operatic work to be published, an allegorical *Singspiel* entitled 'Das geistliche Wald-gedicht oder Freudenspiel genannt Seelewig' (1644). The Sinfonia of this work includes three bassoons.

An extraordinary festival concert of music chiefly by Staden was given at Nuremberg in 1643.[6] Sixteen musical numbers were intended to illustrate *The Origin, Progress, Use and Abuse of Music*. A military march by which Alexander the Great was supposed to be encouraging his troops to join battle, consisted of a vocal duet, tenor and bass, accompanied by two orchestras. The first consisted of military instruments, trumpets, oboes and drums: the second comprised three bassoons, a quart-bassoon, and two pommers—the pitch of these is not stated. It is always a source of confusion when the term basson-quarte or quart-fagott is used. It can mean either a semi-contra bassoon, a fourth below the normal instrument, or a tenor—a fourth above. Only the range of the part will decide. It may be added, however, that in German, quart- and quint-fagott usually denote bassoons of lower pitch. In French, basson-quarte and basson-quinte are diminutives of higher pitch.[7]

Adam Carse in his *History of Orchestration* (1925) cites a work on the subject of John the Baptist by a little-known German named Daniel Bollius and dating from not later than 1628. This contains an introduction for two cornetti and one bassoon.

In the Arien[8] of HEINRICH ALBERT (1604–51), a nephew and pupil of Schütz, bassoons are scored as part of what Carse has described as 'a well-blended group much more suitable for his purpose than the odd and rather clumsy combinations of his more famous uncle'.

MONTEVERDI's *Orfeo* (1607) includes in the score an imposing list of instruments from which the bassoon is absent. It must not, however, be regarded as the basis on which subsequent orchestras were modelled. It was, in fact, an *ad hoc* ensemble gathered on the occasion of wedding festivities under the auspices of Monteverdi's employer, the Duke of Mantua.

It is with CESTI (1620–69) that we find the earliest operatic use of the bassoon, *viz.* in *Il pomo d'oro* (1667–8).[9] Scores of this period occasionally include parts for wind instruments but more often only vague indications suggest that other than stringed instruments are included. Cesti, however, sometimes clearly specifies the wind instruments, as in two ritornelli and in the accompaniment to one long vocal solo, he writes for two cornetti, three trombones and a bassoon. At another point he employs the same group with the addition of a regal to suggest the terrors of Hades.

It has been frequently asserted that the bassoon first appeared in the French opera orchestra in CAMBERT's 'Pomone' (1671). The author has definite information from the Library of the Paris Conservatoire that the fragmentary MS. music of Pomone mentions 'hautbois' but not 'bassons'. It must be remembered, however, that from the end of the seventeenth century to the middle of the eighteenth century, composers frequently adopted a system of wholesale duplication requiring merely a word or two to the specification of instruments at the beginning of a score, *e.g.* 'Violini I e Oboe I' and 'Violini II e Oboe II', while a bass part might be noted 'con fagotto' or 'senza fagotto'. The bassoon may, therefore, have been used in 'Pomone'.

We can be certain of its use by LULLY (1633–87) although bassoons appear irregularly in his scores and have little prominence and no independence. The earliest use is in *Psyché* (1674) and passages for two oboes and bassoon in *La Triomphe de l'Amour* (1681) anticipate similar treatment by Scarlatti, Purcell and Handel.

A. SCARLATTI (1660–1725) has bassoon parts in *Il Prigioniero Fortunato* (1698) though in the overture, for example, the basso-continuo is merely marked 'con fagotto'. PURCELL (1658–95) in his 'Dioclesian' (1691) requires a bassoon and in the *Second Musick* it is accorded a separate line. Towards the close of the century, we have STEFFANI (1655–1729) some of whose scores are remarkable in having an obligato bassoon solo in conjunction with a solo voice, supported only by the basso-continuo. At Hanover, where Steffani was appointed Kapell-meister in 1689, he had an orchestra of French musicians which would seem to have included a very good bassoon-player.

Lavoix[10] cites a mass, 'Le Grand Carme', of 1680 by BENOÎT DE SAINT-JOSEPH, in which the choir is accompanied by strings, three trombones, fagotto and organ.

Finally, BUXTEHUDE (1637–1707) maintained the German Protestant Church style of instrumental music which originated with Schütz and reached its zenith with Bach. Buxtehude still used the bassoon to double the bass strings and his use of instruments was influenced by consideration of similarity of compass rather than of blend or contrast of tone-colour.

So far, we have not referred to chamber-music in which the bassoon was included. The earliest use of it appears[11] to be by BIAGIO MARINI (died 1665), whose Op. 1 *Affetti musicali* (Venice, 1617) includes two sonatas for two solo violins, solo bassoon and continuo: *La Foscarina*, 'Sonata a 3 con il Tremolo, Doi Violini o Cornetti, e Trombone o Fagotto': and *La Aguzzona* containing some solo passages for bassoon. In Op. 8 (Venice, 1626) '*Sonate, Symphonie, Canzoni &c.*' are two sonatas (VIII and IX) 'per 2 Fagotti o Tromboni grossi and continuo'. About the same time, DARIO CASTELLO published two books of *Sonate concertante in stilo moderno* (Venice, 1621–44) for organ or harpsichord with violin, violetta, trombone, bassoon and trumpets; also for voices and instruments. The seventh sonata is for two bassoons and violins.

USPER (1619) composed a work for two solo violins, two solo bassoons and continuo.

RICCIO (1620) wrote for solo 'Flautin e Fagotto' and basso continuo.
Remarkable at this early period are the seven books of Sonatas, Symphonies and Dances of G. B. BUONAMENTE (died 1643). The sixth book (Venice, 1636) is for violin, cornett, dolzaina, viola and basso da brazzo, bassoon and trombone.
The earliest *solo* music for bassoon appears to be an exercise and variations[12] for fagotto solo with basso continuo entitled 'Fantasia Basso solo' by a monk, FRAY BARTOLOMÉ DE SELMA Y SALAVERDE, whose *Libro de Canzoni, Fantasie e Correnti* was published at Venice in 1638. Bartolomé was bassoonist to the Archduke Leopold of Austria and the

florid variations indicate a high technical proficiency at a time when the bassoon had but three keys. The work provides the earliest employment of B♭, for which a bell-joint and third key must have existed.

The author acknowledges Josef Marx's article[13] as the reference to much of his information on early chamber music. Lavoix also cites a number of lesser-known early composers for the bassoon.[14] Others are given by Profeta.[15]

Duets and trios with bassoon occur in the *Olor solymnaeus nascenti Jesu* of MATTHIAS SPIEGLER (1631).

MASSIMILIANO NERI was organist at St. Mark's, Venice, in 1641 and court organist at Cologne in 1664. His Op. 1 (1644) 'Sonate e Canzoni a 4' for church or chamber are for two violins, viola, gamba or bassoon and figured bass. Op. 2 (1651) Sonate for from three to twelve instruments also include the bassoon as alternative solo instrument. It is remarkable to find a collection of nine sonatas for solo bassoon and continuo composed in 1645 by GIOVANNI ANTONIO BERTOLI and published by Alessandro Vincenti, Venice. Bertoli states in his Preface that 'they demand a technical facility previously unexploited'. Brian Klitz[16] comments on the ornateness of the writing, obviously intended for a virtuoso on the two-keyed dulzian. (Compass C–d'.)

PHILIPP F. BÖDDECKER (1615–83), in his early years until 1634 bassoon-player in the Darmstadt Orchestra, published a collection of motets, *Partitura sacra* (Strassburg, 1651) to which is appended a *Sonate sopra La Monica* for violin, bassoon and cembalo. This interesting work has been republished by Histner & Siegel, Lippstadt, and edited by Max Seiffert. The peculiarity of its style consists in that the violin alone carries the melody, repeated four times without variation, except for the last time when it appears in galliard rhythm, while the bassoon plays the accompanying bass with increasing degrees of variation. As the compass is C to c' the piece could have been well played on a dulzian. It is of interest to learn that the melody *La Monica* is taken from a Ballet for the Lute by A. Terzi (1593) but did not acquire its title until before 1614 when it was adapted as a song 'Madre non mi far monaca'. Böddecker's 'Melosirenicum' (1660) is for a choir of six voices accompanied by two violins, bassoons, trombones and trumpets.

PHILIPP F. BUCHNER (1614–69). His trio-sonatas Op. 4 (Frankfurt, 1662) include one for two bassoons and continuo.

JOHANN ROSENMÜLLER (1619–84). His 'Sonate a 2, 3, 4 e 5 stromenti da arco et altri' (Nuremberg, 1682) include one for violin and bassoon with figured bass.

VINCENZO ALBRICI (1631–96) composed a '*Te Deum*' for four voices accompanied by three trumpets, a bassoon and a violoncello.

DIEDRICH BECKER, a composer who settled in Hamburg in 1644 published in 1668 his '*Musicalische Frühlings-Früchte*' which includes, a piece for three stringed instruments, two cornetti and bassoon.

GIOVANNI LEGRENZI (1626–90) deserves mention for his re-organisation of the orchestra of St. Mark's, Venice, when he became Maestro di Capella in 1685. He augmented it to thirty-four performers: eight violins, eleven violette, two viole da braccio, two viole da gamba, one violone, four theorbos, two cornetti, one bassoon and three trombones.

LORENZO AGNELLI (first half of seventeenth century) composed Motets for voices and instruments, including the bassoon.

JOSEPH BODIN DE BOISMORTIER (1691–1755) composed much chamber music, sonatas, trios, suites and concerti, including a concerto for bassoon (or 'cello) and strings. A 'first performance' of the last mentioned was advertised in Paris in 1951 and was played by Fernand Oubradous.

J. E. GALLIARD (c. 1680–1749) composed two sets of six solo sonatas for bassoon and continuo which have gained a place in the repertoire (see Appendix III). Galliard is remembered also by the record of Hawkins who states that in 1745 Galliard had a benefit concert at Lincoln's Inn Fields Theatre, at which a piece for twenty-four bassoons and four double basses was performed.

L. MERCI (c. 1690–c. 1750) composed, c. 1735, solos for the flute and a set of six sonatas for the bassoon (or 'cello). One of the latter has been republished by Schott from the copy in the British Museum.

BENOIST GUILLEMANT (1746), a Paris 'Maitre de Flute et Basson', composed a piece for two unaccompanied bassoons or 'celli (Op. 3).

C. A. P. BRAUN (1788–1835). Op. 6 consists of six sonatas for two bassoons.

VIVALDI (c. 1675–1741) has left a vast quantity of music for solo instruments and concerted items. His 447 concerti include thirty-seven for bassoon, so far published as Series 8 in the Italian complete edition of his works. Much of Vivaldi's output appears to have been written for the Conservatorio dell' Ospedale della Pietà of which he was Maestro for thirty-six years from 1704. This State orphanage provided instruction in singing and in violin, flute, organ, oboe, 'cello and bassoon—possibly the earliest instance of female bassoonists. Pincherle in his thematic inventory cites a concerto in B♭ (No. 382) for bassoon inscribed 'con^{to} p. Gioseppina o sia fagotto' which leads one to picture a youthful Venetian girl fagottist of the early eighteenth century. Dr. Walter Kolneder of Innsbruck, however, declares that examination of the MS. reveals that the dedication is to a Gioseppino Biancardi about whom as yet nothing has been discovered. Vivaldi observed normally a compass of two and a half octaves (C–g′) which would suit the contemporary Chorist-fagott.

Marx lists some thirty seventeenth-century composers, cited in the works of Becker[17] (1855) and Meyer[18] (1934), who included the bassoon in various compositions. Only a few are recorded here but there is ample evidence of the very extensive use of the bassoon in the seventeenth century.

MELCHIOR GLETTLE (died *ante* 1684) composed *Expeditiones Musicae* (1667–70). In five parts the fifth consists of litanies for five voices and five instruments:

Violins or cornettino 1° e 2°
Viola or trombone tenor
Viola or trombone alto
Fagotto or trombone basso
Viol da basso and organo.

J. C. PETZOLD (Petzel or Pezelius) (1639–94) composed works to which he gave very strange titles. Perhaps the strangest was *Bicinia variorum ut à violinis, cornettis, flautis, clarinis et fagotto, cum appendice à 2 bombardinis (vulgo chalumeau), clarinis et fagotto.* (Leipzig, 1674–75 and 1682.)

Other composers of religious music during the century to employ the bassoon include the following:

J. A. HERBST: Loblied (1637).

J. J. HARNISCH: Calliope Mixta (1653).

M. CAZZATI: Motetti e Himni a voce sola con 2 violini e Fagotto ad lib (1658).

J. M. CAESAR: Missa Brevis (1687).
Among operatic composers of the century was M.-A. CHARPENTIER
(1634–1704), whose 'Medée' (1693) includes a chorus supported by
violins, oboes, trumpets, bassoon and timpani. Lavoix remarks on the
very important and effective bassoon part.

MARIN MARAIS (1656–1728). Parisian violist and composer, produced his 'Alcyone' in 1706 and in it his representation of a storm was
notable for its instrumentation which included bassoons.

MONTÉCLAIR (1667–1737), a double-bass player for thirty years
at the Paris Opera, composed an opera 'Jephté' (1732) which includes
in Act I a march for violins, oboes, trumpets, bassoons and basses,
described by Lavoix as 'éclatante et majestueuse'.

KEISER (1674–1739) in his 'Octavia' (1706) scored for five bassoons
and continuo in a soprano aria which recalls Schütz's use of five
bassoons in 1619 already referred to.
At the close of the seventeenth century the orchestral wood-wind had
acquired some independence but no individuality and the bassoon's
tenor qualities were not yet recognised.

With the opening of the eighteenth century, we find rarely a second
bassoon part as an innovation in some scores and the compass employed
was two and a half octaves from C with occasionally B♭, (or even a
factitious A,) not obtainable on all instruments (*i.e.* dulzians). Quantz[19]
prescribes the proportion of bassoons to strings in a well-balanced
orchestra as follows:

  9 strings, 1 bassoon.
  14 strings, 2 bassoons.
  21 strings, 3 bassoons.

Carse[20] has stressed his view that 'one or more bassoons were commonly employed in playing the bass part in all eighteenth-century
orchestras, even though no part was written specifically for this instrument in the score'. The lists given by Carse show that all orchestras
had bassoons, although written parts were few until a start was made
later in the eighteenth century to release the bassoon from its incessant
bass role and to recognise the value of its tenor register. Carse has
devoted considerable space to the use of bassoons in eighteenth-century
orchestras and to the impression gained from examination of very
many scores. Dozens disclose no bassoon parts. 'In operas or oratorios

they may be found in only two or three numbers out of thirty or forty. Hundreds of the printed parts of the eighteenth-century symphonies include no specific bassoon parts. Dozens of Haydn's symphonies in the Breitkopf and Härtel Complete Edition are without them and of Mozart's forty-one symphonies in the same Edition, twenty-eight are without bassoon parts.' When they do occur it is almost entirely in Mozart's later works written from 1778 onwards. Carse made a special study of eighteenth-century music and his amusing comment is well worthy of attention. He continues

> '. . . are we to suppose that these bassoon-players, who were available in every orchestra, sat and did nothing when all these works were played? Did the Archbishop of Salzburg's bassoon-players go out for a drink when a Mozart symphony was played? Did Prince Esterhazy's pair read the evening paper when most of Haydn's early symphonies were played? Did Handel engage two bassoon-players to play in only two numbers in "Esther", and were they allowed to be idle during the overture and in the big full choruses? Of course not. They played with the rest of the bass instruments as a matter of course and only left the track of the bass part when some special melodic or harmonic part in the tenor register was written for them.'

As there can be only one bass part, the composer naturally never troubled to write it out all over again for the bassoons. It was taken for granted that the bassoons would play the bass part unless specially directed to do otherwise. This, then, is the simple and obvious reason for the absence of specific bassoon parts until the close of the eighteenth century. By then all the wood-wind were becoming gradually independent of the strings, and the bassoons, sharing this independence, were accorded separate parts, a fact revealed by practically every score. For the same reason that the bass part was not repeated for bassoons in the score, publishers saved the expense of engraving separate parts and the 'cello and bass part served well enough. Directions were only needed to indicate when the bassoons were to stop playing or to play alone. Carse instances from Arne's printed works: 'Bass, without bassoons'— 'Bassoni soli'—'All the basses, except the bassoons'—and reference has already been made to the terms 'senza Fagotti', 'col Fagotti' or 'Fagotti soli'.

It may seem that this subject is stressed unduly but the fact is that ignorance of it has misled most editors of nineteenth-century reprints of eighteenth-century music. Carse goes so far as to say that 'un-questionably, all the Haydn and Mozart symphonies, ostensibly written for oboes, horns and strings, if they are to be played as they were played in their own time and as their composers intended them to be played, should have bassoon parts'.

The nature of such parts as were written for bassoons in the first half of the eighteenth century depended on whether the composer ranked with the conservative or progressive schools active at that period. The former school maintained their chief concern in the part and not in the instrument. It would seem that it is to German composers of the progressive school that we owe the credit of directing the choice of wind parts 'by technique and colour, accompaniment instead of perpetual polyphony'. It is remarkable that the pioneers of this reform included composers whose music suffered complete and permanent eclipse: Keiser, Telemann, Graun and other so-called 'Zoph' composers.

J. S. BACH (1685–1750) composed for variable and often insufficient resources for performance under his own direction in the various towns where he was employed. His resources in bassoons and the use he made of them have received detailed analysis by C. Sanford Terry.[21] The following is the outline of Bach's career giving his places of employ-ment and the orchestral resources at each:

Arnstadt (1703–7): Count Anton Günther's orchestra of some twenty players with additions including a bassoon-player from Sonders-hausen. The only Cantata composed there (No. 15) does not include bassoon.

Mühlhausen (1707–8): Here he had exceptional resources, both professional and amateur, and for these he composed Cantata No. 71 'Gott ist mein König' using the bassoon for the first time. The score is laid out in four 'Choirs': (i) three trumpets and drums; (ii) two flutes and 'cello; (iii) two oboes and bassoon; (iv) two violins, viola and violone. The bassoon part ranges from B♭, to c′ and occurs in Choruses (1, 6 and 7) and Arioso (4).

No. 131 (1707–8) includes the bassoon in three numbers (C–e♭′) and the part is transposed, sounding a tone below the written notes to adjust the instrument to an organ tuned to *Chorton*—a major tone above *höher Cammerton*, the high chamber pitch in general use for concerted music.

Weimar (1708–17): In ducal service here, Bach became Concert-meister in 1714 with a choir of twelve and the ducal orchestra at his disposal. The twelve musicians included a bassoon-player, Christian Gustav Fischer, who served until his death *c.* 1714 and was succeeded by Bernhard Georg Ulrich who had joined the Capelle before 1714. The twenty-five Weimar chapel cantatas were lightly scored because accommodation in the small roof-gallery was confined and inconvenient for singers and players. All but five of the cantatas, however, are for strings and wood-wind and though flutes and oboes are rarely called for, the bassoon is used as follows:

No.	Date		Compass
18	1714	In 4 numbers	C-eb'
61	1714	In 2 numbers	C-e'
70	1716	In Coro 1 and every movement	C-e'
147	1716 and 1727	In Coro 1	D-e'
150	*c.* 1712	In 6 numbers including obbligato in No. 5. The part is transposed, sounding a minor third lower to adjust to an organ tuned to *Cornett-Ton*	C-f'
155	1716	In duet No. 2. Obbligato—a florid part in semi and demisemiquavers with skips and trills—remarkably advanced	B,-d'
160	1714	In 3 numbers	D-d'
162	1715	In 2 numbers	C-d'
185	1715	In 5 numbers	C♯-d'
Mein Herze schwimmnt	1714	In 5 numbers	C-f'
Sanctus in D(?)			D-f♯'

No. 21 of 1714 and No. 31 of 1715 do not illustrate the resources of the Weimar Capelle. The former was performed at Halle and the second survives as revised in 1731. In No. 21 the bassoon is in eight numbers (C-eb') but in No. 31 the part in three numbers (G,-d') often descends to G, which required a doppelfagott. This cantata is in C major but the oboes and (doppel)fagott are in E flat.

In the secular cantata of 1716 'Was mir behagt', bassoons are used in two choruses, generally 'col violoncello' in the range C-e'.

Cöthen (1717-23): The orchestral resources here were less than at Weimar though as Capellmeister to Prince Leopold of Anhalt-Cöthen, Bach had a group of sixteen including a copyist, eight chamber-musicians, four local players for occasional employment, two trumpeters and a drummer. The chamber musicians included Joh. Christoph Torlee, as bassoonist. The Cöthen period produced, according to Terry, 'especially in the Brandenburg Concertos absolute instrumental music surpassing any in existence in the variety of its colouring, the freedom of its technique and the masterliness of its touch'.

The secular cantata 'Durchlaucht'ster Leopold' (?1718), includes an obbligato bassoon part 'col violoncello' in the bass aria (No. 7) with compass D$\sharp$,–f$\sharp$'.

The Brandenburg Concerto No. 1 in 1721 includes a bassoon part (C–e$\flat$') and of four Ouvertures (undated) one in C has a part for 'Fagotto con Cembalo' (C–f'). The Sinfonia in F contains, in the first Trio, two oboes and fagotti (C–e$\flat$'). At Leipzig Bach had an orchestra of mixed professional and amateur players, varying in size and composition. Except on festal occasions the players rarely exceeded ten or twelve in number, in addition to the organ.

His one bassoon-player was an apprentice Stadtpfeifer, whose name is unknown though the names of the other players are given by Terry.[22] Terry contrasts the lot of Bach, who can seldom have heard his scores with even approximate excellence, with that of Handel who in London had almost unlimited professional players at his disposal.

Leipzig (1723–50).

In the cantatas of this period, the bassoon is included as follows:

Cantata No.	Date		Compass
12	1724–5	In 4 numbers	C–b$\flat$
42	1731	Throughout and obbligato with 'cello in No. 4	B$\sharp$,–a'
44	c. 1725	Throughout	C–f'
52	c. 1730	Throughout	C–e'
63	1723	In 3 numbers	C–e'
66	1731	In Coro 1 'Bassono obbligato' and in Aria 3	C$\sharp$–f$\sharp$'
69	c. 1730	Throughout	B,–f$\sharp$'
75	1723	In Coro 1, fagotti	D–f$\sharp$'

Cantata No.	Date		Compass
97	1734	In Coro 1, fagotti	C–g′
110	*post* 1734	In 2 numbers	C–f♯′
143	1735	In 5 numbers including obbligato to Tenor Aria No. 6	C–f′
149	1731	In 3 numbers incl. obbligato to Duet No. 6	D–g′
159	1729	In 1 number	D–e♭′
165	1724	In 3 numbers	C–c′
172	1731	In 3 numbers	C–d′
174	1729	In Sinfonia	C–e′
177	1732	In 2 numbers including obbligato to Tenor Aria No. 4	E♭–g′
186	1723	In 1 number	C–f′
194	1723	In 1 number, fagotti with 3 oboes	C–f′
197	1737	Obbligato to Bass Aria No. 6	D–e′

In the Easter Oratorio (1736) the bassoon has solo florid passages in the Sinfonia and throughout the work—compass C♯–f♯′.

In the Christmas Oratorio Pt. I of 1734 the bassoon is scored throughout (C–e′).

Bach prescribes 'Continuo pro Bassono grosso' in Coro 1 of St. John Passion of 1723 using the compass C–f′. In the Mass in F (*c.* 1736) he has 'Fagotti col Bassi'—compass F–c′. Finally, in the Hohe Messe (B minor Mass) of 1733 two bassoons have an important obbligato accompaniment (compass 1° C♯–a′: 2° C♯–f♯′) to the Bass Aria No. 10 'Quoniam tu solus sanctus', that notable instance of a solo horn obbligato—the horn's only participation in the Mass.

As Bach's bassoonist at Leipzig was generally an apprentice Stadtpfeifer, obbligato passages were not entrusted to him and occur only within two periods 1731–3 and 1735–7. We may assume that only during these years he had a bassoon-player competent to undertake an independent obbligato.

To summarise, Bach's treatment of the bassoon was conditioned by the degree of competence of his players, but he recognised its value as an orchestral voice to a greater extent than his predecessors. He lived during the period when the dulzian became obsolete and the bassoon became general, and this is shown by the compass he used. In general, he regarded e♭′ or f♯′ as the normal upward limit, and exceeded this only between 1731 and 1734 when the bassoon part rises to g' in three cantatas and to a' in No. 42 and the B minor Mass. At the lower end of the compass, he observed C as the limit with only four exceptions: Nos. 69 and 155—B♮,, and No. 71 B♭,, while No. 31 descends to G, frequently, constituting Bach's single requirement of a doppelfagott.

HANDEL (1685–1759) normally employed a wood-wind group of oboes in two and bassoons in one or two parts, adopting all the current conventions of early eighteenth century in their treatment. The bassoons double the bass part but occasionally rise to the tenor register and at times alternate with other instruments in pairs in imitation. Handel and his contemporaries still adhered to the old *concerto di ouboué* of Scarlatti. Another custom of the time was to use more than one instrument to play each oboe and bassoon part, hence the distinction sometimes found in scores between *solo* and *ripieno* wood-wind parts. The bassoon is used in two distinct ways by Handel. First, in a stereotyped duplication of strings and wind parts varied only where he decided that a less florid version of the string parts was better suited to oboes or bassoons. Secondly, when he distinguishes the three groups, strings, oboes-bassoons, brass and drums. The best example of this is in the *Dettingen Te Deum* (1743). Handel, however, remained conservative throughout his life in his orchestration and his last work, *The Triumph of Time and Truth* (1757), is orchestrated similarly to *The Water Music* (c. 1715). A remarkable exception to his usual use of the bassoon occurs in the oratorio 'Saul' (1739), in the scene between Saul and the Witch of Endor. Two bassoons *soli* accompany the ghostly voice over a sustained bass. The passage is quoted by Prout.[23]

The transition period from Bach's and Handel's manner of treating the bassoon to the beginnings of true orchestration as practised by Haydn and Mozart was spanned by GLUCK (1714–87). His scores of *Orfeo* (1762), *Alceste* (1767), *Iphigenie en Aulide* (1774), *Armide* (1777) and *Iphigenie en Tauride* (1779) reveal the wood-wind supplying harmonic support and sustained oboe and bassoon parts coming clearly through the orchestral mass. Gluck had, of course, the great advantage of clarinets, admitted to the orchestra during his life.

In 'Alceste' a children's duet is accompanied by two cors anglais supported by a bassoon, and this must be one of the earliest instances of the use of the cor anglais. The parts occur in the Vienna score but not in the Paris score as the cor anglais was as yet unknown in France.

PICCINI (1728–1800) deserves the credit of introducing the harmonic combination of clarinet and bassoon tone, a novel and welcome variation from the century-old association of oboe and bassoon.

J. G. MÜTHEL (1728–88) composed a concerto in D minor for cembalo, two bassoons and strings. The bassoons are used in the second movement only and have important and obviously prominent parts.

HENRY HARGRAVE is known only by five concerti with the principal part for bassoon or 'cello. The wording 'Printed for the author and sold by Mr. Walsh' on the title-page enables them to be dated c. 1765.

(ii) PERIOD 1750–1800

The disappearance of the figured-bass continuo began about 1760 and three to six bassoons were common to balance a string orchestra of about two dozen. It would seem that the longer softer reeds used on the eighteenth- and early nineteenth-century bassoons produced a more mellow and less penetrating tone. From a summary given by Carse,[24] showing the number of bassoons, etc., to strings in seven orchestras of the second half of the eighteenth century, three and four bassoons were normal, but five and even six were used at Dresden in 1753 and 1756 when the strings numbered twenty-five and twenty-seven respectively.

HAYDN (1732–1809) had at his disposal at Esterhaz in 1783 seventeen strings, two oboes, two bassoons and two horns with, presumably, two flutes, trumpets and drums, though Forkel[25] does not specify these. Though in his first symphony in 1759 the strings had all essential matter, the wind in his third symphony (c. 1761) commenced to have indispensable parts. He carried this further in Symphony No. 6 (Le Matin) where the wind are indispensable soloists or unite to form six-part harmony (flute, two oboes, bassoon and two horns). Lavoix in 1878 has written of Haydn: 'No composer, even among the moderns knew better than he the character and the timbre of each instrument and he was one of those in whom instrumental genius was most highly developed.' Certainly his use of the bassoon shows the capabilities of the instrument in many moods:

Melodic passages, doubling the 1st violins, in the London Symphony No. 104, (1795): accompaniment by two bassoons in thirds and solo flute and solo bassoon in 'The Clock' Symphony No. 101 (1794): melody in the minuet in The Military Symphony No. 100 (c. 1794) rising to a′: two long solos for bassoon occur in the slow movement of Symphony No. 56 in C (1774): in Symphony No. 85 (La Reine), second movement, a solo bassoon doubles in the octave below a florid chromatic development of the subject. In Symphony No. 86, the trio of the minuet is for bassoon doubling the violins, and in No. 93 the oboe and bassoon play a noteworthy part in the last movement. Ralph Hill[26] refers to Haydn's habit of using the bassoon to reinforce the upper parts rather than to supply the harmonic foundation of the wind ensemble. Even in his very last works the bassoon is scored as a tenor or alto instrument to the almost entire neglect of its lower octave. Haydn had a great affection for the bassoon and 'though he neglected entirely its capacity to portray tragedy, he revelled in its gay, lovable and laughable characteristics'.

With MOZART (1756–91) the development of wind writing reached a state of such perfection that the wind parts remain to this day a joy to play and to hear. Forsyth[27] refers to Mozart's harmonic and melodic doublings in which two bassoons take part, doubling of thirds, of sixths, of fragmentary figures, of held notes and suspensions. He gives credit to Mozart for their invention or consolidation. Forsyth remarks: 'If the student will merely write down on a sheet of paper every bassoon-combination which he can find in the first seven numbers of "Don Giovanni", noting each only once on its first appearance, he will probably be considerably astonished.' An excellent article, 'Mozart and the Bassoon' by Martha Kingdon Ward,[28] reviews Mozart's use of the bassoon in symphonies, serenades, piano concerti and operatic arias. Special reference must be made to a lovely bassoon part which, with flute and oboe, opens the aria 'Nehmt meinen Dank' (K.383) of 1782. The bassoon takes over the eleven closing bars and the entire scoring of this short aria is so perfect that one can but regret it is so seldom performed. The bassoon concerto (K.191) composed in 1774 for Baron von Dürnitz, an amateur bassoonist, has become well known since the advent of radio.* Recordings of a German (Adler) bassoon (G. Brooke) and of a French (Buffet) bassoon (P. Hongne) make a very interesting comparison of the tone-quality of the two types to which reference will be made later. The andante is, in the writer's opinion, the loveliest slow solo ever composed for the bassoon. The 'Sinfonia Concertante' (K. App. 9) for oboe, clarinet, horn, bassoon,

* There also exists a concerto in B♭ (K. 230a) the authenticity of which is disputed.

with strings, two oboes and two horns, dates from 1778 and was composed for the Mannheim Orchestra then numbering forty-six, including four bassoonists, Anton Strasser, Georg Wenzel Ritter (the soloist in the Sinfonia), Sebastian Holzbauer and Joseph Steidel.

REFERENCES

[1] Bukofzer, M.: *Music of the Baroque Era* (1947).

[2] Clercx, S.: *Le Baroque et la musique* (Brussels, 1949).

[3] Schütz, H.: *Sammtliche Werke*, edited by Chrysander and Spitta (Leipzig, 1885–1927), XVIII Volumes. Also: E. Euting: *Zur Getchichte der Blasinstrumente im 16 und 17 Jahrhundert*. Dissert. (Berlin, 1899).

[4] Schein, J. H.: *Sammtliche Werke*, edited by A. Prüfer. Vol. VI, No. 12 (1920).

[5] Kappey, J. A.: *Military Music* (London, 1894), pp. 71–73.

[6] Lavoix, H.: *Histoire de l'Instrumentation* (Paris, 1878), pp. 258–60.

[7] Lavignac: *Encyclopédie* (Paris, 1927), *s.v.* Basson.

[8] Albert, Heinrich: *vide Denk. Deutsch. Tonkunst*, Vols. XII and XIII.

[9] Cesti, P. A.: *vide Denk. Tonkunst in Oesterreich*, Vols. III and IV.

[10] Lavoix: *loc. cit. ante*, p. 247.

[11] Klitz, Brian: Article 'Some 17th century Sonatas for Bassoon' in *Journal of American Musicological Society* (Summer 1962), pp. 199–205.

[12] Lavignac: *loc. cit. ante*, 'La Musique en Espagne' by R. Mitjana, pp. 2085–87 where one variation is given in staff notation.

[13] Marx, J.: 'The Tone of the Baroque Oboe' in *The Galpin Society Journal*, Vol. IV, pp. 3–19.

[14] Lavoix, H.: *loc. cit. ante*, pp. 207 and 245–7.

[15] Profeta, R.: *Storia e Letteratura degli Strumenti musicali* (Florence, n.d.), Chapter XXXVII.

[16] Klitz, B.: *loc. cit. ante*, p. 202.

[17] Becker, C. F.: *Die Tonwerke des XVI und XVII Jahrhunderts* (1855).

[18] Meyer, E. H.: *Die mehrstimmige Spielmusik des 17 Jahrhunderts* (1934).

[19] Quantz: *Versuch, loc. cit. ante*, XVII, Sect. 1, para. 16.

[20] Carse, A.: *Orchestra in the XVIII century*, p. 33, pp. 18–27, pp. 124–6.

[21] Terry, C. S.: *Bach's Orchestra* (London, 1932).

[22] Terry, C. S.: *Ibid.*, p. 14.

[23] Prout, E.: *Instrumentation* (London, 1876), p. 44, Ex. 31.

[24] Carse, A.: *History of Orchestration*, p. 171.

[25] Forkel: *Musikalischer Almanach für Deutschland* (1782).

[26] Hill, Ralph: *The Symphony* (London, 1949).

[27] Forsyth, C.: *loc. cit. ante*, p. 246.

[28] *Music & Letters*, XXX, 1 (January 1949), pp. 8–25.

CHAPTER 6

The Employment of the Bassoon in the Nineteenth and Twentieth Centuries

THE nineteenth century was notable for the increased facilities for musical education both of composers and orchestral players. Important schools of music were established as follows:

Paris Conservatoire	1795	Brussels Conservatoire	1832
Milan Conservatorio	1808	Naples Conservatorio	1808
Prague Conservatorium	1811	Vienna Conservatorium	1821
London R.A.M.	1822	Leipzig Conservatorium	1843

In addition, the printing and publishing of scores and parts and textbooks on instruments and technique of instruments exerted a powerful influence on the study of wind instruments.[1] Reference has already been made to the works of Virdung, Praetorius, Mattheson and others. These were followed by:

1. Francoeur: *Diapason général de tous les instruments à vent* (Paris, 1772).
2. Vandenbroeck: *Traité général de tous les instruments à vent* (Paris, c. 1800).
3. Fröhlich: *Vollständige theoretisch-praktische Musiklehre für alle beym Orchester gebräuchlichen wichtigen Instrumente* (Würzburg, 1810–11).
4. Francoeur-Choron: *Traité général des voix et des instruments d'orchestre* (Paris, 1813). Based on Francoeur (above).
5. Sundelin: *Die Instrumentirung für das Orchester* (Berlin, 1828).
6. Fröhlich: *Systematischen Unterricht . . . Orchesterinstrumente* (Würzburg, 1829).
7. Catrufo: *Traité des Voix et des Instruments* (Paris, 1832).
8. Swoboda: *Instrumentirungslehre* (Vienna, 1832).
9. Kastner: *Traité général d'instrumentation* (Paris, 1837. Suppl. 1844).
10. Gassner: *Partitur-Kenntnis* (Karlsruhe, 1838). *Traité de la partition* (1851).
11. Berlioz: *Traité de l'Instrumentation et d'Orchestration modernes avec supplément 'Le Chef d'Orchestre'* (Trans. M. C. Clarke, London, 1856 and 1904).

BEETHOVEN'S (1770–1827). His use of the bassoon was frequently in association with horns and in his Second Symphony (1802) the clarinets join the bassoons in important passages. When wind instruments are alone, he allots to the second bassoon the solo bass part, a duty it is often hardly strong enough to fulfil satisfactorily.

It is possible to mention only a few of the short *solo* phrases which Beethoven gave the bassoon in his symphonies:

No. 1. In *Allegro con brio*, a little *piano* phrase of four notes, to which the oboe immediately and the flute (an octave higher) reply.

No. 2. In the Finale, both bassoons join the basses in an arpeggio (*ff*) and the 1st bassoon continues it for six bars (*piano* and *decrescendo*). A similar passage occurs later and is preceded by a most expressive solo of eight bars for 1st bassoon accompanied by strings alone.

No. 3. In the slow movement the strings again accompany a short solo for 1st bassoon (oboe and flute), commencing on g'. It is an example of the bassoon's capacity for portraying melancholy.

No. 4. The Finale of this symphony is a cause of concern to nearly every bassoon-player. Letellier and Flament,[2] remark 'Whenever a concert programme includes Symphony No. 4 in B♭, the bassoons are agitated and uneasy. Who would suspect that a simple passage of four bars was the cause of so much anxiety?'. The solo was written entirely staccato (*Allegro ma non troppo*, ♩=80) but at the speed it is frequently taken by certain conductors, it is practically unplayable. The French authors recommend it be played—two semiquavers slurred and two detached: alternatively, if the composer's intention is to be strictly observed, the conductor ought to slow the tempo slightly, seven bars before, and take up the tempo six bars later.

No. 5. In the *Allegro con brio* the horns have a *ff* solo passage which later in the movement the bassoons are given in another key. It has been a subject of argument as to whether it should now be played by the horns, which *could* have played it the second time in Beethoven's time of natural horns employing two stopped notes—¼ and ½ respectively.[3] Certainly, there is a touch of droll anticlimax when even two bassoons *ff* attempt to replace two horns *ff*. The *Andante* includes two lovely short solo phrases. In the first, the 1st bassoon replies to a little phrase given out by the clarinet over a *pp* string accompaniment. In the second case, an eight-note *p* phrase for solo bassoon over soft string accompaniment is continued by a further eight-note phrase delightful both to hear and to play.

In the Scherzo an atmosphere of mystery is created by a solo bassoon *pp* over strings pizzicato, later joined by the second bassoon. Towards the end the 1st bassoon and 'cellos *pizzicati* play the sequence of two crotchets and crotchet rest, *diminuendo*, to bottom C.

A final solo is very striking: three high g' crotchets *pp* (following the first violins), repeated, then ending with four c' crotchets.

The *Allegro* has a very emphatic *ff* phrase for two bassoons and the authors in Lavignac recommend the practice in large orchestras of employing four bassoons for such a passage and as follows:

1° 1st solo, playing the 1st bassoon part.

2° 1st ripieno, assisting the 1st solo and playing with him in passages marked *ff*.

3° 2nd solo, playing the 2nd bassoon part.

4° 2nd ripieno, assisting the 2nd bassoon and playing with him in passages marked *ff*.*

No. 6. Among many bassoon passages is the amusing solo for *2nd* bassoon in the *Scherzo* where it plays dotted minims: F, C, F and after five bars, F, C, C, F, as bass to oboe and horn playing the peasants' dance. On p. 38 (138) of Breitkopf edition of the Pastoral Symphony there occur arpeggi for clarinet and bassoon in octaves. While the clarinet is taken up to bb'', the bassoon's final note is lowered to bb instead of rising to bb'—the reason being that in 1808 few bassoons had a harmonic key for bb'. The higher bb' should always be played now. In the *Finale* is a long semiquaver passage commencing *ff* becoming *p* after 1¾ bars.

No. 7. The *Allegretto* includes a short solo in imitation of a flute and oboe duet and should be played *mf* not *p* to balance with the other two wind instruments.

No. 8. The quaver octave F passage for 1st bassoon is always striking in the *Allegro Vivace*, and recurs an octave lower *pp* as crotchets in the *Finale Allegro Vivace*, doubled by timpani in octaves—a most unusual combination. In the *Minuet*, the 1st solo marked *pp* would never be heard through the surrounding string accompaniment. It must be played *forte* if it is to be heard, for it lies in the third octave where the volume is not great.

No. 9 (Choral). Another example of under-marking occurs when the opening theme is repeated, doubled two octaves higher by the 1st Violins *p*. Though the solo bassoon part is marked *p* it must be played *f*.

The *Scherzo molto vivace* provides a jolly little passage for two

* The Paris Opéra had four bassoons in 1813. As far back as 1828, four bassoons was the normal complement of the French symphony orchestra, *e.g.* Société des Concerts.

bassoons in thirds, restating the theme in E minor. Later the bassoons have a counterpoint passage accompanying a melody on oboes and clarinets. The opening of the *Adagio* is for two bassoons *soli*, and as the 1st enters after the 2nd, he must match his volume with great care.

It has been considered valuable to provide these brief comments on the use of the bassoon in Beethoven's nine symphonies. The author considers that familiarity with them only serves to increase enjoyment of hearing or playing them. A string-player may well be excused for wondering how a bassoon-player can derive any satisfaction from playing only occasional *solo* phrases. It is one of the features of all wind parts that each is in essence *solo* and each player is sub-consciously aware of this as he contributes his share to the orchestral effect. Therein lies the satisfaction.

Apart from his bassoon parts in his Symphonies, Beethoven has given the instrument rising scale passages in the First Movement of the Violin Concerto (bars 18–28 and 400–3). A charming solo occurs in the Rondo (bars 134–58), alternating with the solo violin.

SCHUBERT (1797–1828) as an orchestrator did not become known till about the mid-nineteenth century and this is to be regretted in view of 'the warmth of melody and harmony which lent itself particularly well to orchestration in which colour and blend play the most important parts'. Thus Carse[4] summarises his assessment of Schubert's orchestral work. It is specially noticeable that the bassoons frequently blend in smooth-toned co-operation with the horns and clarinets and bassoons combine to form homogeneous accompanying harmony where oboe tone would prove too assertive. The bassoon, however, was given little or no solo work.

WEBER (1786–1826) gave an immediate and forceful stimulus to dramatic orchestration and, as a result of his friendship with skilled wind-players, he composed much for wind-instruments. For the clarinet he wrote two Concerti (Op. 73 and 74 of 1811) for Heinrich J. Bärmann (1784–1847): for bassoon and orchestra the *Andante e Rondo Ongarese* (Op. 35 of 1813, originally composed in 1809 for viola), and the Concerto for bassoon and orchestra (Op. 75 of 1811). These bassoon compositions were written for G. F. Brandt (1773–1836) then 1st bassoon in the Munich Court Orchestra.

ROSSINI (1792–1868) gave the bassoon numerous duets with flute, oboe or clarinet in many of his overtures but nothing of a purely solo nature. The melodic passages for bassoon, however, are allowed to stand out in strong relief with a judicious accompaniment which never blurs or obscures the melody. His 'Stabat Mater' opens with a telling phrase for the bassoon. In his six quartets for flute, clarinet, horn and bassoon, the bassoon has florid passages in No. 6.

MEYERBEER (1791–1864) demanded a lavish orchestra including sometimes four bassoons. His scores employ low-pitched blends of clarinets and bassoons or of bassoons, trombones and ophicleide. It may be remarked that in his time the contrabassoon was unknown in France where accordingly the normal complement of two bassoons was doubled in an effort to add greater *power* though of course it in no way added depth of *pitch*. That was still to come.

The period of activity of BERLIOZ (1803–69) as a composer—1825–62—coincides with the period in which the wood-wind instruments acquired greatly improved key-mechanism and the bassoon, as we have seen, received its full share of these improvements. His clear perception of the distinctive tone-colour, weight and characters of each type is reflected in his comprehensive *Traité de l'instrumentation et d'orchestration modernes*. His extravagant demands for immense orchestral resources early took shape for, at the age of twenty-four, he wrote the overture to the unfinished opera 'Les Francs-Juges' for an orchestra of 467 which included 16 bassoons with a contrabassoon, then virtually unknown in France. His use of four bassoons in Brander's bass solo in *Damnation of Faust* (1846) is an excellent example of the bassoon's capacity for rollicking fun. On the other hand, his use of its lower register to give sombre colour is to be found in the March to the Scaffold in the *Symphonie fantastique* (1830–1).

BOIELDIEU (1775–1834). His 'La Dame blanche', produced at Milan in 1825, included in the overture a solo, for long dear to bassoon-players.

DONIZETTI (1797–1848) in 'L'Elisir d'Amore' (1832) gives the bassoon a simple and effective melody which was frequently performed in the mid-nineteenth century and referred to in contemporary concert notices—the obbligato to 'Una furtiva lagrima'.

SPOHR (1784–1859) merits inclusion here by reason of his use of the bassoon in his rather undeservedly neglected chamber works. In particular:

Op. 31   Nonet in F major for violin, viola, 'cello, bass, flute, oboe,
clarinet, bassoon and horn.

Op. 52   Quintet in C minor for flute, clarinet, horn, bassoon and
pianoforte.

Op. 147 Septet for flute, clarinet, horn, bassoon, violin, 'cello and
pianoforte.

MENDELSSOHN-BARTHOLDY (1809–47) displayed his competence
as an orchestrator in his first Symphony (1824) and maintained it
until 'Elijah' (1846). His orchestral parts for bassoon are always
admirably suited to the instrument and 'lie' perfectly. He had a
warm affection for its rich cantabile powers, as for example in 'The
Hebrides' and 'Ruy Blas' overtures and in the slow movements of the
'Scottish' and 'Italian' symphonies. The *allegro* movements in these
symphonies include charming short phrases for bassoon and special
mention must be made of the short solo passage for bassoon and
clarinet leading to the last movement of the 'Scottish' symphony. 'The
Hymn of Praise' includes a very effective solo for oboe doubled an
octave lower by bassoon over a *piano* string accompaniment. There is an
amusing 2/4 *Allegro* intermezzo in 'Midsummer Night's Dream' for
two bassoons in thirds to accompany the entry of the Clowns. Prout
cites this in his *Instrumentation*[5] and this may be the origin of his
unjust appellation of the bassoon—'the clown of the orchestra'.

The use of shakes on the bassoon in orchestral music is not common,
and two instances in Mendelssohn's works never fail to strike the
author: in the slow movement of the 'Italian' symphony towards the
conclusion and in the fairy-like *Scherzo* from 'Midsummer Night's
Dream'.

SCHUMANN (1810–56) wrote little of interest for bassoon and his
thick, monotonously full-bodied orchestration seldom allows the individual voices of the orchestra the chance of being heard sufficiently.

Only one or two exceptions concerning the bassoon occur to the
author. In the 'cello concerto (Op. 129), in the slow movement, the
1st bassoon enters in bar 6 with a very expressive phrase repeated by
the soloist and accompanied very lightly throughout. In Symphony
No. 1 in B♭ the bassoon is heard to join the flute, after the flute cadenza
in the Finale.

WAGNER (1813–83) introduced groups of three of each type of
wood-wind instrument and the wood-wind become soloists. He tends
to treat the bassoons as tenor instruments to be used for inside parts

rather than merely as basses of the group. Indeed as regards the wood-wind as a body, Wagner's tendency was to group the flutes, oboes and clarinets in their various sizes together and to ally the bassoons with the horns. Typifying Wagner's disregard of contemporary limitations of compass he wrote up to e″ in the overture to Tannhäuser (1845) but the ascending passage is well covered and doubled by the body of violas and 'cellos. He also asked Heckel to make a bassoon with an extra long bell-joint and extra key for LT to reach A♮,. This note occurs in *Tristan* (1865) and in *The Ring*, *e.g. Walküre* (1870), etc., and it is the 3rd bassoon which has the low A. A similar extension was made to A♮,, in the case of the contra, *c.* 1879, as will be learned later.

L I S Z T (1811–86) gave the bassoon an important solo in the lower octave in the *Lento assai* of his 'Faust Symphony' (1854) where it is heralded by a *ff* bar for timpani.

A M B R O I S E   T H O M A S (1811–96) was perhaps the earliest of French composers to consolidate those very attractive features of French orchestration of which one of the most notable is the piquant treatment of wood-wind with light but always adequate string accompaniment. Solo bassoon passages are rare in Thomas's works but a staccato seven-note figure is prominent in the 'Pantomime' in 'Hamlet' (1868).

G O U N O D (1818–93) in his operatic work gave the bassoon full scope and the parts for two bassoons in 'Faust' (1859) are full of interest. In particular, in the bassoons' accompaniment of the Serenade in Act IV, very effective use is made of the bassoons in sixths and octaves and staccato octaves on B♭, for three bars and octave C's for one bar to imitate the sardonic laughter of Mephistopheles. In the following Andante, 'The Death of Valentine', the final nine bars of 9 are scored over a pedal D on the horns, and the descending harmony including two bassoons in thirds is very effective. Another prominent passage occurs in 'The Funeral March of a Marionette' (1873).

With B I Z E T (1838–75) wood-wind writing advanced to a stage of clarity and economy of colour which makes his orchestration a never-failing joy to hear. His score of *Carmen* (1875) has many solo passages for one or two bassoons and the Intermezzo between Acts I and II is a delightful duet for two bassoons. The two bassoons start soli in G minor and, after twenty-four bars *tacet*, the clarinet repeats the solo, joined by the bassoon in a descending chromatic scale followed by arpeggi. The number ends in typical Bizet fashion with a phrase repeated thrice in descending octaves and ends with three quavers D D G on the bassoons with pizzicato strings. The part includes two bars of an awkward shake on e′/f♯′ for which various fingerings are available on the French bassoon. The best is L1 and the adjacent wing-key for L2. In the first 'L'Arlésienne' suite in the andantino movement the 1st and 2nd bassoons have alternate bars of four staccato triplets as counterpoint to a melody by the 'cellos and horns. In the opinion of MM. Letellier and Flament (in Lavignac) it is preferable if one player can play the whole passage, but the fact is that in performance the bassoons in their middle register marked 'p' can hardly be heard. It would seem to have been a miscalculation on Bizet's part.

VERDI (1813–1901) in the *Requiem* (1874) accompanies the 'Quid sum miser' with four bassoons, a very striking and unusual combination.

BRAHMS (1833–97) employed the wood-wind very fully, frequently doubling one another each in its respective group and when used as a group mostly in conjunction with the horns. His bassoon parts are full of movement, ranging over the whole compass and at times—as in the 1st, 3rd and 4th symphonies—supported by the contrabassoon.

HUMPERDINCK (1854–1921) merits inclusion here for his skilful and understanding employment of the bassoon in 'Hansel and Gretel' (1893). The 'witch' music, in particular, gives full scope to the bassoon.

DELIBES (1836–91) and MASSENET (1842–1912) in the tradition of Parisian theatrical orchestration used the bassoon very effectively in their ballet music. The use of three or even four bassoons became a feature of French orchestration in the late nineteenth and early twentieth century. MASSENET'S 'Scènes pittoresques' No. 4 contains melodic passages of importance for bassoon.

CHABRIER (1841–94), who influenced Ravel, included an effective bassoon solo in his 'España' (1883), a work of wit and brilliance combined with rhythmic and colourful orchestration.

FRANCK (1822–90) in his 'Symphonic Variations' for piano and orchestra (1885) included a rather awkward passage for bassoon in imitation of a passage by the soloist. In performance it is ineffective but it happens to be well covered.

JOHANN STRAUSS (1825–99) is included here as his 'Perpetuum Mobile' includes an attractive short solo for bassoon.

TSCHAIKOVSKY (1840–93) gave the bassoon greater scope more consistently in his symphonies than it had ever received. Many solos, accompanied only by strings, have made the bassoon familiar to many listeners and viewers. It is not possible to do more than refer to a few outstanding solos:

Symphony No. 4. In the opening *Andante*; in the *Andante* of the 2nd movement where the last entrance of the theme is a long solo in five flats at the end of which the first phrase is repeated four times concluding with the bassoon on a long f *morendo*. This is a very striking solo and the final *morendo* calls for breath-control and artistry if it is to be effective.

Symphony No. 5. The subject in the first movement is for solo bassoon in its middle register creating a sombre and melancholy atmosphere. In lighter mood, the third movement in ¾ has a solo which, according to Forsyth,[6] 'affords a very good example of what not to write for the bassoon . . . the big up-and-down *legato* swoops . . . need a good deal of nice adjustment in the *tempo* unless they are to sound merely an awkward scramble'. This is not the general impression, though admittedly the passage benefits by a slight *ritardando* which allows the soloist to adjust his embouchure to the requirements of such a passage.

Symphony No. 6. The opening for bassoon commencing *pp* on E and rising by stages slowly over *divisi* double-basses is a notable example of the lugubrious effect of the very telling lower notes of the bassoon. An equally impressive passage for two bassoons occnrs in the fourth movement where, over sixteen bars with constant change in dynamic marking, the bassoons descend from f♯' through two octaves and a fourth to a *pp* bottom C♯.

The bassoon parts of the 'Casse-Noisette' Suite achieve rich and unusual colouring, *e.g.* in the 'Danse Arabe'. The bassoon's capacity to portray the grotesque is displayed in the persistent staccato bass for two bassoons, alternating F and B♭, quavers, from beginning to end of the 'Danse chinoise'.

GRIEG (1843–1907) gave the bassoon no prominence except in his *Peer Gynt* suite, where two bassoons alternate with the strings in the opening of 'In the Hall of the Mountain Kings', all in the lowest register and staccato and in *Norwegian Dance No. 1*.

RIMSKY-KORSAKOV (1844–1908) will always be associated with his demands upon the bassoon in the three long and important cadenzas in the *Andantino* of *Scheherazade* (1888). The exceedingly rapid turns on high e', f♯', g' and a' were made simple by Wilhelm Heckel.[7] The solo is given special prominence as the sole accompaniment is provided by four double-basses *divisi*. It is related that Tom Wotton, the noted London bassoonist, on meeting the three cadenzas for the first time, told Hans Richter, conducting, that they were impossible. 'Alas! That cannot be', replied Richter. 'I have heard them played on the Continent.'[8]

SAINT-SAËNS (1835–1921) in 'Phryné' (1893) has a curious staccato semiquaver accompaniment for solo bassoon, including skips of as much as 2½ octaves and an arpeggio slurred over two octaves. A solo of sixteen bars staccato in the third octave occurs in 'Phäeton' (1873).

CHARPENTIER (1860–1956), known best for his *roman musical* 'Louise', gave the bassoon a striking phrase in a ¾ Andantino in his 'Impressions d'Italie' (1887).

D'INDY (1851–1931) has an amusing exposition of a fugue for three bassoons in the first of his three symphonic overtures 'Wallenstein' (1873–81). He also included the bassoon in 'Chansons et danses' (1898) for wind instruments and 'Sarabande et menuet' for flute, oboe, clarinet, horn and bassoon (1918).

DUKAS (1865–1935) is associated in the mind of all bassoonists with his scherzo *L'Apprenti Sorcier* (1897) in which three bassoons soli have a rollicking theme over a *pizzicato* string accompaniment. The employment of this piece in a Walt Disney film brought it to the attention of an immense public who also learned to recognise and appreciate the bassoon in its jocular mood.

WEINGARTNER (1863–1942). His orchestral arrangement of Weber's 'Invitation to the Waltz' has a very cleverly contrived counter-melody for bassoon against the strings playing the second subject.

DOHNÁNYI (1877–1960) has aroused very mixed opinions, *e.g.* in Grove's *Dictionary*, 4th edit. and 5th edit. The humour of his 'Variations on a Nursery Song' for piano and orchestra undergoes criticism but did he not dedicate it 'to the enjoyment of lovers of humour and to the annoyance of others'? In any case, as one might expect, the bassoon and contrabassoon have their share in some of the ten variations, the fourth in particular for two flutes and piccolo against two bassoons and contra. In the ninth variation, the odd *Scherzo* includes

H

a unison passage for piccolo and contrabassoon and the fugal *Finale* is amusingly rounded off by flute, piccolo, bassoon and contrabassoon in succession.

SULLIVAN (1842–1900) had a great affection for the bassoon and there can be little doubt that through his father, a band-instructor, he gained a first-hand knowledge of the instrument. This is confirmed by the way in which his bassoon parts, both in the comic operas and in extra-theatrical compositions, 'lie' conveniently and can be so much the more effective. If he exploited the bassoon's comic features, *e.g.* *Grotesque Dance* in his 'Masquerade' Suite, he also gave it very effective harmonic and melodic passages—often but a phrase, alternating with one or other of the wood-wind—and occasionally an outstanding bass part as in Ruth's song in 'The Pirates of Penzance' Act I, and the Colonel's song in 'Patience' Act I. In the overture 'Di Ballo' (1870) Sullivan gave the bassoon a prominent bass part—an 'Alberti bass' in rapid time.

RICHARD STRAUSS (1864–1949) employed first three and soon after four of each type of wood-wind which in the bassoons included the contra in passages to which reference is made later. In *Ein Heldenleben* (1898) he has a florid solo for bassoon in tenor clef rising in d♭′ with harp accompaniment. Similar florid ascending bassoon passages occur in 'Till Eulenspiegel' and 'Don Juan'.

In *Don Quixote* (1898) Variation VIII has a prominent passage for three bassoons and contra, while Variation IX has a more remarkable passage of fourteen bars for two bassoons, unaccompanied except in the last two bars.

MAHLER (1860–1911), like Strauss, demanded ever larger orchestral forces and from thirteen wood-wind in his 1st Symphony (1904) he scored for twenty in his 6th Symphony, including four bassoons and contra.

DEBUSSY (1862–1918) was much more restrained in his demands upon orchestral resources, though his 'Gigues' require sixteen wood-wind including three bassoons and contra. Solo passages for wood-wind are frequent and he appears to have been attracted by the veiled quality of high notes on the bassoon. The author chanced to acquire a copy of a letter written by Debussy to his friend André Caplet dated 24 July 1909. In it he writes: 'Ma seule bonne journée me fut procurée par le concours des instruments à vent. Ah! mon ami! quelles clarinettes . . .

et quels Hautbois et des Flutes en velours. Quant aux Bassons, ils sont purement admirables . . .! pathétiques comme Tchaikowsky, ironiques comme Jules Renard. Tout cela dans une Fantaisie de H. Büsser, écrite comme s'il était né dans un basson . . . ce qui ne veut pas dire qu'il est né pour faire de la musique.'

The 'Fantaisie' to which Debussy refers was the 'pièce de concours' set by the Administration of the Paris Conservatoire. In the year 1909 the set piece for bassoon-pupils was 'Récit. et thème varié de Henri Büsser'. It may be added that André Caplet, to whom Debussy was writing, composed a piano and wind quintet (flute, oboe, clarinet and bassoon) (1898) and a 'Suite Persane' for two flutes, two oboes, two clarinets, two horns and two bassoons (1900). In the opening to Debussy's *Pelléas et Mélisande* the 3rd bassoon has a low D requiring such a pianissimo that in France a pocket-handkerchief is placed in the bell as a makeshift 'mute'.

ELGAR (1857–1934) has been said by Forsyth to have lavished the greatest attention on his bassoon parts which 'always appear to be peculiarly present to his consciousness'. In the opening of the 3rd 'Pomp and Circumstance' March he marks the score *Fagotti preponderate*. In the 'Enigma Variations' (1899) there are numerous passages, often very florid as in Variations III, VII and X. In Variation VIII two bars of solo staccato skips are alternated with two legato bars of the theme. In Variation XI the bassoons have a very rapid staccato version of the first part of the theme.

MASCAGNI (1863–1945) employs the bassoon with dramatic effect in *Cavalleria rusticana* (1890), e.g. in the Romance and Scena No. 4, the 1st bassoon has a very telling solo of eighteen bars *largo* in the middle register, giving great scope and satisfaction to the player.

In the following Andante No. 5 in $\frac{6}{8}$ the 1st bassoon has twenty bars of arpeggio accompaniment in A flat and the passage is both awkward and tiring. Later, both bassoons have five bars solo in octaves, *Largo molto sostenuto* in A flat, and the effect is sombre and ominous. A similar tragic four-bar passage for the 1st bassoon occurs in the Finale No. 8. Later, two bassoons have seven bars *fff* in $\frac{2}{4}$, followed by a solo passage in $\frac{2}{4}$, largely chromatic and going down to B♮ʼ.

HARTY (1879–1941) produced in 1924 a completely re-written version of his early Irish Symphony the Scherzo of which alone has been recorded. It includes a comical little falling arpeggio solo for

bassoon which, it has been said,⁹ represents the stumbling gait of a
drunken Irishman returning from a fair! It requires skill to bring it off
successfully.

STRAVINSKY (1882) is known to bassoon-players for his unreason-
able demands upon them in 'The Rite of Spring' (1913). As if it were
not sufficiently trying for the solo bassoon to open the work, the
eighteen-bar passage commences on c″ and rises to d″ more than once
requiring a hard reed and considerable strength of embouchure. In
'The Soldier's Tale' (1918) he has another difficult solo in the range a′
to b″ with semi and demisemiquavers. In 'The Firebird' (1910) there
is a sixteen-bar passage in six flats in the range b♭′ to f″. In 'Pulcinella'
(1920) a very long and trying semiquaver accompaniment (two slurred
and two detached) ranges over the compass D to a′.

DVOŘÁK (1841–1904) in the Symphony 'From the New World'
(1893) has a counter-subject for bassoon solo in the form of a Czech
dance near the end of the last movement. The conductor must use care
lest the bassoon be obscured at this point. A further passage in the
Largo of the same Symphony has always delighted the author. The cor-
anglais plays the solo for ten bars when the bassoon joins it in unison
an octave lower, creating a subtle change in tone-colour which is always
fascinating to detect.

RAVEL (1875–1937) in 'Bolero' (1927) has a very trying solo in the
range d′ to d♭″—an example, in the author's opinion, of a solo quite
out of the range to ensure characteristic bassoon quality. In the piano
concerto, Ravel gives the bassoon continuous bars of slurred arpeggi
in the range C to g′ followed by a cantabile solo marked 'vibrato'. In
the Presto movement a florid passage in semiquavers is marked *presto*.
In 'Rapsodie espagnole' (1907) a very difficult passage occurs for two
bassoons in florid semiquavers in the third and fourth octaves. At times
the 1st bassoon is playing groups of four against the second bassoon's
groups of six. A less difficult and consequently much more effective
solo in the range b to a′ occurs in 'Alborada del gracioso' (1905). Finally
mention must be made of another difficult scale passage, though it is
within the third octave, in 'L'Heure espagnole' (1907).

IBERT (1890) has several compositions of wind chamber-music and
among his orchestral works is *Escales* (1922) which contains some
difficult florid passages though entirely within the second and third

octaves. In his ballet *Diane de Poitiers* (1934) there are at least five difficult passages marked 'Vif', 'animé', or 'allegro scherzando', but they
never rise above a'.

SMETANA (1824–84) in the overture to *The Bartered Bride* (1863–6)
makes severe demands on the orchestra. The opening unison for strings
and all the wood-wind demands the utmost precision and a high standard of proficiency with each player. The passage is always included
among those a student must master.

PIERNÉ (1863–1937) was for a time a member of the directing com-
mittee of studies at the Paris Conservatoire and he composed a 'solo
de concert' for bassoon in 1898. Solo bassoon passages of some
difficulty occur in his ballet *Cydalise et le Chèvre-pied* and in *Preludio
et Fughetta*.

LEONCAVALLO (1858–1919). The score of *Pagliacci* (1892) with its
many dramatic passages includes several for bassoon.

PUCCINI (1858–1924) has written a passage of importance before
the rise of the curtain in *Gianni Schicchi*, the third of the one-act operas
in his *Trittico* (1918). It may be noted that earlier, *e.g.* in *La Bohème*
(1896), he substituted the bass-clarinet for the bassoon as bass of the
wood-wind.[10]

SIBELIUS (1865–1957) makes continuous use of the lower octave
in *Finlandia* (1899). Indeed, the second bassoon part is quite fatiguing.
In the *4th Symphony* (1911) bassoon passages of importance occur in
the 2nd and 3rd Movements and in the 1st Movement of the Violin
Concerto (1903).

BARTOK (1881–1945) in his Concerto for orchestra opens the second
movement with a passage for two bassoons (bars 8–24) and three
bassoons are used in bars 164–81.

VAUGHAN WILLIAMS (1872–1958) has very prominent bassoon
parts in the overture *The Wasps* (1909) and in *Five Tudor Portraits*
(1936) a bassoon cadenza *andante doloroso* occurs.

PERCY GRAINGER (1882–1963) has given the bassoon a characteristic whimsical part in the orchestral arrangement of his *Children's
March*.

BAX (1883–1953). His 3rd Symphony (1928–9) opens with an
important solo passage for bassoon, unaccompanied. At the first

performance under Sir Henry Wood (to whom the Symphony was dedicated) the solo was played by Richard Newton, 1st bassoon of the provisional B.B.C. Symphony Orchestra, prior to its foundation in October 1930.

CARL ORFF (1895–   ) in his first stage work *Carmina burana* (1937) has written in No. 12 'The Song of the roasted cygnet', a difficult solo for bassoon. A passage employing d″/c″ seven times in five bars ends with a *sforzando* C.

WALTON (1902–   ) makes great use of the bassoon in his orchestral parts. A notable solo passage occurs in his 1st Symphony rising often to c″. Another is the solo in Suite No. 2 *Façade* No. 5, Popular Song (1938), where a passage played by a saxophone is repeated on the bassoon. It provides a rare and interesting opportunity of assessing the comparative orchestral timbre of the two instruments. The Comedy Overture, *Scapino* (1941) has unison passages for two bassoons in bars 246–50 and again in bars 263–8.

SHOSTAKOVITCH (1906–   ) in the 5th Symphony (1937) has written in the 2nd movement (Allegretto) a passage for two bassoons and another for bassoons and contra. Outstanding solos occur in nearly all his symphonies, particularly in the Finale of the 8th and in the slow movement of the 9th and 10th symphonies.

MALIPIERO (1914–   ). His Symphony No. 1 'The Four Seasons' (1934) opens with a very prominent bassoon solo.

BENJAMIN BRITTEN (1913–   ). His Op. 34 *The Young Person's Guide to the Orchestra* (1946) gives a prominent passage to two bassoons. The more recent Op. 60, *Nocturne* for Tenor and Orchestra (1958), has a florid and difficult obbligato to a setting of Tennyson's 'The Kraken'.

J. M. DAMASE (1928–   ) in his *Dix-sept Variations* (Op. 22) for wind-quintet has given No. V to bassoon solo and No. XI contains a florid part.

THE BASSOON IN THE THEATRE

Some reference will be expected to be made to the use of the bassoon in small and incomplete orchestras, more and more rarely to be heard in theatres today. The author recalls his boyish enjoyment of the orchestras in the Edinburgh theatres pre-1914. It will surprise many readers to learn that an orchestra of at least sixteen was maintained at four theatres and smaller groups in two others. Economic causes after 1920 have resulted in the total disappearance of any theatre orchestra in the capital city and, even more regrettable, the almost total disappearance of wholly professional players of harp, oboe, bassoon, clarinet, horn, while the trumpets and trombones available are seldom orchestrally trained. The author's delight in the bassoon was first derived in the theatre and it may well be impossible for the younger generation to realise how effective an instrument it proved in the light music of the theatre. Francis M. Collinson, from long experience as conductor and orchestrator in London theatres, has listed in his *Orchestration for the Theatre*[11] a dozen functions of the bassoon in the theatre. These recall to the author many examples of which opportunities of hearing them today are very rare indeed outside London and rare even there.

If we have reason to be thankful that the bassoon has not shared the debasement which has beset the clarinet, saxophone, trumpet and trombone, we have to recognise that the absence of the bassoon from all dance music is due in large measure to its technical difficulty and its unsuitability for 'doubling'. This has meant that the demand for the professional bassoon-player has become much less. Added difficulties are the popularity of the German System and the prohibitive price of imported bassoons (until lately), also the lack of teachers familiar with the French system which is still that of a considerable number of 'school' bassoons in Britain.

Bassoon-playing has reached a stage when opportunities for the professional are unlikely to increase and only young people interested in serious music will devote their studies to the instrument.

REFERENCES

[1] *Text-Books on Orchestration before Berlioz*, by A. Carse, in *Music & Letters* XXII, No. 1, Jan. 1941.
[2] Lavignac: *Encyclopédie, loc. cit. ante*, p. 1573.
[3] Kindly communicated by R. Morley-Pegge.
[4] Carse, A.: *History of Orchestration*, p. 235.
[5] Prout, E.: *Instrumentation, loc. cit. ante*, Ex. 32.
[6] Forsyth, C.: *Orchestration, loc. cit. ante*, p. 238.
[7] Heckel, W.: *Der Fagott, loc. cit. ante*, 1st edit., p. 30.
[8] Kindly communicated by A. R. Newton.
[9] Kindly communicated by A. Camden.
[10] Grove's *Dictionary*, 5th edit., *s.v.* Puccini, Vol. VI, p. 989.
[11] Collinson, F. M.: *Orchestration for the Theatre* (London, 1st edit., 1941; 2nd edit., 1949).

CHAPTER 7

Higher-pitched Bassoons

As has been shown in Chapter 2, the early seventeenth century was a period during which whole families of instruments were made in imitation of the divisions of the human voice. The type instrument in the bassoon family was the chorist-fagott (compass C–g′). The others of lower pitch will be treated as contrabassoons in Chapter 8. Those of higher pitch continued to be made from at least 1600–1890, although singularly little music was written for them. Baines[1] has suggested that some may well have been made for boys to learn upon. The stretch for the fingers and thumb of the right hand on the ordinary bassoon is considerable. It is known, for example, that Wenzel Ritter (1748–1808), the noted bassoonist at Berlin and Mannheim, commenced to learn at the age of eight.

In Praetorius there were fagottini (a convenient term to cover all types above the chorist), *viz.* tenor in G, alto in d and discant in g. The alto and discant appear to have been little used in the dulzian shape, unique survivals being the Spanish 'bajoncillos' in Brussels: Nos. 2328–30 and an anonymous No. 990 in A which Mahillon considers to have been in C of the period, but seems more likely to have been in G, as in height it agrees with No. 2327 in G. The tenor fagott, which acquired the name tenoroon in the nineteenth century has been made in a variety of pitches. An anonymous original in G is in the German National Museum, Nürnberg (No. MI 124) and a facsimile is in Brussels (No. 991).

The Denners (father—died 1705, and son—died 1735) are the earliest known makers of three-keyed bassoons which they produced while still making two-keyed dulzians. A fine three-keyed octave-bassoon by Denner is No. 146 in the Fine Arts Museum, Boston, U.S.A. (ex Galpin). The catalogue refers to the inverted conoidal course of the bore of the bass-joint, a device to soften the lower notes. Other fagottini survive bearing makers' names:

3 *keys:* C. Kraus; J. Kuteruf.

106

4 *keys:* H. C. Tölcke; C. Kraus; Scherer; Tuerlinckx; Kraus; Müller.

5 *keys:* M. Lot, Paris.

7 *keys:* I. Leiberz, Coblenz, dated 1700 (4 keys not original); Delusse, Paris (2 or 3 keys not original); Buhner & Keller, Strasbourg.

12 *keys:* Savary Jeune. dated 1827.

16 *keys:* Hawkes, London.

The normal tenor bassoon was originally in G, a fifth above the bassoon (*Fr.* basson quinte) but after *c.* 1830 the tenor in F gained popularity. In Germany, the nomenclature became so confused that the word 'Hoch' was often prefixed to distinguish the Quart or Quint-fagott higher than the bassoon from those lower. The following list of surviving tenoroons indicates pitch and number of keys:

In E♭   Tuerlinckx, 5; Tauber, 9.

In F   Blockley, 4; Kraus, 4; Babb, 6; Kies, 9; Adler, 10; Savary Jeune, 11–15; Stehle, 12; Buffet-Crampon, 16; Morton, 16; Hawkes, 16.

In G   Peale, 7; Cahusac, 6.

Pierre[2] states that although the cor anglais was introduced at the Opéra in 1808, it was much longer before it was used in the provinces in France. It was, therefore, replaced by a tenoroon ('basson en fa') notably at Bordeaux where Reickmans settled *c.* 1833 after leaving the Opéra in Paris. M. Espaignet of the Orchestra of the Opéra Comique (in 1890) had also played the tenoroon in Bordeaux. When two cors anglais were needed, as in the ritornello of the air 'Rachel quand du Seigneur' from 'La Juive', the oboist transposed the first part and the bassoonist played the second on an instrument usually in F. This procedure continued for a long time. Solo bassoonists also used the higher bassoons, *e.g.* Eugène Jancourt, then (1890) professor at the Paris Conservatoire, played between 1838 and 1840 several solos on an instrument in E♭ by Savary. Pierre was of opinion that such exceptional cases no longer occurred and higher bassoons had no purpose. The few qualities they possessed could not outweigh the inconvenience inherent in their nature. If the pitch of the instrument is raised, it may gain readiness of response, but with the loss of much of its sonority. The timbre differs at the two extremities of the compass: above, the notes become thin—those of the F tenoroon are strangely like those of the saxophone—below, they have neither roundness nor volume and in no way whatever do they resemble the tone-character of the bassoon. 'What need is there', inquired Pierre, 'to extend the bassoon into the range of higher instruments?' Its highest notes could never be compared with the low and middle notes of the clarinet and oboe. These notes had no longer a sufficiently marked and pleasant quality to provide a special colour in orchestration. Having thus expressed this frank opinion (and, be it noted, Constant Pierre was a competent bassoonist), he accused Evette and Schaeffer of 'pure coquetterie de facteurs' in having made for the 1889 Exhibition useless instruments. They presented four, in Db, Eb, F and G—a semitone, a minor third, a fourth and a fifth above the bassoon. Each had fifteen keys and was much better than any tenoroon produced until then. Nevertheless, Pierre considered that it would have been far better to make a semi-contra—mid-way between bassoon and contrabassoon. This will be considered in Chapter 8.

Even earlier than the Paris 1889 Exhibition, Morton, an excellent London bassoon-maker, was supplying tenor bassoons and these were included in the Catalogue of Lafleur, London, c. 1870.[3] A sixteen-keyed tenoroon by Morton is listed *supra*. It is quite remarkable that so much confusion has arisen over the tenoroon. The following references will show this:

1849 Chambers' *Information for the People*: 'The tenoroon played with a reed is seldom employed.'

1879 Stainer. *Music of the Bible*: 'The tenor oboe or tenoroon.'

1884 Dr. W. H. Stone in Grove's *Dictionary of Music*: 'The tenor bassoon or alto fagotto.'

1898 Stainer and Barrett: *Dictionary of Musical Terms* and

1911 Stokes' *Cyclopaedia of Music and Musicians*: 'Tenoroon: The name of an old tenor oboe with a compass extending downwards to tenor C.'

1913 Sachs' *Real Lexikon*: 'Tenoroon: a super octave Bassoon made by Lazarus in London c. 1820, with pronounced cone and blown with a single reed. The term Tenoroon is applied otherwise to all smaller bassoons.'

Note: Lazarus was a noted clarinettist not a maker and he was aged five in 1820!

Stainer was certainly influenced by Stone who held the very definite but equally unjustified opinion that the oboe da caccia of Bach was the tenoroon (*i.e.* a bassoon raised a fourth) and not the cor anglais (*i.e.* an oboe lowered a fifth). His erroneous contention that tenoroon and oboe da caccia were identical was based on no stronger evidence than a similarity of treatment in transposition.[4]

Stone was consistent in his viewpoint for he owned a pair of Savary tenoroons and played on one the oboe da caccia parts in Bach Concerts in London *c.* 1885. At the International Inventions Exhibition in London in 1885, Stone lent his pair of tenoroons but insisted on having them catalogued as 'A pair of Oboi da Caccia or Alti Fagotti by Savary.' The alto fagotto was a small bassoon-shaped instrument, an octave above the bassoon and played with a single reed. How Dr. Stone, a skilled amateur bassoon and contra player, could confuse the alto fagotto with the true tenoroon or either with the obsolete oboe da caccia is very strange. For those who care to study this in greater detail, there are two articles: 'The Saxophone before Sax' by the late F. G. Rendall[5] and 'The Alto-Fagotto—misnamed Tenoroon—its original, the Caledonica and their Inventor' by L. G. Langwill.[6]

EMPLOYMENT OF HIGHER-PITCHED BASSOONS

The earliest score, so far noted, to specify a high-pitched bassoon would appear to be *Concentus in duos distincti choros* Lib. I by Giovanni Pietro Flaccomio (d. 1617) published in Venice in 1611.[7] The author is indebted to Mr. Brian Klitz of the Music Department of the University of Connecticut for photo-copies of the altus and bassus parts of the Secundus Chorus, Quinque vocum. The altus in alto clef is marked 'Con basoncico alias fagotto piccolo' with the range a to a'. The bassus in tenor clef is marked 'Con sacabuche alias trombone'. The fagotto piccolo here is evidently of higher pitch than the variety so designated by Praetorius in *De Organographia* (*vide* Chap. 2, Plate 4, No. 4) and must denote the discant fagott or the intermediate alt-fagott (not included by Praetorius in the compass table). It is understandable that the nomenclature of the smaller varieties of bassoon had not yet been agreed in the early seventeenth century.

An interesting article by H. Jean Hedlund, 'Ensemble Music for small Bassoons'[8] concerns a MS. composition in the Ratschulbibliothek in Zwickau (Catalogue No. 738), listed by two authorities as *Parthia No. IV* by Johann Kaspar Trost. It is not certain which of a number of seventeenth-century Trosts composed the music, but examination of it indicates that it was written probably in the eighteenth rather than the seventeenth century. Confusion arises, however, from the fact that the title-page gives the composer as J. G. M. Trost, initials which differ from the bibliographical listings of Eitner and Meyer. Mr. Hedlund concludes that J. G. M. Trost was probably an eighteenth-century descendant of the Trosts listed by Eitner. Be that as it may, the title-page reads:

'No. IV/Parthia/à/2 Corni in C/
2 Fagotti-octavo/2 Fagotti-quarto/et/
2 Fagotti/del/J. G. M. Trost.'

The ranges of the bassoon parts (actual pitch) are as follows:

Fagotto-octavo I: g to f″
Fagotto-octavo II: e♮ to c″
Fagotto quarto I: c to c″
Fagotto quarto II: G to g′
Fagotti I & II: C to g′

In addition to this very remarkable work, Cantata No. X of Zachau (1663–1712)[9] includes parts for two 'Bassonetti', a term found nowhere else but presumably denotes fagottini. This Cantata is scored thus:

In this, as in most of the other Cantatas, oboes and bassoons are written a minor third above the strings and voices to accommodate the wood-wind to an organ in Cornett-Ton. Similar treatment by Bach in his Cantata No. 150 has been noted in Chapter 5. A problem arises in the case of Zachau's bassonetti, however, as the range of the parts is d′–c‴—too high for an octave bassoon (fagottino). We can only conclude that the parts were for two octave-bassoons written an octave above the real sounds. The author is indebted to Mr. A. C. Baines who examined the scores and supplied notes on which the foregoing is based.

Mention must be made of Haydn's parts for 'Fagotti in E♭' in his *Stabat Mater* (1771). The full score published by John Bland *c.* 1784 indeed specifies 'Fagotti in E♭' in two numbers, but examination of the parts reveals that these are for instruments in F not E♭.

The full score by Breitkopf and Härtel in 1803 has 'Corni Inglesi' instead of 'Fagotti in E♭', and the clef, signature and notes are identical. The parts are unsuited to tenoroons in F and musically must sound at the cor anglais range: b♭–b♭″, sounding e♭–e♭″.

REFERENCES

[1] Baines, A. C.: *Woodwind Instruments, loc. cit.*, p. 290.

[2] Pierre, C.: *La Facture, loc. cit.*, pp. 25–28.

[3] Baines: *Woodwind Instruments, loc. cit.*, pp. 336–7.

[4] Forsyth, C.: *Orchestration, loc. cit.*, pp. 221–2, where the three obsolete notations and the now universal modern notation are explained.

[5] *Musical Times*, 1 December 1932.

[6] *Musical Progress and Mail*, April 1934: and Grove's *Dictionary*, 5th edit., *s.v.* Tenoroon.

[7] Preserved in the Library of the Hispanic Society of America in New York City.

[8] *Galpin Society Journal* XI (1958), pp. 78–84.

[9] Denkmäler deutscher Tonkunst, Vols. XXI and XXII.

CHAPTER 8

The Contrabassoon

PASSING reference has been made in Chapter 1 to Ludovico Zacconi's *'Prattica di Musica utile et necessaria si al compositore . . . si anco al cantore'*, the first part of which was published at Venice in 1592 and reprinted in 1596. The second part, also printed at Venice, first appeared in 1619. The contents are divided into four books and Chapter 56 of Book IV gives a table of instruments which supplies information unobtainable elsewhere on the musical instruments of the sixteenth century. The work is extremely scarce and no facsimile has yet appeared. Copies are, however, in the Reid Library, Edinburgh University, the British Museum and the Royal College of Music, London. The table in the concluding chapter shows on a great stave of eleven lines the compass of 'the instruments which are usually employed in making concerti'. On p. 219 he gives the compass of the *Fagotto chorista* in the old Bass Clef:

and adds the remark: 'The Fagotto Chorista goes from the octave of C fa ut of the bass to the B fa b mi above. They call it Fagotto Chorista because there are others which are not of its pitch but a little higher or a little deeper.'

He is referring to the doppel fagott, a fourth lower (G,) or a fifth lower (F,), and to the piccolo fagott, a fifth higher (G), which are Nos. 1, 2 and 4 in Praetorius' table (see Chapter 2).

The next detailed account of bassoons of deeper pitch than the type instrument is Praetorius's *De Organographia* (1619) (see Chapter 2). Both varieties were two-keyed dulzians, differing merely in size:

Quint-fagott F,–e♭ (or, possible, g).
Quart-fagott G,–f (or, possible, a).

Praetorius's reference to the Meister who made the octave trombone refers to Hans Schreiber, Kammermusikus of the Electoral Court of Berlin. He was said to be attempting a fagot contra an octave below the fagotto-chorista. He may well have succeeded, for a contrafagott is specified in 1626 in the Inventory of the Barfüsserkirche, Frankfurt a/M.[1]

Curt Sachs has pointed out that to bore wooden trunks of such large size is a task which can be undertaken only with difficulty and imperfectly without special machinery. Writing in 1920 he states that old wood-wind instrument-makers still recalled having, as apprentices, dragged the rough trunks to the well-sinker to be bored. Apart from this, however, the note-holes had to be bored through the tube-wall disproportionately small and obliquely so that the fingers could reach and cover them. As a result the contrafagott pleased neither the performer nor the audience and Heckel informs us that, for over two centuries, the contra (a convenient contraction) was the 'Schmerzenskind' (child of affliction) of instrument-makers.

Two superb specimens of doppelfagott, considered to be of late sixteenth-century Italian workmanship, are preserved with six contemporary dulzians in the Kunsthistorisches Museum, Vienna, depicted and described in Schlosser's Catalogue of the Collection.[2] Both are held with right hand above left, contrary to the modern bassoon and, though Schlosser states they are pitched in A, a minor third below the contemporary choristfagott, it is almost certain that they were in G. (Quartfagott.)

> No. 198   Marked 'Hier. S.' Two brass keys, covered by brass shields. Height 4 ft. 5 ins.
> No. 199   Marked 'Hier. S.' Two brass keys, covered as above. More ornamental band around the middle. Possibly in two sections. Height 4 ft. 4 ins.

Schlosser is in error in referring to Bach's use of a fagott in low A in Cantata 150. As explained in Chapter 5, the part is transposed sounding a minor third lower to adjust to an organ tuned to Cornett-Ton.[3] At Weimar, where Bach was c. 1712 when Cantata No. 150 was composed, the organ of the ducal chapel was tuned to Cornett-Ton, i.e. a minor third above höher cammerton, the pitch in general use for concerted music. As a result, in Cantata No. 150 in which the strings and continuo are in B minor, the bassoon is in D minor. This, therefore, does not signify the use of a bassoon in low A, but merely the employment of a normal instrument in conjunction with an organ tuned a minor third higher.

In Chapter 4 reference is made to the use of a quart-fagott at Nürnberg in 1643, but we cannot be certain of the pitch of that instrument.

There is no doubt in the case of Bach's use of a doppel fagott in Cantata No. 31 of 1715 revised in 1731. The range of the part is G'–d' (*i.e.* a quart-fagott). In one of the versions of the *St. John Passion* of 1723, Bach prescribes 'Continuo pro Bassono grosso' but curiously demanding a compass of only C–f'. Terry (founding upon Stone's article 'Double Bassoon' in Grove's *Dictionary*, 1st and 2nd edit.) has attributed the disuse of deeper bassoons to their faulty construction and weak rattling tone. It would be equally reasonable to attribute this to the frequently slender instrumental resources at Bach's disposal.

One other seventeenth century doppel fagott is in the Heyer-Leipzig Collection (No. 1361) and a facsimile is in the Heckel Collection.[4] It is a large two-keyed dulzian, 4 ft. 5 ins. high, descending to F, or G,. Kinsky is not precise on the point[5] and Heckel states A♭,.

It must have been an instrument of this type which Bach employed in 1715, although we have puzzling evidence of an improved Italian contra of 1732. The Salzburg Museum No. 209 is a contra of dark-stained maple, 6 ft. high, with a bell representing a dragon-head with flexible tongue. This 'instrument de fantaisie' has a spike for support and is stamped 'Joannes Maria Anciuti/invenit et fecit/Midiolani/ MDCCXXXII', and, above, a winged lion. Anciuti of Milan is known by other instruments, dated from 1722 to 1740, but clearly this contra has been improved by the addition of keys now numbering nine, whereas no bassoon of the period had more than four.

Burney's *Account of the Musical Performances in Westminster Abbey . . . in commemoration of Handel* (1785) reports the earliest recorded use of the contra in England, *viz.* in Handel's *Hymn for the Coronation* (1727). The passage is as follows:

'The Double Bassoon . . . is . . . a tube of sixteen feet. It was made, with the approbation of Mr. Handel, by Stainsby [*sic*], the flute-maker, for the coronation of his late majesty, George the Second (*i.e.* 1727). The late ingenious Mr. Lampe, author of the justly admired music of "The Dragon of Wantley", was the person intended to perform on it; but, for want of a proper reed or for some other cause, at present unknown, no use was made of it at that time; nor, indeed, though it has been often attempted, was it ever introduced into any band in England till now, by the ingenuity and perseverance of Mr. Ashly (*i.e.* Ashley) of the Guards.'

The proportions of this giant contra were misunderstood by H. Lavoix who states:[6] 'Burney prétend qu'il avait seize pieds, ce qui est exagéré . . .' From the account given below, it will be seen that Burney was correct in his statement that the tube-length *from reed to bell* was sixteen feet.

An announcement in the *London Daily Post and General Advertiser* of 6 August 1739 states:

> 'Marybone-Gardens. This day, and to be continued. The usual concert. To which will be added (for the better Entertainment of Gentlemen and Ladies, the Undertaker being desirous to make the concert the most complete), Two Grand or Double Bassoons, made by Mr. Stanesby, jun. the Greatness of whose sound surpasses that of any other Base Instrument whatsoever. Never perform'd before.'

In quoting this Canon Galpin[7] made one of his exceedingly rare slips of the pen, for he stated that the contras were made by Stanesby, *senior*.

As Stanesby Senior died in 1734 it had always puzzled the author why five years after Stanesby Senior's death the contras were advertised as 'never performed with before'. By a mere chance, a copy of a similar advertisement of 17 August 1739 from the *London Daily Post and General Advertiser* came into the author's hands. In attributing the 'Two Grand or Double Bassoons' to 'Mr. Stanesby, jun.' it confirmed the author's suspicions.

As Stanesby, junior (1692–1754), placed his stamp and date 1739 on the sole surviving English contra of eighteenth century (now preserved in the National Museum of Ireland, Dublin) this is almost certainly one of the two played at Marylebone Gardens in 1739. Nothing is known of the contra made either by Stanesby father or son for the Coronation in 1727.[8]

This unique contra (Plate 17, Fig. 1) has four brass keys in saddles giving $B\flat_{,,,}$ $D_{,,}$ $F_{,,}$ $G\sharp_{,}$. The bell has an outward bulbous shape, expanding slightly at the top and the long brass crook is recurved downwards, parallel to the wing for nearly three-quarters of its length, before bending out and upwards to receive the reed. The fingerholes are necessarily very much smaller than acoustical demands require and, although bored obliquely in the usual manner, are so far apart as to cause the player inconvenience.

Handel employed the contra in the *Fireworks Music* (1749) and in *L'Allegro* (1740) it is scored in two of the choruses: No. 42 and No. 53. For the most part the contra within the written compass F to b♭ (sounding an octave lower) doubles the second bassoon an octave below. It is significant that Handel avoids the notes below F, which it may be assumed were uncertain or of bad quality.

A further announcement in the *General Advertiser* of 20 October 1740 was intended as a skit on the large orchestras of the period. Announcing the opening of Handel's season at the Haymarket, the advertisement forecasts:[9]

'A concerto of twentyfour Bassoons accompanied on the violoncello, intermixed with duets by four double Bassoons accompanied by a German flute, the whole blended with numbers of violins, hautboys, fifes, trombonys [sic], French horns, trumpets, drums and kettledrums.'

No more is heard of the contra in England until 1784 at the first Commemoration of Handel in Westminster Abbey. Burney's account of 1785 describes the orchestra of 250 which included 6 flutes, 26 oboes, 26 bassoons and a double bassoon. A second contemporary account is that of W. T. Parke, 1st Oboe at the Theatre Royal, Covent Garden, who took part. In his *Musical Memoirs* he records:[10]

'At these musical performances Mr. Ashley, a sub-director, and first bassoon at Covent Garden Theatre, played for the first time on a newly-invented instrument called a double bassoon, an appropriate appellation, it being double the size of the common ones. This instrument, which rested on a stand, had a sort of flue affixed to the top of it, similar (with the exception of smoke) to that of a Richmond steamboat. I am ignorant however, whether it produced any tone, or whether it was placed in the orchestra to terminate the prospect. The name of this double bass and gigantic instrument, which was only fit to be grasped by the monster Polyphemus, did not transpire, and the double bassoon, which had never been heard, was never again seen after these performances were ended.'

Parke, however, in this as in other cases was not correct, because the contra was included in the orchestra of 307 performers at the Fourth Handel Festival in Westminster Abbey in 1787.

John Crosse in his *Account of the Grand Musical Festival held in September 1823 in York Minster*[11] remarks:

'Notwithstanding what is said in the Account of the Commemoration, we have always understood that the double bassoon was not found to be a serviceable instrument and it does not appear to have been used in 1791' (The Sixth Festival).

At Worcester in 1788,[12] in presence of George III and the Royal Family, 'Ashley[13] with the double bassoon and his four sons . . . aided by the powerful support of His Majesty's private band' took part; and yet again at Worcester in 1803 Jenkinson played the double bassoon. After this, however, the contra appears to have gone completely out of use in England until the close of the nineteenth century. There is no reference to it at the Festivals at York (1823–5–8–35), Birmingham (1823), Liverpool (1823) or Gloucester (1825).

The only English attempt to construct a practical contra in normal bassoon shape was that of J. Samme, London, c. 1855, whose eight-keyed quart-bassoon in low G is preserved in the Donaldson Collection in the R.C.M. London.

DEVELOPMENT IN BELGIUM

Some unique information concerning the business of musical instrument-making in Belgium at the end of the eighteenth and in the early nineteenth centuries has been collated by R. van Aerde.[14] Four successive generations of the Tuerlinckx family exercised their craft extensively in Malines, making both wood-wind and brass instruments and keeping, from c. 1782 onwards, voluminous and careful records which have fortunately survived. At least one contrabassoon stamped Tuerlinckx (the successive generations unfortunately used the same maker's mark) is preserved. Made of maple, 5 ft. 8 ins. high, with five brass keys for D,, E♭,, F,, F♯,, G♯,, it is of bassoon-shape with a long coiled brass crook and descends to C,; between the two groups of three finger-holes for the left and right hands respectively, a curious loop of brass tubing has been interposed—Mahillon asserts—to bring the hands nearer each other. M. van Aerde remarks[15] upon Tuerlinckx's opportunities for examining contras of other countries:

'At the time when Austrian troops were scattered all over our country (1785) the Malines instrument-maker had ample opportunity to familiarise himself with the new types of instrument. It was probably this that enabled him to study the bore of the contrabassoons used in the Hanoverian infantry bands. Later, when the Allies paraded in Belgium, he got his ideas from the German, Swiss, French, English, Austrian, etc., models used in regimental bands.'

It would also seem that to Tuerlinckx is due the credit of certain improvements in compass and tone of the contra. Van Aerde continues:[16]

'He also made contrabassoons the potentialities of which, according to Canon de Smet,[17] he increased by adding two notes and by reducing the size of the instrument. These two extra notes were in the low register and appear to have been obtained by means of keys.'

It is possible that the extra two notes were C, (left thumb-hole) and D, (left thumb-key) which would not be obtainable on the German quint-fagott in low F, with E♭, sounding as its lowest note. By making the contra in C, an octave below the bassoon, all difficulty as regards transposition was removed and fingering became uniform on both types of bassoon. One further extract from van Aerde[18] reveals the range of bassoons available c. 1830, the approximate date of a sale-list of Tuerlinckx:

> Fagotto—Petit basson octave
> Fagotto—Petit basson quinte
> Fagotto—Basson ordinaire 8 clefs
> Fagotto—Basson ordinaire 14 clefs
> Contrafagotto—Basson basse
> Contrafagotto—Anches

The following extract from the price-list of 1826 of B. Schott Söhne, Mainz, shows the range of bassoons on offer. It will be noted that the serpent is included under 'Fagotte'. All instruments were made of maple and, except the last, had brass keys and brass mounts:

Fagotte	*Number of Keys*
Serpent in Fagott-Form	6
Serpent mit Drachenkopf	6
Contra-fagott	9
Fagott (1 wing and 1 crook)	10
Fagott (2 wings and 2 crooks)	10
Fagott (2 wings and 2 crooks) (new model)	15
Fagott (2 wings and 2 crooks and ivory mounts and silver keys)	15

EARLY USE OF THE CONTRA IN GERMANY AND AUSTRIA

It would seem that, up to about 1850, the inclusion of the contra in scores depended entirely on whether it was locally available. As Vienna seems to have been the centre where the contra was always procurable, we find it in the scores of Haydn and Beethoven. It received little attention, however, from Mozart and less from Schubert, and it rarely occurs in German scores as it was first considered more suitable for military music. Gassner[19] in 1838 states that the contrafagott, which included the low quart-fagott, was then very rarely used in Germany (since the serpent and ophicleide had been so much improved) and then only in military bands. As an orchestral substitute for the contra, the serpent, the upright serpent or the ophicleide was used, and it was perhaps more than a coincidence that when these instruments had, each in turn, become obsolete, the contra underwent improvement and re-construction until the early years of the present century (Plate 18, Figs. 3, 4, 5 and 6). It is not always possible to rely upon continental references to a contrafagott as being in reality to that instrument. The Russisches fagott, a form of upright serpent (but of wood, made in bassoon-form, and blown, of course, with a cup-mouthpiece) was often called a 'double bassoon' in Germany and in France. In Michel Brenet's 'La Musique Militaire'[20] an obvious basson russe is designated 'Basson à tête de dragon', the crook without a mouthpiece being mistaken for the crook of a bassoon. Kastner[21] designates No. 9 an obvious bass-horn, 'contra-basson autrichien' and No. 6, an Austrian double-bassoon, he named 'Basse d'harmonie (instrument autrichien)'. Berlioz[22] when at Brunswick in 1842, found the same confusion:

'. . . a Russian bassoon, called by the performer a double-bassoon. I had much trouble in undeceiving him as to the nature and name of his instrument, which emits the sound just as it is written, and is played with a mouthpiece like the ophicleide, whilst the double-bassoon, a transposing reed-instrument, is simply a large bassoon reproducing almost the entire bassoon scale an octave lower.'

The same doubt does not exist in regard to Viennese references, for actual instruments (bearing the Viennese makers' names) are preserved and there are records of their use in Vienna in Beethoven's time and after. L. Köchel[23] gives a pay-roll of the Imperial Orchestra at Vienna which included '1 Contrafagott' in 1807. Kastner[24] records the use of two contras in a performance of Handel's Timotheus at Vienna in 1812.

Beethoven's use of two contrabassoons is mentioned in a memoran-dum by the composer concerning the orchestra at a concert in Vienna on 27 February 1814[25] when two contras were added to seventy-nine strings.

No less than four contras, one being of brass, were used for perform-ances in the Riding School, Vienna, of Haydn's The Seasons in 1839 and *The Creation* in 1843, according to Gassner.[26] Castil-Blaze,[27] on the other hand, records the use of four serpents in a performance of *The Creation* at the Opéra, Paris, in 1800, and two ophicleides in 1844. Franz Stöber's plan of the orchestra of the Kärntnerthor Theatre, Vienna, in 1821 provides a place for a contra-player.

Mozart rarely used the contra, *e.g.* in the *Mauerische Trauermusik* (Masonic Dirge) (K. 477) in C minor composed at Vienna in July 1785. Here the contrabassoon is not obbligato, and contra C is the lowest note, occurring thrice—in bar 4, and in the seventh last and last bars. g is the upper limit.

In Haydn's *Die Sieben Worte . . . am Kreuze* (composed in 1786), one of the Intermezzi is a Largo in A minor for twelve wind instruments including two bassoons and contrabassoon. Contra C is the lowest note for the latter—occurring in bar 13. In *The Creation* (composed 1795–8) Haydn ventures down to B♭,,, in No. 22, 'Now Heaven in fullest glory shone', at the well-known passage 'By heavy beasts the ground was trod' (on the word 'trod'): and again in No. 34 'Sing to the Lord, ye voices all'. In *The Seasons* (composed 1799–1800) he appears to have reverted to contra C as the downward limit, *e.g.* No. 19, 'Ach! das Ungewitter naht' in C minor, where the contrabassoon has a pedal C near the opening.

Schubert only once included the contra, and this was in the *Trauermusik* for two clarinets, two bassoons, contrabassoon, two horns and two trombones. The original MS. is dated 19 September 1813. As to whether he had any practical experience of the contrabassoon, nothing is known: it is not likely that it had a place in the very capable but limited orchestra of the Imperial Seminary, where he remained until the month following. It is not used in his First Symphony which they performed on the eve of his departure, nor does it appear in any of his subsequent scores.

Beethoven employs the contrabassoon in the Fifth and Ninth Symphonies, in the Mass in D, in the Overture to *King Stephen* (1811), in *The Ruins of Athens* (1811), in two military marches in F (1809), a march in C (1809), a Polonaise in D, Ecossaise in D (1810) and a march in D (1816). Cecil Forsyth has remarked[28] upon 'the elaborate double-bassoon part in the Finale of the Choral Symphony'. He considers 'it may have been written by Beethoven for a smaller and more flexible instrument than the one used at the present day. We have no knowledge that such an instrument existed.'

The contra is scored continually with the double-basses, even in the

Prestissimo, and the extreme compass is used B♭, to a, sounding an octave lower. Prout remarks[29] that 'it is doubtful whether the effect is ever entirely satisfactory'. Forsyth also comments upon the *pp* entry of bassoons, double-bassoon and bass drum for the first eight bars of the *Allegro assai vivace* which 'unless very carefully played, only just misses being grotesque'. The contra has one note-worthy passage in the grave-digging scene in *Fidelio* where it is scored *pp* with the double-basses.

EARLY USE OF THE CONTRA IN FRANCE

The limited orchestral use of the contra is confirmed by nineteenth-century French records. In 1794, at the Paris Conservatoire, it was proposed to form a class for contrabassoon, but the scheme did not materialise.[30] In 1813, A. Choron edited a second edition of L. J. Francoeur's *Traité général des voix et des instruments d'orchestre*, stating in the Introduction that he does not deal with the contra 'attendu qu'on n'en fait plus d'usage'. In 1822, however, Nicolo's *Aladin* was produced and the score contained quite an important part for contra.[31] By 1825 the contra was much in demand in French military bands, following the custom of German and Austrian bands in which bassoons and contrabassoons were supplemented by serpents, upright or con-voluted, and in France, the practice continued, until the saxhorns, appearing in 1846, supplanted the other bass instruments.

Constant Pierre, a bassoon-pupil of the celebrated Eugène Jancourt, quotes an interesting passage from his unpublished *Histoire de l'orchestre de l'Opéra depuis Cambert jusqu'à nos jours*. After expressing the opinion that the contrabassoon was introduced into France in 1800 for the performance of *The Creation*, he cites a statement in a monograph on the serpent, published in 1804,[32] to the effect that it replaced with advantage the contrabassoon 'aux sons sourds et criards' (muffled and harsh) used in England. Until 1863, when the Société des Concerts du Conservatoire acquired the only contra made in France,[33] the contra was replaced by the ophicleide as the part could not be dispensed with. It was only in the eighties of last century that French composers scored freely for it and that the parts were played on the instrument lent by the Société des Concerts. The following list is given by MM. Letellier et Flament:[34]

1867 Don Carlos (Verdi)
1867 Les Barbares (Saint-Saëns)
1867 Les Noces de Prométhée (Saint-Saëns)

1877 Samson et Dalila (Saint-Saëns)
1879 Etienne Marcel (Saint-Saëns)
       At the production in Lyons, there being no contra available,
       the part was played on a contrabass sarrusophone.
1882 Françoise de Rimini (Ambroise Thomas)
1883 Henri VIII (Saint-Saëns)
1884 Sigurd (Reyer)
1885 Le Cid (Massenet)
1889 Esclarmonde (Massenet)
1890 Ascanio (Saint-Saëns)
1890 Salammbô (Reyer)
1894 Thaïs (Massenet)

DEVELOPMENT IN GERMANY

The use of the instrument in military music in German-speaking
Europe led makers there to make a series of attempts to construct a
satisfactory metal contrabassoon. Evidence is somewhat conflicting as
to which of these makers led the way.

JOHANN STEHLE'S METAL CONTRABASSOON

Mendel[35] informs us that the wooden contra was weak in tone and
that this fact led Stehle, instrument-maker in Vienna, in the thirties
of the nineteenth century[36] to make a contra of brass—5 ft. 6 ins. high[37]
(Plate 18, Fig. 7). The holes were apparently all covered by keys—fifteen
in number—with a compass of two octaves, and the technique was
difficult, but the tone was said to be three times as strong as that of
the usual contrafagotti.[38] Wieprecht states that in order to simplify the
difficult technique of Stehle's contra, Carl Wilhelm Moritz (1811–55),
celebrated instrument-maker in Berlin, invented at the end of 1845
the ingenious claviatur-contrafagott.

In 1838 Wieprecht's reformed German infantry bands included two
bassoons and two contras. In 1848 Austrian infantry bands had four
bassoons and two contras. The popularity of the contra in Germany
and Austria in the first half of the nineteenth century may be contrasted
with the complete absence of the instrument in France and Britain.

C. W. MORITZ'S CLAVIATUR-CONTRAFAGOTT

Though it had but a brief existence, this type of contra embodied the
keyboard as we have it today on the piano-accordion. Fifteen keys were
operated by the finger-board which had black and white touches as on

the piano. The tube of the instrument had the same proportions as those of Stehle's model, the tube was conical, the reed a bassoon one, and a slide-key, raised by a special touch-piece, assisted production of the upper octave. Moritz's contra was warmly commended by the Berliner Tonkünstlerverein on 18 October 1845, and by the Berlin Akademie der Kunste on 22 March 1855, as well as by distinguished musicians including Meyerbeer and Graf Redern. Moritz thereupon applied for a German patent which, however, was not granted until 1856, a year after his death.[39] A drawing in *Soldatenfreund* (Plate 20, Fig. 14) of the 'sixties shows a bandsman of the 2nd Garderegiment of Foot carrying a claviatur-contrafagott.[40] No surviving specimen is known.

SCHÖLLNAST'S TRITONIKON

Although Mendel considers Moritz's invention was an improvement upon Stehle's metal contra, there are statements to the effect that his improvement was upon a brass contra invented in 1839 by Schöllnast und Sohn of Pressburg (now Bratislava, Czechoslovakia), and named *tritonikon* or *universal-kontrabass*. The instrument had a total tube-length of 14 ft. 11½ ins. folded on itself five times, and had fifteen large keys of which only the first was open. This arrangement facilitated fingering which resembled that of the piano, and gave a chromatic compass of sixteen notes from D, to F.[41] Sachs comments that the preference for simpler fingering entailed the disadvantages of restricted volume of tone and imperfect intonation.

ČERVENÝ'S METAL CONTRA

V. F. Červený (1819–96), a skilful maker at Königgrätz in Bohemia, was the next to attempt an improvement on the contra, and in 1856 he produced his fourteen-keyed *tritonikon* in Eb, claiming it to be an improvement upon the Stehle model of the previous year. Pierre has given a description of the fingering[42] and a drawing of the instrument[43] which is shaped like a slender tuba—the form adopted later for the lower sarrusophones. Červený next made a tritonikon in Bb, a fourth lower than his model of 1856 and this instrument, first exhibited at the Paris Exhibition of 1867, was shown again at the Paris Exhibition of 1889. Pierre informs us that this Bb contra was the only instrument of the renowned Bohemian maker to be heard at the Paris Exhibition of 1889. With a compass of two octaves it could be played without fatigue. The tone was powerful but very vibrant, having little analogy with that of the true contrabassoon. This was largely due to the construction which differed considerably from that of the bassoon. Indeed Pierre considered that the name 'Contrebasse-à-anche', given by M. Mahillon to an instrument presented by him and constructed on the same system, was more appropriate.

ČERVENÝ'S SUBKONTRAFAGOTT

An unbelievable depth of pitch is said[44] to have been reached in 1873 by Červený, when he invented his fourteen-keyed subkontrafagott in B♭—an octave below the contrabassoon—with the compass B♭,,, to B♭. Now B♭,,, is a tone below C,, which has only sixteen vibrations, and, although Dr. Scholes states[45] that 'a "perfect" ear can take in pitches as low as ten vibrations per second', it is difficult to imagine how such a giant contra could be manipulated. From its pitch—B♭— and the fact that Červený was a brass-maker, we may conclude it was designed for military band use—assuredly not for use on the march!— doubled in the upper octave by other brass basses. So far as is known, no specimen of such a contra survives.

The author is convinced that Sachs erred in his *Real-Lexikon* where he gives the compass as B♭,,, to B♭—*i.e. three* octaves. Pierre, as a bassoon-player, heard the instrument in 1889 and, therefore, a more reliable authority, informs us that the compass was *two* octaves and, as a catalogue of Červený (*c.* 1897) shows the upper limit as B♭ in the bass-clef, two octaves down would reach B♭,, not B♭,,, and the instrument would be in fact a metal contrabassoon with the modern normal downward limit of B♭,,.

C. MAHILLON'S CONTREBASSE-À-ANCHE

This brass contra[46] (Plate 19, Fig. 8) was invented in 1868 by Charles Mahillon, the noted Brussels maker. It had as its lowest note D, instead of B♭,, but in other respects was identical alike in mechanism, appearance, and arrangement with Červený's contra. Of the seventeen keys, two were octave keys and all were closed keys except the first, and the fingering was the same as for Červený's model. The first four notes from D, to F, were not overblown; the others from F♯, to C were overblown using one octave-key, and the remainder of the scale from C♯ to f using the second octave key. Pierre had the opportunity of hearing the Mahillon contra and states[47] that the timbre was not so good as that of Červený's contra. The vibrations produced a disagreeable sound which seemed to be due to insufficient thickness of the metal.

Both Mahillon's and Červený's contras had the disadvantage of particular mechanism, and were not, in the literal sense of the term, contrabassoons, as they did not reproduce the notes of the bassoon in the contra octave *with the fingering of the bassoon*. Hence arose the difficulty of persuading bassoon-players to adopt them, having regard to the special study required. Pierre concludes by agreeing that bassoon-players had grounds for objection, but one had to consider these brass instruments as being named to denote that they filled the place of the old, inadequate and awkward contrabassoon and not to denote their nature or their construction.

Schlesinger in 1910[48] specified Mahillon's brass contra and Heckel's wooden contra but adds that the Haseneier–Stone–Morton contra was then almost exclusively used in English orchestras. An illustration of the latter is given and a similar block appeared in the earlier editions of Grove's *Dictionary* and was repeated in Prout's *The Orchestra* (1897). As the Haseneier type has been completely obsolete for over half a century there can be no excuse for repeating the illustration in a recent reprint of Prout's work.

It is worth noting that the Hallé Orchestra first had a contra-player in 1881 and he was Morton, son of the London maker who carried out Stone's suggestions.

Forsyth in 1935[49] still included the three types (1) Mahillon–Schöllnast; (2) Haseneier–Stone–Morton; and (3) German, which he correctly forecast as 'likely to oust both the above'. It has two great advantages over the others. Its quality is much more refined and much less obtrusive, the vibrations in its lowest fifth not being nearly so apparent to the ear and the tone-colour homogeneous. Secondly, its compass is chromatic down to sub-contra B♭ and it 'speaks' easily even down to this note.

LOUIS MULLER'S MULLERPHONE

It was in 1855 that Louis Muller of Lyons invented a French contre-basse-à-anche (Fr. Pat. 12728 of 3 March 1955). Muller was a nephew of François Sautermeister (d. 1830) who had been inventive (*e.g.* basse-orgue in 1812, basse d'harmonie in 1827) and Muller on succeeding to his uncle's business, proved even more inventive. In 1846 he constructed a bass clarinet in bassoon-shape, descending to C, and this instrument he proposed should replace the bassoon. In 1855 he was a medallist at the Paris Exhibition, and he brought out his Mullerphone which was coiled in parallel tubes in bassoon-shape, and descended an octave below the bassoon. The bore of wood was chiefly cylindrical, the bell of metal, and the twenty-one keys were arranged in a new manner. No specimen appears to have survived, and only a brief reference is made by Pierre.[50] Examination of the *Brevet d'Invention* (for fifteen years) and the drawings of the instrument show it to have been a contra-bass-clarinet and not a contrabassoon. It was, in fact, similar to, if not the same as, his uncle's basse-orgue of 1812 which was patented for only five years. It is worth noting that the name 'Muller-phone' does not occur in the patent specification and the present short account is given to correct a misapprehension as to the real nature of the instrument. Both Sachs' *Lexikon* and Wright's *Dictionnaire* err in describing the Mullerphone as a contrabassoon.

H. J. HASENEIER'S CONTRABASSOPHON

In 1847 H. J. Haseneier, of Coblenz, first designed a wooden contra of an entirely new type[51] (Plate 19, Fig. 9). In an account[52] of this new type named *contrabassophon*, it was stated that Haseneier had submitted it in December 1849 to the most diverse tests. His model was copied very closely by several makers, *e.g.*:

(*a*) Ch. Geipel, Breslau—seventeen keys.[53]

(*b*) C. Fr. Doelling & Sohn, Potsdam—twenty keys.[54]

(*c*) Georg Berthold & Söhne, Speyer-am-Rhein (a firm founded in 1849 by Georg Jacob Berthold (1824–1904)) endeavoured to reduce the weight of Haseneier's wooden model and produced it of papier-mâché. At least two survive: in the Heckel Museum, and in the Heyer-Leipzig Collection (No. 1407).[55]

(*d*) Anonymous, unique improved model *c.* 1855–60 with only three-fold tube, but taller and descending to sub-contra B♭.[56]

(*e*) A copy of Haseneier's model was made, *c.* 1875, by Alfred Morton,[57] London, and was lent at the Royal Military Exhibition, No. 172. Said by Pierre to be one of three[58] or four[59] made by Morton, one was played by Morton's eldest son at the Crystal Palace, at Richter's Concerts and at the Opera. Other two were used by the Coldstream and Grenadier Guards and one by the Scots (Fusilier) Guards—as we must interpret Pierre's reference to 'Scotch Cusseley' [*sic*].[60]

Morton also made a contra in F[61] identical in design with the preceding contras, but a fourth higher in pitch.*

* Efforts to trace this instrument since it was lent by Sullivan to the Royal Military Exhibition in 1890 have failed. The author has a letter from the late Sir Henry Wood dated 15 October 1943 stating that never in his time was a contra used in the Orchestra of the Savoy. Sullivan employed the contra *inter alia* in *The Martyr of Antioch* (1880) and *The Golden Legend* (1886), but does not indicate a transposition for a contra in F.

(*f*) A contra on the Haseneier model with fourfold coil was made in 1888 by W. Bradka (1822–1907) of Gumpoldskirchen, near Vienna. This contra (Plate 19, Fig. 10) descends to contra C and has twenty-two keys.[62]

(*g*) M. Fontaine-Besson decided to manufacture contras on Morton's model (*i.e.* Haseneier's) to meet French requirements and patented it in 1890. Pierre describes and depicts Besson's model,[63] which descended to sub-contra B♭.

DEVELOPMENT IN FRANCE SINCE 1860

About 1850 F. Triébert and A. Marzoli of Paris made a contra of bassoon-shape and consequently nearly 8 feet in height. This contra was used by the Société des Concerts du Conservatoire until 1863.[64] P. Goumas, a Paris maker, had also experimented and Evette and Schaeffer, who succeeded him in 1885, made a similar wooden contra with fifteen keys and covered holes, descending to contra C, but having the same disadvantage of being nearly 8 feet in height—'like a tall factory-chimney emerging into space'. Pierre was not favourably impressed with this instrument which he heard at the Paris Exhibition of 1889. At that exhibition Martin Thibouville aîné presented his first attempt at an improved brass contra, which he had designed in collaboration with Lucien Jacot, bassoonist at the Opéra Comique. By coiling the tube of 17 ft. 8 ins. in four parallel lengths, Thibouville succeeded in reducing the height to under 5 ft. and the weight was 11 lbs. All holes were covered and there were nineteen keys and six plates, so arranged that the fingering of the French bassoon was successfully retained.[65] It was probably this type which led Evette and Schaeffer, who took over the old-established business and trade-mark of Buffet-Crampon et Cie., to make a similar brass contra corresponding in height and fingering to the bassoon.[66] The progress of the Heckel contra, however, soon led Evette and Schaeffer (now trading as Buffet-Crampon & Cie), to build a contra of wood, in most respects similar to the German type except that, of course, the French fingering was retained. Their new contra was heard for the first time about 1906 at the performances of Richard Strauss' *Salomé* at the Académie Nationale de Musique, Paris, and it gave great satisfaction. Strauss has scored in that work a contra-bassoon solo of considerable difficulty, played at the Opéra by Marcel Couppas.

The modern French contra, like the German, has a wooden bell-rim for use when contra C is the lowest note required, and an inverted metal bell which can be slipped on when sub-contra B♭ is required.[67]

DR. W. H. STONE'S INTEREST IN THE CONTRABASSOPHON

At this point it may be convenient to refer to the important part taken by Dr. W. H. Stone (1830–91)[68] who was an accomplished amateur performer on the tenoroon, bassoon and contrabassoon, and wrote the articles on these and other instruments in the first and second editions of Grove's *Dictionary of Music*. Writing of the double bassoon he states: 'It has been considerably improved by Herr Haseneier of Coblenz and subsequently improved by the writer who has introduced it into English orchestras . . . as made on the writer's design by Haseneier.' It would appear that Morton of London carried out Stone's improvements.

Referring to the double bassoon in general, he indicates that it had gone completely out of use until the Handel Festival of 1871—at which, presumably, he played it. The present writer had the good fortune to have on loan the actual Haseneier contrabassophon owned and played by Dr. Stone, exhibited at the International Inventions Exhibition, 1885, and at the Royal Military Exhibition, 1890.[69] It is perhaps unfair to judge the tone produced with an original reed (in a case containing a visiting card bearing the name of Dr. W. H. Stone). The reed must date from *c.* 1890 and is remarkable on account of its size. The following measurements show the comparative sizes of the reed of the contrabassophon, and of those of the modern German contrabassoon:

	Contrabassophon	*Contrabassoon*
Total length	3⅜ ins.	2¹⅜ ins.
Breadth at wide end	1¹⁄₁₆ ins.	1⅜ ins.
Inside diameter of lower end	¼ ins.	³⁄₁₆ ins.

In the first edition of Grove's *Dictionary*, Dr. Stone gives some details of the contrabassophon: tube, 16 ft. 4 ins. long, truly conical in bore, enlarging from ¼-inch diameter at the reed to 4 inches at the bell, and curved four times on itself so that the height of the instrument is 4 ft. 8 ins.—only a little more than the ordinary bassoon, and the weight some 18 lbs. The extreme compass is three octaves from C, to c' (middle c), but g is recommended as the upward limit. The scale, which is chromatic throughout, is produced as follows:

C, to F,: a single sound is obtained by each key.

F, to F and F to f: the fundamental scale is repeated in the octave harmonics by simple overblowing and change of embouchure.

f♯ to c′: seven semitones, which are the twelfths of the funda-
mentals from B♮, with further increased wind pressure, carry the
scale up to middle c.

The sound-holes, all covered by keys, are of graduated size, increasing (from 1½-in. diameter to 2⅝ ins.) downwards with the size of the
bore, and placed as a rule in their correct positions so as to cut off the
appropriate tube length. The key mechanism is very ingenious and
solid, and incorporates a device to distinguish 'open' from 'closed'
holes. The touches of the open holes, *i.e.* those covered by keys operated
by the first three fingers of each hand, are saddle-shaped, whereas the
keys for the two little fingers and the thumb have cushion-shaped
touches. Dr. Stone, who was a physician as well as a musician with
profound acoustical knowledge, remarks that this device not only facili-
tates technique for a performer accustomed to the ordinary bassoon,
but, by the saddle-shaped touches, 'serves to support the upper joints
of the finger, and to throw the labour of closing the hole more on the
powerful muscles of the forearm than on the weaker fabric of the hand
itself'. A stout leather supporting strap, 4 feet long, passes over the
shoulder round the body and swivels are attached to two eyelets on the
instrument. It must be stated, however, that playing the contrabassophon is very exhausting, although this was not the main reason
for its disuse. In the second edition of Grove's *Dictionary*, Mr. D. J.
Blaikley mentions the objections made against Dr. Stone's contra, that
its tone is too 'open' lacking some of the characteristic 'closeness' of
bassoon tone, and that it is difficult to obtain a good piano quality.
W. H. Heckel, describes[70] the tone in true German fashion as *ophikleiden-
artig-kurzklingend und nicht fagottartig-tragend.*

STRITTER SYSTEM CONTRA

It was, however, in imitation of the outward shape of the contrabassophon, that J. A. Heckel (1812–77) commenced with his son W.
Heckel (1856–1909) in 1876 to transform his contrabassoon—until then
of bassoon-shape and descending only to contra D[71] (Plate 19, Fig. 11).
He divided the tube into three parallel tubes, altered the shape of the
crook, and adopted a curious arrangement by which the instrument was
played left-handed, *i.e.* it was held at the left side of the player, the
left hand lowermost where the wing, finger-plates and keys lay on the
underside. The fingers of both hands had, however, the same movements as on the regular bassoon, and only the manner of holding the

hands differed. This type descended to contra C, and its design was termed 'System Stritter'.[72] Being unable to find any biographical notes concerning Friedrich Stritter, the writer communicated with the late Herr W. H. Heckel in 1939 and obtained an interesting reply from which the following is an extract:

'Stritter was a young workman during my grandfather's latter years from 1871 to 1877, and when my grandfather died in 1877 and my father was only twenty years old, Stritter took the opportunity of patenting in his own name my grandfather's latest idea. . . . This . . . was the left-handed contra, *i.e.* the short type which was not long in use—c in the illustration on page 16 in "Der Fagott".'

In the Patent Office, London, may be seen the abridgment of the specification of the Patent[73] in favour of Fr. Stritter of Biebrich. The following is a translation:

Contrafagott entirely of Wood

This Contrafagott is about 2 ft. 3 ins. shorter than the contrafagott hitherto customarily in use, in so far as it is composed not as before of two long tubes, but of three shorter ones. It has the advantage of a compass from high g down to contra C, and responds quite clearly in the lowest notes—which is not the case on the usual contrafagott.

This new contra is made of wood, weighs only 7¾ lbs., and is generally on that account not only very light to handle, but also particularly adapted for the performance of marches and military music.

The connecting of the tube-lengths is accomplished not by metal elbow-joints, as hitherto customary, but by wooden bends. This affords a special softness to the tone of the instrument, otherwise in itself very powerful, full and pure.

It is blown with a cane reed (a large bassoon-reed), 'speaks' extraordinarily easily, and is therefore very well suited to be a solo instrument.

The manipulation of this contrabassoon is different from that of all contras hitherto in use, as, in performance, the right hand lies uppermost and the left hand below, whence there results in marching a much more convenient mode of handling.

It is not clear why there should be any greater convenience! Few instruments bearing Stritter's name are known, and no textbook mentions his system which was, in any event, quickly superseded by Heckel's improved types.

BRAUENLICH'S CONTRABASSOON

Another attempt to produce an improved contra was made in 1886 by Professor Adolf Brauenlich of Dresden.

A very flattering account of this inventor and his instrument appeared in *Musical Opinion* of 1 May 1886.[74] The article contains certain interesting references, *e.g.* to contras of bassoon-shape by Bradka of Vienna and those of fourfold shape by Heckel of Biebrich, in all of which a relatively small bore was maintained. The original contrabassoon, on account of its narrow bore, had been regarded simply as an octave to the smaller instruments; it had no characteristic passages of its own, possessing both the form and scale of the smaller, excepting the lowest B♮,, and B♭,, which no manufacturer had until then been able to produce. Up to that time (1886) the instruments of Haseneier of Coblenz and of Heckel of Biebrich on 'Stritter's System', had been accepted as the best and most practical. The article proceeds to record that long and persevering experiments, made with Haseneier's instruments in the Hoftheater, Dresden, led to the conclusion that this type was not in any way suited to orchestral use, however well it might suit the military band. The bore proved to be too large, making the lower register imperfect, and preventing such a *piano* as is required in the Opera. Notwithstanding all efforts to suppress it, the contrabassophon overpowered the *piano* of the other wood-wind. The same thorough and systematic experiments were made with the Heckel contra on Stritter's system, but the same imperfections were just as apparent. The narrower bore was considered to cause a dull tone and weakness in *forte* passages. The manner of holding the instrument was tiresome and awkward, and, to one accustomed to playing the bassoon, both contrary and annoying. These and other criticisms were said not to be personal but were made by competent judges assembled to hear *Fidelio*, *Thusnelda*, *Rattenfänger* and *Andreasfest*. Professor Brauenlich's invention is then described. The tube for 16-ft. C was exactly once again as large as that required for 8-ft. C on the ordinary bassoon made by Meyer in Hanover, and with this exact measurement, the faults of the other systems disappeared. The compass was from B♭,, to c' or d', great emphasis being laid on the availability of B♭,, and B♮,,—of such undoubted value in works such as *The Creation* (Haydn), *Missa Solemnis* (Beethoven), and the later works of Wagner, such as *Parsifal*. So far as is known, no specimen of the Brauenlich contra exists in any collection.

THE SARRUSOPHONE

Adolphe Sax, of Paris, in 1846 patented the saxophone, and his group of seven sizes, alternately in E♭ and B♭, may have suggested to Sarrus, bandmaster of the French 13th Regiment of the Line, a similar

K

family of double-reed brass instruments. His idea was that a group of six such instruments should replace oboes and bassoons in military bands, and the Paris maker, P. L. Gautrot, designating them *sarruso-phones*, took out a French patent[75] for them in 1856—not 1863 as stated in Grove's *Dictionary*, 4th edit., and elsewhere. Sarrus' hopes for these instruments were not fulfilled as only the contrabass in E♭ (Plate 20, Fig. 13), and another contrabass in C, made later for orchestral use, have survived. The orchestral model has a compass of two octaves and a fifth from sub-contra B♭ and Saint-Saëns was the first composer to use it to play the contrabassoon part in his *Les Noces de Prométhée* in 1867.[76] Later, in 1879, he had one made at his own expense for performances of *Etienne Marcel* at Lyons, and another which he gave to a Paris musician who used it in concert work and also in 1884 in the Paris production of *Etienne Marcel*. The sarrusophone is not, however, prescribed by name in his scores, presumably on account of its rarity.

Massenet was next to employ it in *Esclarmonde* in 1889. Pierre gives an interesting account of the instrument and states that Jancourt, when serving as a bandmaster in the Garde Nationale from 1867–70, acquired an E♭ contrabass sarrusophone[77] which was played at first by Coyon (a bassoon-player and author of a tutor[78] for sarrusophone) and later by Eugène Bourdeau, 1st Bassoon at the Opéra Comique. In 1889, when Pierre was writing his *La Facture Instrumentale*, Couesnon and Cie., successors to Gautrot, were striving to popularize the sarruso-phone and, in the musical press, there was lively controversy over its merits and defects. The instrument has a wide bore and large note-holes which give it a powerful but unrefined tone, and however valuable it may be in a military band, it has been very rarely used in the orchestra, *e.g.* Ravel's *Rapsodie espagnole* (1907), Delius's *Dance Rhapsody* (1908) and *Eventyr* (1917) and Holbrooke's *Apollo and the Seaman* (1908).*

In the U.S.A., curiously, the sarrusophone is used to some extent, being first made there by Messrs. C. G. Conn at the request of the U.S. Government for military use. The fact that the fingering is very similar to that of the saxophone may account for this American adoption. Pierre accounted thus for the difficulty of introducing a new instru-ment into the orchestra. A composer does not write for an instrument which is not played and a player is not interested in practising upon an instrument which is not required.[79]

---

* In his autobiography *A Mingled Chime* (Chaps. 14 and 15), Sir Thomas Beecham gives a vivid and humorous account of the sarrusophone's employ-ment in *Appollo*.

HECKEL CONTRAFAGOTT

It is to the firm of Heckel of Biebrich that we owe the production of a series of contras from *c.* 1834 until 1879 when the modern contra may be said to have been perfected. The successive types are depicted in *Der Fagott*, p. 16, and are the following:

(1) *Circa* 1834: A contra of normal bassoon shape but over 5 feet high with an unusually long butt joint and a large looped crook. Such contras were normally stamped 'B. Schott' but were the work of J. A. Heckel. The lowest note was contra D. (Illust. *a.*)

(2) *Circa* 1849: A contra, also of bassoon shape, but even taller than (1) and stamped 'Heckel-Biebrich'. The compass was chromatic down to contra D. (Illust. *b.*)

(3) *Circa* 1876: A left-handed contra, coiled to reduce its height to less than that of the bassoon, but played left-handed and descending to contra C. This is the 'Stritter System' to which reference has already been made, but the instrument is stamped 'Heckel-Biebrich'. (Illust. *c.*)

(4) *Circa* 1879: Original type of the modern contra, right-handed, and having a vertical wooden bell rising above the coils of the tubing. The instrument, however, descended still only to contra C. It was this type, the work of Wilhelm Heckel, which was played to Wagner at Bayreuth in October 1879, when the composer was much impressed.

W. H. Heckel has explained[80] that as Wagner, after this, composed only *Parsifal*, it is only in that score that he employed the contra.

It is not known when the contra was enlarged to descend to sub-contra B♭, but Heckel refers[81] to improvements in the bore and the introduction of two octave-keys on the large crook to facilitate fingering in the middle register. It was on the advice of Wagner that Heckel constructed a bassoon with an extended bell enabling the production of contra A, and about 1900 the contra was made to descend to sub-contra A, the lowest note on the pianoforte and among the lowest in the orchestra. For the downward extension from contra C, the bell is made either of long upright shape (Plate 19, Fig. 12), or with a large wooden bend terminating in both cases in an inverted metal bell. There are, however, half a dozen variations in shape, and all the bells to $A_{,,}$ or $B♭_{,,}$ are detachable and may be replaced by an additional wooden bell rim for contra C (Plate 21, Figs. 15 and 16). The large metal crook has a tuning-slide to regulate the pitch, as the contra, on account of its large dimensions (19 ft. 5 ins. to sub-contra A), is sensitive to variations of temperature.

DEVELOPMENT IN ENGLAND SINCE 1871

Pierre states[82] that in 1890 there were in London only two performers on the contra—one, R. Morton, the eldest son of Alfred Morton to whose work and association with Dr. Stone reference has already been made; the other, presumably Dr. Stone himself. Morton's few contras and Haseneier's original (owned by Dr. Stone) were the only contras in use until the early years of this century. Naturally the improved tone and easier manipulation of the French and German contras of Buffet and Heckel respectively quickly gained approval. At first the French type was most general because bassoons on the French system were then the most popular, but the taste for German bassoon-tone grew steadily and professional bassoon-players even changed over to the German system. The adoption of German contras followed naturally, and the Heckel type or copies of it are those in common use in British orchestras today.

ORCHESTRAL USE

One does not expect to have frequent opportunities of hearing the contra, for it is normally used to support the orchestral mass in *tuttis*. The treatment by Haydn and Beethoven and others has been mentioned above and we may now consider the extent of its employment in the nineteenth century always bearing in mind that composers were greatly restricted by the comparative rarity of the contra (except in Austro-Hungary) for most of the century.

MENDELSSOHN scored for contra and serpent or bass-horn in a few works. In such cases the composer was obviously seeking merely reinforcement of the bass. The contra, reading from the non-transposing parts for serpent or bass-horn, would sound an octave lower. As it could not always be counted on being available, the part was doubled in the octave higher. An exception occurs at one point in the *Trauer Marsch* (Op. 103) (1836) where the part is marked '*C. Fag*' and later '*unis*'.

GLINKA (1804–57) included an excellent contra part in the Overture to *Russlan and Ludmilla* (1842) and it must appear remarkable that so many subsequent Russian composers, including notably TCHAIKOVSKY (1840–93), ignored the contra and preferred the tuba.

RIMSKY-KORSAKOV (1844–1908) gave the contra an important part in *Coq d'Or* (1906).

SHOSTAKOVITCH (born 1906) included the contra in his Fifth Symphony (1937) and his Sixth Symphony (1st movement) (1939).

WAGNER became favourably impressed with the Heckel contra in 1879 and wrote in its favour a short testimonial commending its facility of legato in the lowest register. As, however, Wagner composed only *Parsifal* after this date the contra appears only in that score. In other works it has been added, partly at the instance of Hans Richter. It may be noted that Wagner, for some obscure reason (and certainly without consideration for the player), writes the contra part at its actual pitch and not an octave higher.

BRAHMS included the contra in his Symphony No. 1 (1876) and its tone is heard to wonderful effect in the impressive chorale-subject in the *Più Andante* of the last movement. The passage scored *p. dolce* for bassoons, horns and three trombones, has the contra doubling the bass trombone in the octave below. It occurs twice, descending on the first occasion to contra C and the second time to sub-contra B♭. Forsyth in his *Orchestration* remarks on the telling effect and the author would add that, of all the contra passages he has played, he finds this one of the most thrilling.

In Symphony No. 2 (1877) Brahms replaced the contra by the tuba, but appears to have preferred the contra to which he resorted again in Symphony No. 3 (1883) and No. 4 (1885). Earlier, in 1873, he had included it in several of the *St. Anthony Variations*.

STRAUSS included it in most of his works giving it difficult solos in *Salomé* (1904) and *Elektra* (1906) and a remarkable descending glissando over a ninth (written: e♭ to D) in *Don Quixote* (1897) (where the knight falls asleep).

In *Tod and Verklärung* (1889) Strauss has an A♭ minor chord for cor anglais, bassoon, contra and trombones. In performance, the composer could often hear a C, evidently a harmonic of bassoons or contra, and he records this experience in his treatise on the 'Instrumentation' of Berlioz.

RAVEL has a solo for contra in *Ma Mère l'Oye* suite (La Belle et la Bête) ascending to a′ (beyond the *effective* range of the contra). In an American recording, the contra has been replaced by the tuba but the tone of the latter is too hard and aggressive for this particular passage.

In the Piano Concerto for the left hand, the contra opens the work (written compass B♮,–b♭) and later has three sextuplets in demisemi-quavers.

DUKAS has written perhaps the best-known short passage for contra in *L'Apprenti Sorcier*. A repeated slurred four-note phrase, commencing on contra F, introduces the ⅜ theme for three bassoons in unison.

The contra has been included in nearly every large-scale work since about 1880, thus mention can be made of its use by only certain composers.

SULLIVAN included a contra part in *The Golden Legend* (1886) and in *The Martyr of Antioch* (1880) there is an extensive (but not solo) contra part (compass E (written) to d' (written)) which would be playable on a semi-contra in F. There are many occasions inviting low D's but the part is taken up an octave. The player must, of course, have transposed, but this contra part is interesting in view of the F-contra said to have belonged to Sullivan. (See earlier in Chapter 8.) Other instances occur in Holst's *The Planets* (1918): Respighi's *The Pine Trees of Rome* (1924): Elgar's *Dream of Gerontius* (a five-bar phrase, *pp molto rit.*, descending F,, C♭,, B♭,, slurred)—very telling in effect: Bax, Parry, Stanford, Delius and Vaughan Williams (*e.g.* in 'Job' and in the 4th Symphony in the trio of the 3rd movement where bassoons, contra and tuba lead off in unison for the *fugato* section).

ALBAN BERG has given the contra a solo in 'Wozzeck' Act I, bars 108–17.

WALTON also employs the contra freely, writing parts often of difficulty.

STRAVINSKY has scored for 1st and 2nd contras in *Le Sacre de Printemps* and gives the 1st contra a series of solo top f"s.

BENJAMIN BRITTEN in his symphony for 'cello and orchestra Op. 68 (1964) has given the contra an extended solo in the opening section of the first movement.

The tone in the lowest register (sounding sub-contra B♭ to E) in sustained notes is soft and smooth, becoming easy and flexible as far as E. The instrument is capable even of rapid and staccato passages though the effectiveness of very rapid passages is certainly questionable. From E to G the tone commences to lose resonance, and though the compass can be extended from G to f, this portion is better avoided, as the notes sound forced and dull, and can be blown with less effort and more effectively on the bassoon.

Notwithstanding this, Beethoven, Brahms, Ravel and others write up to a, where the contra is quite useless.

AEROPHOR[83]

Passing reference must be made to an extraordinary instrumental accessory patented in Germany[84] in 1911 by Bernhard Samuel, a flautist in Schwerin. Named aerophor, it was intended to enable a wind-instrumentalist to sustain notes indefinitely without effort of breath-pressure. This was achieved by the use of a small foot-bellows connected to a small flexible tube held in the mouth beside the reed or mouthpiece. Incredible as it may seem, the aerophor was recognised by Strauss who made use of it in his *Alpensinfonie* and *Festliches Praeludium*. In the latter it is prescribed for the contra, the 3rd and 4th bassoons, 7th and 8th horns and tuba. The following note appears in the score:

> 'Um in den Blasinstrumenten die langen Bindungen ohne Atem-unterbrechung auszuführen, ist Samuel's "Aerophor" zu gebrau-chen.'

> 'Samuel's 'aerophor' is to be used by the wind-instruments in playing the long 'held' notes without a break.'

Needless to say the apparatus never found acceptance and is probably unknown to most wind-players today.

Historically the aerophor is of interest as it embodies the very ancient custom of using the mouth as a 'wind-chamber'. The primitive Eastern folk-instruments arghul, zummara and other medieval types were blown thus.

SUMMARY

The successive stages in the evolution of the contra appear to have been:

I. Low-pitched dulzians

Sixteen and early seventeenth centuries: single wooden shaft with twin bores connected at the foot to form a continuous conical tube. Small squat bell and short crook:

(*a*) Quart-fagott descending to contra G.
(*b*) Quint-fagott descending to contra F.

(*Cf.* Vienna Kunsthistorisches Museum, Nos. 198 and 199. *Illust. Mus. Times*, April 1937.)

II. *Contrabassoons* (Plates 17–21)

(1) Tall bassoon-shape, entirely of wood except for metal crook of
large size, sometimes bent back on itself more than once:

(*a*) In C, descending to sub-contra B♭, *e.g.* Stanesby Junior, London,
1739. (H. 8 ft. 4 ins.) (Fig. 1.)

(*b*) In C, descending to contra C, *e.g.* Doke, Linz. (H. 5 ft. 8 ins.)
(Fig. 3.)

(*c*) In F (quint-bassoon), descending to contra E♭, *e.g.* H. Grenser,
Dresden, *c.* 1790. (H. 6 ft. 1 in.)

(*d*) In G (quart-bassoon), descending to contra F, *e.g.* Samme,
London, *c.* 1855. (H. 5 ft. 7 ins.)

(2) Bassoon-shape: long butt; large bell of metal and widely flared.
This type is almost exclusively Viennese or Bohemian; in C, descend-
ing to contra C, *e.g.* Stehle of Vienna (Fig. 2) and Uhlmann of Vienna;
Horák and Rott of Prague; Schöllnast of Pressburg. (Fig. 6.)

(3) Similar to (1) but having a second butt-joint, inverted and lying
side by side with the bell. This permitted the construction of a contra
pitched in C, with normal fingering but reduced to little over five feet
in height:

(*a*) To contra C, *e.g.* Lempp, Vienna. (H. 5 ft. 2 ins.); Horák, Prague.
(H. 5 ft. 1 in.) (Fig. 4.)

(*b*) To contra D, *e.g.* Schott, Mainz (*i.e.* Heckel), *c.* 1830–50. (H.
5 ft. 7 ins.).

(4) Fourfold shape, wide bore, narrow rim instead of a bell; all
holes very large and bored at approximately acoustically correct
intervals and all covered by keys. In C, descending to contra C; height
reduced to about 4 ft. 7 in.:

(*a*) Of wood—contrabassophon, *e.g.* Haseneier, Coblenz (1849).
(H. 4 ft. 8 ins.). (Fig. 9.)

(*b*) Of papier-mâché—contrabassophon, *e.g.* Berthold, Speyer-am-
Rhein.

(5) Fourfold shape; narrow bore; of wood; holes of more normal
bassoon size; all covered by keys, with bassoon fingering.

(*a*) Descending to contra C (H. 5 ft. 4 ins.). Heckel, Biebrich.

(b) Descending to contra C (H. 4 ft.). Stritter System (left-handed). (Fig. 11.)

(c) Descending to contra C (H. 4 ft. 5 ins.), W. Bradka, Vienna. (Fig. 10.)

(d) Descending to sub-contra B♭ (H. 6 ft. 4 ins.). Inverted metal bell. (Fig. 12.)

(e) Descending to sub-contra B♭ and A. Inverted metal bell. (Figs. 15 & 16.) *e.g.* Heckel, to contra C, 1879; later to sub-contra B♭ and *c.* 1900 to sub-contra A.

III. Metal Types

All holes covered, not bassoon-fingering. The sarrusophone alone has survived.

(a) Ophicleide shape:

To contra D, *e.g.* Stehle, Vienna, *c.* 1850 (H. 5 ft. 6 ins.). (Fig. 7.)

(b) Slender tuba-shape:

Tritonikon in E♭ (Schöllnast, Pressburg, 1839 and 1855) (H. *c.* 3 ft. 3½ ins.)

Tritonikon in E♭ (Červený, Königgrätz, 1856).

Tritonikon in B♭ (Červený, Königgrätz, 1867).

Contrebasse-à-anche, to contra D (*e.g.* Mahillon, Brussels, 1868). (Fig. 8.)

Claviatur-contrafagott (*e.g.* C. W. Moritz, Berlin, 1845–56). (Fig. 14.)

Contrabass sarrusophone in E♭ or C (*e.g.* Gautrot, Paris, 1856). (Fig. 13.)

REFERENCES

[1] Sachs, C.: *Handbuch der Musikinstrumentenkunde* (Leipzig, 1920), p. 323.

[2] Schlosser, J.: *Catalogue of Kunsthistorisches Museum* (Vienna, 1920), Nos. 198 and 199.

[3] Terry, C. S.: *Bach's Orchestra* (1932), p. 114.

[4] Heckel, W. H.: *Der Fagott* (2nd edit.), p. 7, Illust. *b.*

[5] Kinsky, Dr. G.: *Kleiner Katalog der Sammlung . . . Heyer in Cöln* (1913), p. 160.

[6] Lavoix, H.: *Hist. de l'Instrumentation, loc. cit.,* p. 269.

[7] Galpin, F. W.: *Old English Instruments, loc. cit.,* p. 169.

[8] For notes on the Stanesbys (father and son), *vide Galpin Society Journal,* XII, pp. 49–51, and XIII, pp. 59–69. Both articles by E. Halfpenny.

[9] Galpin, F. W.: *Old English Instruments, loc. cit.,* p. 169.

[10] Parke, W. T.: *Musical Memoirs (1784–1830)* (London, 1830), 2 Vols., I, p. 42.

[11] Crosse, John: *Account of . . . Festival . . . in . . . 1823 in York Minster* (York, 1825), pp. 174–5.

[12] Lysons, Rev. D.: *Origin and Progress of the Meeting of the Three Choirs* (Gloucester, 1895), p. 69.

[13] Ashley, John (died 1805): a London bassoonist and assistant conductor at the Handel Commemoration in 1784 who, with his four sons, gave concerts in various parts of England. The names of the father and four sons occur in Doane's *Musical Directory* for 1794: address, No. 4 Pimlico Terrace. It is a coincidence that another 'Ashly [sic] of the Guards' (1740–1809) played the contra at the same Handel Commemoration as recorded by Burney, *supra*. It is generally considered that this was Jane Ashley (1740–1809), brother of John (above) and, like him, a bassoonist.

[14] *Bulletin of the Cercle Archéologique de Malines*, Tome XXIV: 'Les Tuerlinckx, luthiers à Malines.'

[15] *Bulletin of the Cercle Archéologique de Malines*, Tome XXIV, p. 110.

[16] *Ibid.*, p. 138.

[17] Van der Straeten: *La Musique aux Pays-Bas*, Tome 5, p. 181.

[18] *Bulletin . . . Malines, op. cit. ante*, p. 165.

[19] Gassner, F. S.: *Partiturkenntnis* (Carlsruhe, 1838).

[20] Brenet, M.: *La Musique militaire* (Paris, n.d.), p. 72, and illust., p. 65.

[21] Kastner, G.: *Manuel général de Musique militaire* (Paris, 1848), pl. xiii, Nos. 6 and 9.

[22] Berlioz, H.: *Memoirs* (English translation) (London, 1884), Vol. II, p. 79.

[23] Köchel, L.: *Die Kaiserliche Hofmusikkapelle zu Wien von 1543–1867* (Vienna, 1869), p. 32.

[24] Kastner, G.: *Cours d'Instrumentation* (Paris, 1837), p. 5.

[25] Thayer, A. W.: *The Life of Beethoven* edited by H. E. Krehbiel (New York, 1921), Vol. II, Chap. XIV, p. 268.

[26] Gassner, F. S.: *Dirigent und Ripienist* (Carlsruhe, 1844). Plan of orchestra reproduced in Schunemann's *Geschichte des Dirigierens*, p. 310.

[27] Castil-Blaze: *L Académie impériale de musique* (Paris, 1855), Vol. II, p. 372.

[28] Forsyth, C.: *Orchestration*, 2nd edit. (1935), p. 249.

[29] Prout, E.: *The Orchestra*, 2nd edit. (1897), p. 144.

[30] Lavignac: *Encyclo., loc. cit.* (Paris, 1927), p. 1563; *ibid., loc. cit. ante*, p. 1562.

[31] Pierre, C.: *La Facture*, p. 29 *et seq*.

[32] *Essai sur le serpent* by Cocatrix, from 'Correspondance des professeurs et amateurs de Musique', 2e Année, 1804, pp. 331, 339 and 345.

[33] This single contra was apparently made by Goumas, later improved by his successors Evette and Schaeffer. A full description is given by Pierre in *La Facture*, pp. 31–33.

[34] Lavignac: *Encyclo., loc. cit.*, p. 1564.

[35] Mendel, H.: *Musikalisches Conversations-Lexikon* (Berlin, 1872), *s.v. contrafagott*.

[36] Pierre, C.: *La Facture, loc. cit.*, p. 36, states 'in 1855'.

[37] *Cf.* Heyer-Leipzig Coll., Catal. No. 1404.

[38] 'Reisebriefe' of W. Wieprecht in *Berliner Musikzeitung*, Jhg. 1845, No. 43.

[39] Preuss. Patent No. 13043 of 24 October 1856.

[40] Illust. in Sachs' *Handbuch . . .*, *loc. cit.*, p. 324.

[41] Sachs, C.: *Real-Lexikon, s.v.* Tritonikon. *Cf.* Berlin Colln. No. 821.

[42] Pierre, C.: *La Facture*, p. 34.

[43] Pierre, C.: *ibid.*, p. 35; also Lavignac, *Encyclo., s.v.* Basson, p. 1562, fig. 678.

⁴⁴ Sachs, C.: *Real-Lexikon, s.v.* Subkontrafagott.

⁴⁵ Scholes: *Oxford Companion to Music, s.v.* Ear and Hearing.

⁴⁶ Illust. of back and front in Day's Catal. of Royal Military Exhibition (1890), p. 34.

⁴⁷ Pierre, C.: *La Facture*, p. 36.

⁴⁸ Schlesinger, K.: *Instruments of the Orchestra* (1910), Vol. I, pp. 25–28.

⁴⁹ Forsyth, C.: *Orchestration, loc. cit.*, 2nd edit., pp. 247–8.

⁵⁰ Pierre, C.: *Les Facteurs, loc. cit.*, p. 345. Pontécoulant: *Organographie*, Vol. II, p. 507.

⁵¹ Heyer: Leipzig Coll. No. 1403 and Brussels No. 1003.

⁵² *Neue Zeitschrift für Musik* (Leipzig, 1850), p. 154.

⁵³ Ann Arbor, Stearns Colln. Catal. No. 684, Illust., Pl. VI.

⁵⁴ Berlin Colln., Catal. No. 1067, p. 288.

⁵⁵ Heyer-Cöln, Kleiner Katalog No. 1407, Dr. Kinsky attributes it to *c.* 1875, whereas Heckel suggests 1888 (in *Der Fagott*, p. 23, caption of illust. (a)).

⁵⁶ Heyer-Cöln, *loc. cit. ante*, No. 1405, p. 161.

⁵⁷ Morton was born in 1827 and went to Vienna as apprentice to Joseph Uhlmann & Sons. In 1847 he returned to London and finally settled in Clapham Park Road as a maker of excellent oboes, cors anglais, tenoroons, bassoons and contras. He died in London 2 January 1898.

⁵⁸ Pierre, C.: *La Facture, loc. cit.*, p. 37, Illust. p. 39; also Lavignac, *Encyclo. s.v.* Basson, p. 1562, fig. 679.

⁵⁹ ——: *op. cit.*, p. 255.

⁶⁰ By an amazing series of coincidences, the author acquired over many years various scraps of information and finally learned that the Donaldson Coll., R.C.M., London, had been given a contra by descendants of Wm. ('Rooty') Davis (1846–1927) for long the only contra-player in London, both in orchestras and in the band of the 'Scots (Fusilier) Guards'. The contra is marked 'Made by Alfred Morton for F(ontaine) Besson, London' and 'S.F. Gds./No. 1/1876'. This proves the date and the instrument must have been made in low pitch because Mr. Frank Rendell, the London bassoon-player and teacher, recalls seeing in a case in the small museum of Boosey & Co. (when at Frederick Mews, Stanhope Gate, W.) a slice of twin bores, some 4 inches in height with a notice that this portion had been cut off the butt of the contrabassoon used by Mr. Davis in the Scots Guards Band, 'to put it in tune'!

⁶¹ Day, C. R.: Catal. of Royal Mil. Exhib. (1890), No. 173, p. 82.

⁶² Schlosser, J.: Catalogue of Vienna Colln., No. NE 532, Illust., pl., LIV.

⁶³ Pierre, C.: *La Facture, loc. cit.*, pp. 38–40 with illust.

⁶⁴ ——: *ibid.*, pp. 30–32.

⁶⁵ ——: *ibid.*, pp. 33–34 and illust. p. 35; also Lavignac, *Encyclo., s.v.* Basson, p. 1562, fig. 677.

⁶⁶ Lavignac: *Encyclo., loc. cit.*, fig. 676.

⁶⁷ ——: *ibid., loc. cit.*, fig. 680.

⁶⁸ Grove's *Dictionary*, 5th edit., *s.v.* Stone, Dr. W. H.

⁶⁹ Day, C. R.: Catal. of Royal Mil. Exh. No. 171, pp. 81–82 and Pl. VIII, B. Now in the P. A. T. Bate Collection.

⁷⁰ Heckel, W. H.: *Der Fagott*, 2nd edit., p. 21.

⁷¹ ——: *ibid.*, p. 16, illus. (a) and (b).

⁷² ——: *ibid.*, illust. (c) and *Zeitschrift für Instrumentenbau* (1898–99), pp. 340–341, 'Zur Geschichte und Statistik des Heckel-Fagotts' by Wilh. Altenburg.

⁷³ Deutches Reich Patent No. 1131 of 24 October 1877.

⁷⁴ Being a translation of an article by Hermann Starcke in the *Deutsche Musik Zeitung*.

[75] French Brevet d'Invention, No. 16212 of 9 June 1856.

[76] Pierre, C.: *La Facture, loc. cit.*, pp. 40–47.

[77] Chouquet, G.: *Catal. du Musée* . . . Paris, No. 512 bis.

[78] Coyon: *Méthodes élémentaires de Sarrusophones* . . . (Paris, 1867), 2 vols.

[79] Pierre, C.: *La Facture, loc. cit.*, p. 42.

[80] Heckel, W. H.: *Der Fagott*, 2nd edit., p. 20.

[81] ——: *ibid.*, p. 21.

[82] Pierre, C.: *La Facture, loc. cit.*, p. 255.

[83] *Zeitschrift für Instrumentenbau*, XXXII, 5, 46: Sachs: *Real-Lexikon, s.v.* Aerophor: Grove's *Dictionary*, 5th edit., *s.v. idem.*

[84] Deutsches-Reich Patent No. 242807 of 12 April 1911.

CHAPTER 9

Acoustics

OBSERVATIONS on the behaviour of musical pipes have been recorded at intervals over more than two thousand years.

Julius Pollux in his *Omnasticon* (*c.* A.D. 177) describes the wind instruments of his day, the aulos and syrinx. He mentions the three divisions of the instrument-makers' craft; the aulos-maker, the reed-maker and the wood-turner. The material could be one of several substances: reed-cane, bronze, 'lotos' (a North-African tree from the hard black wood of which auloi were made), box-wood, horn, bone, or dwarf-laurel branches hollowed out. Pollux states that for a time the aulos had only four holes, but Diodorus, the Theban, made it with many holes bored obliquely. This very ancient reference to oblique boring which survives in the bassoon to the present day is remarkable.

Two centuries later, Macrobius (*c.* 378–423) in his commentary *in Somnium Scipionis*, Book II, Chap. IV, dealt with the Music of the Spheres and draws an analogy in the case of 'tibiae' (flutes). The passage is as follows:

> 'From the holes in these which are near to the mouth of the player, a high note is emitted; while from those that are farther away and placed at the far end, a deeper note is produced; also, the note is of higher pitch through the wider holes and deeper through the narrow holes. In each case there is only one explanation; the breath is stronger where it begins and weaker where it ceases; and it sets in motion a greater rush of air through the wider hole; but the contrary is the case where the holes are small and placed at a distance.'

Again, we observe that the ancients were well aware of a principle which has enabled the fingers of the two hands to control a number of lateral holes which would otherwise be too widely spaced to be reached.

With Aristoxenus (*c.* 330 B.C.) we need not be concerned here since his *Elements of Harmony*, in three books, deal with the philosophy of Music. In Book I, paras. 20 and 21, however, in reference to compass there is a remarkable reference to the highest note of an aulos-player performing with the 'speaker-key' open and the lowest note of such a player performing with the 'speaker-key' closed. We see here the basis of Denner's experiments *c.* 1700 leading to the 'discovery' of the clarinet. Similar 'harmonic keys' were applied to all wood-wind instruments including the bassoon—two thousand years after we first hear of the device.

It is to Helmholtz (1821–94) that we owe our first real insight into the structure of complex tones. His *On the Sensations of Tone* (1873) gave a complete study of sound with the limited apparatus then available, *i.e.* his investigations were necessarily largely qualitative. With Graham Bell's invention of the telephone in 1876, Edison's invention of the phonograph in 1877 and Berliner's gramophone in 1887, quantitative research became possible. Dayton Miller of Cleveland, Ohio, a happy combination of scientist and musician, developed about 1909 a very sensitive instrument which he named a 'Phonodeik'. With this he carried out a long and comprehensive series of investigations into the nature of musical sounds. The late Professor Bernard Hague of Glasgow University, another example of a scientist-musician, has acknowledged that though Miller's results 'have been superseded in recent years by those obtained by modern electronic techniques of superior sensitiveness, accuracy and ease of application, his work remains as a permanent memorial to his genius and superlative skill as an experimenter'.

Musicians interested in the science of acoustics owe a debt of gratitude to Professor Hague whose friendship throughout many years the author was privileged to enjoy. In April 1947 he read to the Royal Musical Association his paper *The Tonal Spectra of Wind Instruments*[1] and much that follows is taken from that source, by kind permission of his daughter, Mrs. Mackay, London.

We must first recognise the features common to all instruments:

(1) The *generator* or *exciter* by means of which sound is initiated and maintained. In the case of the bassoon this is a double-reed held between the lips while air is forced between the reed-blades causing them to vibrate.

(2) These vibrations are communicated to the *resonator* which consists of the column of air contained within the tube of the instrument. The generator and resonator constitute a coupled dynamic system in which the mode of vibration of each is associated with the other in a complex and intimate way. The resonator is, however, predominant and both stabilises and determines the pitch of the note produced. This

is facilitated by the relatively large mass of the air column and the fairly tight coupling to the light flexible generator, *i.e.* the reed.

(3) The tube is provided with means for adjusting the length of the air column or resonator so that a chromatic scale can be produced. In the bassoon this is achieved by providing *lateral holes* covered by the fingers or by keys which, raised in sequence, shorten the air-column allowing the air to escape and raising the pitch to the desired extent. In the bassoon, to an even greater extent than in other wood-wind instruments, the effect of opening a lateral hole does not have the effect of reducing the sounding column to the portion *above* the open hole. In fact, the lower portion of the column continues to exert an influence.

(4) Finally, the generator is coupled to the air-cavities in the head, throat and chest of the player setting into vibration the air within these cavities as well as the air of the resonator. The reality of the phenomenon is easily demonstrated with the aid of a stethoscope.

We may now consider some general observations based on an article by Dipl. Ing. Franz Groffy of the Heckel firm relating to sound production on the bassoon.[2]

We may with advantage remind ourselves that in the traditional church organ each note of the musical scale demands its own separate pipe, whether a flue pipe or a reed pipe, so that in a large organ several hundred pipes may be required, each of which will have its own generator and resonator. On this account it becomes necessary to supply air to the pipes from a common reservoir, hence the wind-pressure remains constant for each pipe. Thus the organ, from its very nature, assumes the character of a mechanical sound-producer.

How different is the case of the bassoon. The player must acquire artistic virtuosity and adaptability to the multifarious possibilities of breath-control and skill of fingers. Bassoon-playing demands unerring mastery of a chromatic sequence in temperament over three and a half octaves. In other words, some forty-two notes must be produced from a single wooden pipe and to do so eight fingers and two thumbs have to control eighteen tone or semi-tone holes as well as three harmonic holes. (Additional tone-holes serve to produce special trills, etc.) While it is true that the positions of the holes may be calculated from general acoustical principles, as was done, for example, by Gottfried Weber early in the nineteenth century and subsequently by Theobald Boehm, nevertheless, the results are insufficiently exact for musical purposes such as good intonation; moreover, there are often matters involved, not the least of which is the practical convenience of the player. Similar acoustical difficulties occur with other wood-wind instruments and even with the much simpler organ pipe. In the first place, the lowest note B♭, requires a tube-length of 2·59 m. (102 ins.) requiring sub-division into the bell, long-joint, butt, wing and crook. Secondly, the holes out-number the digits to cover them so that certain holes must be operated by keys arranged in groups for easy manipulation by the fingers and thumbs of both hands. This again gives rise to a series of compromises in the strict acoustical sub-division of the tube by tone-holes.

Firstly. The lateral sub-division of the tube length of the bassoon requires displacement of the tone-holes for F, G♯, A, c, c♯, as otherwise these would occur in the socket and tenon or in the U-bend of the butt. To correct the intonation it is, therefore, necessary to bore oblique holes with varying depth of penetration and diameter. For this purpose, on the German bassoon, additional resonance-holes are bored in the wide-bore of the butt to assist tone-holes in the narrow bore (*e.g.* B♭ and A resonance-holes).

Secondly. In general it is customary to employ for the six-hole scale (L123 and R123) hole-intervals which suit the normal spread of the fingers. Acoustically this suits small instruments such as flutes, oboes and clarinets, but it does not suit the bassoon. Therefore, very oblique tone-holes are bored and the penetration of these is artificially length-ened by thickening the tube at the points, *e.g.* the bulge of the wing joint. For the two thumbs and two little fingers, key-combinations of an intricate kind are provided to attain the ultimate aim—the greatest possible uniformity in intonation and tone-colour throughout the entire compass. It will be observed that the player at times makes use of two tone-holes bored in different places, operating simultaneously, to sound one and the same note.

On the bassoon, using the eighteen whole-tone and semi-tone holes from low B♭, we reach middle f. From there onwards the octaves begin by 'overblowing' the fundamental scale an octave higher. This over-blowing succeeds on the bassoon in practice only for f♯, g, g♯, a, b♭, c′, c♯′ and d′ after which, as a result of the compromises in placing the tone-holes (as stated above), considerable differences in intonation and tone-equality can emerge.

These differences can be compensated by auxiliary fingerings both on the French and German bassoons. Normally low tone-holes are opened or closed as far as the availability of the thumbs or little fingers admit of this.

For the notes d♯″, e″, f″ auxiliary fingering must be used in conjunction with the a′ and c″ octave-keys as well as by opening and closing the crook-hole which is also an octave-key-hole. A better term for these holes is 'harmonic-holes' as they assist in the production of twelfths, etc., as well as octaves.

Bore. The bassoon has an apparently continuous conical bore and, throughout the history of the instrument, the degree of 'conicity' has constantly been altered to accord with improvements otherwise. Certain portions of the bore are parabolic rather than conical. The most vital portion is obviously at the narrow part, so the taper of the bore of the crook and of the wing is of supreme importance. The crook has been described in German as 'die Seele' ('the soul') of the instrument. There is a wide variety of crooks each possessing some or other advantage for the particular instrument to which it is fitted. Thus one will facilitate the production of low notes, another will suit only for producing the highest notes d♯″, e″, f″. Even the smallest deviations in the course of the bore result in an alteration in the theoretical length of the instrument and, accordingly, upset its pitch. Theorists and even bassoonists often underestimate the influence which the construction of the tube has upon both the intonation and tone-colour of the bassoon.

The skilled player usually makes his own reeds or has these made by a skilled reed-maker to suit him. Such reeds can nevertheless be unsuitable for another player because he may have a different embouchure, different breath-control and different breath-volume. The quality of the reed cane, its provenance and age play an important part; finally, a player should have a sound knowledge of the acoustical conditions under which a reed sets in vibration the air-column in the instrument. With long experience of wind technique, the skilled player almost unconsciously produces with the reed all frequencies necessary to obtain all chromatic notes of the $3\frac{1}{2}$ octaves. There is, therefore, no generally suitable model reed, but this much can be said—the frequency of the reed itself in making it 'croak' should give approximately the pitch of f,, f♯,, g, or g♯.

Herr Groffy carried out a long series of experiments with reeds and tested some forty different types of construction and makes of the best-known bassoons. It appears, moreover, that different lengths of the 'shape', of the bore and of the breadth of the 'shape' cause differences in the pitch of the instrument, to a degree which cannot be made apparent by mere objective measurements. The varying strength (stiffness or flexibility) of the two vibrating reed-blades is of tremendous

L

significance and is conditioned by the growth and quality of the reed-cane employed. There are bassoonists who use no tools for measuring thickness but know precisely from the transparency and structure when the correct strength has been reached. These musicians, however, have it also in their power, from testing the reed, to improve it subsequently quite considerably and to make it conform to particular requirements, *e.g.* light response in the lower register, uniform middle register, improved high register and by no means least a beautiful even tone-colour of the instrument throughout the whole register.

Something more must be said about the tone-colour of the bassoon. The artistic lengthening of the bassoon downwards—normally the instrument must give out the note F or E—has for result that, although one always hears the fundamental, this has only a fraction of the power of the entire sound volume. Herr Groffy measured the strength of the partials in the individual registers and found that, *e.g.* from low B♭ to about G the 5th harmonic possesses about 60 per cent, the fundamental only 2 per cent of the whole power. From G♯ to e the 3rd harmonic has 60 per cent of the whole power, the fundamental about 4 per cent; from C♯ to c′ the 2nd harmonic has 95 per cent and the fundamental 3 per cent; from c♯′ to c″ the 1st harmonic (*i.e.* the fundamental) about 90 per cent and the other harmonics the remainder of the power.

In other words the prominent partials with the greatest power lie between 330–550 cycles per second.

It is therefore obvious that the tone-colour of the bassoon is actually different in the three octaves. It is precisely to this difference in tone-colour in the separate registers that the artist within living memory has accustomed himself and it has become the characteristic of bassoon-tone and constitutes its chief charm.

Confirmation of these findings is contained in Professor Hague's article above-mentioned, in which he reproduces several of the 'tonal spectra' first recorded by E. Meyer and G. Buchmann.[3] The tonal spectrum of the bassoon sounding low C and the spectra of the three octave C's above are shown in Plate 22, Fig. 1. In his comments on the spectrum, Professor Hague describes the bassoon as 'an acoustical phenomenon of great complexity, chiefly because of the form of its resonator which is long, slowly tapered and of narrow "scale". The oblique holes are not simple openings as in the case of the flute, oboe or clarinet, but are auxiliary tubes branching from the main resonator.[4] Their influence on the resonance properties of the air-column is very marked and they are largely responsible for the exceedingly uneven character of the timbre at different parts of the compass. In the illustrations of the tonal structure, it will be noted that, in all except the highest notes, there is a very small proportion of fundamental in the spectra and there is a large number of harmonics in the low register. These conclusions are also true of the contrabassoon.

'Simple theory suggests that harmonic structure should depend only upon the generator and resonator and that tone-quality is determined by the relative proportion of harmonics to fundamental set up in the resonator by the generator.' If this were so, the relation should remain constant whatever the note sounded, but this is far from being so. Another factor must be taken into account.

'The air column is confined within an almost rigid wall of wood' which has 'certain natural frequencies of its own and to some extent a measure of damping'. With lateral holes, in which the air 'has mass, "elastance", and is in close dynamical connection both with the air column within the tube and with the atmosphere outside the tube, the bassoon possesses certain selective frequency characteristics and behaves as an "acoustic filter"'. These factors of construction and configuration are constant and 'harmonics falling within one or more ranges of pitch' become specially prominent and independent of the particular fundamental being generated. 'Those fixed-pitch ranges of harmonics constitute a "formant", a characteristic feature of a particular instrument and a determining factor of its timbre.' In the tonal spectra reproduced in Plate 22, Fig. 1 we note that the bassoon has a particularly strong formant at about 500 cycles per second.

Another feature requires mention. One can find difficulty in distinguishing two instruments with quite similar steady tone, *e.g.* horn and bassoon, but immediately there is movement from one note to another, the different articulation is perceptible. Tonal spectra analyse the structure of steady unvarying tone. In music, however, the passage from one note to another occurs with great rapidity. We must recognise that in this very short interval the vibration of the air-column changes transiently 'in a manner determined by the method of articulation used by the player'. The use of staccato, for example, so characteristic of and effective on the bassoon creates one kind of transient behaviour, while legato sostenuto playing causes quite another. These changes are termed 'transients'.

It has been proved that there is approximate correspondence between 'the tonguing technique used by wind instrument players for various kinds of phrasing' and 'the use of dental consonants in speech'. Indeed 'the parallel between articulate speech and wind-instrument playing is sufficiently close to justify on physical grounds the soundness of teaching such instruments upon a vocal basis'.

A question put to the author many years ago from U.S.A. was the following: Why does the bassoon, with a tube-length of approximately 8 feet, give as its fundamental note B♭, which should require a tube-length of over 9 feet?

I am indebted to my friend Mr. G. A. S. Dibley, Edinburgh, for the following solution which has not so far been challenged!

To solve the problem, measurements were made on a bassoon by I. Lot and gave the following data:

Length of crook 12 inches, tapering one in 55 ⎫
Length of wood 83¼ inches, tapering one in 79 ⎬ Total 98½ inches.
Effective length of reed; about 2¼ inches ⎪
End correction for open end: about 1 inch ⎭

The instrument is thus by no means a perfect cone, but is a tube with an over-all length of about 98½ inches.

Now remembering that the pitch of a note is indicated by the frequency of vibrations, the theoretical frequency for a true cone of the above length works out at about 69—wave-length about 197 inches— C♯, about a tone and a half too high! For the frequency of bottom B♭ is in the neighbourhood of 58—wave-length 234 inches—and should require a cone of length 117 inches (half the wave-length of the note).

Again, the taper of the main part of the instrument being 1 in 79 and the diameter of the bell-end about 1¾ inches, for the bore to be truly conical throughout and to taper off to zero, it can be calculated that the length must be 116 inches, a result well within 1 per cent of the theoretical length for B♭. The diagram (exaggerated) will make this clear. (Plate 22, Fig. 2.)

To sum up: the tube of a bassoon consists of (*excluding* the reed) a short cone tapering 1 in 55, a long cone tapering 1 in 79, and a short cylinder; the whole being 96¼ inches long. This behaves harmonically as though it were a single true cone 117 inches long, and gives a fundamental note of frequency 58, *i.e.* bottom B♭, near enough.

As a postscript to this chapter, the following anecdote is recorded[5] of Darwin, who, when studying earthworms, put them to a curious use. Earthworms are devoid of the sense of hearing, yet they move away from the footfall of birds and other enemies, and especially at the approach of their arch enemy, the mole.

Like the blind, they are intensely sensitive to vibrations. One day a physician called to see Charles Darwin. The great naturalist was in the library with an iron tray containing earthworms. The worms took no notice of the jingling of keys, the shrill note of a whistle, or similar sounds, but when Darwin's son played to them on a bassoon they felt the vibration and immediately began to wriggle.

REFERENCES

[1] *Proceedings of Royal Mus. Assoc.*, LXXIII, pp. 67–83, including an extensive list of references.

[2] (a) On the use of a clarinet mouthpiece on the bassoon.

(b) The limits of altering the length of wood-wind instruments as influenced by temperature variations.

(c) Further problems of instrumental pitch. Three papers in German (with English versions) by Dipl. Ing. Franz Groffy, proprietor of the firm of Wilhelm Heckel.

The author is indebted to Herr Groffy for permission to quote from these articles.

[3] *Sitzungsberichte der Preuss. Akad. der Wissenschaft*, pp. 735–78 (1931): 'Die Klangspektren der Musikinstrumente'.

[4] *Physical Review*, Vol. 17, pp. 534–5 (1921): 'Broken tone from reed instruments' by J. B. Taylor.

[5] Bland-Sutton, Sir John: *Selected Lectures and Essays* (London, 1920), p. 270.

For further reading on the general subject of *Acoustics of Woodwind Instruments* the reader is referred to two articles by P. A. T. Bate in *Research*, Vol. 15, September and October 1962.

CHAPTER 10

Materials and Reeds

MUCH controversy has surrounded the question of the effect of the material of the tube or resonator upon timbre. Divergence of opinion exists not only among acousticians but also between theorists and players. During the eighteenth and nineteenth centuries the view was held that at least in the case of certain instruments, *e.g.* the trumpet, the material exercised considerable influence on the tone. The opinions of Perrault (1680), Bernoulli (1762), Lambert (1763), Riccati (1767), Chladni (1809), Biot (1816), Herschel (1830), Müller (1840), Zamminer (1852), Seebeck (1870), and Helmholtz (1885), all more or less in agreement, are summarised by Rockstro (1890).[1] With the advent of V. Mahillon (1841–1924) and D. J. Blaikley (1846–1936) vigorous opposition was offered to the theory. Both were practical musical instrument-makers with opportunities for minute research so their opinions were entitled to respect. In the present century, however, informed opinion is in favour of the material exercising subtle influences upon the tone.

These influences are of two kinds: quantitative (effect on pitch and intensity of sound), and qualitative (effect on timbre). The former can be appreciated by a player who feels the vibration of his instrument in playing. A tube with thick walls of a dense hardwood will not vibrate readily and will produce a dull tone lacking brilliance. Conversely, a thin-walled tube will vibrate to excess. In both cases much of the player's energy will be wasted. The ideal is achieved where the thickness of the tube wall is proportioned to the density of the wood. As wood varies from billet to billet, mass production must inevitably give rise to occasional poor instruments.

As regards qualitative effect we must recognise that it has been proved that the timbre of a note is conditioned by the presence and intensity of certain partials aided to some extent by a formant. (See Chapter 9.) Organ-builders have found that certain timbres are best obtained from certain metals or alloys. In the same way, wood-wind makers, until the mid-nineteenth century, chose boxwood which

Mersenne in 1637 stated was more frequently employed than any other wood. Boxwood gave a sweet tone and Cocus and African blackwood give a full and brilliant tone.

In the bassoon, where four joints are involved, it would seem necessary that the joints should be cut from the same log or carefully matched in regard to resonance. It was to this care in matching the joints that the bassoons of Savary jeune owed their singing tone.

A survey of the kinds of wood used for wood-wind instruments in fourteen representative European collections, selected at random, gave remarkable results. Their accuracy, however, can be seriously questioned for a number of reasons. Certain catalogues make no attempt to identify the wood: others do so without the very specialised knowledge necessary and the identification may well be wrong. In the case of 781 specimens the following was the material:

Boxwood	406	Palissander	21
Ebony	106	Pear	15
Maple	100	Cocus	12
Grenadilla	37	Cherry	7
Ivory	31	Walnut	4
Plum	22		

Others with less than four examples were mahogany, apple, bamboo, crystal, glass, rosewood, jacaranda, hornbeam, malacca, 'fruit-wood' and sanctus-holz, *i.e. Lignum vitae* or guaiacum. Needless to say, bassoons were not made of such a wide variety of materials.

Writing in 1855, von Gontershausen[2] stated that opinion was divided as regards the best wood for bassoons. The majority, however, preferred medium-hard, porous, 'geflammt' maple (*Acer pseudo-platanus*). This is the European maple, also called sycamore in England and plane-tree in Scotland. Almenräder chose North American black maple (*Acer nigrum*). Others preferred the sugar-maple (*Acer saccharinum*) which has a brown or brownish-black colour. The pores are long and coarse but the grain is firm and durable, and bassoons made from this wood have a bright clear tone.

Grenadilla (a species of *Dalbergia melanoxylon*), Ebony and Palissander (*Lignum violaceum*) were then used largely for bassoons and von Gontershausen remarked that apart from the fact that the use of these woods made the bassoons uncomfortably heavy, it was evident from the tone that solid non-porous woods were less suited for bassoons than softer porous wood. Thus the tone of bassoons of ebony in particular was always rather dull and while instruments of ebony and grenadilla were more durable than those of maple the tone from the latter was to be preferred. This statement holds good today in Germany though, in France, Palissander (commercial rosewood) continues to be preferred by makers.

The author consulted timber experts and it appears that *Palissandre* is the French name for South American Rio Rosewood (Brazilian Rosewood). The tree is of the genus *Dalbergia* of which there are several varieties, the principal being *Dalbergia nigra*. This wood varies in colour from chocolate or violet-brown to rich purplish-black. When cut, irregular streaks of dark red are conspicuous and the wood appears oily with a faint but distinct rose perfume whence it is called *Rosewood*. It has of course, no connection with the rose plant but had a long vogue in Victorian days in cabinet-making, veneering, etc., ranking second only to mahogany in the mid-nineteenth century. It is recorded that in 1867 Britain imported some 560 tons of this timber chiefly from Para and Maranham. Trunks twenty feet long were cut in two and then split to be sure they were sound. Experts include with *Dalbergia*, *Machaerium incorruptibile, M. legale, M. allemani* and *M. violaceum.*

Another kind of rosewood of East Indian origin is *Bombay Rosewood Dalbergia latifolia*, also called *Blackwood*; but this is *not* known as Palissander. Today in England Jamaican Rosewood is imported from Honduras and used for Xylophone notes, as French-system bassoons are very rarely made in England. Heckel informs us that he uses maplewood almost exclusively for bassoons. The process of preparation of the wood was briefly described by Herr Groffy in the *Handbuch der Musikwissenschaft.*[3] Maple trunks are cut into thick planks, selected for lightness and uniformity of growth. Gentle steaming follows in a special room to kill the living cells. Thereafter the planks must dry for many years in the open air but care must be taken to exclude the direct rays of the sun. Only then are the planks cut into square billets suitable for bassoon-joints and the first narrow hole is bored in their long axis. By yearly stages, the joints are gradually reduced to their exact final dimensions and any showing a flaw are rejected. Intricate and accurate tools are employed in shaping the wing and butt in particular and the utmost precision is required as each tone-hole requires its own particular thickness of wood in the wall of the instrument. This is a requirement which cannot be corrected subsequently. A special lathe for oval turning enables the butt to be shaped without subsequent hand-work. To ensure uniformity in turning the bell-joint, a contrivance is affixed to another guide-spindle lathe which automatically and accurately turns the wood to the recognised proportions.

The U-shaped water-outlet is then fixed to the base of the butt, two requirements being ease of removal and absolute accuracy of fit. The applied metal surfaces are ground one on the other so that, without any rubber or cork packing, no air can escape. It may be remarked that the U-bend is conical in bore and is punched with a die from a single brass plate and pressed into shape. A perforated plate is soldered, polished and provided with guide-holes and tenons. Such is the precision of the machinery that no other work is needed on this accessory.

Metal 'mounts', to strengthen sockets and prevent splitting, are next fitted to the wing, butt and bell, after which the wood is filed all over to an exact model, ground, stained and polished.

A special process then follows during which the joints are saturated with a suitable oil which closes the pores and renders the wood better acoustically and more durable as those parts of the bore which are not lined are thus rendered capable of withstanding moisture. The ebonite lining is next inserted in the bore of the wing and the narrow tube of the butt.

One of the most important processes follows; that of boring the tone-holes and the holes for the screw-pillars to support the keywork. The lathe for boring the tone-holes exact to a tenth of a millimeter was built to a special design to enable the boring 'bit' to be inclined through nearly two right angles for the obliquely bored finger-holes. For each tone-hole, in fact, and for the bed-hole for each key-pad, there are special 'bits', all hand-made and of irreplaceable value.

A revolving lathe is used to screw in the 'pillars' (or 'key-posts') but the key mechanism is mounted by hand. This can never be done by machinery as special fitting of individual keys is required for every bassoon, depending on the peculiarity of the wood.

Depending on the movement of the key-mechanism, leaf-springs or needle-springs are next fitted and the entire metal parts after being cleaned are brought up to a high brilliancy by one of several electric polishing-motors each provided with two 'buffs'.

The nickel-plating or silver-plating of the keys and rings is undertaken in a galvanising department.

The tenons are then cotton-bound or cork-padded and tested to ensure perfect fitting in the sockets. The bore is tested again with a 'Prototype-borer', varnished and polished. The keys are padded and the under-surfaces of the rods cork-lined where they bear on the wood.

The whole mechanism then undergoes rigorous scrutiny for completely noiseless action and perfect adjustment.

The manufacture of the crook[4] is a delicate process because the conical course of the tube must be carefully continued from the reed to the wing-joint. The metal is cut from a flat sheet of soft German silver or sheet brass, then rolled and seamed. It is filled with a substance to allow the exact bend to be made without altering the cone. After removal of the packing, the inner surface must be smooth as a mirror. This is especially important in the narrow part of the bore if correct tone-production is to be achieved.

DOUBLE-REED

In Chapter 1 the double-reed of the bassoon is mentioned. Some account of this very important component is now essential. The term double-reed refers to the two slips of cane which compose the reed. Confusion is unavoidable in English where we employ the word 'reed' for the 'generator' (see Chapter 9) and for the plant from which the reed is obtained (*Arundo donax* or *A. sativa*).

For centuries the best reeds have come from the South of France, near the mouth of the Rhone, particularly from three small and separate areas of the Province of Var, *viz.* Fréjus, Cogolin and Hyères, a district of vineyards and orchards. There we find in the wide flat alluvial valleys, reed-beds, in French, *roseaux*. Although during summer all except the largest rivers are dry, water is to be found a few feet below ground and thus the reeds, enjoying almost continuous sunshine for most of the year, are in a dry sandy soil within a few feet of water. In winter, however, the district suffers from the 'Mistral' which Alphonse Daudet describes in his *Lettres de mon Moulin*. This strong dry cold wind blows from the north-west with a violence which is increased by the configuration of the Rhone Valley. This wind is accompanied by brilliant sunshine, intense dryness and piercing cold. It is difficult to analyse the effect of these conflicting climatic conditions, but the fact remains that nowhere else are reeds grown to compare with those of Var.

In most cases the reeds are grown on the banks of small streams which intersect the low land and while some have been deliberately planted, in many cases they grow wild. The reeds grow to about eighteen or twenty feet and are cut when two years old, usually in late winter. The reeds are gathered into bundles about a foot thick and are stacked against poles fixed horizontally to two other supporting poles. Occasionally, these are placed against a tree or building. Here they remain for about fifteen months after which the bundles are untied and sorted according to quality. In one case, the grower stated they were for making baskets or 'chips' as they are called in the fruit-trade in certain districts in Britain. Other reeds are made into fishing rods, but those for musical instruments are cut into lengths of about four feet and placed on racks for about a week in the hot sun. The reeds are turned every evening and take on a golden hue. The reeds are now what we may term 'canes' and are sawn into lengths of nine or ten inches and are again sorted, this time according to diameter, the largest for contra and bassoon and the smaller for clarinet, oboe, etc. Much of the foregoing information it taken from an article by Mr. T. K. Dibley, 'Roseaux pour Pêche et Musique'.[5]

As long ago as 1829 Almenräder wrote a short article[6] on the maintenance of bassoon reeds. He recommended strong cane tubes about ¾ inch in diameter because a double-reed made from a weaker tube turns out too arched which is detrimental to soft artistic expression. A practice of steeping the cane in oil, he found not only useless but damaging because the oil, through warmth, saturates the pores of the cane thus restricting free vibration of the cane fibres. He considered that much reed-cane was unusable because it had been cut at the incorrect season when the sap was still in the shoots and more often if stored in a damp or ill-ventilated place. As this can be detected by an unpleasant musty smell and lack of elasticity in the cane, no one will readily make use of it. It is of supreme importance to avoid cane with crooked growth. No matter how it may be trimmed, it will, after some use, warp again and lose the requisite arching of the two sides. In advising that the cane be not cut too thickly in the region of the middle, where the wire binding-rings are, and that in cutting, the utmost evenness be observed, Almenräder quaintly commends the advantage of doing the work in the evening 'when on account of the sharp shadows cast by the candle-light, every unevenness and inequality can be detected with ease'. He declared that a reed fashioned according to such basic principles would, from the start, have a good tone, respond readily both above and below and continue consistently good, even with long use.

Dealing with preservation, he attributes the gradual deterioration of both single and double reeds to the slimy scum which adheres to the walls of a reed in frequent use. The cane putrifies as a result and loses its natural elasticity. He, therefore, always cleaned his reed after use, passing a chicken-feather or pigeon-feather through it, so that no scum remained.

Ozi in his *Méthode de Basson* had already commended this procedure. A second very powerful cause of deterioration is in the treatment of reeds after use. The normal procedure is to shut up the reed in a reed-case to which the air cannot penetrate to dry the saturated reed. In consequence, the cane rots and must soon be ruined. Almenräder would have nothing to do with a case of metal or leather, which retain dampness to a greater or lesser extent. He preferred a pasteboard box with the reed-blades next the lid which should be perforated all over. As soon as practicable the reed should be removed to a position where it can dry naturally. He states that since he adopted this method, he kept a reed—although in daily use—one, one-and-a-half, up to two years 'in the best and most usable condition'. When we consider that Almenräder was a virtuoso on his instrument, such a statement must amaze professional players today.

Finally, he advocates thorough drying of a reed and painting it with pure rape-seed oil, when it is not to be used for a time. Any other fine oils caused a crust which could not be removed without risk of damage to the reed.

The practice of many bassoonists is to make their own reeds, obtaining for the purpose reeds ready 'gouged' or even gouged and 'shaped'. Others procure ready-made reeds which require only slight adjustment. Early tutors which give detailed and illustrated instructions for reed-making are Ozi, Almenräder, Fröhlich, Jancourt and Weissenborn.

Two recent studies deserve mention. First, that of Edouard Flament (died 1958), Basson solo de la Société moderne d'instruments a vent, entitled *Étude sur le Grattage des Anches de Basson* (Paris, 1919). Printed in French and English, it is clearly illustrated. An even better account of the process is given by A. C. Baines.[7]

Of all writings on reed-making, by far the most detailed, technical and comprehensive account is that of Don Christlieb, the distinguished Los Angeles bassoonist. In 1945 he produced his 'Notes on the Bassoon Reed'[8] for the Musicians Congress of America. This excellent treatise, amended in 1954 and again in 1964, deals with all aspects of the bassoon reed—botanical and microscopic details of the cane, bindings, varnish, machines to gauge, shape and profile the reed, the jig for folding and wiring, the mandrel and reamer. The extensive study and experience of this eminent bassoonist and capable engineer are thus presented for all who face the endless reed problem.

A remarkable feature of bassoon reeds is their reduction in size since c. 1800. Baines gives[9] a comparison of reeds commencing with an old English bassoon-reed which was much longer and thinner than the modern reed. The cane was gouged thinner, the throat was wider and the reed had only one wire (above the binding). Doubtless, the reed was thus made to suit the wider bore of the crook at that period. The heavy brass crook of a Cahusac bassoon dated 1769 in the author's collection increases from $1\frac{3}{8}$ in. to $1\frac{6}{8}$ in. as compared with $1\frac{2}{8}$ in. to $\frac{6}{8}$ in. in the case of a modern French crook. The old crook is much less arched and measures $12\frac{1}{2}$ in. against $13\frac{1}{2}$ in. of the French crook. The wider crook and wing, the narrower butt and long-joint and bell-'choke', in association with a long reed of the kind described above, combine to produce a sweet soft tone partaking of 'cello quality and not unlike a modern French bassoon. This is the expert opinion of A. C. Baines who has played old English bassoons professionally, cf. The Evolution of the Bassoon in England 1750–1800 by E. Halfpenny.[10]

REFERENCES

[1] Rockstro, R. S.: A Treatise on . . . the Flute . . . (London, 1890), para. 242.
[2] von Gontershausen, W.: Magazin musikalischer Tonwerkzeuge (Frankfurt a/Main, 1855), pp. 379–80.
[3] Handbuch der Musikwissenschaft edited by Dr. Ernst Bücken (Potsdam, 1929), Lieferung 29, Heft 2, p. 39.
[4] Handbuch . . . op. cit. ante, p. 41, with illustration.
[5] The Hallé Magazine (April 1952).
[6] Caecilia: Band XI, Heft 41, pp. 58–62.
[7] Woodwind Instruments . . . (London, 1957), Chapter III.
[8] Christlieb, Don: Notes on the Bassoon Reed (1964), 40 pp., obtainable from the author, 3311 Scadlock Lane, Sherman Oaks, California 91403, U.S.A.
[9] Woodwind Instruments, op. cit. ante, Pl. VI.
[10] Galpin Society Journal, Vol. X (May 1957).

CHAPTER 11

Technique, Capabilities, Tutors

THE purpose of the present volume is not to provide instruction in playing the bassoon. Students can confidently turn to *Bassoon Technique* by Archie Camden, the well-known soloist who has written the book in the Oxford University Press series on technique of orchestral instruments. It deals with the German system (which Mr. Camden plays) and has chapters on breath-control and tone; finger technique; intonation, etc., and a useful account of reed-making and the 'finishing' of hard or unfinished reeds. The Appendix compiled by William Waterhouse (co-principal Bassoon of the B.B.C. Symphony Orchestra) is a valuable list of music for bassoon and orchestra, bassoon and piano, bassoons only, chamber-music for bassoon and strings, etc. A much more extensive list forms an Appendix to the present work and the author is indebted for its compilation to Mr. Graham Melville-Mason.

As to the capabilities of the bassoon, it is well to commence by recalling the dictum of F. A. Gevaert in his *Nouveau Traité d'Instrumentation* (1885): 'De nos jours le basson n'a plus la prétention de briller au concert. . . . Il se contente d'être à l'orchestre un serviteur utile, infatigable: de tous les instruments à vent, c'est celui qui repose le moins.'

'Nowadays (1885) the bassoon no longer has any ambition to shine on the concert platform. . . . It is satisfied to be a useful and tireless servant in the orchestra: of all the wind instruments, it is the bassoon that has the least rest.'

To explain why this useful and tireless servant rests the least, we have only to consider its capacity to portray a wide variety of moods. A *Times* critic on 15 August 1925 contributed one of the best assessments of the bassoon, entitled 'The Gentleman of the Orchestra'. The occasion was the performance by Mr. Richard Newton in Queen's Hall of Mozart's Bassoon Concerto.

The unusual sensibility and versatility of the bassoon is revealed by countless passages, frequently of such short duration that only the listener who trains his ear to learn and to love the colours of the orchestral palette can fully appreciate the beauties of each instrument and the artistry of composer and performers alike. Some of these characteristics are its ability to give rhythmic definition or whimsical grace, to portray melancholy, drollery, roguishness, mystery, pathos, drama and poetry. Examples of each will be found among the many compositions listed in Chapters 4 and 5.

Two unusual aspects of technique have received attention from specialists in dentistry and physiology respectively. In the *British Dental Journal* of 5 August 1952, Mr. Maurice M. Porter, L.D.S., contributed an illustrated article entitled 'Dental aspects of orchestral wind instrument playing with special reference to the embouchure'. Mr. Porter, himself an amateur clarinettist, cites authorities for the statements that: (1) 'dentistry has been of some appreciable service to musicians playing wind instruments'; (2) that 'the use of wind instruments is of value in correcting certain facial and dental defects'; (3) that 'certain respiratory disorders have been treated by the use of such musical instruments since careful control of breathing is absolutely necessary in order to play a musical piece successfully'.

Progressive dental troubles have been responsible, directly or indirectly, for a deterioration in tone produced often as a result of prolonged study and practice. In other cases, a beginner may have a dental defect which may hinder his progress or even make it impossible to acquire a good tone. 'The dentist is, by virtue of his knowledge and experience, in a position to help both the experienced wind instrumentalist and the beginner' and may even advise on the choice of wind instrument best suited to his oral and dental anatomy.

Technique of itself, however skilled, is not enough unless it is accompanied by a good tone and this in turn is largely dependent on a good 'embouchure', *i.e.* 'the method of applying the lips and mouth to a wind instrument'. Mr. Porter discusses the relationship of embouchure to tone but, unfortunately, the wood-wind instruments mentioned do not include the bassoon.

It is rarely that a player is known to have contributed to the development of the bassoon. Exceptions have been Almenräder and Jancourt, whose work has been described, and today we have William Waterhouse, co-principal Bassoon of the B.B.C. Symphony Orchestra. If we agree that quality and quantity of breath are paramount for tone and successful execution of many technical effects, then efficient operation of the respiratory system is basic. Correct posture is therefore vital and

Mr. Waterhouse has for some years been endeavouring to find the correct position of the bassoon in relation to the lips and hands. The reed must enter the lips at the angle required by the individual lay of jaw. He decided that, if the weight of the bassoon could be removed from the hands and neck, a greater degree of freedom from tension would result in a larger and better tone. With most players, posture and embouchure are determined by the shape of the instrument. If a player's dimenions differ from the average, the result is contortion in varying degrees. Over the past ten years Mr. Waterhouse has evolved a straightened crook and spike which suit his particular dimensions and result in his holding the bassoon at an unusual angle. (See Plate 23.) To achieve optimum results, each player must hold the instrument in the correct position demanded by his dimensions and build: this the use of a spike enables him to do. Other advantages are better response from a straight crook and, during rest, the reed remains only a couple of inches away from the mouth, ready for instant recommencement of play. A number of players, amateur and professional, have since adopted the spike to support their instruments and the device is now being marketed by Schreiber of Nauheim.

Another technical aspect of bassoon-playing concerns the medical and physiological problems connected with breathing and blowing. In the Netherlands, Professor Roos, himself a flautist, studied a number of flute and oboe players from 1936 to 1940. His main conclusion from his measurements of mouth-pressure during play and estimated volume of air expired through the instrument, was that flute- and oboe-playing do not surpass in any way the limits of performance to be expected from persons with normal lungs and breathing muscles.

A very interesting article, 'Breathing and Blowing in Wind Instruments' by Dr. Arend Bouhuys of the School of Medicine, Emory University, Atlanta, U.S.A., formerly of the University of Leiden, appeared in *Sonorum Speculum* of 1 December 1962 (Amsterdam). Dr. Bouhuys has very kindly permitted the author to quote extracts from this article.

'The common belief that wind instrumentalists, by creating a high pressure to play their instrument, strain their lungs excessively is based upon a faulty conception of the mechanics of breathing. Actually the lung tissue is not subject to any significant extra strain during blowing . . . because the lungs are supported by the bony cage of the thorax and its muscles, including the powerful diaphragm. As recently as 1960, a German physician averred that "increased lung volume in wind players . . . is very often only the result of a faulty technique of blow-ing. . . . Long term wind instrument playing can cause a decrease of elasticity, even an atrophy of the alveolar walls, by the repeated expira-tory decrease of the lung volume" .' Dr. Bouhuys considered it essential to compile factual data concerning the function of the lungs in wind-instrument players. In this way it would be possible to decide 'whether or not pulmonary emphysema occurs with undue frequency in these artists'. For good performance, co-ordination of breathing is essential to ease of playing and this results from skilled instruction and long practice. A preliminary study was made at Bentvelt in the Netherlands in July 1962 under the auspices of the Eduard van Beinum Foundation when more than forty wood-wind and brass instrumentalists took part.

Lung function tests were performed on all participants and compared with tests made previously in groups of other healthy persons who were not wind instrument players. Factors such as age and smoking habits were taken into account. From other studies there is 'evidence that heavy smoking, in particular cigarette smoking, has in the long run an unfavourable effect on the functional performance of the lungs'.

'None of the tests performed gave any evidence to believe that wind instrument players are liable to develop pulmonary emphysema as a consequence of their profession.'

'Even in healthy persons, however, the performance of the lungs, as measured with the tests described, shows a gradual decline with advancing age. . . . The decline of the functional performance of the lungs with age in wind instrument players appears to be similar to that in other healthy persons.'

Dr. Bouhuys 'found that in male persons above the age of forty-five years, the degree of unequal distribution of inspired gas in the lungs correlates with the amount of tobacco these subjects said they usually smoked. This finding is of particular importance to wind instrument players who want to have optimal capacities for performance also when they grow older. Such artists would be well advised not to smoke; at least, not cigarettes.'

Playing a wind instrument requires 'rapid and deep inspirations followed by prolonged and intermittent expirations'. The chest move-ments of seven flautists playing Debussy's 'Syrinx' were recorded and very similar results were obtained 'in spite of marked differences in the qualities of the performance between these different artists. This shows that the composer controls to a large extent the breathing of the performers of his work who are only allowed to inhale at moments when

M

inspiration does not interfere with the correct musical performance.'
Estimates of the carbon dioxide in blood before, during and immediately
after half an hour playing on different instruments by young musicians
with several years' experience 'showed no significant changes'.

'The player appears to adjust, unconsciously, the average volume of
air he breathes in such a way that, over longer periods of time, there
are no demonstrable changes in the carbon dioxide level in his blood.

'The strain which a person experiences during physical exercise
may be estimated approximately from the heart rate found during this
exercise. . . . Continuous records of the heart rate in most participants
in the study, while they played their instruments during five minutes
"revealed that the heart rate during the last minute was no higher
than about 120 per minute . . . the category of moderate exercise".'

To ascertain the energy required to play different instruments, the
pressure in the mouth was measured during play. 'In woodwind
players, mouth pressures of up to about 60 mm. mercury were recorded.'
. . . In reed instruments, the condition of the reed appeared to be a major
factor influencing mouth pressure during playing. The differences in
pressures obtained in individual musicians playing the same instrument
were considerable and there were some indications that more experienced players develop lower pressures for the same note at the same
strength than less experienced artists.'

Measurements of sound levels made with the help of the Laboratory
of Acoustics of the Netherlands Radio Union at Hilversum 'allow a
calculation of the sound output of the instruments in terms of energy
produced'.

'Simultaneous measurements of mouth pressure and volume expired
through the instrument' make it possible to estimate the approximate
energy which the player expends on his instrument. 'Such calculations
allow an estimate of the efficiency of playing a wind instrument, *i.e.*
of the ratio of the sound energy output and the input of mechanical
energy. The mechanical efficiency varied from about 0·005 per cent
to about 1 per cent in one professional bassoon-player, which means
that for each 100 energy units the player expends on his instrument,
the return in sound energy is less than 1 unit. . . . Of the total amount
of energy generated by the player, less than 0·2 per cent is finally emitted
as sound waves by the instrument. . . . Wind instrument playing is very
wasteful in terms of energy. . . .

'Musicians may feel distressed to learn that their instruments are so
inefficient as measured in prosaic mechanical terms, but they need to

be reminded that the spiritual joy of music cannot be measured quantitatively. Perhaps one should look upon the low mechanical efficiency of wind instrument playing as a physical and physiological expression of the sacrifice the artist has to make, throughout his life, to bring the joys of music to his fellow-man.'

In a subsequent letter to the author, Dr. Bouhuys remarked that he found no extremes of pressure in bassoon-players. A point which emerged from measurements of air-flow rate and pressure in a bassoonist was that when playing a note (at high or low pitch) first pp and then ff the pressures differed but little, which is contrary to findings in most other instruments. To play more loudly one generally has to apply more pressure. This seemed not to be so in the bassoon, where pressure was found to be nearly independent of loudness, but air-flow rate increased markedly with loudness. The highest pressure found in a bassoonist, at high notes, was about 80 mm. mercury, which indeed is pretty high compared with pressures in other woodwinds but lower than those required in brass (up to 160 mm. mercury).

Dr. Bouhuys has recently compiled a further study on 'Lung Volumes and Breathing Patterns in Wind Instrument Players' and this will appear in *The Journal of Applied Physiology*.

TUTORS

To obtain a conspectus of the evolution of the bassoon since the close of the seventeenth century, we can select from an extensive list of tutors (Ger. *Schulen*: Fr. *Méthodes*), many accompanied by fingering-charts which are invaluable in revealing the development of fingering as the keys multiplied. Many of the works listed are unfortunately of great rarity. Over forty (marked 'P') are in the Library of the Conservatoire de Musique, Paris, and the author wishes to express his thanks to the librarian for supplying a microfilm of the titles. Others (marked 'BM') are in the British Museum.

The Hochschule für Musik, Berlin, is using the *Methods* and *Studies* of Almenräder, Bourdeau, Weissenborn, Piard and Schaefer. A Hungarian bassoon soloist and teacher, Mr. Otto Oromszegi of Budapest, published in 1962 ten modern bassoon-studies. In his English Preface, he stresses the importance of training students to read and perform passages of the kind they will certainly meet in the modern orchestral repertoire. Mr. Oromszegi is highly critical of the generally accepted instruction which is confined to performance of the purely classical repertoire, important as that may be.

BASSOON TUTORS AND CHARTS

P denotes a copy in Library of Paris Conservatoire. BM = British Museum.

1687	Speer, D.: *Grundliches Unterricht* . . . (2nd edit., 1697) (for two-keyed dulzian).
1730	*Musica Bellicosa*, (published by Walsh) including '*Scale of the Gamut for the Bassoon*', which was evidently the original for the scale in *Apollo's Cabinet* (1754) *infra*, (for a four-keyed bassoon).
1732	Majer, J. F. B. C.: *Music-Saal* (2nd edit., 1741) (for three-keyed bassoon).
1738	Eisel, J. P.: *Musicus autodidactus* (for two-keyed dulzian and four-keyed bassoon).
1751	Diderot and D'Alembert's *Encyclopédie*, Vol. II, Article: 'Basson de Hautbois', Tablature, p. 128 (for four-keyed bassoon).
1754⎫ 1756⎭	*The Compleat Tutor* (Henry Purcell, London, 1754). *Apollo's Cabinet or The Muses' Delight* (John Sadler, Liverpool) (2nd edit., 3rd edit., 1757). *The Gamut or Scale for the Bassoon*, p. 45 (for four-keyed bassoon).
1762	Tans'ur's *Elements of Music Displayed*, Bk. III (7th edit., London, 1829. Scale, etc., pp. 233–4 (for four-keyed bassoon).
1770	*Complete Instructions for the Bassoon* . . . (Longman, Lukey & Co.), six keys.
c. 1765	Bailleux, Antoine: *Méthode . . . par Mr. Hotteterre le Romain . . .* Nouvelle Édition augmentée . . . des Tablatures de la Clarinette et du Basson . . . etc. (Paris, c. 1765). Gamme, p. 25 (for five-keyed bassoon).
1780	Laborde's *Essai sur la Musique* by Pierre Cugnier (Paris, 1740–?).
c. 1780	Abrahame (1764–1805): *Principe de Basson* (Frère, Paris, n.d.). Gamme (for five-keyed bassoon).
c. 1780 BM	*Complete Instructions for the Bassoon* . . . (Longman & Broderip).
1784⎫ or ⎬ 1786⎭	Joseph Gehot: *The Complete Instructor or Complete Instructions for every Musical Instrument.* Various editions 1784–c.1840 (for four-keyed bassoon).
1788	*Méthode nouvelle et raisonnée pour le Basson*, par M. Ozy (Boyer, Paris).
1800 P	*Méthode de Basson*, par E. Ozi (Nadermann, Paris, 2nd edit., 1800).
P	—— (Paris, Imprimerie du Conservatoire. An XI = 1802–3).
P	—— (Paris, J. Meissonnier, 1843). Revised edit. 1898.
c. 1790 BM	*Complete Instructions for the Bassoon* . . . (Preston & Son, London).
1795	*Muzijkaal Kunst Woordenboek* (J. Verschuer Reeynvaan, Amsterdam). Pl. 3 for two-keyed dulzian.
c. 1796	Blasius, M. F.: (1758–1829) *Nouvelle méthode* . . .
c. 1800 P	Van den Broeck, O. J.: *Traité général . . . basson* (Paris, Boyer, n.d.).
c. 1805	*Complete Instructions for the Bassoon* (printed and sold by Wm. Dover, London).

c. 1806		*Complete Instructions for the Bassoon or Fagotto* (printed by G. Goulding, 5 Pall Mall, London) (for four-keyed bassoon).
c. 1810		*Tutor for the Bassoon by Charles Eley* ('cellist) (in Goulding's Catalogue).
1810 and 1811		*Vollständige . . . Musikschule* (Joseph Fröhlich) (1780–1862).
1820		Rees's *Cyclopaedia* (Chart dated 1807), Vol. III (London and Philadelphia, 1810–24): 'Scale of the Bassoon' (eight-keyed bassoon).
c. 1820		Almenräder, C.: *Traité sur le perfectionnement du Basson* (Schott, Mainz).
1825		G. Weber in *Caecilia*, Band II, Heft 6.
1828		—— *ibid.*, Band IX, Heft 34.
1829		C. Almenräder on bassoon reeds in *Caecilia*, Band XI, Heft 41.
c. 1832	P	Cokken, J. F. B. (1802–75): *Nouvelle édition du Méthode de Berr en deux parties* (E. Gérard, éditeur, Paris), also (Paris, Alphonse Leduc, n.d.).
1834		Schneider, W.: *Historisch Technische Beschreibung.*
1836	P	Berr, F. (1794–1838): *Méthode complète de Basson* (Paris, J. Meissonnier, 1836).
1839		Choron & Lafage (in *Encyclo.*—Roret).
1840	P	Neukirchner, W.: *Fagottschule* (Leipzig, F. Hofmeister).
c. 1840	BM	*New and Improved Bassoon Tutor* by Geo. Mackintosh (published by Z. T. Purday, London).
1840	P	Blumer: *Méthode de Basson* (Paris, Schonenberger).
1841		C. Almenräder's *Fagottschule* (Mainz, Schott).
1844	BM P	Willent-Bordogni, Jean Baptiste: *Méthode complète* (Paris, Troupenas). *Metodo completo* (*v. Organo*, p. 450 (1847)). (Milan, Ricordi, 1884.)
1850?		Hofman, F. H.: *Fagott-Schule* (Leipzig, Merseburger).
	P	Krakamp, Emanuele (1813–83): *Metodo per Fagotto* (Napoli, T. Cottrau, n.d.).
1854	P	Cornette, V.: *Méthode de basson* (Paris, Colombier, also Gallet).
1847	BM P	Jancourt, E.: *Méthode théorique et pratique pour le basson en 3 parties.* Op. 15 (Paris, G. Richault).
1869	P	—— *ibid.* (2nd edit.).
1879	P	—— *ibid., Étude du basson perfectionné à . . . 22 clés* (Paris, P. Goumas).
1911	BM	—— *ibid.*, Trans. by C. O'Neill. Edit. by J. Fitzgerald and E. F. James (Hawkes & Son, London, 1911).
?	P	Jancourt (Eugène) et Bordogny: *Grand Method for the Bassoon* (London, J. R. Lafleur & Son, n.d.).
?		Romero y Andia, Antonio (1815–86): *Metodo completo de Fagot.*
1870?		Orselli, Luigi: *Metodo completo per Fagotto.*
		Gebauer, F. R. (1773–1845): *Méthode.*
1885	BM	Langey, Otto: *Practical Tutor for Bassoon* (Hawkes & Son, London). Numerous editions up to the present day.
1887	BM	Weissenborn, J. (1837–88): *Fagott-Schule.*
1890?		Kling, H.: *Leichtfassliche praktische Schüle für Fagott* (Berlin, L. Oertel).
1895	P	Parès, P. C. G.: *Méthode de basson* (Paris, H. Lemoine).
1899	P	—— *Metodo de fagot* (Paris, E. Lemoine).

1896?		Metzler: *Tutor.*
1900		Satzenhofer, J.: *Neu praktische Fagott-Schule.*
1938–39	BM⎱ P ⎰	Oubradous, F.: *Enseignement complet du Basson.* 3 cahiers (Paris, A. Leduc, 1938–9).
	P	Küffner, Joseph K. (1776–1856): *Principes élémentaires . . . et gamme de basson . . .* Fr. and Ger. text (Mayence, Fils de B. Schott).
1905		Haubold, O.: *Fagott-Schule* (Hamburg).
1908	P	Fontbonne, L.: *Méthode complète* (Paris, Costallat).
1942	P	Dhérin, Gustave and Pierné, P.: *Nouvelle technique de basson.*
1942	P	Pierné, P.: *vide* Dhérin.
1946	P	Bourdeau, E.: *Grande Méthode complète de basson.* Eng. and Fr. text (Paris, A. Leduc). 1st edit., 1890?
1955	P	Haultier, J.: *Le Débutant Bassoniste* (Paris, A. Leduc).
1959	P	Beauregard, Jean: *Méthode de Basson* (Paris, A. Zurfluh).
1900?		Hawkes, *Tutor.*

ALTO FAGOTTO

| 1825? | BM | Wood, George: *Complete Instructions for Alto Fagotto.* |

STUDIES

All in the Library of Paris Conservatoire.

Bitsch, Marcel: *Vingt Études pour le basson* (Paris, A. Leduc, 1949).

Bourdeau, Eugène: *Receuil de gammes et arpèges mesurés pour le basson en deux suites* (Paris, Evetee and Schaeffer, 1894 and 1895).

Bozza, Eugène: *Quinze Études journalières pour basson* (Paris, A. Leduc, 1945).

Defer, A.: *Étude pour . . . basson* (Paris, Gras, 1951).

Dhellemmes, A.: *25 Études polyphoniques . . . pour basson* (Paris, H. Lemoine, 1961).

Dubois, P. M.: *Douze Études pour basson* (Paris, A. Leduc, 1957).

Flament, E.: *Quinze Études pour le basson* (Paris, H. Lemoine, 1951).

——: *Exercices techniques . . . suivis d'une étude sur le grattage des anches* (Paris, Evette and Schaeffer, 1919).

Gambaro, J. B.: *Études pour le basson* (Paris, H. Lemoine et Cie, 1935).

Jancourt, E.: *Étude du basson perfectionné à . . . 22 clés* (Paris, P. Goumas, 1879).

——: *24 Exercices mélodiques . . . 2 parties* (Paris, Evette & Schaeffer, 1888).

Martelli, H.: *Quinze Études pour basson* (Paris, H. Lemoine, 1954).

Orefici, A.: *Studi melodici per fagotto* (Paris, A. Leduc, 1946).

Ozi, E.: *Gammes variées en études . . . extraites de la méthode du Conservatoire* (Paris, Ph. Petit, n.d.).

Parès, P. C. G.: *Gammes et exercices . . .* (Paris, H. Lemoine, 1896).

Piard, M.: *90 Études pour le basson,* 1er receuil (1942); 2e receuil (1943); 3e receuil (1946) (Paris, edit., Costallat).

Porret, J.: *24 Déchiffrages manuscrits . . . pour . . . basson . . .* (Paris, le Chant du Monde, 1946).

CHAPTER 12

Some Noted Bassoon-players Past and Present

IT was suggested that this chapter should include some account of players who have contributed to the technique of the bassoon. It appeared, however, from perusal of a list of some hundreds of bassoon-players included in British and foreign books of reference that only Almenräder in Germany and Jancourt in France can be said to fulfil the requirement and a detailed account of the part played by each has been given in Chapter 6. One must recognise that it is to the instrument-makers we owe the technical improvements, although these have doubtless been mainly initiated by players whose identity remains unknown. One must also acknowledge the part played by performers whose technique and artistry have raised the bassoon to its present status. Unfortunately, references to the playing of noted bassoonists of the past are rare. The following small selection includes some of those whose playing received favourable comment.

The London Pleasure Gardens* provided considerable employment for orchestral musicians in the eighteenth century and the bassoon-players in 1794 are recorded in Doane's rare *Musical Directory* of that year. This directory includes both London and provincial players giving the names and addresses of 202 wind instrumentalists, many of whom played more than one instrument. It is remarkable that bassoon-ists—forty-nine of them—outnumber any other class of wind-player.

Mortimer's rare *London Directory* of 1763 gives a list of twenty-eight wind-instrumentalist teachers of whom six were bassoonists.

CARL ALMENRÄDER (1786–1843). From the age of thirteen he taught himself to play the bassoon. When he settled in Cologne in 1808 he had become a soloist and from 1810 professor in the newly-founded Cologne Music School. In 1812 he entered the Frankfurt Theatre Orchestra and issued his first composition—a Rondo for bassoon. The war years, however, so reduced his income that he was compelled to return to Cologne in 1814. As bandmaster of the 3rd

* Marylebone, Vauxhall, Ranelagh, Apollo and The Circus in St George's Fields.

Prussian militia he saw service in France and on his return in 1816 he accepted a similar position with the 34th Regiment at Mainz. A year later, having formed a friendship with Gottfried Weber, the Opera Director, he resigned his military appointment to play in the Mainz Theatre. He was deeply impressed by the acoustical theories of Weber and immediately set himself to reform the bassoon in accord with these. He experimented in the instrument factory of B. Schott & Sons who published his *Treatise, c.* 1820. (*Vide* Chapter 6.) In 1822 he became 1st Bassoon in the Duke of Nassau's Court Orchestra at Biebrich and Wiesbaden, meantime continuing his researches at Schott's factory. In 1829 J. A. Heckel, a youth of seventeen, arrived in Mainz and found employment beside Almenräder, now a man of 43. The two formed a partnership in 1831 thus founding the Heckel firm known throughout the world to this day. In 1841, Schott published Almenräder's *Fagott-schule* in German and French. Almenräder, therefore, ranks as the founder of the German or Heckel system. He died in 1843 leaving in manuscript many unpublished compositions.

JOHN ASHLEY, Senior, was 1st bassoon at Covent Garden Theatre and a sub-director at the Handel Commemoration of 1784. He was given a prominent position on the platform and entrusted with a contra made by Stanesby, Junior. Unfortunately, the instrument, or more probably the reed, failed and Parke remarks, 'the double bassoon which had never been *heard*, was never again *seen* after these perform- ances were ended'. This is not correct, however. Ashley played the contra at the Three Choirs at Worcester in 1788.

FRIEDRICH BAUMANN was born in Ostend in 1801, gained the Premier Prix at Paris Conservatoire in 1822 and was brought to England by Jullien. He soon attained great popularity in London musical circles, and his portrait and an acrostic on his name are to be found in *Illustrated London News* of 13 January 1844. He was rather vain, priding himself on his resemblance to Napoleon. He played in the orchestras of the Haymarket and Covent Garden Theatres and at the Three Choirs Festival in 1846–50–52. Welch records a Benefit Concert at the King's Theatre Concert Rooms on 15 April 1831 when Baumann and Barret, the noted oboist, combined in a trio by Brod and also played a set of variations by Berr. *Musical World* of 6 May 1836 declared that: 'Mr. Baumann has not so pure a quality of tone as Messrs. Mackintosh or Denman; nevertheless, he is an excellent orchestral player.' He died in London in 1856.

PAOLO GIROLAMO BEZOZZI (born Parma, 1704—died Turin, 1778). Son of a military band bassoon-player, gained fame through his association with his elder brother Alessandro, an oboist. The two were members of the Compagnia Militare irlandese (a military band instituted by Duke Antonio Farnese in 1702). The brothers travelled little but visited Paris in 1735 when they played at the Concert Spirituel. Settling in Turin, the brothers were visited by Burney in 1770 when the two old virtuosi played duets for oboe and bassoon. Burney highly praised their exquisite performance.

ROGER BIRNSTINGL (1932–   ). Gaining a piano scholarship at the R.C.M., he studied bassoon with Archie Camden. Awarded the Tagore Gold Medal in 1955, he became 3rd bassoon in the Philharmonia Orchestra (1955–6), principal in the London Philharmonic Orchestra (1956–8), principal with Radio Svizzera Italiana, Lugano (1958–61), Royal Philharmonic Orchestra (1962–3), then joined the L.S.O. in which he continues as principal. As a member of the London Wind Soloists he has recorded the complete wind works of Mozart and those of Beethoven are to follow.

GWYDION BROOKE, one of the leading British bassonists today, played his first public solo at the age of thirteen and secured his first orchestral contract with Basil Cameron at seventeen. He studied under Richard Newton at the R.A.M. and became successively 2nd in Beecham's London Philharmonic Orchestra in 1932 and principal in the B.B.C. Scottish Orchestra in 1935. After military service 1939–45, he joined the Liverpool Philharmonic Orchestra in 1946 and a year later transferred to Beecham's Royal Philharmonia Orchestra. In 1961 he became principal in the Philharmonic Orchestra.

Brooke has organised several chamber music ensembles and has recorded the Weber concerto with Sargent and the Mozart with Beecham. He is now a member of the Wigmore and the Prometheus Ensembles and of the London Wind Quintet. As a soloist he has played at the Promenade concerts and the Edinburgh and Strasbourg Festivals. He plays a much modified Adler bassoon of the 1930's.

PAUL DRAPER (1898–   ). Son of the late Charles Draper, the noted clarinettist and a founder of the Royal Albert Hall Orchestra. Paul became a pupil of the late W. H. Foote, almost the first London player to adopt the Heckel bassoon. Winning a scholarship at the R.C.M. in 1921 Paul was a pupil of Wilfred James. As a military bandsman

1915–21 he played an Adler sharp-pitch bassoon, and from 1918–21 he played in the Reid Orchestra, followed by the Royal Albert Hall Orchestra; the B.B.C. Military Band (until 1943); the R.P.O. 1930–4; L.S.O. and Glyndebourne 1934–9; Royal Opera, Covent Garden, 1946–51; Philharmonia 1953–5; L.S.O. again 1955–8. From 1926–50 he used a Mollenhauer with a tenor joint specially made by Louis & Co. in rosewood with Heckel proportions and fingering giving a distinctive tone. He now plays at Sadlers Wells Opera using a Mollenhauer bassoon and contra.

ARCHIE CAMDEN (1888–) studied at the Royal Manchester College of Music 1904–8 gaining his diploma with distinction. He adopted the German system (Adler) which he still plays and was principal with the Hallé and the Liverpool Philharmonic Orchestras 1914–33 while also professor at the Royal Manchester College. He then joined the B.B.C. Symphony Orchestra (1933–46) and on retiring he became professor at the Royal College of Music from 1946–58, returning again in 1963. He conducted Lancashire Orchestras from 1922–33 and in 1937 became conductor of the London Stock Exchange Symphony Orchestra. Well known as a soloist, he has done much to popularise the bassoon on the concert platform and on radio and gramophone recordings. Concertos by Eric Fogg and Gordon Jacob are dedicated to him and his mastery of elaborate staccato is equalled by his sustained cantabile.

EDMUND DENMAN, who, with his brother Henry, played at the Abbey in 1784, was principal at Worcester in 1836 and in the Philharmonic in 1837. Denman played the introductory symphony and accompaniment to 'Odi grand'Ombra' on 2 May 1830 at the Oratorio concert. It drew from 'his brother-fagotto Mackintosh, who sat in a box, strong marks of approbation'. So we read in The Harmonicon for May 1830. Denman succeeded Mackintosh as first bassoon in the Philharmonic in 1835 until 1839 when Baumann took over.

CHARLES GODFREY (1790–1863) joined the Coldstream Guards in 1813, becoming in turn bassoon-player and in 1825 bandmaster. He filled this position with distinction till his death after fifty years' service—latterly from 1834 as a civilian bandmaster. In 1831 he was appointed Musician in Ordinary to the King. The Royal Society of Musicians, of the Court of Assistants of which he was a member, possesses Godfrey's eleven-keyed Milhouse bassoon. He edited

Jullien's *Band Journal* from 1847. His grandson, the late Sir Dan Godfrey, stated that his grandfather was a contrabassoon player in the London Orchestra.

JOHN HEBDEN. At Vauxhall Gardens *c.* 1740–50 the bassoonists included John Hebden whose portrait was painted by Mercier in 1741 and engraved by Faber. Busby states that in the summer of 1745, Tyers, proprietor of Vauxhall Gardens, extended the performances of his orchestra to vocal music: 'Sometimes the principal violoncello and sometimes the first bassoon was ably managed by the abilities of Hebden.'

ERNEST W. HINCHCLIFF (1879–1963) had a long and interesting career. Pre-1914 he became 2nd bassoon in the Beecham Orchestra and subsequently 1st bassoon in the Royal Albert Hall Orchestra, later the New Symphony Orchestra, under Sir Landon Ronald: 1st bassoon in the original 2LO B.B.C. Orchestra: second principal with Richard Newton on the founding of the B.B.C. Symphony Orchestra 1930 and from 1933 until 1950 he played the contra in the B.B.C. Symphony Orchestra. As a founder-member of the L.S.O. he played at their initial concert under Hans Richter in 1904. After two years at Sadler's Wells, he retired. He was joint professor with Wilfred James at the R.C.M. 1931–7 and sole bassoon professor there 1937–46. He was also professor at Guildhall School of Music and Kneller Hall Royal Military School of Music (1920–46).

THOMAS HOGG was a prominent London player in the last quarter of the eighteenth century. We hear of him playing at 'The Nag's Head' and 'The King's Arms' from 1772 to 1778. *The Leics. and Notts. Journal* of 15 August 1778 announced him as visiting principal bassoon at a concert at Ashby-de-la-Zouch. The Churchwardens' Accounts of Swalcliffe, Oxon., record the purchase on 12 December 1782 of a bassoon from Thomas Hogg for £5 5s. The agent for the purchase in London, Joseph Tett, wrote: 'Should anything be wanting to it or out of order Mr. Hogg will put it to rights at any time.'
Hogg appeared again as one of the four principal bassoons at the Handel Commemoration of 1784 but may be presumed to have died before 1794 as his name does not occur in Doane's *Directory*. He can probably be identified with Hoog whose name figures in orchestral lists at the time.

JAMES HOLMES played at Vauxhall, Ranelagh, the Opera, Oratorios at Drury Lane, the Abbey in 1784, the Oxford Meeting in 1793, the Salomon Concerts (including a first performance of Haydn's Sinfonia Concertante) and the King's Theatre. He made his first appearance at the Three Choirs at Worcester in 1794, became principal in 1796 and continued until 1817. He died in 1820. *Vide* reference to Holmes, *s.v.* Miller.

(EDWIN) FRED. JAMES (1860–1920), elder brother of Wilfred James (*q.v.*), was born at Swindon in 1860 and began his professional career in the orchestra of the then fashionable Brighton Aquarium as a bass-player but soon changed to the bassoon, teaching himself. A player of great distinction, he used a Savary sharp-pitch bassoon and became 1st bassoon of the Royal Italian Opera and the German Opera Seasons at Covent Garden and later 1st in the Queen's Hall Orchestra. He was one of the small group of distinguished London musicians who formed the London Symphony Orchestra in 1904. He was 1st bassoon in the L.S.O. and Chairman of its Board of Directors. He was a member of Queen Victoria's private orchestra holding the appointment of 'Musician in Ordinary to H.M. The Queen'. He was bassoon professor at the R.A.M. from 1906 to 1918 jointly with T. E. Wotton and alone from 1918 until his death in 1920. He held the corresponding position at the Guildhall 1912–16: at the R.C.M. from 1912–20 and at Trinity College from 1897–1920. About this time he transferred to a Morton low-pitch bassoon. He also occasionally played solos on a rosewood Morton tenoroon with brass keys. Two years before his death, he resigned his position in the L.S.O. for health reasons and rejoined the Queen's Hall Orchestra as 2nd bassoon to his brother Wilfred.

A man of great musical ability and personal charm, he did much to raise the standard of bassoon-playing in his day.

WILFRED JAMES (1872–1941) was born at Swindon and came to London at the age of seventeen, having won a scholarship at the R.C.M.—the first bassoon scholar there. He was a gifted violinist as well, but decided to make his career as a bassoonist. His bassoon professor at the R.C.M. was William Wotton. His first appointment was 2nd bassoon in the newly-formed Queen's Hall Orchestra (his brother E. F. James being 1st bassoon). Succeeding his brother in 1904 he played in the Queen's Hall Orchestra for twenty-nine years, the last twenty as principal bassoon. Concurrently he was also 1st in the Beecham Orchestra, taking part in Sir Thomas's historic Mozart Opera Seasons. Wilfred James's first instrument was a sharp-pitch Savary bassoon and later he changed to a flat-pitch Mahillon. He was an innovator and was the first player of distinction to adopt *c.* 1900 the Buffet bassoon which he used until his retirement in 1930. He succeeded his brother as professor at the R.A.M. 1921–8 and at the R.C.M. 1921–37. For the last seven of these years at the R.C.M. he was joint professor with E. W. Hinchcliff. He held the same position at Kneller Hall (1914–18) and at Trinity College (1916–22). Like his brother, he was a member of Queen Victoria's private orchestra and later of King Edward VII's private orchestra, holding the appointment of 'Musician in Ordinary' to their Majesties.

CECIL JAMES (1913–) at the age of sixteen won a scholarship at Trinity College, studying bassoon under his father, first on a Morton bassoon but a year later with a scholarship to the R.C.M. he changed to a Buffet, again studying under his father and later under E. W. Hinchcliff. Leaving the R.C.M. in 1934 he was invited to join the L.S.O. as 2nd bassoon to Paul Draper and was a member of the original Glyndebourne Opera Orchestra, occupying these positions until 1939. After war-service with the R.A.F. he became 1st bassoon in the New London Orchestra and played much chamber music besides appearing as soloist. He joined the Philharmonia Orchestra in 1951 as 1st bassoon and, after nine years, left to join the Royal Philharmonic Orchestra in 1961. A brief spell of free-lance playing followed and he became a founder member of the New London Wind Ensemble. He has now returned to the Royal Philharmonic Orchestra as 1st bassoon and with A. E. Wilson as 2nd they maintain the best tradition of French bassoon tone.

JOHANN FRIEDRICH LAMPE (1703–51) came to London from Helmstedt, Saxony, in 1725. He was at first bassoonist at the King's Theatre and later became a composer of some note as the list of his compositions from 1730–45 bear evidence (*cf.* Grove's *Dictionary*, 5th edit.). He played at Vauxhall Gardens and in Handel's Orchestra and it is said that Handel had a contra made by Stanesby, senior, for use by Lampe in 1727. In 1745 Lampe became a friend of John and Charles Wesley, publishing in 1746 a set of tunes to twenty-four of Charles' hymns. About 1738 he married Isabella Young, sister of Mrs. Arne, both of whom were accomplished singers. Lampe and his wife toured England concert-giving, Lampe acting as accompanist. In 1751, while playing in 'The Beggars' Opera' in which his wife played Lucy, they reached Edinburgh where Lampe contracted fever and died on 28 July

1751. It is regrettable that his handsome memorial in the Canongate Churchyard is in disrepair and the inscription now largely illegible.

THOMAS LING, who lived at Helmet Court, Strand, in 1794, is listed as player of violin, oboe and bassoon. He was a reed-maker and was highly praised by William Bainbridge in a booklet published in 1823. He was one of the twenty-six bassoons at the Handel Commemoration in 1784 and played the oboe at the York Festivals of 1823-5-8. The Accounts of the Churchwardens of Fingringhoe, Essex, for 1823 record 'J. Chaplain, Colchester, for 3 Ling's bassoon reeds 6/-'.

JOHN MACKINTOSH (1767-1844) was the virtual successor to Holmes, on whose death in 1820, he became principal at the Three Choirs from 1823-35. In 1823 he became first professor of bassoon at the Royal Academy of Music. He played at the Opera, Antient and Philharmonic Concerts in 1823 and 1835, the Abbey oratorios, the Apollo Gardens and was a member of the Royal Society of Musicians for half a century. At the Festival in York Minster in September 1823 he was first of eight bassoons and played the obbligato to Dr. Boyce's song 'Softly arise, O Southern Breeze'. He retired about 1830, having married a lady of means, and died 23 March 1844 in his seventy-eighth year.

MILLER—described by Burney as 'the best bassoon I can remember'—was a London soloist from c. 1750. The Public Advertiser of 17 March 1760 announced the first of a series of Subscription Concerts at the Little Theatre in the Haymarket when the programme included a bassoon concerto by 'Mr. Miller'. Miller was principal at the Three Choirs, Worcester, in 1755 and continued to take part in the Festival until 1768. His second, throughout, was Adcock. About 1750 morning concerts were instituted in London and Busby recounts that 'Miller, the superior bassoon of his time, contributed to enrich the band'. He was principal at the 'Messiah' performed at the Foundling Hospital, 3 May 1759, and also played at Ranelagh. Jones' Encylo. Londoniensis (1797-) states 'In the last age, Miller was the most esteemed performer on the bassoon at all public places in England. At present, Holmes is the favourite'.

RICHARD NEWTON (1895-) first studied, 1911-13, under Paul Draper (elder brother of Charles Draper the famous clarinettist), and in 1914 gained a scholarship at the R.A.M. Starting on a Hawkes 'Morton' model French-system bassoon he shortly after changed to a

Buffet. His scholarship was interrupted by war-service 1915–19. After completing his course he was appointed 4th bassoon in the L.S.O. and a year later organist as well for the L.S.O.

Beginning with the Promenade Concerts of 1924 he was appointed 1st bassoon of the New Queen's Hall Orchestra by Sir Henry Wood in succession to Wilfred James. From 1923–30 he was 1st in the London Chamber Orchestra under Anthony Bernard. In 1930, on the formation of the B.B.C. S.O. which, in that year, took over the Proms., he became 1st bassoon. In 1931 he changed over to the Heckel bassoon—being influenced in this by the B.B.C. From 1933–46 he was 2nd principal and principal from 1946 until his retirement in 1959. Before removing to Yorkshire, where he now lives in the peace of Wensleydale, he was co-principal with Roger Hagger at the Royal Opera, Covent Garden, for the 1959–60 season.

KARL OEHLBERGER (1912–) was born in St. Pölten, Austria, and from the age of eight received instruction in piano and violin from his father, a music teacher who had an amateur orchestra. In this group, for which all instruments were provided by his father, Karl learned much about both strings and wood-wind. At the weekly practices he had to take the place of missing players and later conducted his own small orchestra and became choir-master of three choral societies. When his father completed his orchestral resources by adding a bassoon, Karl began his study of the instrument in 1930 under Professor Karl Strobl at the Vienna Academy of Music. In 1936 he passed his final examination and was at once appointed 1st bassoon at the Vienna State Opera and the Vienna Philharmonic Orchestra, thus becoming a member of the Wind Ensemble of the Vienna Philharmonic. In 1938 he followed in the steps of his teacher by becoming professor at the Academy of Music. He counts among his pupils many noted European players and American bassoonists have gone to Vienna to benefit by his instruction.

JOHN PARKER, besides playing oboe and bassoon, was a wood-wind maker at 52 Long Lane, Southwark, *c.* 1770–1804, and at 3 Angel Court, Strand, 1804–*c.* 1815. Nearly a dozen of his six-keyed bassoons have been recorded, besides flutes, flageolets and even a six-keyed clarinet. Canon Galpin credited Parker with having invented the cross-blown flageolet, a rare specimen of which is in Buxted Church, Sussex. Parker played in concerts of the New Musical Fund, the Handel Society and in Westminster Abbey.

JEREMIAH PARKINSON, about whom Parke relates an amusing incident at Yarmouth, played at Hanover Square Rooms in 1791. Parke played at a concert here with Parkinson and refers to 'his great and neat execution . . . his tone was remarkably sweet, having none of that nasal quality which occasioned a medical friend of mine to observe that the upper notes of the bassoon, in general, appeared to him like a hautboy labouring under a cold'. Parke described Parkinson as 'generally acknowledged to be one of the first bassoon-players in Europe'.

JOHN PARR (1869–1963). This notable bassoonist had a very long and interesting career. Born in Sheffield, 6 March 1869, he first became a chorister until, at the age of twenty-one, he commenced to learn the bassoon under F. Foulds (of the Hallé Orchestra 1884–95). He sang at the First Sheffield Triennial Festival under August Manns and played the bassoon at the Second Festival under Henry J. Wood. He formed a collection of wood-wind instruments and played solos on the baritone oboe, the tenoroon and double-bassoon. For nearly sixty years he played as an extra in orchestras, including the Hallé, the Liverpool Philharmonic, B.B.C. Northern, Scottish and Scottish Variety Orchestras and the L.S.O. He recalled having seen Sullivan conduct 'The Golden Legend' at Leeds Festival in 1889.

In 1930 he commenced an annual winter series of six Chamber Concerts of unfamiliar music for wind instruments with and without piano and with vocalists. At these concerts during twenty-seven years, he played solos besides taking part in ensembles. He travelled widely in Europe and copied out unpublished works for bassoon and other woodwind for his Winter concerts. In 1960, at the age of ninety-one, he fulfilled his last engagement. When he wrote to the author sending the notes from which this biography is compiled, he was still practising daily and holding house parties for ensemble playing. In 1963 he died peacefully in hospital in London at the ripe age of ninety-four. All who knew him retain the memory of a genial kindly old musician, full of pawky humour and bonhomie. He donated a part of his collection to Weston Park Museum, Sheffield. The remainder was dispersed in 1964.

In 1899 Hans Richter became conductor of the Hallé Orchestra and soon decided to introduce the German-system bassoon. OTTO SCHIEDER (died in Vienna 1950) arrived first from Vienna in 1903 remaining until 1914. In 1904 WICHTL arrived to join Schieder, retiring with Richter in 1913. In 1904 Richter gave two five-year

Bassoon Scholarships to the Royal Manchester College of Music where Schieder had become professor, and the awards were made to Archie Camden and Maurice Whittaker.

SOL SCHOENBACH (1915–) is among the best-known American bassoonists. Starting to learn the piano at age five, he commenced bassoon at age ten at the Hecksher Foundation, New York. He received a scholarship at fifteen to the Institute of Musical Art (later merged with the Julliard School of Music). He then became staff bassoonist with the Columbia Broadcasting Company and in 1937 he joined the Philadelphia Orchestra as 1st bassoon, a position which he held for twenty years; including membership of the Army Service Forces Orchestra 1944–6. Sol Schoenbach has had much to do with Children's Orchestral Concerts and in 1950 he was among the organisers of the Philadelphia Woodwind Quintet, known for its virtuoso performances and recordings. The Quintet has toured extensively since 1954. He now teaches at the Curtis Institute of Music, Philadelphia, and at the Settlement Music School, Philadelphia, besides making frequent appearances as guest soloist in concerts.

GEORGE FREDERICK SCHUBERT was another of the bassoonists at the Abbey in 1784. According to Doane's *Directory* he lived in King Street, Soho, and played both trombone and bassoon at concerts of the New Musical Fund established in 1786. Parke in his *Memoirs* (II, 215) records an incident at Drury Lane Theatre *c.* 1785 when Schubert had in his bassoon part a long held note of several bars which he was unable to sustain. When he stopped, the leader called to him 'Hold out that note'. Schubert replied in his quiet way: 'It is very easy for you, Mr. Baumgarten, to say hold out that note, but who is to find *de vind?*'

A. G. SCHWARZ (1743–1804). First mentioned by Burney who heard him in 1772 at Ludwigsburg. Schwarz came to London in 1784 for Lord Abingdon's Concerts and played with Holmes at the King's Theatre, at Vauxhall and at the Haydn-Salomon Concerts. Returning to Germany in 1787, he joined the Berlin Court Orchestra.

CHRISTIAN GOTTLIEB SCHWARZ, eldest son of the foregoing, was born in Württemberg in 1768. He received his early instruction on the bassoon from his father whom he accompanied to London in 1784. Although only sixteen years of age, he was engaged for the band of the Prince of Wales (later George IV) till it was disbanded in 1787.

N

Thereafter he joined the Berlin Court Orchestra, was pensioned in 1826 and died in Berlin in 1829.

WILLIAM HENRY STONE (1830–91). This remarkable man was a physician and amateur musician of varied and brilliant attainments. Educated at Charterhouse and Balliol College, Oxford, he devoted study to the physics of music and electricity, becoming meanwhile a skilful performer upon the tenoroon, bassoon and contra as well as the clarinet and basset-horn. Between 1856 and 1861 he travelled widely in Europe and may then have met with the contrabassophon invented by H. J. Haseneier of Coblenz in 1849. (*Vide* Chapter 8.) Acquiring one of these contras, he introduced it to English orchestral music at the Handel Festival of 1871. In 1879 he played oboe da caccia parts on the tenoroon in F at the Three Choirs at Hereford. In 1881 he became lecturer in Acoustics at Trinity College of Music and contributed many articles on wood-wind instruments to the first edition of Grove's *Dictionary*. In addition to papers on medical and electrical subjects, including the Harveian Oration of 1887, he was author of *Sound as Music* (1876): *The Scientific Basis of Music* (1878); and *Elementary Lessons in Sound* (1879).

GEORGE W. TROUT was a well-known London bassoonist in the 1870's. He took part in the Fourth Leeds Festival in 1880 and was professor at the R.A.M. from 1880–3. Two of his sons became London theatre and orchestral players in the 1890's, one being also a reed-maker. Richard Newton recalls 'Trout reeds' *c.* 1914, the large bassoon reeds still then in use, bound with bright red waxed thread.

J. G. WAETZIG was 1st of the four bassoons in the private band of George IV. His bandmaster, Christian Kramer, in 1826 said of him that he was 'a most respectable man and the best bassoon-player in England'. He continued in the private band of Queen Victoria in 1837 and in 1846 became bandmaster of the 2nd Life Guards. In 1861 he was 1st bassoon at Hereford in succession to Baumann and played at the Philharmonic Concerts in the 'sixties. In 1875 he received the sinecure appointment of Sergeant-Trumpeter at the Court of St. James.

WESTON was bassoonist in the Duke of Chandos' private band at Cannons in 1720.

JOHN WINTERBOTTOM (1817–97), bassoonist, with his brothers

A. Winterbottom (double-bass) and William (trombone) were all members of Jullien's Orchestra between 1840 and 1852. After some years as a bandmaster in Melbourne and Sydney, Australia, he became bandmaster successively of the Royal Marine Artillery (1870) and of the Artists' Rifle Corps (1892).

RONALD WALLER (1916–   ). Commenced to learn the bassoon in the band of the Duke of York's School. Then followed study at Trinity College of Music, London (1937–9) under Edward Dubrucq, and at the R.A.M. (1939–44) under Richard Newton. After serving in the band of the Grenadier Guards he was appointed principal bassoon in the London Symphony Orchestra, resigning after seven years in 1955. As a free-lance player, he became a founder member of the Virtuoso Chamber Ensemble of London and of the Sinfonia of London Orchestra. Later he joined the New Philharmonia Orchestra, in which he still plays, and in 1962 became a professor at the R.A.M.

WM. R. WATERHOUSE (1931–   ). Started by learning piano, clarinet and bass clarinet. In 1946 took up the bassoon and won a scholarship at the R.C.M. in 1948 where he studied for three and a half years. Played in the R.A.F. Central Band (1949–51). Joining the Philharmonia Orchestra as 4th Bassoon, he played during foreign tours. Then followed two years with the Royal Opera, Covent Garden. He then joined Radio Svizzera Italiana, Lugano (1955–8), after which he became first in the L.S.O. and joined the Melos Ensemble. In 1964 he became co-principal in the B.B.C. Symphony Orchestra where he is still. His interest in bassoon repertoire led to his compilation of a list of works appended to A. Camden's *Bassoon Technique*. He gave the first performance of Skalkottas' Sonata Concertante at Leeds Festival 1964 and has given radio performances of rare works. During the past ten years he has completely altered his playing technique and now plays with a special straight crook and spike supporting the bassoon (see Chapter 11).

A. EDWARD WILSON (1901–   ). Had bassoon lessons from the age of thirteen from his father and played a ♭ pitch Mahillon with covered holes made to order for a child's use. Studied at R.C.M. (1915–18) under Tom Wotton and later Fred. James, changing to a ♯ pitch Buffet. He joined the Old Vic. Opera Company in 1919 and later as 1st played with the B.N.O.C. He played at Savoy Hill in the early days of broadcasting, and in the London Chamber Orchestra, and

Royal Albert Hall Orchestra; the B.B.C. Symphony Orchestra as 2nd (1930–46); the English Opera Group (1946–50), and the Royal Philharmonic Orchestra from 1946. He played on two American Tours with the R.P.O. and elsewhere with both the English Opera Group and the R.P.O. He is still with the R.P.O. as 2nd to Cecil James and, like him, has not allowed himself to be persuaded to transfer from the French bassoon.

WILLIAM B. WOTTON (1832–1912) joined the band of the 1st Life Guards, having learned the flute, cornet and, under John Hardy, the bassoon. Grove writes of Wotton's 'artistic style and charm of tone'. He studied orchestral playing at the R.A.M. under Charles Lucas. His first appearance as a soloist was at Windsor. On the death of Baumann in 1856, Wotton was forbidden by Waddell, his bandmaster, to accept the position and he was transferred to the saxophone, of which he was the earliest player in England. In 1866 his colonel allowed him to join the orchestra of the Crystal Palace in which he played first bassoon until his retiral in 1897. He played in the orchestras of the Philharmonic, Albert Hall, Three Choirs, and the Festivals at Leeds, Sheffield and Birmingham. He was professor of bassoon at the R.C.M. 1883–1905 and at the R.A.M. 1883–1912, for the last six years jointly with E. F. James. W. B. Wotton was faithful to his high-pitch brass-keyed Savary bassoon throughout his long life.

THOMAS E. WOTTON (1852–c. 1918) was the much younger brother of W. B. Wotton and like him began his musical career in the 1st Life Guards. Second only to his brother he excelled as a bassoonist in chamber-music. He was for many years from 1879 2nd to his brother in the Crystal Palace Orchestra, succeeding to the 1st chair on his brother's retiral in 1897. He was professor at the R.C.M. from 1906 to 1918. Like his brother he played a high-pitch Savary bassoon with brass keys and a low-pitch Triébert.

Bassoon and Contra Makers and Dealers

* = Born   † = Died   (C) = Contra-maker

Name	Place	Date	No. of Keys or Source
Adler, K. F.	Bamberg	*1795 †1888	11
Adler, F. A.	Paris	*1813	—
Adler, F. G.	Paris	..1809 †1854	8/13
Adler, Oskar & Co.	Markneu-kirchen	Founded 1885	German system
Albert, Jacques fils	Brussels	Founded 1846	16/19
Aldorf	Linz	Early 19th century	10
Amlingue, Michel	Paris	c. 1782–c. 1826	5/8
Anciuti, Joh. M. (C)	Milan	c. 1717–40	9-keyed contra
Ashbury, John	London	pre-1690–post 1699	Trade-card, B.M.
Astor, Geo. & Co.	London	1784–1826	6/8
Auger, I.	Rouen	—	7
Babb, G.	?	—	6-keyed tenoroon
Bachmann, G. C.	Brussels	*1804 †1842	Made Willent-Bordogni bassoon
Baesler, H.	Memmingen	*1781 †1850	8
'Barbier'	Paris	Modern	Trade-name
Baumann (C)	Paris	1800–30	7. Advertised contras in 1825
Beltrami	Lugano	c. 1835	10
Berthold, G. & Söhne (C)	Speyer a/Rh.	1849–88	19/20 and contra
Besson & Co.	London	1869–	17
Bilton, R. J. 'apprentice & foreman to Cramer, London'.	London	1826–55	12/13/15
Blockley, John	Ullesthorpe, Leics.	*1735 †1798	4 & 4-keyed tenoroon
Boosey & Co., later Boosey & Hawkes	London London	Founded 1816⎱ Founded 1930⎰	18 Full German or French systems
Bradka, Wenzel	Gumpolds-kirchen, near Vienna	1822–1907	Contra
Bruggemann, F. G. B.	Leiden	? †1899	12/13
Buffet, A. Jne.	Paris	1831–85	16
Buffet-Crampon & Cie (C)	Paris	1836–	17/20 and 16-keyed tenoroon and contra

Name	Place	Date	No. of Keys or Source
Buhner & Keller	Strasbourg	*c.* 1780–*c.* 1837	7/13 and 7-keyed octave-bassoon
'Buisson, F.'	Paris	Modern	Trade-name
Bunau	?	?	4
Cahusac, Thos.	London ⎱	†1798	4 '1769'; 6 tenoroons,
Cahusac, W. M.	London ⎰	1755–1814	4, '1788'
Carlström, I.	Stockholm	*c.* 1806	6 '1806'
Catlin, Bliss & Co.	Hartford, Conn.	*c.* 1827	6
Červený, V. F. (c)	Königgrätz	*1819. Founded 1842	Contras: brass
Chappel, S. A., late Jullien & Co.	London	Founded 1812	Fr. system (agent for Courtois)
Christman, C. G.	New York	1828–57	6
Clementi, M. & Co.	London	1802–	8
Coigne, Joshua	?	?	3-keyed fagottino
Collier, T.	London	*c.* 1773	5/9
Conn, C. G.	Elkhart, Ind.	1890–	
Corcoran, Matthew	Dublin	1840–42	11
Cotton, William	London	*c.* 1763	Trade-card in B.M.
Couesnon & Cie	Paris	*c.* 1884–	
Cowlan	Liverpool	1823–4	6
Cramer & Key	London	1805–7	9
Cramer & Son	London	1807–24	6
Crone, I. A.	Leipzig?	?	8
Cuvillier	St. Omer	early 19th century	8/11
D'Almaine & Co.	London	1835–58	6/9
Deloose	Ghent	?	7
Delusse, Christopher	Paris	1783–9	7-keyed octave bassoon
Delusse, Jacques	Paris	1752–69	—
Denman	London	*c.* 1784–94..	7/8
Denner, Jacob	Nürnberg	†1735	—
Denner, Joh. Chr.	Nürnberg	*1655 †1707	3
Des Costeaux	Paris	..1692..	Livre commode
Distin, Henry John	London	..1857–68..	14 (by Gautrot?)
Doelling, C. Fr. & Sohn (c)	Potsdam	'1850'	Contrabassophon
Doke, Alois	Linz	..1823..	10
Doke, Karl (c)	Linz	*c.* 1778–1826	11 and contras, 5/6
Dondeine	?	?	4
Dujariez, E. J. M.	Paris	1831–1855	16
Dupré, Joseph	Tournai	*c.* 1825	At Haarlem Exhib. 1825
Dupré, P. P. G. J.	Tournai	*1790 †1862	8
Durrier & Muller	Strasbourg	—	7
Eichentopf, Andreas	Nordhausen	*c.* 1670–1721	3-keyed contra, dated 1714

Name	Place	Date	No. of Keys or Source
Eichentopf, Joh. Heinr.	Leipzig	*1678 †1769	4
Eisenbrant, C. H.	Göttingen	*1790–	7-keyed tenoroon
Eisenmenger, Joh. G.	Mannheim	*1698 †1742	5 wooden keys
Estrella, D. José	Madrid	..1786..	Dict. B. Saldoni (1868)
Evette & Schaeffer (c)	Paris	1885–	*Vide* Buffet-Crampon
Esposito, Giosué	Naples	c. 1913	24
Felix, C. H.	Paris	c. 1840	7. Inventor-mechanic
Finke, F. H. (c)	Dresden	c. 1822	8/9, contra, 7
Floth, J. F.	Dresden	pre-1807	6/7
Folgmann, J.	?	?	8
Fontaine Besson (c)	London and Paris	c. 1890	Contra
Fox Products Corpn.	So. Whitley, Ind., U.S.A.	Modern	—
Freyer, J. G.	Potsdam	..1775..	8
Freyer & Martin	Potsdam	..1816..	7
Fröhlich	Mittelbach	18th century	4/5
Franklin, Charles	London	1805–9	8
Galander	Paris	1835–55	19-keyed galandronome
Garrett	London	..1826–62	11
Gautrot, P. L. aîné	Paris		Paris Exhib. 1867
Gautrot aîné Durand & Cie	Paris	1847–82	Paris Exhib. 1878
Gautrot-Marquet (c)	Paris		19; brass contra, 17
Gedney, Caleb	London	..1754–†69	4/6
Gehring (*cf.* Jehring)	Adorf	c. 1788	5
Geipel, C. (c)	Breslau	c. 1850	Contrabassophon, 17
Geisler, C. G.	Amsterdam	1801–84	16
Gerock, C. (& Co.)	London	1804–21	6/9
Gerock & Wolf	London	1831–7	8
Goeppert	Meleyn?	—	Fleischer's Berlin Catal.
Goulding, Geo.	London	1786–98	6/9
Goulding, Wood & Co.	London	1799–1806	5/8
Goulding & Co.	London	1806–10	6
Goulding d'Almaine (Potter) & Co.	London	1811–23	6/11
Goumas, P. et Cie (c)	Paris	1865–85	*Vide* Buffet-Crampon
Grenser, Karl Aug.	Dresden	*1720 †1805	5/7/8
Grenser, Joh. Heinrich Wilhelm (c)	—	*1764 †1813	5-keyed contra in F 6-keyed fagottino
Grenser & Wiesner	Dresden	—	5/8/9/11/13-keyed bassoons
Greve	Mannheim	..1830–55	14
Griessling & Schlott	Berlin	1808–35	7

Name	Place	Date	No. of Keys or Source
Gritschker, J.	?	?	7
Grundmann, J. F.	Dresden	*1727 †1800	4
Haka, Richard	Amsterdam	1645–1709	Trade-card, 4
Hale, John	London	1784–1804	6
Hamich	Dresden?	?	5
	—Neustadt		
Hanken, G. J. F.	Rotterdam	*1849 †1935	14
Hart, Joseph	London	1830–58	7
Hartmann, J. G. L.	Hamburg	*1773 †1835	14
Haseneier, H. J. (c)	Coblenz	*1835 †1921	16/20; contrabasso-phon, 19
Hasler, John	London	1830–44	6/8
Hawkes (& Son), (& Co.)	London	1860–1930	French system
Heckel (c)	Biebrich a/Rh.	1831–	16/21 ; contra
Heerde, J. J. van	Amsterdam	c. 1731	Danzig Inventory
Heinze, I. G.	Leipzig	—	8
Hell, F.	Brünn	c. 1854	11
Helwert, Jacob	Stuttgart	c. 1851	19
Hess, W.	Munich	c. 1873	16
Hirsbrunner	Sumiswald ⎫	Founded 1847	8/12
Hirsbrunner, F.	Grünen ⎭		6
Hohl	Lutzenberg	—	6
Horák, Johann	Prague	*1817 †1884	10/16
Horák, Wenzel (c)	Prague	*1788 †1854	Contras, 5/7
Hörmann	?	?	6 (error for Börmann?)
Howarth, George	London	*1860 †1933	Made for Boosey
Howell, David	London	c. 1898 †1914	13
Hüller	Germany	Modern	—
Huttl, Ignaz	Graslitz	—	8/9
I. IR.	Swiss?	..1777..	3
Jacoby fils	Auch	?	5
Jeantet	Lyon	?	7
Jehring, C. F. A.	Mainz	*1798 †1837	13/16/17
Jehring, Julius	Adorf	*1824 †1905	8
Jung	Marseilles	c. 1830	Léry Coll. Sale
Kaiser	Zug	?	6/8
Kenigsperger, J. W.	Roding	†1752	3
Key, Thos. (& Co.)	London	1807–53	12/15/16
Kies, W. (c)	Vienna	c. 1820	9; tenoroon 9/10; contra 6
Kirst, F. G. A.	Potsdam	*1750 †1806	5/6/7
Kleinert	Breslau	—	20
Knikker, I v.d.	Tilborch	*1731 †1815	4
Koch, Stephan (c)	Vienna	*1772 †1828	Contra
Kohler, John	London	1790–3	8
Kohlert, V. Söhne	Graslitz	Founded 1840	—
Kohlerth, Ignatz	Graslitz	?	11
Kraus, C.	?	?	4-keyed fagottino 4-keyed tenoroon

Name	Place	Date	No. of Keys or Source
Kraus, J.	?	?	5; fagottino 3
Krauss, E.	?	?	3-keyed tenoroon
Kress, W.	?	?	5-keyed dulzian
Kretzschmann, C.	Strasbourg	c. 1830	7
Kruspe, E.	Erfurt	—	20
Kusder	London	..1762–1799..	5
Kuss, Wolfgang (c)	Vienna	..1811–38	11/15; contra 5
Kuteruf, J.	?	?	3
Lafleur, J. R. (c)	London	..1870–1910..	French system: contra
Lange, C. O. (c)	St. Petersburg	c. 1875	Contra, 9
Lange, Reinhold	Wiesbaden	c. 1892	18/21
Laussmann, I. A.	Linz	c. 1855–67	16
Lavenstein, C.	?	?	3
Lecomte, A. & Cie	Paris	*1818 †1892	Brass bassoon, 17
Lehner, Martin	Munich	19th century	Brass bassoon, 18
Leiberz	Coblenz	'1700'	7-key fagottino
Lempp, Martin (c)	Vienna	..1788–1822..	8; contras, 5/6
Lesher, Wood-Wind Co.	Elkhart, Ind.	Modern	German system
Lienecke, C.	Leipzig	?	5
Lindemann	Strasbourg	?	8
Lindholm	Stockholm	c. 1805	7
Lindner, Leonhard	Augsburg	c. 1820	4
Linton Mfg. Coy.	Elkhart, Ind.	Modern	German system
Lot, Isodore	Paris	..1867–1878..	19
Lot, Martin	Paris	c. 1785	5-keyed fagottino
Lot, Thomas	Paris	c. 1740–85..	Tablettes de Renommée
Lott, D.	?	?	4
Louis Mus. Inst. Co. Ltd.	London	1923–	French system Merged with Rudall Carte
Ludwig, F.	Prague	?	13
Lutz, Bartholomaeus	Wolfhalden	c. 1800	6
Luvoni, U.	Milan	?	7
Mahillon, C.	Brussels	*1813 †1887	French system
Mahillon & Co. (c)	Brussels London	Founded 1836 Founded 1844	18; brass contra, 15
Maino & Orsi	Milan	c. 1880	21
Majorano, Fratelli	Naples	—	21
Maldura, A.	Milan	..1871–85..	8/9, Cremonesi system
Martin frères	Paris	1840–1939	German system
Marzoli, A.	Paris	c. 1850	28/29, Boehm system
Mayer, H.	Lienz	Late 18th century	Contra (incomplete)
Meacham, J. & H.	Albany, N.Y.	1824–8	4
Medel, J.	Graslitz	—	8
Meinhart	?	Modern	German system
Meissner, K. Herm.	Hof (Bavaria)	Modern	German system

Name	Place	Date	No. of Keys or Source
Melchor, R. S.	?	17th century	Bajoncillos
Metzler, V. (& Co.)	London	1788–†1840	6/8/10
Meyer, H. F.	Hanover	..1864..	16/18
Milhouse, W.	Newark	..1763–88	4/5/6
Milhouse, W. (& Son)	London	1789–1838	5/6/7/8/9/10/11
Mollenhauer, J. (& Söhne)	Fulda	Founded 1822	10/11/13
Mollenhauer, G. & Söhne	Cassel	Founded 1864	20
Mönnig, Gebrüder	Markneu-kirchen	Modern	German system
Moritz, C. W. (c)	Berlin	*1811 †1855	13; contras, 13/20; klaviaturkontrafagott
Morton, A. (& Sons) (c)	London	*1827 †1898	18; tenoroon, 16; contras in C and F
Müller	?	?	Fagottino, 4
'Muraeus'	?	mid-18th century	Maker's mark? On Stanesby bassoon dated 1747
Nechwalsky, A.	Vienna		11
Ott, F.	Wurzburg		9
Pace, Charles	London	1834–49	6/12
Pace, Frederick	London	1831–65	6
Parent, Michel	Amsterdam	†1711	Dutch newspaper advert.
Paridaens, Désiré	Paris	1829–56	Simple French system
Parker, John	London	c. 1770–c. 1815	5/6/8
Pask, John (& Co.)	London	1840–72	8
Peale, T.	?	?	7-keyed tenoroon
Pelitti (c)	Milan	c. 1853	Contra
Peuckert & Sohn (c)	Breslau	..1802–35..	10/15; contra, 6
Pezé	Paris	1800–30	6
Philidor	Paris	Livre Commode 1692	cf. Rousselet
Piana, P.	Milan	—	7
Piele, C. A.	Rudolstadt	?	? De Wit Coll. No. 388
Polisi, W. Bassoon Corpn.	New York	Modern	German system
Porthaux, Dominique	Paris	c. 1782–1824	5/6/7
Preston, John (& Son)	London	1773–1834	6/9
Proser	London	..'1795'..	4/5
Prowse	(Dublin)?	(1816–68)	9. Error for London?
Prudent, père et fils	Paris	c. 1769–1830	5/6, cf. Thierriot
Püchner, Josef (c)	Nauheim	Founded 1897	German system bas-soons and contras

Name	Place	Date	No. of Keys or Sour
Raingo, Nicolas Marcel	Mons	*1746 †1823	7
Rastouil	Toulouse	..1829–31..	Bottin (Directory)
Riedl, E. K.	Graslitz	Modern	German system
Riedl, I. V.	(Vienna?)	?	4
Rijkel, Coenraad	Amsterdam	*1667	4 (Trade-card)
Robert, Alexandre	Paris	1868–1920	—
Roberts, Alfred	Birmingham	c. 1900	—
Roeder, Charles	Vienna	..1862..	Internal. Exhib. 1862
Rorarius, Augustin	Vienna	..1813–48	5/7
Roth, J. F.	Adorf?	—	3
Rott, Vincenz Josef (c)	Prague	pre-1854	Contra, 8
Rousselet	Paris	..1692..	cf. Philidor supra
Roome, F.	Derby	..1794..	4 (originally); dealer
Rosa, R. de	Naples	—	(Dealer) tenoroon, 11
Roth, Ferd.	Milan	Modern	French system
Royan, A. D.	London	..1907–†1922	13
Rudall-Carte & Co.	London	1878–	French imports
Rust	Lyons	—	7
Rust, Veuve et Dubois	Lyons	—	7
Samme, J. (c)	London	c. 1855	Semi-contra in G: 8
Sautermeister & Müller	Lyons	1830–	6 and 1 wing-key
Savary père	Paris	c. 1788–1826	9
Savary jeune	Paris	c. 1823–50	Full French system
Sax père	Brussels	*1791 †1865	Improved bassoon, 1830
Sax, Adolphe	Paris	*1814 †1894	Improved bassoon, 1840 and 1851
Saxton, Thomas	Nottingham	c. 1799	G tenoroon, 4
Schadenberg, Franz	Dresden	19th century	14
Schamal, Wenzel (c)	Prague	c. 1854	Contra, 20
Schaufler, Carl August	Stuttgart	*1792 †1877	10/14 Neukirchner's model
Scherer, I.	Paris	c. 1750	4; tenoroons, 4
Schiele, W.	?	—	9
Schimmel, J.	Vienna	—	11(perhaps Schemmel)
Schöllnast, F. (c)	Pressburg		Contra, 6
Schott, B. Söhne (c)	Mainz	1780–	Contra, 6
			16, Almenräder Bassoon; contras, 6/8
Schreiber, W. & Söhne	Nauheim	1946–	German system
Schubert, Geo.	Paris	1854–7	Bought up Adler, Savary & Galander
Schuster, G. (c)	Vienna	—	Contra, 7
Schuster, Gottfried	Markneu-kirchen	—	Fagottino, 6
Seelhoffer (c)	Berne	—	Contra (incomplete

Name	Place	Date	No. of Keys or Source
Seidel, Joseph	Mainz	1820–62	Internat. Exhib. 1862
Selmer, Henri	Paris	1890–	—
Silvani & Smith, Ward & Sons	London	1884–	Lavignac, p. 1559 Importers of wood-wind
Simiot, Jacques François	Lyons	c. 1803–35	9
Sioli, L. (c)	Milan	Modern	French system bassoons and contras
Spada, Gaetano	Bologna	..1873–88..	Exhibs. Vienna 1873 and Bologna 1888. Metal bassoon
Stanesby, Thomas, senior	London	†1734	—
Stanesby, junior (c)	London	*1692 †1754	4; contra, 4
Stecher, Josef I	Vienna	*1874 †1932	—
Stecher, Josef II	Vienna	*1914–	—
Stecher, Karl	Vienna	*1820 †1904 Founded 1865	At Vienna Exhib., 1873, bassoons and a tritonikon
Steegmans, Benoit Antoine	Malines	*1784 †1848	—
Stehle, Johann (c)	Vienna	c. 1840–1855	15/19; contra, 15
Stengel, Joh. Samuel	Bayreuth	c. 1810–54	8/11/16/17
Streitwolf, Joh. Heinrich Gottlieb	Göttingen	*1779 †1837	14
Stritter, Friedrich	Biebrich a/Rh.	1871–96	Heckel workman. 'Stritter Syst.', contra 1877
Sutter	Appenzell	..1788..	4
Tauber, Kaspar (c)	Vienna	..1799–1836..	7/9; contras, 5/7
Thibouville, Martin fils ainé (c)	Paris	c. 1820–83	Metal contra, Paris Exhib. 1889
Thierriot, Prudent	Paris	c. 1775	cf. Prudent, supra
Tölcke, H. C.	Brunswick	c. 1775	4
Triébert, Frédéric (c)	Paris	*1813 †1878	19; also Boehm system and contras
Tuerlinckx, J. A. A. (c)	Malines	*1753 †1827	4/5/7 and contras
Tuerlinckx, C. J. J. (c)	Malines	*1783 †1855	
Truška, S. J. (c)	Praga, Poland	1735–1809	5/6; contra, 6
Uhlmann, Leopold	Vienna	.1830–95..	19
Uhlmann, Joseph & Sons	Vienna	..1800–51..	7/17/18
Uhlmann, Joseph Tobias (c)	Vienna		Contra, 7
Vezzelli, Pietro	Bologna	..1883–88..	Boehm bassoon, key-work
Vidal, J.	Barcelona	..1914..	(Dealer) Brass bassoon

Name	Place	Date	No. of Keys or Source
Ward, Cornelius (& Sons)	London	c. 1836–70	Bassoon patent 1853
Weber, Karl (c)	Graz	—	Contra, 8
Werner, C. C.	Leipzig	—	8/10
Wernicke	Berlin	—	16
Whitaker	London	..1770–78..	6
Wiesner	Dresden	c. 1810–c. 1830	6/12/13/16; successor to Grenser
Wietfelt, Erich	Burgdorf?	early 18th century	4
Wietfelt, Philipp Gottlieb	Burgdorf?	early 18th century	4
Wietfelt, Harmen	Burgdorf?	early c. 1720	4
Wijne, Robert	Nymwegen	*1698 †1774	4
Willis & Goodlad	London	1825–9	8/16
Winckler, J. C.	Leipzig	—	6
Winnen, Jean (fils)	Paris	*1795 †1867	'Bassonore' at Paris Exhib., 1844, for military use.
Winnen, Nicolas W. (père)	Paris	..1788–†c. 1834	7
Wood, James	London	1799–1819	8; made bassoons for other makers
Wood, James & Son	London	1819–29	9; alto fagotto, 7
Wood & Ivy (late Geo. Wood)	London	1837–47	8
Wrede, Herman	London	c. 1810–c. 1820	6
Wrede, Herman, junr.	London	c. 1832–49	
Wrede, W.	London	c. 1815–36	
Wünderlich, C. A.	Siebenbrunn	Founded 1854	German system
Wussinger, F.	Klagenfurt	—	9 keyed-quint-fagott
Ziegler, Johann (c)	Vienna	Founded 1820–47	10/15; contra, 9-keys
Ziegler, Joh. & Sohn	Vienna	1847–55	8–16 in 1855

APPENDIX II

Inventories of Musical Instruments

Students of the history of the bassoon will derive much information from the lists of collections in the sixteenth–eighteenth centuries. To facilitate reference to these, the following selective list is offered.

D.D.T.   Denkmäler deutscher Tonkunst.
G.S.J.   Galpin Society Journal.
O.E.I.   Old English Instruments of Music (F. W. Galpin).
M.f.M.   Monatshefte für Musikgeschichte.
Z.f.M.   Zeitschrift für Musikwissenschaft.

Segovia (Queen Isabella)	1503	G.S.J. IV, p. 30. Van der Straeten, *La Musique aux Pays-Bas*, Vol. VII.
Augsburg Town	1540	D.D.T. Bayern, second series, Vol. V, lvii.
Henry VIII's Collection	1547	O.E.I. Appendix 4 from Brit. Mus. Harl. 1419.
Marie of Hungary (Flanders)	1555	Van der Straeten, *op. cit. supra*, Vol. VII, p. 439.
Fugger Collection, Augsburg	1566	Peter's Year-Book (abridged list).
Accademia Filarmonica, Verona	1569	A. C. Baines, *Wood-wind Instruments and their History* (1962), p. 239.
Weimar Capell	1573	M.f.M. Jahrgang 29, 1897.
Hesse-Cassel Hofkapelle	1573	Zulauf, *Beiträge zur Geschichte der Hofkapelle*, also G.S.J. IV, pp. 31–32.
Graz Hofkapelle	1577/1590	J. Schlosser, *Die Sammlung alter Musikinstrumente* (Vienna, 1920), pp. 19–20.
Baden-Baden Hofkapelle	1582	Z.f.M. 12.
Berlin, Kurbrandenburg Hofkapelle	1582	C. Sachs, *Musik und Oper.*, 205. Also A. C. Baines *op. cit. supra*, p. 240.
Stuttgart Hofkapelle	1589	G. Bossert, *Württembergische Vierteljahrhefte für Landesgeschichte* (1912).
Dresden Schloss	1593?	H. J. Moser, *Heinrich Schütz*, p. 123.
Innsbruck (Ambras) (*cp.* 1665)	1596	J. Schlosser, *op. cit. supra*, pp. 11–12.
Innsbruck (Ambras: Ruhelust)	1596	J. Schlosser, *op. cit. supra*, pp. 12–13.
Philip II of Spain	1598	Jahrbuch für kunsthistorisches Sammlungen, Jahrgang 19 (2), cxxxii: also van der Straeten, *op. cit. supra*.
Modena (Este)	{1600 / 1625}	Van der Straeten, *op. cit. ante*, Vol. VI, 117.
Hengrave Hall, Essex	1603	J. Gage, *History and Antiquities of Hengrave* (1822).

192

Hesse-Cassel Hofkapelle	1613	Zulauf, *Beiträge zur Geschichte der Hof-kapelle*: also G.S.J. IV, pp. 32–34.
	1638	Zulauf, *Beiträge zur Geschichte der Hof-kapelle*: also G.S.J. IV, p. 30.
Weimar Capell	1662	A. Aber, *Die Pflege der Musik unter den Wettinern* (Leipzig, 1921).
Settala Museum	1664	Scarabelli, *Museo ò Galeria del Sig. Manfred Settala*: also J. Schlosser, *op. cit. supra*, pp. 17–19.
Innsbruck (Ambras) (*cp.* 1596)	1665	Waldner, *Studien zur Musikwissenschaft*, Leipzig, Heft 4.
Berlin Hofkapelle	1667	C. Sachs, *Musik und Oper* . . .
Leipzig St. Thomas Kirche	1678	C. S. Terry, *Bach's Orchestra* (1932), p.
	1701	19: also Bach-Jahrbuch 1907, p. 38: also A. Schering, *Musikgeschichte Leipzigs* . . . (Leipzig, 1926), p. 114.
Dresden	1681	Z.f.M. 4.
Cöthen	1706	Bach-Jahrbuch, 1905.
Ossegg, Bohemia	1706	Bach-Jahrbuch, 1921, p. 96: also Z.f.M. 4.
Krems	1739	*Monatshefte für Musikgeschichte*, XX, 1888.
Sayn-Wittgenstein	1741	*Freiburger Studien zur Musikwissenshaft*, Reihe 2, Heft 1–2, 66: also A. C. Baines, *op. cit. supra*, p. 302.
Detmold	1780	Freiburger Studien, *op. cit. supra*.

Solo Music for Bassoon and Double Bassoon

T H I S list is a guide to the vast quantity of bassoon literature, from earliest known pieces to the present day. Initially it was intended to publish tables including chamber music (from duos upwards) in which the bassoon has a part, but this grew to a work as large as the rest of the book, thus Appendix III is a compilation of solo music for the bassoon. It cannot claim to be complete and most items where neither source nor publisher was known have been omitted, so have all arrangements and potpourris unless these are of interest as an example of a composer's use of the instrument.

The compiler is indebted to the publishing houses for their help in supplying information from their catalogues. His sincere thanks are due to his friends William Waterhouse (from whose collection of early bassoon literature much has been taken), Gerald Corey and Don Christlieb (both of whom diligently sought out and provided information from the Americas for this appendix and Appendix IV).

G. M.-M.

Abbreviations

* = Items no longer in print or not readily obtainable. Where known the, source of a copy is given. Ms. = Manuscript.
A.M.V. = Archiv Der Musikfreunde, Vienna
A.M.Z. = Bibliothek der Allgem. Musikgesellschaft, Zurich
B.M. = British Museum, London
F.B. = Fürstlich Fürstenbergischen Hofbibliothek, Donaueschingen
F.M. = Fitzwilliam Museum, Cambridge
M.L.B. = Mecklenbergische Landesbibliothek, Schwerin
O.W.B. = Öffenliche Wissenschaftliche Bibliothek, Berlin
T.T.H. = Thurn und Taxis'sche Hofbibliothek, Regensburg

bn = bassoon	pf = pianotorte
ca = cor anglais	rec = recorder
cbn = contrabassoon	tbn = trombone
cl = clarinet	timp = timpani
db = double bass	tp = trumpet
fl = flute	va = viola
hn = horn	vad'am = viola d'amore
hpsch = harpsichord	vad'g = viola da gamba
ob = oboe	vc = violoncello
perc = percussion	vn = violin

Section 1. Bassoon(s) Alone

Composer	Title	Publisher/Source and Date
Alcock, J. (b. 1715)	Duets	*Longman and Broderip
Alfven, H. (b. 1872)	Trio	Gehrmann
Almenräder, K.	Duo, Op. 8	*Schott
(b. 1786)	Duo, Op. 10	*Schott
Anonymous	Quartet	*Ms. Paris Conservatoire
Apostel, H. E. (b. 1901)	Sonatine Op. 19, No. 3	Universal
Bantock, G. (b. 1868)	Dance of the Witches (Trio)	Swan
	The Witches' Frolic (Trio)	Goodwin
Barreli	Duets	*Longman
Bentzon, J. (b. 1897)	Studies in Variation Form Op. 34	Skandinavisk
Bergt, A. (b. 1772)	Trio	Hofmeister
Blasius, M. F. (b. 1758)	Three Duos, Op. 30	*Leduc
	Six Duos	*British Museum
Blume, O.	Twelve Duets	Fischer
Boismortier, J. B. de (b. 1619)	Six Sonatas, Op. 14 (Duo)	*Boismortier (B.M.)
	Five Sonatas, Op. 26 (Duo)	Moeck
	Six Sonatas, Op. 40 (Duo)	*Boismortier (B.M.)
	Six Sonatas, Op. 50 (Duo)	*British Museum
	Six Petites Sonates (Duo)	*Paris National Bibl.
Bozza, E. (b. 1905)	Fifteen Etudes, Op. 64	Leduc
	Duettino (Duo)	Leduc
	Divertissements (Trio)	Leduc (1954)
Braun, C. A. P. (b. 1788)	Six Sonatas (Duo)	*Paris Conservatoire
Buchner, P. F. (b. 1614)	Sonata, Op. 4, No. 9 (Duo)	*Ms. Breslau Stadbib.
Carolo (fl. 18 Cent.)	Sonatas (Duo) (1710)	*Ms. Durham Univ. Lib.
Castil Blaze, F. H. J. (b. 1784)	Trio, Op. 17	*Paris Conservatoire
Catelinet, P. B. (b. 1910)	Suite (Duo)	Hinrichsen (1952)
Cherubini, L. (b. 1760)	Morceau pour basson (1823)	*Ms. Berlin O.W.B.
Chinzer, G. (b. 1695)	Sonata, Op. 1 (Duo) (1745)	*British Museum
Cornette, V. (b. 1795)	Eighteen Duos	Costallat
Corrette, M. (b. 1709)	Sonata (Duo)	Moeck
Couperin, F. (b. 1668)	Thirteenth Concert	Oiseau Lyre
Delcambre, T. (b. 1766)	Six Duos, Op. 2 (1796)	*Paris Conservatoire
	Six Duos, Op. 3 (1798)	*Paris Conservatoire

o

Composer	Title	Publisher/Source and Date
Devienne, F. (b. 1759)	Six Duos, Op. 3	*Paris Conservatoire
	Duos Concertantes	Kneusslin
Dhérin, G.	Sixteen Variations	Eschig
	(20 Cent.)	
Dieter, C. L. (b. 1757)	Six Duos, Op. 1	*Naples Conservatorio
	Six Duos, Op. 2	*Nageli (Zurich, A.M.Z.)
	Sechs Kleine Duetten	*Nageli
Dotzauer, J. J. F.	Three Duos, Op. 10	*Peters
(b. 1783)	Three Duos, Op. 15	*Publisher not known
Dubensky, A. (b. 1890)	Prelude and Fugue	Ricordi (1938)
	(Quartet)	
	Fugue (Octet)	Ricordi
Dumonchau, C. F.	Three Duos, Op. 27	*Vienna, A.M.V.
(b. 1775)		
Enosko-Borowski, A.	Scherzo, Op. 13	Russian State
(b. 1889)		
Erbach, F. C. (b. 1573)	Six Duos	Bärenreiter (1954)
Fesch, W. de (b. 1687)	Sonata, Op. 1 (Duo)	*LeClerc
	(1738)	
	Sonata, Op. 2 (Duo)	*LeClerc
	Sonata, Op. 3 (Duo)	*LeClerc
Fougas (b. c. 1783)	Six Duos	*Schonenberger
Fuchs, G. F. (b. 1752)	Six Trios, Op. 1	Lemoine
Gambaro, J. B.	Eighteen Etudes	International
G.A.S. (fl. 1686)	Sonata (1646)	*Ms. Modena Bibl.
Gebauer, F. R.	Twelve Airs and	*Zurich, A.M.Z.
(b. 1773)	Variations (Duo)	
	Twelve Duos	*Zurich, A.M.Z.
	Concertantes	
	Six Duos Concert-	*Sieber
	antes, Op. 25	
Geviksman, V.	Prelude and Fugue	Russian State
	(Quartet)	
Guignon, J. P. (fl. 1737)	Six Sonatas, Op. 2	*Paris, National Bibl.
	(Duo)	
Guillemant (fl. 1740)	Pieces, Op. 3 (Duo)	*Paris, National Bibl.
Haan, S. de	Suite (Trio)	Hinrichsen (20 Cent.)
Holland, T. S. (b. 1878)	Cortège (Quartet)	Hinrichsen
Jacobi, C. (b. 1756)	Two Duos, Op. 5	*Simrock
	Six Caprices	International
Jacobson, M. (b. 1896)	Three Bagatelles (Trio)	Mills
Jancourt, E. (b. 1815)	Nine Sonatas (Duo)	Costallat
	Twenty-six Etudes,	International
	Op. 15	
Küffner, J. (b. 1770)	Twenty-four Duets	Schmidt
Kummer, G. H.	Twelve Trios, Op. 11	Hofmeister
(b. 1777)	Trios, Op. 12	*Peters
	Trios, Op. 13	*Breitkopf
	Duos, Op. 1	*Leipzig, Stadtbibl.
	Duos, Op. 2	*Leipzig, Stadtbibl.
	Duos, Op. 5	*Leipzig, Stadtbibl.

Composer	Title	Publisher/Source and Date
Kunc, B. (b. 1903)	Buffoonery	Rongwen (1958)
Lapis, S.	Six Duets	*Paris, National Bibl.
Mancinelli, D. (b. 1848)	Two Sonatas (Duo)	Ricordi
Marini, B. (*fl.* 1626)	Sonata, Op. 8 (Duo)	*Ms. Breslau, Stadtbibl.
Masse, J. B. (*fl.* 18 Cent.)	Sonata, Op. 1 (Duo)	*Paris, National Bibl.
	Sonata, Op. 2 (Duo)	*Paris, National Bibl.
	Sonata, Op. 3 (Duo)	*Paris, National Bibl.
Milde, L.	Thirty Etudes, Op. 26	International
Moortel, A. van de	Partita, Op. 1	Moortel (1939)
Mulder, E. W. (b. 1898)	Trio (1942)	Donemus
Muller, P. (b. 1791)	Thirty-five Duets	Spratt
Orselli, L.	Six Grand Adagios, Op. 11	Ricordi
Osborne, W.	Rhapsody	Peters
Ozi, E. (b. 1754)	Air and Variations (Duo) (1793)	*Paris, National Bibl.
	Twenty-four Duos (1798)	*Paris, National Bibl.
	Six Duos (1800)	*Paris, National Bibl.
	Duos	*Vienna, A.M.V.
	Potpourri	*Jouve
	Six Grand Sonatas	Ricordi
	Drei Kleine Sonaten (Duo)	Hofmeister
	Twenty-four Caprices	Musica Rara
	Sonates faciles	Breitkopf
Philidor, M. D. (b. *c.* 1665)	Four Pieces	Zurfluh
Piard, M.	Sixteen Characteristic Pieces	International
Prokofiev, S. (b. 1891)	Scherzo Humoristique (Quartet)	Forberg
Ritter, G. W. (b. 1748)	Duetto	*Schwerin, M.L.B.
Saggione, G. F. (*fl.* 1733)	Six Sonatas (Duo)	*Paris, National Bibl.
Satzenhofer	Twenty Duets	International
Schiltz	Eight Duos	*Paris Conservatoire
Schmitt, N. (*fl.* mid 18 Cent.)	Air and Variations (Duo)	*Pleyel
Schneider, G. A. (b. 1770)	Three Duos	*Breitkopf
	Duette	Hofmeister
Schobert, J. (b. 1720)	Duets	*Longman and Broderip
Schröder, H. (b. 1896)	Music for Bassoon	Lienau (1958)
Schuman, W. (b. 1910)	Quartettino	Rongwen
Simonet, F. (*fl.* 1723)	Duos, Op. 1 (1791)	*Paris, National Bibl.
Stumpf, J. C. (b. 1760)	Airs (Duo)	*Paris Conservatoire
	Twelve Duos	*Simrock
Telemann, G. P. (b. 1681)	Duet	Kallmeyer
Ticciati, N.	Variations on 'Voi che sapete'	Hinrichsen (20 Cent.)

Composer	Title	Publisher/Source and Date
Tulou, J. P. (b. 1749)	Six Duos (1798)	*Paris Conservatoire
	Twelve Airs and	*Sieber
	Variations (Duo)	
Vogell, J. C. (b. 1756)	Six Duos	*Leduc
Weissenborn, J.	Six Pieces, Op. 4	*Merseburger
(b. 1837)	(Trio)	
Wellez, E. (b. 1885)	Suite, Op. 77	Rongwen

Section 2. Bassoon and Keyboard

Agafonnikov, N.	Russian Dance	Russian State (1960)
Almenräder, K.	Potpourri, Op. 3	*Schott (1824)
(b. 1786)		
Ammeler, A.	Fagotin	Hinrichsen (1960)
Amon, J. A. (b. 1763)	Sonata Concertante,	*Berlin, O.W.B.
	Op. 88	
André-Thiriet, A. L.	Theme and Variations	Leduc
	(1954)	
Antjufjev, B.	Deux Pièces, Op. 83	Russian State
	(1954)	
Bachelet, A. (b. 1864)	Ballade	Musica Rara
Bacon, E. (b. 1898)	The Woodchuck	Rongwen
Baines, F. (b. 1917)	Introduction and	Schott
	Hornpipe	
Baird, T. (b. 1928)	Four Preludes (1954)	Polish State (1955)
Balaleinikoff, V.	Three Pieces	Belwin (1939)
Balantschivadse, A.	Concertino (1954)	Russian State
Bariller, R.	Fantasio (1960)	Leduc (1960)
Bartoš, J. Z. (b. 1908)	Concertino	*Ms. copy Waterhouse
		Colln.
Beekhuis, H. (b. 1889)	Sonatine	Donemus
Ben-Haim, P. (b. 1897)	Three Songs Without	Israel Mus. Pub. (1953)
	Words	
Benson, W.	Song and Dance	Boosey (1955)
Berghmans, J.	Les Oursons Savants	Leduc
	(1958)	
Bergmann, W.	Prelude and Fugue	Schott (1950)
Bernier, R. (b. 1905)	Bassoonerie	Leduc
Berr, F. (b. 1794)	Deux Cavatibes	*Meissonnier (Schott)
	Variations on 'Ma	*Schott
	Céline'	
	Quatre Aires Variées	*Schott
Bertelin, A. (b. 1872)	Introduction and	Evette
	Rondo (1905)	
Bertoli, G. A. (fl. 1645)	Nine Sonatas (1645)	*Ms. Bologna Bibl.
		(Vincenti)
Bertoni, U.	Concerto	Bongiovanni
	Capriccio	Ricordi
Besozzi, G. (b. 1713)	Sonata	Oxford Univ. Press (1963)
Bielfeld, A.	Divertissement	Sikorski

Composer	Title	Publisher/Source and Date
Binet, J. (b. 1893)	Variations	Henn (1957)
	Morceau de Concours (1938)	Henn
Bitsch, M.	Concertino (1948)	Leduc
	Rondoletto	Leduc (1949)
	Passepied	Noël
Bloch, A. (b. 1873)	Fantasie Variée	Leduc
	Dancing Jack	Fourgéres (1957)
	Goguenardises	Noël
Blømdahl, K. B. (b. 1916)	Little Suite (1945)	Könstforlag
Boerlin, H. E.	Soliloquy	Musica Rara
Boismortier, J. B. de (b. 1691)	Sonata No. 5	Siècle Musicale (1950)
Bonnard, G.	Sonata (1937)	Ricordi
Bossi, M. E. (b. 1861)	Improvviso	Bongiovanni
	Feuillets d'album, Op. 111	Rieter-Biedermann (1897)
Bourdeau, E.	Three Solos	Leduc (Evette 1907)
Bourgault-Ducoudray, L. A. (b. 1840)	Fantasie	Evette
Boussagol, E.	Serenade	Evette
Bozza, E. (b. 1905)	Concert Etude	Leduc
	Recitative, Silicienne and Rondo	Leduc (1935)
	Burlesque	Leduc
	Fantasie (1945)	Leduc
	Espieglerie	Leduc
	Duettino	Leduc
Brakhinskas, S.	Sonatine	Russian State
Brogi, R. (b. 1873)	Visione Veneziana	Ricordi
Bruns, V.	Sonata, Op. 20	Ed. Pro Musica
Buchtel, F. L.	Crescent March	Musica Rara
Büsser, P. H. (b. 1872)	Concertino, Op. 80	Leduc
	Recitative and Thème Variée, Op. 37 (1909)	Leduc
	Pièce de Concours, Op. 66 (1917)	Leduc
	Cantiléne et Rondo, Op. 75 (1925)	Leduc
	Portuguesa, Op. 106	Leduc
Büttner, M. (P.) (b. 1870)	Improvisationen, Op. 22	Hofmeister
Cadow, P.	Variations on a Finnish Folk-song (1941)	Grosch
Carre, J. F.	Doodling	Musica Rara
Casadesus, R. (b. 1899)	Deux Pièces (1961)	Durand
Cascarino, R.	Sonata (1950)	Arrow
Castellucci, L.	Intermezzo	Musica Rara
	Capriccioso	
Chabrano, G.	Six Sonatas	*Paris, National Bibl.

Composer	Title	Publisher/Source and Date
Challan, H.	Suite	Selmer
Chapuis, A. P. (b. 1858)	Fantasie Concertante	Durand
Childs, B.	Sonata (1938)	C.C.C. New York
Clèrisse, R.	Notturno	Leduc
	Theme de Concours	Leduc
Cockshott, G.	Three Pieces on Appalachian Folktunes	Novello
Coenen, J. M. (b. 1824)	Sonata (1864)	Weygand
Cohn, A. (b. 1910)	Declamation and Toccata	Elkan-Vogel
	Hebraic Study (1944)	Elkan-Vogel (1946)
Colaco Osorio-Swaab, R. (b. 1889)	Cavatina	Donemus
	Sonatina	Donemus
Cools, E. (b. 1877)	Concertstück, Op. 80	Evette
Corrette, M. (b. 1709)	Sonatas, Op. 20 (1766)	*Paris, Bibl. l'Assenale
	Le Phenix (4 bns.)	*Paris, National Bibl.
	Sonata in D Moll	Müller
Corticelli, G.	Fantasia	Cipriani
Couprevitch, V.	Scherzino	Russian State (1956)
Dahmen, J. A. (b. 1760)	Duetto, Op. 45	*London, Dahmen (19 Cent.)
Dallier, H. (b. 1849)	Sonata in B♭	Evette
Damase, J. M. (b. 1928)	Aria, Op. 7	Salabert
Dard (fl. 1767)	Six Solos, Op. 1 (1767)	*Paris Conservatoire
	Six Solos, Op. 2 (1767)	*Paris Conservatoire
David, F. (b. 1810)	Concertino, Op. 12	Kistner, Costallat
Decruck, F.	Scherzo Fantastique	Selmer (1934)
DeLamarter, E. (b. 1880)	Folksong and Scherzetto (1950)	Witmark
	Arietta (1950)	Witmark
Delaunay, R.	Scherzando	Selmer
Delcroix, L. (b. 1880)	Prelude and Caprice	Evette
Demersseman, J.	Introduction and Polonaise, Op. 30	Costallat
Demuth, N. (b. 1898)	Sonata (1955)	*Ms. London, Demuth
Desportes, Y. B. (b. 1907)	Chanson d'Antan	Leduc (1951)
Dieter, C. L. (b. 1757)	Three Sonatas, Op. 3	*Nageli
Dodd, P.	Two Rhythmic Interludes	New Wind Music Co.
Domenico, O. di	Sonatina	Leduc
Dominschen, K.	Scherzo	Russian State (1958)
Dubois, P. M.	Sérénades	Leduc
	Virelai (1961)	Leduc (1961)
Dubrucq, E. (fl. 1900)	Humoresque	Mahillon
Duclos, R.	Fagottino	Leduc (1946)
	Three Nocturnes	Leduc
	Quadrilles	Noël
Dunhill, T. H. (b. 1877)	Lyric Suite, Op. 96	Boosey
	Intermezzo	Williams

Composer	Title	Publisher/Source and Date
Dutilleux, H. (b. 1916)	Sarabande and Cortège	Leduc
Dvarionas, B.	Theme and Variations (1952)	Russian State (1952)
Eder, H. (b. 1916)	Sonatina, Op. 34, No. 3	Doblinger
	Sonatina, Op. 36, No. 2	Doblinger
Elgar, E. (b. 1857)	Romance, Op. 62	Novello
Enosko-Borowsky, O. (b. 1889)	Poem-Nocturne, Op. 15 (1952)	Mistetstvo
Essex, K.	Suite (1952)	Ms. Essex
Etler, A. D. (b. 1913)	Sonata (1955)	American Mus. Pub.
Falcinelli, R. (b. 1920)	Berceuse (1956)	Leduc
Farkas, F. (b. 1905)	Sonatine	Musica Rara
Fasch, J. F. (b. 1688)	Sonata in C	Peters
Finkelstein, I. B.	Three Concert Pieces (1958)	Soviet Composers (1958)
Flament, E. (b. 1880)	Concertstück	Evette
	Elegie, Op. 1	Ms. copy Waterhouse Colln.
Foret, F.	Prelude, Aria and Fugue	Costallat (1936)
	Pièces Brèves (1938)	Buffet
Foster, I.	Two Simple Pieces, Op. 10	Williams (1930)
Gabaye, P.	Toccatina	Leduc
Gagnebin, H. (b. 1886)	Scherzetto	Leduc
Galliard, J. E. (b. 1680)	Six Sonatas	McGinnis, Hinrichsen
Gallois-Montbrun, R. (b. 1918)	Improvisation	Leduc
Gallon, N. (b. 1891)	Recitative and Allegro (1939)	Oiseau-Lyre
Gartenlaub, O.	Sonatine	Musica Rara
Gedda, G. C. (b. 1899)	Sonata Umoristica (1925)	Genovese
Geiser, W. (b. 1897)	Capriccio, Op. 33	Bärenreiter (1947)
Glière, R. M. (b. 1875)	Two Pieces, Op. 35, Nos. 8 and 9	Jurgenson
Goepfart, K. E. (b. 1859)	Zwei Charakterstücke, Op. 31	Hofmeister
Golz, W.	Romance	Musica Rara
Górecki, B.	Etiuda, No. 1	Czytelnik (1953)
Grimm, F. K. (b. 1902)	Sonata, Op. 113	Wrede
Groot, C. de (b. 1914)	Bassonerie (1962)	Donemus
Groot, H. de	Kleine Suite	De Wolfe
Grovlez, G. M. (b. 1879)	Sicilienne and Allegro giocoso	Costallat (1931)
	Sarabande and Allegro	Costallat
Guide, R. de	Élégie and Consolation, Op. 32	Leduc (1958)
Guillou, R.	Ballade	Gras (1936)
Haan, S. de	Scherzo	Schott (20 Cent.)
Haletzki, P.	Intermezzo and Scherzo	Musica Rara

Composer	Title	Publisher/Source and Date
Halsey, L.	Sonata	American D.C.
Harrison, P.	Faggot Dance	Chappell (1963)
Hennessy, S. (b. 1866)	Pièce Celtique, Op. 74	Eschig
Hess, W. (b. 1859)	Seven Recital Pieces	Hinrichsen
Hilmera, O. (b. 1891)	Con Umore: Three Pieces	Hudebni (1943)
Hindemith, P. (b. 1895)	Sonata	Schott (1939)
Hlobil, E. (b. 1901)	Divertimento, Op. 29	Artia (1953)
Hoffmann	Habanera	Boosey
Horder, M.	Hornpipe and Trio	Hinrichsen (1963)
Hurlstone, W. Y. (b. 1876)	Sonata in F	Cary (1907)
Ibert, J. (b. 1890)	Carignane (Arabesque)	Noël
Jacobi, C. (b. 1756)	Introduction and Polonaise, Op. 9	Schott
	Variations on a Scottish Folk Song	Ed. Pro Musica
	Potpourri, Op. 13	*Breitkopf (1834)
Jancourt, L. M. E. (b. 1815)	Eighteen Solos	Costallat
	Ninth Solo	Evette
	Duo Concertante, Op. 6	Richault
	Fantasie and Variations, Op. 11	Richault
	Neapolitan Air Variée, Op. 28	Hawkes
Jeanjean, P.	Prelude and Scherzo (1911)	Leduc
Jelescu, P.	Rapsodie Dobroglana (1956)	Rumanian State
Kaporale, A.	Sonata in D Moll	Musgis
Karosas, J.	Suite	Russian State (1959)
Kennaway, L.	Dance Arabesque	Williams
	Interrupted Serenade	Hinrichsen
Kerrison, J.	Three Young Pieces	Mills (1958)
	Suite of Dances	Mills (1958)
Kesnar, M.	Concerto (1954)	Cundy-Bettoney
Koch, H. C. (b. c. 1749)	Fantasie and Variations, Op. 27	*Schott
	Bolero en Forme de Rondo, Op. 40	*Schott (1830)
Kocken, J. F. B.	Drei Kleine Fantasien	Breitkopf
Koechlin, C. (b. 1867)	Three Pieces, Op. 34	Ms. Koechlin
	Sonata, Op. 71	Ms. Koechlin
Kohs, E. B. (b. 1916)	Sonatina (1953)	Merrymount
Kolomietz, A.	Scherzo	Russian State (1959)
Kortchmaroff	Esquisse (1924)	Russian State (1927)
Kostic, D.	Sonatina	Musik Naklada
Kostlan, M.	Two Concert Etudes	Musica Rara
Kremlev, U.	Sonata (1961)	Russian State
Krufft, N. F. von (b. 1779)	Grand Sonata in B♭, Op. 34	*Brietkopf (1818) (B.M.)
	Grand Sonata in F.	*Merchetti (1809) (B.M.)

Composer	Title	Publisher/Source and Date
Kuprewitsch, W. W.	Scherzino	Musgis
Labate, B.	Humoresque (1948)	Alfred
Lajtha, L. (b. 1892)	Intermezzo	Leduc
Lamarter, E. de (b. 1880)	Arietta and Scherzetto	Musica Rara
Lange, H.	Suite, Op. 17 (1940)	Lange
Lantier, P.	Danse Bouffonne (1949)	Leduc
Lavagne, A. (b. 1914)	Steeple-chase (1954)	Noël
Lecail, C. (fl. 1921)	Fantasie Concertante	Leduc
Levy, F.	Suite of Eight Pieces	Musica Rara
Liste, A. (b. 1774)	Sonata in F, Op. 3 (1804)	Costallat
Longo, A. (b. 1864)	Suite in G Moll, Op. 69 (1915)	Ricordi (1915)
Lovell, K.	Swing, Train and Summer Song	Elkan
Lucas, L. (b. 1903)	Orientale	Chester (1957)
Lysenko, N. (b. 1842)	Serenade and Album Leaf	Russian State (1957)
M.G.	Sonata	*Ms. Modena, Bibl. (Harburg)
Maingueneau, L.	Suite Brève	Durand (1947)
Maixandeau, M. V.	Lied and Rondo	Leduc
Makarov, E. (b. 1912)	Scherzo, Op. 12	Russian State (1950)
Marescotti, F. A. (b. 1902)	Fantaisie, Giboulées	Joubert (1949)
Markiewiczowna, W.	Toccata	Polish State (1957)
Martelli, H. (b. 1895)	Sonata, Op. 50 (1941)	Moeck (1960)
	Thème Variée, Op. 74 (1950)	Eschig (1950)
Maugüe, J. M. L.	Divertissements Champêtres	Costallat
Mazellier, J. (b. 1897)	Prelude and Dance	Leduc (1931)
Medin, H.	Suite Brève	Medin (1957)
Merci, L. (b. c. 1690)	Six Sonatas, Op. 3 (1735)	*Weaver (British Museum)
	Sonata in G Moll	Schott
Mignon, E.	Sonata (1954)	Mignon
Migot, G. (b. 1891)	Prelude (contrabassoon)	Leduc
Milde, L.	Andante and Rondo, Op. 25	Lienau
Milhailovici, M. (b. 1898)	Novelette	Leduc
Miroshnikov, D.	Sonata, Op. 76	Heugel (1958)
Mocker (fl. 1790)	Scherzo	International
Montfeuillard, R.	Nocturne, Op. 3	Arnaud
Moritz, E. (b. 1891)	Lamento and Finale	Philippo
Mortari, V. (b. 1902)	Scherzo, Op. 104b	Zimmermann (1960)
Moscheles, I. (b. 1794)	Marche Fériale	Leduc
	Grand Duo Concertante in B♭, Op. 34	Breitkopf
Moser, R. (b. 1892)	Suite, Op. 97	Moser (1957)
Mouquet, J.	Ballade, Op. 34 (1912)	Evette
Mulder, H. (b. 1898)	Sonata No. 5, Op. 54	Donemus

Composer	Title	Publisher/Source and Date
Neukirchner, W. (*fl.* 1805)	Acht Etuden	*Hofmann
	Burleske	*Diabelli (*c.* 1844)
Nicolov, L.	Two Pieces (1951)	Bulgarian State (1951)
Nowka, D.	Sonatina	Litolff
Nussio, O. (b. 1902)	Variazione	Universal
Ollone, M. d' (b. 1875)	Romance and Tarantelle (1922)	Leduc (1928)
Orban, M. (b. 1884)	Sonate	Costallat (1950)
Orefice, A.	Adagio	Evette
Oubradous, F. (b. 1903)	Recitative and Variations (1938)	Leduc
	Cadence and Divertissement	Oisen Lyre
	Divertissement	Noël
Owen, A.	Bagatelle	Arcadia
Ozi, E. (b. 1754)	Grand Sonata in C	Siècle Musicale
	Adagio and Rondo	Siècle Musicale
	Sonata, Op. 1	*Jouve
	Sonatas (Bk. 1 and 2)	*Breitkopf
	Six Grand Sonatas	Ricordi
	Sonatas Faciles	Ricordi
Paciorkiewicz, T.	Sonatina (1956)	Polish State
Pauer, J. (b. 1919)	Capriccio	Artia (1953)
Paxton, S. (b. 1735)	Six Easy Solos, Op. 3 (1780)	*British Museum
Petit, P. (b. 1924)	Guilledoux	Leduc (1951)
Pfeiffer, F. A. (b. 1754)	Five Sonatas	*Schwerin, M.L.B.
Philidor, M. D. (b. *c.* 1665)	Livre de Pièces	*Ms. Paris Conservatoire
Piantoni, L.	Pastorale and Rondeau (1943)	Conservatoire de Genève
Pierné, G. (b. 1863)	Solo de Concert, Op. 35 (1898)	Leduc
	Prelude de Concert, Op. 53	Salabert
Pierné, P. (b. 1874)	Theme and Variations (1941)	Costallat (1941)
Pixix, J. P. (b. 1788)	Duo Concertante	Costallat
Poot, M. (b. 1901)	Ballade	Leduc
Presle, J. de la (1888)	Petite Suite in F	Leduc
	Orientale	Leduc
Puget, P.	Solo de Basson (1899)	Leduc
Rakov, N. (b. 1908)	Etude (1956)	Russian State (1956)
Raphael, G. (b. 1903)	Berceuse (1959)	Leduc
	Sonata, Op. 46, No. 9	Leduc
Ratez, E. (b. 1851)	Barcarolle and Impromptu, Op. 67	Andrieu
	Variations, Op. 72	Hamelle
Rathaus, K. (b. 1895)	Polichinelle	Belwin (1939)
Reicha, A. (b. 1770)	Sonate	*Ms. Paris Conservatoire
René, C.	Solo de Concert (1901)	Lemoine
Reutter, H. (b. 1900)	Serenade (1957)	Leduc

Composer	Title	Publisher/Source and Date
Revel, P.	Petite Suite	Leduc (1952)
Roscher, J.	Andante and Allegretto, Op. 81	Schott
	Twelve Vortragsstücke, Op. 88	Schott
Rose, J. L. (b. 1928)	Capriccio, Elegie and Scherzetto	Galliard
Ruthenfranz, R.	Divertimento (1960)	Metropolis (1960)
Saint-Saëns, C. (b. 1835)	Sonata in G, Op. 168	Durand
Sauguet, H. (b. 1901)	Barcarolle (1936)	Ed. Sociales (1936)
Schaefers, A.	Capriccio	Sikorski
Schäfer, C. (b. 1899)	Capriccio	Zimmermann (1908)
Schindler, G. (b. 1921)	Baba Yaga	Bosworth (1962)
Schmid, H. K. (b. 1874)	Ode, Op. 34, No. 3	Schott
Schneider, F. L.	Humoresque, Op. 71	Schott
Schoeck, O. (b. 1886)	Sonata, Op. 41 (orig. bcl.)	Breitkopf
Schollum, R.	Sonatine, Op. 55, No. 3	Doblinger (1956)
	Sonatine, Op. 57, No. 3	Doblinger
Schouwman, H. (b. 1902)	Romanza and Humoresque, Op. 33	Donemus
Schreck, G. (b. 1849)	Sonata in E♭, Op. 9	Hofmeister
Selma, B., de (b. 17 Cent.)	Canzoni (1638)	*Ms. Breslau, Stadtbibl.
Semler-Collèry, J.	Recitatif and Final	Eschig (1951)
Skalkottas, N. (b. 1904)	Sonata Concertante, Op. 67	*Skalk Foundation
Spindler, F. (b. 1817)	Sonata in F, Op. 347	Kistner
Spohr, L. (b. 1784)	Adagio in F, Op. 115	Schott
Stadio, C.	Serenata	Ricordi
	Burlesca	Ricordi (1931)
Starokadomsky, M.	Four Pieces, Op. 25	International
Stekel, E. P. (b. 1898)	Mélodie (1953)	Leduc
Stevens, H. (b. 1908)	Three Pieces	Hinrichsen
Stolte, S.	Spielmusik (1957)	Peters
Stratton, H. W.	Impromptu (Tarantella)	*Waterhouse Colln.
Suchanek	Concertino (1948)	Russian State (1948)
Tak, P. C.	Variations (1944)	Donemus
Takacs, J.	Sonata Missoulana, Op. 66	Doblinger
Tanner, P.	Sonata (1956)	Tanner
Tansman, A. (b. 1897)	Sonatine	Eschig (1952)
Taudou, A. (b. 1846)	Morceau de Concours (1904)	Evette
Tchemberdzhie, N. (b. 1903)	Humoresque (1936)	Russian State (1936)
Tcherepnin, N. (b. 1873)	Variations Simples (1935)	Schirmer
	Esquisse, Op. 45,	Chester
Telemann, G. P. (b. 1681)	Sonata No. 3 in F Moll	International
	Sonata	*Ms. Rostock, Univ. Bibl.

Composer	Title	Publisher/Source and Date
Templeton, A. (b. 1905)	Elegy	Leeds
Theuss, K. T. (fl. 1785)	Sonata (1820) (six bns.)	*Hofmeister (B.M.)
Thilman, J. P. (b. 1906)	Sonatine	Hofmeister
Thiriet, A. L.	Theme and Variations	Leduc
Tiehl (Thiel) (fl. 18 Cent.)	Twenty-two Sonatas	*Ms. Schwerin, M.L.B.
Tillmetz, R.	Romance and Burleske, Op. 37	Rahter (1903)
Tomasi, H. (b. 1901)	Danse Guerrière (1960)	Leduc (1960)
Tuskia, J.	Trio (two bns.)	Musford
Vachey, H.	Trois Pièces Faciles	Delrieu (1962)
Vidal, P. (b. 1863)	Adagio and Saltarelle (1929)	Leduc (1929)
	Mélodie	Leduc
Vinter, G.	The Playful Pachyderm	Boosey (1942)
	Reverie	Cramer (1952)
Vivaldi, A. (b. 1675)	Sonata in A Moll	International
Vladiguerov, P. (b. 1899)	Caprice (1951)	Bulgarian State (1951)
Walthew, R. (b. 1872)	Introduction and Allegro	Hinrichsen
Webber, L.	Country Impressions: Northington Farm	Ascherberg
Weber, A.	Sonatine	Leduc
Wehding, H. H.	Scherzo	Musica Rara
Weinberger, J. (b. 1896)	Sonatine (1940)	Fischer
Weissenborn, J. (b. 1837)	Romance, Op. 3	Forberg
	Sechs Vortragsstücke, Op. 9	Forberg
	Drei Vortragsstücke, Op. 10	Breitkopf
	Capriccio, Op. 14	Hofmeister
Wichtl, A. M.	Concerto, Op. 2 (1911)	Hawkes
Willent-Bordogni, J. B. J. (b. 1809)	Sonata in F, Op. 17	Costallat
	Sonata in C, Op. 30	Costallat
	Solo, Op. 3	Richault
Wlassow, V. (b. 1903) and Fehre, V.	Four Pieces (1932)	Russian State (1932)
Zbinden, J. F. (b. 1917)	Ballade, Op. 33	Breitkopf
Zinsstag, D.	Elégie	Henn (1957)

Section 3. Bassoon and Orchestra

Adaskin-Murray	Concerto	Musica Rara
Aimon, P. L. F. (b. 1779)	Two Concertos	*Frey
Almenräder, K. (b. 1786)	Potpourri, Op. 3	*Schott (1824)
	Concerto in C Moll	*Schott
	Concerto in A Moll	*Publisher not known
	Concerto in D	*Publisher not known
	Concerto in F	*Publisher not known

SOLO MUSIC FOR BASSOON AND DOUBLE BASSOON 207

Composer	Title	Publisher/Source and Date
Andriessen, J. (b. 1925)	Concertino (bn. and wind)	Donemus
Anselm	Concerto	Montserrat
Appold, V.	Concerto	*Donaueschingen F.B.
Bach, J. C. (b. 1735)	Concerto No. 1 in B♭	Sikorski
	Concerto No. 2 in E♭	Sikorski
Bärmann, K. (b. 1811)	Grand Concerto in C, Op. 1	*Breitkopf
	Concerto	*Berlin, O.W.B.
Batka, W. (c. 1747)	Concertos	*Ms. source not known
Berr, F. (b. 1794)	Two Concertinos	*Meissonnier (Leduc)
Berwald, J. F. (b. 1787)	Concertstuck (Concerto), Op. 2	*Ms. Uppsala Bibl.
Bielfeld, A.	Divertissement	Fischer
Bitsch, M.	Concertino	Leduc
Blasius, M. F. (b. 1758)	Concerto	*Source not known
Blazevitsch, V.	Concerto No. 5 in E♭	Russian State
Blondeau, P. A. L. (b. 1784)	Concerto in C	*Paris, National Bibl.
Bodart, E.	Concerto in E♭	Müller
Boismortier, J. B. de (b. 1691)	Concerto in D, Op. 26	Ricordi
Bond, C.	Concerto No. 6 in B♭ (1766)	Boosey
Bozza, E. (b. 1905)	Concertino, Op. 49	Leduc
Brandl, J. (b. 1760)	Concertino in F	*Ms. Donaueschingen F.B.
Braun, C. A. P. (b. 1788)	Concerto in C, Op. 56	*André
	Concertino in F	*Donaueschingen F.B.
Bruns, V.	Concerto No. 1, Op. 5	Breitkopf
	Concerto No. 2, Op. 15	Hofmeister
Buhler, S.	Concerto	*Longman and Broderip
Couperin, F. (b. 1668)	Concerto for 2 bns.	Musica Rara
Danzi, F. (b. 1763)	Concerto in F	*Donaueschingen F.B.
	Concerto in F	*Munich. Bayer. Standbibl.
	Concerto in G Moll	*Donaueschingen F.B.
	Concerto for 2 bns. (1820)	*Source not known
Dalcambre, T. (b. 1766)	Concerto in C	*Paris Conservatoire
David, F. (b. 1810)	Concertino, Op. 12	Kistner
Devienne, F. (b. 1759)	Concerto in C	Hofmeister
	Concerto No. 1 in C	*Imbault
	Concerto No. 2	*Nadermann
	Concerto No. 3 in F	*Sieber
	Concerto No. 4 in C	*Sieber
	Concerto No. 5	*Pleyel
Dieter, C. L. (b. 1757)	Concerto	*Berlin O.W.B.
	Concerto in F	*Nageli
	Concerto No. 1 for 2 bns.	*Nageli
	Concerto No. 2 for 2 bns.	*Darmstadt, Landesbibl.

Composer	Title	Publisher/Source and Date
Dieter, C. L.—cont.	Two Sinfonias Concertante for 2 bns.	*Hug
Dobrowolski, A.	Concerto (1953)	Moeck
Donatoni, F. (b. 1927)	Concerto (1952)	Drago (1961)
Dotzauer, J. J. F. (b. 1783)	Variations, Op. 40 (1817)	*Hofmeister
Durnitz, Baron von	Concerto	*Schwerin, M.L.B.
Eichner, E. (b. 1740)	Concerto	*Schwerin, M.L.B.
Elgar, E. (b. 1857)	Romance, Op. 62	Novello
Eriksson, N.	Concerto (1949)	Musik Könstforlag
Fasch, J. F. (b. 1688)	Concerto	Noetzel
Feld, J.	Concerto (1961)	Leduc
Fernström, J. A. (b. 1897)	Concerto	Musik Könstforlag
Fesch, W. de (b. 1687)	Concerto in B♭	Musica Rara
Fiala, J. (b. 1748)	Concerto	*Schwerin, M.L.B.
Fischer, F. (b. c. 1665)	Concerto	*Schwerin, M.L.B.
Fischer, J. (b. 1646)	Concerto	*Schwerin, M.L.B.
Fischer, M. G. (b. 1773)	Concerto in F, Op. 8	Breitkopf
Flament, E. (b. 1880)	Capriccio	Schott
Fogg, E. (b. 1903)	Concerto	Elkin
Fürstenau, K. F. (b. 1772)	Potpourri, Op. 31	Simrock
Gebauer, F. R. (b. 1773)	Thirteen Concertos	*Paris, National Bibl.
Geminiani, F. (b. 1687)	Concerto Grosso, Op. 7, No. 6	*British Museum
Graun, J. G. (b. 1703)	Concerto in B♭	Sikorski
Graupner, C. (b. 1683)	Concerto in C	Leuckart
	Concerto in C Moll	Bärenreiter
	Concerto in E Moll	Bärenreiter
	Fifty Concertos	*Darmstadt, Landesbibl.
Grøndahl, L. (b. 1886)	Concerto (1942)	Dania
Haack, C. (b. 1751)	Concerto	*Hummel
Hargrave, H. (fl. 18 Cent.)	Concerto No. 1 (1760)	*British Museum
	Concerto No. 2	*British Museum
	Concerto No. 4	*British Museum
Hässler, L. (b. 1564)	Concerto in C Moll, Op. 14	Oertel
Hendrich (fl. 18 Cent.)	Concerto	*Schwerin, M.L.B.
Henneberg, C. A. T. (b. 1901)	Concerto	Musik Könstforlag
Hertel, J. W. (b. 1727)	Concerto in B♭	*Brussels Conservatoire
	Concerto in G Moll	*Brussels Conservatoire
	Concerto	*Brussels Conservatoire
Heymann	Two Concertos	*Washington, Library of Congress
Hodgson, P.	Concerto	Lopez
Hoffmeister, F. A. (b. 1754)	Concerto No. 1	*Darmstadt, Landesbibl.
Holbrooke, J. (b. 1878)	Concerto in B♭, Op. 88	Boosey

Composer	Title	Publisher/Source and Date
Hubschmann	Five Variations	*Breitkopf
Human, A.	Polonaise	*Breitkopf
	Polonaise in D Moll	*Peters
Hummel, J. F. (b. 1855)	Concertstück, Op. 201	Breitkopf (1915)
Hummel, J. N. (b. 1778)	Concerto	*Ms. British Museum
Humphries (*fl.* 18 Cent.)	Concerto No. 9 for 2 bn.	*British Museum
	Concerto No. 11 for 2 bn.	*British Museum
Jacob, G. (b. 1895)	Concerto	Williams
Jacobi, C. (b. 1756)	Two Concertos, Op. 1	*Breitkopf
	Potpourri, Op. 6	*Simrock
	Concertino, Op. 7	*Breitkopf
	Variations, Op. 8	*Breitkopf
	Introductions and Polonaise, Op. 9	*Breitkopf
	Variations, Op. 10	*Breitkopf
	Divertimento, Op. 11	*Breitkopf
	Potpourri, Opp. 12, 13, 14 and 16	*Breitkopf
	Fantasie, Op. 17	*Schott
Jancourt, L. M. E. (b. 1815)	Fantasie No. 1, Op. 5	Richault
	Fantasie No. 2, Op. 8	Richault
	Air and Variations	Richault
	Concertino, Op. 40	Costallat
Jiranek, A. (b. 1712)	Concerto in G Moll	*Darmstadt, Landesbibl.
Jolivet, A. (b. 1905)	Concerto	Heugel
Kahtel	Concerto	*Schwerin, M.L.B.
Kalliwoda, J. W. (b. 1801)	Introduction, Theme, Variations and Rondo, Op. 57	Peters
Kelemen, M.	Concerto	Universal
Koch, C. (b. 1749)	Concerto in F, Op. 11	*Simrock
Kozeluch, J. A. (b. 1738)	Concerto	Russian State
Kreibe, B. F. F. (b. 1772)	Concerto, Op. 3	*André
Küchler, J. (b. 1738)	Two Symphonies with bn. obbl.	*Paris, National Bibl.
	Concerto	*Ms. Schwerin, M.L.B.
Kummer, G. H. (b. 1777)	Concerto No. 1 in F, Op. 7	*Breitkopf
	Concerto No. 2 in F, Op. 10	*Breitkopf
	Concerto No. 3, Op. 11	*Breitkopf
	Concerto No. 4 in B♭, Op. 16	*Breitkopf
	Concerto No. 5 in F, Op. 24	*Breitkopf
	Concerto No. 6 in C, Op. 25	*Breitkopf
	Concerto No. 7 in D, Op. 27	*Breitkopf

Composer	Title	Publisher/Source and Date
Kummer, G. H.—cont.	Concerto, Op. 3	*Berlin, O.W.B.
	Concerto, Op. 9	*Berlin, O.W.B.
	Variations on a Mazurka	*Costallat
	Variations in B♭, Op. 15	*Breitkopf
Kunkel, M. J.	Concertino in E♭	Schmidt
Lachner, N. A.	Variations (1815)	Breitkopf
Landowski, M. (b. 1915)	Concerto	Choudens
Larsson, L. E. (b. 1908)	Concertino	Gehrmann
Lassen, E. (b. 1830)	Zwei Fantasiestücke, Op. 48	Ries
Laube, A.	Concerto	*Prague, Bibl.
Levy, F.	Concerto	Musica Rara
Lier, B. van (b. 1906)	Concerto (1950)	Donemus
Lindpainter, P. J. von (b. 1791)	Rondo, Op. 8	*Breitkopf
	Rondo, Op. 24 (1820)	*Breitkopf
Lizio, F.	Concerto (1759)	*Naples Conservatorio
Louel, J. (b. 1914)	Burlesque (1943)	Cebedem
Lutyens, E. (b. 1906)	Concerto Grosso, Op. 83	Chester
	Concerto No. 3	Chester
Maconchy, E. (b. 1907)	Concertino	Legnick
Maessen, A. (b. 1919)	Divertimento (1960)	Donemus
Maingueneau, L.	Suite brève	Durand
Malipiero, G. F. (b. 1882)	Serenata	Ricordi
Marescotti, A. F. (b. 1902)	Fantaisie, Giboulées	Joubert
Maros, R. (b. 1917)	Concertino	Zenemukiado (1960)
Matz, A.	Concerto	Breitkopf
Meister, K.	Concerto	Ars Viva
Mengis, C. (fl. 1760)	Two Concertos	*Breitkopf
Meulemans, A. (b. 1884)	Rhapsodie (1942)	Cebedem
Meuser, E. H.	Concerto Orientale	Donemus
Milde, L.	Adante and Rondo, Op. 25	Schlesinger
	Concerto No. 2	Schlesinger
Mozart, W. A. (b. 1756)	Concerto in B♭ (K. 191)	Breitkopf (1881)
	Concerto in B♭ (K.A. 230a)	Peters
Mühling, A. (b. 1782)	Theme and Variations, Op. 14	*Breitkopf (1819)
	Concerto in E♭, Op. 24	*Breitkopf
Müller, F. (b. 1786)	Theme and Variations, Op. 29	*Breitkopf
Müller, S. W.	Concerto, Op. 56	Eulenburg (1938)
Müthel, J. (b. 1718)	Concerto	Bote
Neukirchner, W. (c. 1805)	Burlesque (Neapolitan)	Cranz
	Fantasia	Cranz
	Fantasie: Scène Villageoise	Schott

Composer	Title	Publisher/Source and Date
Orlamünder	Concertino	*Washington, Library of Congress
	Concerto	Schmidt
Ozi, E. (b. 1754)	Eight Concertos	*Darmstadt, Landesbibl.
	Sinfonia Concertante for 2 bn.	*Paris, National Bibl.
Pauer, J. (b. 1919)	Concerto	Artia (1949)
Pfeiffer, F. A. (b. 1754)	Ten Concertos	*Ms. Schwerin, M.L.B.
Phillips, B. (b. 1907)	Concert Piece	Fischer
Pichl, W. (b. 1741)	Concerto	*Groswardein Chapel Library
Pierné (b. 1863)	Solo de Concert	Leduc
Ponse, L. (b. 1914)	Concerto da Camera, Op. 34	Donemus
Praag, H. C. van	Fantasie (1962) (bn. and wind)	Donemus
Prati, A. (b. 1750)	Concerto	*Paris, National Bibl.
Reichenauer, A.	Concerto	*Darmstadt, Landesbibl.
	Three Concertos	*Dresden, Landesbibl.
Rethaler, A. (b. 1800)	Concerto	*Paris Conservatoire
Richens, J.	Rondo	*Ms. Richens
Rimsky-Korsakov, N. (b. 1844)	Concerto, Op. 33	Russian State (1952)
Ritter, G. W. (b. 1748)	Two Concertos	*Bailleux
Ritter, P. (b. 1763)	Concerto	*Washington, Library of Congress
Romberg, A. (b. 1742)	Concerto	*Paris Conservatoire
Ron, J. M. de (b. 1789)	Andante and Polonaise Op. 2	*Breitkopf
Rössler, F. A. (b. 1746)	Four Concertos in B♭	*Schwerin, M.L.B.
	Concerto in B♭	Schott (1955)
Schacht, T. von (b. 1748)	Concerto in B♭	*Regensburg, T.T.H.
Schier	Concerto	*Longman and Broderip
Schmitt, N. (fl. 18 Cent.)	Concerto	*Brussels Conservatoire
	Three Concertos (1792)	Cochet
Schmittbach, C. (c. 1832)	Andante, Variations and Rondo (1827)	*Breitkopf
	Andante and Variations, Op. 2	*Nagel
Schmittbauer, J. A. (b. 1717)	Concerto	*Schwerin, M.L.B.
Schneider, G. A. (b. 1770)	Grand Concerto	*Berlin, O.W.B.
	Concerto, Op. 67	*Schlesinger
	Concerto, Op. 85	*Hofmeister
	Concerto, Op. 104	*Simrock
Schoemaker	Concerto in B♭	Bärenreiter
Schönebeck, C. S. (b. 1758)	Concerto, Op. 4 (1800)	*Hummel
Schwarz, A. G. (b. 1743)	Concerto	*Schwerin, M.L.B.
Sehlbach, E.	Concerto	Möseler

Composer	Title	Publisher/Source and Date
Sperger, J. M. (*fl.* 1780)	Concerto in F	*Schwerin, M.L.B.
Spisak, M. (b. 1914)	Concerto (1944)	Ricordi
Stamitz, K. (b. 1745)	Concerto in B♭	Sikorski
	Concerto in C	*Schwerin, M.L.B.
	Concerto in F	Sikorski
	Concerto No. 17	*Schwerin, M.L.B.
Stumpf, J. C. (b. 1760)	Concerto No. 1	*Simrock
	Concerto No. 2	*Simrock
	Concerto No. 3	*Simrock
	Concerto No. 4	*Simrock
Suhl	Concerto (1761)	*Breitkopf
Sukhanek	Concertino	International
Thilman, J. P.	Sonatine	Hofmeister
	Concerto	Hofmeister
Tomasi, H. (b. 1901)	Concerto	Leduc
Vanhal, J. B. (b. 1739)	Concerto in C	Bärenreiter
	Concerto for 2 bn.	Bärenreiter
Villa-Lobos, H. (b. 1887)	Ciranda das Sete Notas	Southern
Viola	Concerto	Edition Espaniola
Vivaldi, A. (b. 1675)	Concerto in A Moll, Vol. 8, No. 2	Ricordi
	Concerto in A Moll, Vol. 8, No. 7	Ricordi
	Concerto in A Moll, Vol. 8, No. 10	Ricordi
	Concerto in A Moll, Vol. 8, No. 12	Ricordi
	Concerto in B♭, Vol. 8, No. 1 (La Notte)	Ricordi
	Concerto in B♭, Vol. 8, No. 24	Ricordi
	Concerto in B♭, Vol. 8, No. 35	Ricordi
	Concerto in B♭, Vol. 8, No. 36	Ricordi
	Concerto in C, Vol. 8, No. 3	Ricordi
	Concerto in C, Vol. 8, No. 4	Ricordi
	Concerto in C, Vol. 8, No. 9	Ricordi
	Concerto in C, Vol. 8, No. 13	Ricordi
	Concerto in C, Vol. 8, No. 16	Ricordi
	Concerto in C, Vol. 8, No. 17	Ricordi
	Concerto in C, Vol. 8, No. 18	Ricordi
	Concerto in C, Vol. 8, No. 21	Ricordi

Composer	Title	Publisher/Source and Date
Vivaldi, A.—*cont.*	Concerto in C, Vol. 8, No. 26	Ricordi
	Concerto in C, Vol. 8, No. 28	Ricordi
	Concerto in C, Vol. 8, No. 31	Ricordi
	Concerto in C, Vol. 8, No. 33	Ricordi
	Concerto in C, Vol. 8, No. 34	Ricordi
	Concerto in C Moll, Vol. 8, No. 14	Ricordi
	Concerto in D Moll, Vol. 8, No. 5	Ricordi
	Concerto in E♭, Vol. 8, No. 27	Ricordi
	Concerto in F, Vol. 8, No. 8	Ricordi
	Concerto in F, Vol. 8, No. 15	Ricordi
	Concerto in F, Vol. 8, No. 19	Ricordi
	Concerto in F, Vol. 8, No. 20	Ricordi
	Concerto in F, Vol. 8, No. 22	Ricordi
	Concerto in F, Vol. 8, No. 25	Ricordi
	Concerto in F, Vol. 8, No. 32	Ricordi
	Concerto in G, Vol. 8, No. 29	Ricordi
	Concerto in G, Vol. 8, No. 30	Ricordi
	Concerto in G, Vol. 8, No. 37	Ricordi
	Concerto in G Moll, Vol. 8, No. 11	Ricordi
	Concerto in G Moll, Vol. 8, No. 23	Ricordi
Vogell, J. C. (b. 1756)	Concerto	Leduc
	Concerto No. 3	*Paris Conservatoire
	Concerto No. 4	*Paris Conservatoire
Wagner, J. K. (b. 1772)	Concerto	*Ms. Darmstadt, Landes-bibl.
Weber, C. M. Von (b. 1786)	Concerto in F, Op. 75	Lienau
	Introduction and Rondo, Op. 35	Lienau
Weinzweig, J.	Divertimento No. 3	Leeds
Wessely, J. (b. 1762)	Concerto	*Vienna, National Bibl.
Whettam, G.	Concerto a Cappriccioso, Op. 22	de Wolfe

Composer	Title	Publisher/Source and Date
Widerkehr, J. C. M. W. (b. 1730)	Sinfonia Concertante for 2 bn.	*Paris Conservatoire
Willent-Bordogni, J. B. J. (b. 1809)	Four Fantasies	*Paris, National Bibl.
Winter, P. von (b. 1754)	Concertino	*British Museum
	Rondo and Variations	*British Museum
Wittgenstein-Berlebourg, G. von (b. 1819)	Theme and Variations, Op. 3	Simrock (1811)
Wolf, A. (b. 1817)	Concerto	*Ms. Schwerin, M.L.B.
Wolf-Ferrari, E. (b. 1876)	Suite-Concertino in F, Op. 16	Ricordi (1932)

Section 4. Concertos for Bassoon with other Solo Instruments and Orchestra

Ahnert (*fl.* 1758)	Concerto for cl. and bn. (1758)	Breitkopf
Beck, C. (b. 1901)	Concertino for cl. and bn.	Schott
Beethoven, L. van (b. 1770)	Romance for fl. bn. and pf.	Breitkopf
Biscogli, F.	Concerto in D for ob. bn. and tp.	*Paris Conservatoire
Blacher, B. (b. 1903)	Concerto for cl. bn. hn. and tbn.	Bote
Blezard, W.	Variations for cl. and bn.	*Ms. Composers Guild
Boccherini, L. (b. 1743)	Sinfonia Concertante, Op. 41, for ob. bn. and hn.	Novello
Boismortier, J. B. de (b. 1691)	Concerto in D for bn. 2 vn. and hpsch.	Musica Rara
	Concerto in E Moll for fl. ob. bn. and vn.	Siri
Brautigam, H.	Concerto for fl. ob. and bn.	Breitkopf
Brescianello, G. A. (b. 1717)	Concerto for bn. and vn.	*Darmstadt, Landesbibl.
Breval, J. B. (b. 1756)	Sinfonia Concertante in F, Op. 31, for fl. and bn.	*Devienne
Brunetti, G. (b. 1740)	Air and Variations for ob. and bn.	*Paris, National Bibl.
Burkhard, W. (b. 1900)	Toccata, Op. 86, for fl. cl. bn. tp. and perc.	Bärenreiter
Crussell, B. (b. *c.* 1778)	Sinfonia Concertante No. 3, Op. 3, for cl. bn. and hn.	Peters
Danzi, F. (b. 1763)	Sinfonia Concertante for fl. ob. bn. and hn.	Schott (1938)
	Sinfonia Concertante No. 1 for cl. and bn.	Simrock

Composer	Title	Publisher/Source and Date
Danzi, F.—cont.	Sinfonia Concertante No. 2, Op. 47, for cl. and bn.	*Breitkopf
	Sinfonia Concertante in E♭ for fl. ob. bn. and and hn.	*Berlin, O.W.B.
	Sinfonia Concertante in B♭ for cl. and bn.	*Paris, National Bibl. Musica Rara
Devienne, F. (b. 1759)	Sinfonia for cl. and bn.	*Vienna, A.M.V.
	Sinfonia Concertante No. 1 (1792) for bn. hn.	*Paris, National Bibl.
	Sinfonia Concertante No. 2 (1793) for ob. cl. and bn.	*Paris, National Bibl.
	Sinfonia Concertante No. 3 for fl. cl. and bn.	*Paris, National Bibl.
	Sinfonia Concertante No. 4 (1794) for fl. ob. bn. and hn.	*Paris, National Bibl.
	Sinfonia Concertante No. 5 (1800) for fl. ob. bn. and hn.	*Paris, National Bibl.
Eberwein, T. M. (b. 1775)	Sinfonia Concertante, Op. 47, for ob. bn. and hn.	*Breitkopf (1820)
Eckhardt-Gramatté, S. C. (b. 1902)	Triple Concerto for cl. bn. and tp.	Universal
Eler, A. (b. 1764)	Sinfonia Concertante (1796) for fl. cl. bn. and hn.	*Paris, National Bibl.
	Sinfonia Concertante for fl. bn. and hn.	*Ozi
Fesch, W. de (b. 1687)	Concerto in B♭, Op. 3, No. 2, for 2 fl. bn. and 2 vn.	Siri
Fischer, M. G. (b. 1773)	Concerto in C, Op. 11, for ob. and bn.	*Breitkopf (1808)
Gallon, N. (b. 1891)	Concerto for ob. cl. and bn.	Leduc
Garnier, F. J. (b. 1755)	Sinfonia Concertante, Op. 4, for fl. ob. and bn.	*Nadermann
Gatterman	Fantasie Concertante for ob. and bn.	Costallat
Gebauer, F. R. (b. 1773)	Sinfonia Concertante No. 1 for cl. and bn.	*Jouve
	Sinfonia Concertante No. 2 for fl. cl. and bn.	*Jouve
	Sinfonia Concertante No. 3 for bn. and hn.	*Jouve
	Sinfonia Concertante No. 5 for fl. and bn.	*Paris Conservatoire

Composer	Title	Publisher/Source and Date
Gebauer, F. R.—*cont.*	Eight Sinfonias Concertante for fl. cl. bn. and hn.	*Jouve
Goepfart, K. E. (b. 1859)	Concertante for cl. and bn.	*André
Gresnick, A. F. (b. 1755)	Sinfonia Concertante (1797) for cl. and bn.	*Pleyel
Hargrave, H. (*fl.* 18 Cent.)	Concerto No. 3 for ob. and bn.	*British Museum
	Concerto No. 5 for ob. and bn.	*British Museum
Haydn, F. J. (b. 1732)	Sinfonia Concertante for ob. bn. vn. and vc.	Brietkopf
Helm, E.	Concerto for fl. ob. bn. tp. and vn.	Schott
Hertel, J. W. (b. 1727)	Concerto for 2 ob. 2 bn. and tp.	Musica Rara
Hindemith, P. (b. 1895)	Concerto for bn. and tp.	Schott
	Concerto for fl. ca. cl. and bn.	Schott
Holbrooke, J. (b. 1878)	Quadruple Concerto for fl. ob. cl. and bn.	de Wolfe
Humphries (*fl.* 18 Cent.)	Concerto No. 5, for ob. and bn.	*British Museum
Hurlebusch, C. F. (b. 1696)	Concerto for 2 ob. bn. and vn.	*Vienna, A.M.V.
Jadin, L. E. (b. 1768)	Sinfonia Concertante for fl. bn. and hn.	*Dufaut
	Sinfonia Concertante for cl. bn. and hn.	*Sieber
Lefèvre, J. X. (b. 1763)	Two Sinfonias Concertante for cl. and bn.	*Sieber
	Sinfonia Concertante for ob. cl. and bn.	*Janet
Levy, F.	Concerto for ob. bn. hn. and timp.	Musica Rara
Lindpainter, P. J. von (b. 1791)	Sinfonia Concertante, Op. 36, for fl. ob. cl. bn. and hn.	*Schott
	Sinfonia Concertante, Op. 44, for fl. ob. cl. bn. and hn.	*Schott
Machonchy, E. (b. 1907)	Duo-Concertante for ob. and bn.	Lengnick
Martelli, H. (b. 1895)	Concertino for ob. cl. bn. and hn.	Ricordi
	Double Concerto for cl. and bn.	Moeck
Martinn, J. J. B. (b. 1755)	Sinfonia Concertante No. 1 for 2 fl. and bn.	Frey

Composer	Title	Publisher/Source and Date
Martinn, J. J. B.—*cont.*	Sinfonia Concertante No. 2 for fl. ob. bn. and hn.	Martinn
	Sinfonia Concertante for fl. cl. and bn.	Martinn
Martinů, B. (b. 1890)	Sinfonia Concertante for ob. bn. vn. and vc.	Boosey
Mengs (*fl.* 18 Cent.)	Concert for bn. and vn.	*Darmstadt, Landesbibl.
Meyer, C. H. (*c.* 1772)	Fantasie Concertante, Op. 20, for fl. cl. bn. and hn.	Hofmeister
Molter, J. M. (b. *c.* 1695)	Sinfonia Concertante for 2 ob. bn. 2 hn. and tp.	*Karlsruhre, Landesbibl.
Mozart, W. A. (b. 1756)	Sinfonia Concertante in E♭ (K. 297b) for ob. cl. bn. and hn.	Breitkopf
Müller, F. (b. 1786)	Sinfonia Concertante, Op. 31, for cl. and bn.	Breitkopf
Müthel, J. G. (b. 1718)	Concerto in D Moll for 2 bn. and hpsch.	*Brussels Conservatoire
Nohr, C. F. (b. 1800)	Potpourri, Op. 3, for fl. cl. bn. and hn.	Breitkopf
Ozi, E. (b. 1754)	Sinfonia Concertante, Op. 5, for cl. and bn.	*Paris, National Bibl.
	Sinfonia Concertante, Op. 7, for cl. and bn.	*Paris, National Bibl.
	Sinfonia Concertante, Op. 10, for cl. and bn.	*Paris, National Bibl.
Panny, J. (b. 1794)	Sinfonia Concertante, Op. 7, for ob. and bn.	Artia
Pfeiffer, F. A. (b. 1754)	Concerto for ob. bn. vn. and vc.	*Berlin, O.W.B.
Pleyel, J. (b. 1757)	Sinfonia Concertante No. 4 for fl. ob. bn. vn. va. and vc.	*Pleyel
	Sinfonia Concertante No. 5 for fl. ob. bn. and hn.	*Nadermann
Praag, H. C. van (b. 1880)	Fantasia Concertante for fl. and bn.	Donemus
Prowo, P.	Concerto No. 1 in F for 3 ob. and bn.	Musica Rara
	Concerto in D Moll for 2 fl. 2 ob. and 2 bn.	Musica Rara
Reichenauer, A.	Eight Concerti for ob. bn. and vn.	*Dresden, Landesbibl.
Rieti, V. (b. 1898)	Concerto for fl. ob. cl. bn. and hn.	Universal
Saeverud, H. (b. 1897)	Rondo Amoroso for ob. and bn.	Mills

Composer	Title	Publisher/Source and Date
Schneider, G. A. (b. 1770)	Sinfonia Concertante, Op. 84, for cl. and bn.	Bote
	Sinfonia Concertante, Op. 106, for cl. and bn.	*Simrock
	Sinfonia Concertante, Op. 107, for cl. and bn.	*Simrock
Schubert, J. F. (b. 1770)	Sinfonia Concertante, Op. 4, for ob. and bn.	Peters
Scott, C. (b. 1879)	Concertino for fl. and bn.	Elkin
Seyffert, M. (fl. 1720)	Three Concertos for ob. and bn.	*Dresden, Landesbibl.
Stamitz, A. (b. 1754)	Sinfonia Concertante for ob. and bn.	Kneusslin
Stamitz, K. (b. 1745)	Double Concerto in B♭ for cl. and bn.	Sikorski
	Sinfonia Concertante for fl. bn and 2 vn.	*Paris, National Bibl.
	Concerto in D♯ for ob. bn. hn. and vn.	*Darmstadt, Landesbibl.
Stegmann, K. D. (b. 1751)	Concerto for ob. bn. and pf.	*Brussels Conservatoire
Strauss, R. (b. 1864)	Duett-Concertino for cl. and bn.	Boosey
Telemann, G. P. (b. 1681)	Concerto in D for 2 fl. and bn.	*Darmstadt, Landesbibl.
	Concerto in A Moll for 2 fl. and bn.	*Darmstadt, Landesbibl.
	Concerto in B Moll for fl. bn. and vad'g.	*Darmstadt, Landesbibl.
	Concerto in C for fl. bn. and vad'g.	*Darmstadt, Landesbibl.
	Concerto in F for rec. and bn.	Germany (1964)
Tulou, J. L. (b. 1786)	Sinfonia Concertante No. 1 for fl. ob. and bn.	*Lemoine
	Sinfonia Concertante No. 2 for fl. ob. bn. and hn.	*Pleyel
Vejvanovsky, P. J. (b. 1640)	Intrada con Altre Ariae for 3 ob. bn. 2 clarini and hpsch.	Musica Rara
Vivaldi, A. (b. 1675)	Concerto in C, Vol. 12, No. 24, for fl. ob. bn. and vn.	Ricordi
	Concerto in D, Vol. 12, No. 7 for fl. bn. and vn.	Ricordi
	Concerto in D, Vol. 12, No. 9, for fl. ob. bn. and vn.	Ricordi
	Concerto in D, Vol. 12, No. 25, for fl. ob. bn. and vn.	Ricordi

Composer	Title	Publisher/Source and Date
Vivaldi, A.—*cont.*	Concerto in D, Vol. 12, No. 27, for fl. bn. and vn.	Ricordi
	Concerto in D, Vol. 12, No. 29, for fl. ob. bn. and vn.	Ricordi
	Concerto in E Moll, Vol. 12, No. 22, for bn. and vc.	Ricordi
	Concerto in F, Vol. 12, No. 21, for fl. bn. and vn.	Ricordi
	Concerto in F, Vol. 12, No. 26, for fl. ob. bn. and vn.	Ricordi
	Concerto in F, Vol. 12, No. 32, for 2 ob. bn. 2 hn. and vad'am.	Ricordi
	Concerto in G, Vol. 12, No. 36, for ob. and bn.	Ricordi
	Concerto in G Moll, Vol. 12, No. 5 (La Notte), for fl. and bn.	Ricordi
	Concerto in G Moll, Vol. 12, No. 6, for fl. ob. bn. and vn.	Ricordi
	Concerto in G Moll, Vol. 12, No. 8, for fl. bn. and vn.	Ricordi
	Concerto in G Moll, Vol. 12, No. 20, for fl. ob. bn. and vn.	Ricordi
Vogel, J. C. (b. 1756)	Sinfonia Concertante No. 1 for ob. cl. and bn.	*Paris, National Bibl.
Vogt, G. (b. 1781)	Duetto for ob. and bn.	*Costallat
	Duo Concertante for ob. and bn.	*Costallat
Wagner, C. (b. 1772)	Two Sinfonias Concertante for ob. and bn.	*Darmstadt, Landesbibl.
Westenholz, F. (*fl.* 1800)	Sinfonia Concertante, Op. 7, for ob. and bn.	*Schlesinger
Whettam, G.	Variations for ob. and bn.	Ascherberg
Widerkehr, J. C. M. W. (b. 1730)	Sinfonia Concertante No. 1 for cl. and bn.	*Pleyel
	Sinfonia Concertante No. 2 for cl. and bn.	*Pleyel
	Sinfonia Concertante No. 3 for bn. and hn.	*Pleyel
	Sinfonia Concertante No. 4 for fl. ob. cl. 2 bn. hn. and vn.	*Paris, National Bibl.

Composer	Title	Publisher/Source and Date
Widerkehr, J. C. M. W. —cont.	Sinfonia Concertante No. 5 for bn. and hn.	*Sieber
	Sinfonia Concertante No. 6 for ob. and bn.	*Sieber
	Sinfonia Concertante No. 7 for fl. cl. and bn.	*Erard
	Sinfonia Concertante No. 9 for fl. ob. and bn.	*Erard
	Sinfonia Concertante No. 10 for bn. and hn.	*Schlesinger
	Sinfonia Concertante No. 11 for ob. and bn.	*Schlesinger
	Sinfonia Concertante No. 12 for ob. and bn.	*Schlesinger
	Sinfonia Concertante for ob. and 2 bn.	*British Museum
	Sinfonia Concertante for bn. and hn.	*Paris Conservatoire
	Two Sinfonias Concertante for ob. and bn.	*British Museum
Winter, P. von. (b. 1754)	Sinfonia Concertante, Op. 11, for cl. bn. hn. and vn.	*Berlin, O.W.B.
	Sinfonia Concertante, Op. 20, for ob. cl. bn. vn. va. and vc.	*Breitkopf

Section 5.   Chamber Music for Bassoon and Strings

(bn. vn. va. and vc. unless otherwise indicated)

Almenräder, K. (b. 1786)	Introduction and Variations for bn. 2 vn. va. and vc.	Alisky
	Variations on an Ancient Melody, Op. 4	Schott
Bax, A. E. T. (b. 1883)	Threnody and Scherzo for bn. hp. 2 vn. va. vc. and db.	Chappell
Blasius, M. F. (b. 1758)	Overture for bn. vn. va. and db.	*Schwerin, M.L.B.
	Quartet for bn. vn. va. and db.	*Schwerin, M.L.B.
Brandl, J. (b. 1760)	Quintet, Op. 14, for bn. vn. 2 va. and vc.	*André
	Two Quintets, Op. 56, for bn. vn. 2 va. and vc.	*André (1823)
Danzi, F. (b. 1763)	Three Quartets, Op. 40	*André (1815)
	Quartet, Op. 40, No. 3	Musica Rara
Demerseman	Introduction and Polonaise for bn. 2 vn. va. and vc.	Costallat

Composer	Title	Publisher/Source and Date
Devienne, F. (b. 1759)	Three Quartets, Op. 73 (1800)	*Erard
	Quartet, Op. 73, No. 1	Musica Rara
	Six Trios, Op. 17 (1795), for bn. vn. and vc.	*Imbault
Dotzauer, J. J. F. (b. 1783)	Quartet, Op. 36 (1816)	*Breitkopf (1816)
Ducreux, E. (b. 1765)	Variations 'Les Folies d'Espagne' for bn. and vc.	*Corbaux
Dukelsky, V. (b. 1903)	Etude for bn. and vn.	Sprague-Coleman
Elliott, S.	Poem for bn. 2 vn. va. and vc.	Musica Rara
Engelberth, A.	Variations for bn. 2 va. and vc.	*Breitkopf
Flament, E. (b. 1880)	Fantasie, Op. 54, for bn. vn. and vc.	Evette (1942)
Françaix, J. (b. 1912)	Quintet for bn. 2 vn. va. and vc.	*Ms. Paris, Grandmaison
Gal, H. (b. 1890)	Divertissement for bn. and vc.	*Ms. Edinburgh, Gal.
Gebauer, F. R. (b. 1773)	Three Quartets, Op. 40	*Jouve
	Three Trios, Op. 33, for bn. vn. and vc.	*Sieber
Graf, F. H. (b. 1727)	Six Quartets	*British Museum
Gumlich, F.	Two Quartets	*Simrock (1822)
Heiden, B. (b. 1910)	Serenade	International
Hindemith, P. (b. 1895)	Stuck (1942) for bn. and vc.	*Ms. Hindemith estate
Holbrooke, J. (b. 1878)	Quintet, Op. 134, for bn. 2 vn. va. vc.	Modern Music Ltd.
Jacobi, C. (b. 1756)	Quartet, Op. 4	*Simrock (c. 1828)
Krommer, E. (b. 1759)	Two Quartets, Op. 46, for bn. 2 va. and vc.	*Vienna, Bureau des Arts (1804)
Küchler, J. (b. 1738)	Six Quartets, Op. 13	*Paris, National Bibl.
Lange, H.	Quintet (1937) for bn. 2 vn. va. and vc.	Lange
Lindley, R. (b. 1776)	Trio, Op. 7 (1810), for bn. va. and vc.	*Clementi
Malzat, J. M. (b. 1730)	Three Quartets (1775) for bn. vn. va. and vc.	*Publisher not known
Mozart, W. A. (b. 1756)	Sonata (K. 292) for bn. and vc.	Breitkopf
Ozi, E. (b. 1754)	Six Sonatas for bn. and vc.	Afranius
Pfeiffer, F. A. (b. 1754)	Six Quartets, Op. 1	*Hummel
	Divertimento for bn. vn. and vc.	*Ms. Schwerin, M.L.B.
	Two Quartets	*Ms. Schwerin, M.L.B.
Reicha, A. (b. 1770)	Quintet (1826) for bn. 2 vn. va. and vc.	*Berlin, O.W.B.
Ritter, G. W. (b. 1748)	Six Quartets, Op. 1	*Sieber (1777)

Composer	*Title*	*Publisher/Source and Date*
Rolla, A. (b. 1757)	Concertino for bn. va. and vc.	*Milan Conservatorio
Rössler, F. A. (b. 1746)	Quartet	*Lübeck, Bibliothek.
Roussel, A. (b. 1869)	Duo for bn. and db.	Durand
Satter, G.	Sextet, Op. 109 (1869), for bn. 2 vn. va. and 2 vc.	Forberg
Schmitt, N. (*fl.* 18 Cent.)	Three Quartets, Op. 2 (1793)	*Cochet
Schneider, G. A. (b. 1770)	Eighteen Quartets	*Ms. Berlin, O.W.B.
	Quartet No. 1, Op. 43	*André (1808)
	Potpourri No. 2, Op. 48, for bn. vn. 2 va and vc.	*Peters (c. 1810)
Searle, H. (b. 1915)	Variations for bn. 2 vn. va. and vc.	Williams
Spisak, M. (b. 1914)	Duo for bn. and va.	Ricordi
Spitzmueller-Harmersbach, A. (b. 1894)	Divertimento, Op. 6, for bn. 2 vn. va. and pf.	Universal
Stamitz, K. (b. 1745)	Two Quartets, Op. 19, Nos. 5 and 6	*Sieber (c. 1777)
Stumpf, J. C. (b. 1760)	Quartet (1804)	*Simrock
Vinter, G.	Quintet (1964) for bn. 2 vn. va. and vc.	Polyphonic
Vogell, J. C. (b. 1756)	Three Quartets, Op. 5	*Leduc
Vogt, G. (b. 1781)	Sextet for bn. 2 vn. va. vc. and db.	Costallat

APPENDIX IV

Discography of Bassoon Players

This appendix is intended to give audibly available examples of the various styles of bassoon playing and players from 1920 onwards. Each player is listed with the works he has recorded together with the known record numbers, which include British, American and European pressings. No attempt is made to list other artists (or works not including bassoon) which are recorded on the same disc as such information is available from the catalogues once an initial reference is made. Recordings by wind ensembles and chamber groups where the bassoon players are not named have also been excluded.

The compiler is indebted to those two indispensable sources of discography —the *World Encyclopaedia of Recorded Music* by F. F. Clough and G. J. Cuming and the '*Gramophone' Long Playing Catalogue* edited by Stanley Day, as well as to information supplied by individual players listed. Other information is from his own index of wind music.

G. M.-M.

JOHN ALEXANDRA
Mozart: Quintet in E♭ (K. 452) for piano and wind — NGS 121/3
Mozart: Divertimento No. 16 in E♭ (K. 289) for 2 ob. — HLP 19
  2 hn. 2 bn. (Menuet and Adagio only) — 7er 5096

MAURICE ALLARD
Bach, C. P. E.: Trio Sonatas in B♭ and E♭ (W. 92) for — CHS 1074
  cl. bn. hpsch. — Clc 6084
Beethoven: Quintet in E♭ (Op. 16) for piano and wind — Pol. 566326/8
  — AmVox. PLP 6040
Bitsch: Passepied for bn. and pf. — Pat. G 1055
Bloch, A.: Goguenardises (1954) for bn. and pf. — Pat. G 1055
Couperin, F.: Les Goûts Réunis No. 5 in F for fl. bn.
  hpsch. — CFD 11
Couperin, F.: La Steinkerque for 2 ob. bn. and strings — TWV 91092
Ibert: Carignane (1954) for bn. and pf. — Pat. G 1055
LaLande: Symphonies pour les Soupers du Roi — TWV 91092
Lavagne: Steeple-Chase (1954) for bn. and pf. — Pat. G 1055
Lully: Marches and Fanfares — TWV 91092
Mouret: Fanfares (1st Suite Symphonique) for vns.
  obs. bns. tpts. and timps. — TWV 91092
Mozart: Bassoon Concerto in B♭ (K. 191) (with — CFD 52
  Salzburg Mozarteum, cond. Paumgartner) — RSX 13
Mozart: Bassoon Concerto in B♭ (K. 191) (with — DGG 18631
  Lamoureux Orch., cond. Markevitch) — DGG 138131
Oubradous: Divertissements (1954) for bn. and pf. — Pat. G 1055
Poulenc: Trio for ob. bn. pf. — Veg. C35A 181
Sauget: Divertissement de Chambre for fl. cl. bn. va. — Charl. CCPE 2
  and pf.

223

RAYMOND ALLARD

Mozart: Serenade No. 10 in B♭ (K. 361) for 2 ob. 2 cl.
    2 bst-hn. 2 bn. cbn. 4 hn., (cond. Koussevitzky)
    (1st, 3rd, 4th, 6th and 7th Movts.)

Vic. 12-0897/900
set M 1303
LM 1077

Stravinsky: L'histoire du Soldat for voices, vn. cl. bn.
    cnt. tbn. db. perc. (cond. Bernstein)

Vic. 12-0136/8
set M 1197
ItV.A12R 0091

Stravinsky: Octet (1923) for fl. cl. 2 bn. 2 tp. 2 tbn.
    (cond. Bernstein)

Vic. 12-0139/40
set M 1197
LM 1078
ItV.A12R 0091

HERBERT ANTON

Bach: Brandenburg Concerto No. 1 in F

LXT 5512

Mozart: Harmonie-Musik 'Die Entführung aus dem
    Serail' (for 2 ob. 2 ca. 2 hn. and 2 bn.)

APM 14141
SAPM 198023

HANS BÄRR

Haydn: Sinfonia concertante in B♭ (Op. 84) for ob.
    bn. vn. vc.

Or. MG 20068
Or. SMG 20069

VIRGINIO BIANCHI

Vivaldi: Bassoon Concerto in C (P. 69)

PL 10740
STPL 510740

Vivaldi: Bassoon Concerto in A Moll (P. 70)

PL 10740
STPL 510740
GBY 12480

Vivaldi: Bassoon Concerto in C (P. 71)

PL 10740
STPL 510740

Vivaldi: Bassoon Concerto in B♭ (P. 401)

PL 10740
STPL 510740

    (all with Accademici di Milano, cond. Santi)

Vivaldi: Concerto for oboe and bassoon (P. 129) (with
    Accademici di Milano, cond. Santi)

VDL 450
STDL 500450
GBY 12480

KAREL BIDLO

Beethoven: Sextet in E♭ (Op. 71) for 2 cl. 2 bn. 2 hn.

SUA 10293

Beethoven: Octet in E♭ (Op. 103) for 2 ob. 2 cl. 2 bn.
    2 hn.

Amad. VVRS 6159

Dvořák: Serenade in D Moll (Op. 44) for 2 ob. 2 cl.
    2 bn. cbn. 3 hn. vc. db.

SUA 10326

Janáček: Mládí for fl. ob. cl. bcl. bn. hn.

LPM 400
Merc. 15009

Krommer-Kramář: Harmonie (Op. 71) for 2 ob. 2 cl.
    2 bn. cbn. 2 hn.

U. H 13121/3
LPM 60
U 5041C
SUP 20217

Mozart: Bassoon Concerto: in B♭ (K. 191) (with
    Czech Philharmonic Orch., cond. Ancerl)

U.H 24205/7
LPV 66
PLP 104
SUP 10208

Mozart: Serenade No. 11 in E♭ (K. 375) for 2 ob. 2 cl.
    2 bn. 2 hn.

Amad. VVRS 6159

Pauer: Bassoon Concerto (with Czech Philharmonic Orch., cond. Ancerl) ALPV 366
SUP 10310
Telemann: Quartet in D Moll for fl. ob. bn. and cont. (T.M.2) SUA 10500
Weber: Bassoon Concerto in F (Op. 75) (with Czech Philharmonic Orch., cond. Redel) LPEM 19129
ALPV 366
SUP 10310

ROGER BIRNSTINGL

Bach: Musical offering (BWV 1079)	XID 5237
Beethoven: Sextet in Eb (Op. 71) for 2 cl. 2 bn. 2 hn.	LXT 6170
	SXL 6170
Beethoven: Octet in Eb (Op. 103) for 2 ob. 2 cl. 2 bn. 2 hn.	LXT 6170
	SXL 6170
Beethoven: Rondino in Eb (Op. posth.) for 2 ob. 2 cl. 2 bn. 2 hn.	LXT 6170
	SXL 6170
Handel: Concerto Grosso (Op. 3, No. 1)	RG 400
Mozart: Divertimento No. 3 in Eb (K. 166) for 2 ob. 2 ca. 2 cl. 2 bn. 2 hn.	LXT 6050
	SXL 6050
Mozart: Divertimento No. 4 in Bb (K. 186) for 2 ob. 2 ca. 2 cl. 2 bn. 2 hn.	LXT 6051
	SXL 6051
Mozart: Divertimento No. 8 in F (K. 213) for 2 ob. 2 bn. 2 hn.	LXT 6050
	SXL 6050
Mozart: Divertimento No. 9 in Bb (K. 240) for 2 ob. 2 bn. 2 hn.	LXT 6052
	SXL 6052
Mozart: Divertimento No. 12 in Eb (K. 252) for 2 ob. 2 bn. 2 hn.	LXT 6052
	SXL 6052
Mozart: Divertimento No. 13 in F (K. 253) for 2 ob. 2 bn. 2 hn.	LXT 6051
	SXL 6051
Mozart: Divertimento No. 14 in Bb (K. 270) for 2 ob. 2 bn. 2 hn.	LXT 6053
	SXL 6053
Mozart: Divertimento No. 16 in Eb (K. 289) for 2 ob. 2 bn. 2 hn.	LXT 6053
	SXL 6053
Mozart: Divertimento Bb (K.A. 227) for 2 cl. 2 bn. 2 hn.	LXT 6053
	SXL 6053
Mozart: Divertimento in Eb (K.A. 266) for 2 ob. 2 cl. 2 bn. 2 hn.	LXT 6052
	SXL 6052
Mozart: Serenade No. 10 in Bb (K. 361) for 2 ob. 2 cl. 2 bst-hn. 2 bn. cbn. 4 hn.	LXT 6049
	SXL 6049
Mozart: Serenade No. 11 in Eb (K. 375) for 2 ob. 2 cl. 2 bn. 2 hn.	LXT 6050
	SXL 6050
Mozart: Serenade No. 12 in C Moll (K. 388) for 2 ob. 2 cl. 2 bn. 2 hn.	LXT 6051
	SXL 6051

CARL BLOCH

Bozza: Variations sur un thème Libre (Op. 40) for wind quintet	D. LXT 2803
	Lon. LL 734
Haydn: Sinfonia Concertante in Bb (Op. 84) for ob. bn. vn. vc. and orch. (with Danish Radio Orch., cond. Busch)	G. C 4122/4
	DB 20134/6
Holmboe: Notturno (Op. 19) (1940) for wind quintet	G. DA 5258/9

CARL BLOCH—*cont.*

Ibert: Trois Pièces Brèves for wind quintet	D LXT 2803
	Lon. LL 734
Mozart: Divertimento No. 14 in B♭ (K. 270) for 2 ob. 2 bn. 2 hn.	G. DA 5260/1
Nielsen: Wind Quintet in A (Op. 43)	G. KALP 7
	MOAK 30004
	Od 30004
	D. LXT 2803
	Lon. LL 734
	Mer. MG. 15046
Poulenc: Trio for ob. bn. and pf. (1926)	Mtr. CL 3000/1
	Mtr. MCEP 3002
Schultz: Une Amourette for wind quintet	Mer. MG. 15046

HENRI BOUCHET

Moser: Suite for ob. cl. bn.	CT 64–15
Müller von Kulm: Suite (Op. 57) for 2 fl. cl. bn.	CT 64–23

MANFRED BRAUN

Beethoven: Septet in E♭ (Op. 20) for cl. bn. hn. vn. va. vc. db.	LPM 18887
	SLPM 138887
Mozart: Sonata in B♭ (K. 292) for bn. and vc.	LPM 18887
	SLPM 138887

AAGE BREDAHL

Jersild: Music-Making in the Forest (1947) for wind quintet	C. KC 1
Rossini: Quartet No. 4 in B♭ for fl. cl. bn. hn.	C. SELK 1001
Stravinsky: Octet (1923) for fl. cl. 2 bn. 2 tp. 2 tbn.	C. KC 1

GWYDION BROOKE

Beethoven: Symphony No. 4 in B♭—bassoon passage from 4th Movt.	CLP 1523
	7eg 8673
Instruments of the Orchestra: Demonstration of Bassoon Compass	CLP 1523
	7eg 8673
Mozart: Bassoon Concerto in B♭ (K. 191) (with Royal Philharmonic Orch., cond. Sir Thomas Beecham, Bart., C.H.)	ALP 1768
	ASD 334
	Cap. G 7201
	SG. 7201
	FALP 657
	ASDF 225
Rimsky-Korsakov: Scheherazade—Bassoon cadenza	CLP 1523
	7eg 8673
Weber: Bassoon Concerto in F (Op. 75) (J. 187) (with Liverpool Philharmonic Orch., cond. Sargent)	C. DX 1656/7
	GQX 11402/3
Weber: Bassoon Concerto in F (Op. 75) (J. 187) 1st Movt. (with orchestra, cond. Sargent)	LXT 5573

MARTIN BÜLOW

Bach: Cantata: 'Was Gott tut' (BWV 100)	Cant. 641208
Bach: Cantata: 'Er rufet seinen Schafen' (BWV 175)	Cant. 641208

EBERHARD BUSCHMANN

Mozart: Divertimento in B♭ (K. 196f) for 2 cl. 2 bn. 2 hn.	APM 14141
	SAPM 198123

ALFRED BUTLER (Contrabassoon)
Dohnányi: Variations on a Nursery Song, Var. IV arr.
cbn.   LXT 5573

F. BUURMANN
Bach: Cantata: 'Gleich wie der Regen' (BWV 18)   Tel. AWT. 9442-C
Bach: Cantata: 'Tritt auf die Glaubensbahn' (BWV   Tel. AWT 9442-C
    152)

ARCHIE CAMDEN
Bach, J. S.: Musical Offering (BWV 1079) (with Bath   ALP 1893
    Festival Orch., cond. Menuhin)   ASD 414
Bach, J. S.: Aria from Anna Magdelena Book (arr. bn.
    and pf)   G. C 3621
Beethoven: Septet in E♭ (Op. 20) for cl. bn. hn. vn. va.   G. DB 3026/30
    vc. db.   Vic. 12450/4
                                                       set M 571
Galliard: Sonata No. 1 for bn. and cont.   7ep 7078
Galliard: Suite in four movements for bn. and cont.   7ep 7187
Godfrey: Variations on Lucy Long   7ep 7078
Kerrison: Lullaby and Fairy Clock   7ep 7078
Mozart: Bassoon Concerto in B♭ (K. 191) (with Hallé   AmC 67328/30D
    Orch., cond. Sir Hamilton Harty)   C. L. 1824/6
Mozart: Bassoon Concerto in B♭ (K. 191) (with   DLP 1153
    London Mozart Players, cond. Blech)   Elec. E 80770
Sammartini: Sonata in G for vn. and cont. (arr. bn.
    and pf.) (Gigue only)   G. C 3621
Senallié: Sonata in D Moll (Bk. II No. 5) for vn. and   C. L. 1826
    cont. (Allegro Spiritoso only. Arr. bn. and orch.)   AmC 67330D
    (with Hallé Orchestra, cond. Sir Hamilton Harty)   in set M 71
Senallié: Sonata in D Moll (Bk. II No. 5) for vn. and
    cont. (Allegro Spiritoso only. Arr. bn. and orch.)
    (with London Mozart Players, cond. Blech)   7ep 7078
Senallié: Sonata in D Moll (Bk. II, No. 5) for vn. and
    cont. (Allegro Spiritoso only. Arr. bn. and pf.)
    (with Gerald Moore—pf.)   7ep. 7187
Stamitz: Bassoon Concerto in F (with London Mozart   DLP 1153
    Players, cond. Blech)   Elec. E 80770
Tscherepnine: Esquisse for bn. and pf.   7ep 7187
13th Century Manuscript: Lamento di Tristan for bn.
    and cont.   7ep 7187

ELIAS CARMEN
Beethoven: Quintet in E♭ (Op. 16) for pf. and wind   STR 616
                                                      MC 20062
Powel: Divertimento for wind quintet   CRI 121
Schubert: Octet in F (Op. 166) for cl. hn. bn. 2 vn. va.   STR 603
    vc. db.   MC 20073
Spohr: Nonet in F. (Op. 31) for fl. ob. cl. hn. bn. vn.
    va. vc. db.   STR 609
Weber: Andante e Rondo ongarese (Op. 35) (J. 158)   YPR 1009

LEO ČERMAK
Beethoven: Trio in G for fl. bn. and pf.   SPA 28

Q

LEO ČERMAK—*cont.*

Mozart: Bassoon Concerto in B♭ (K. 191) (with Vienna Pro Musica, cond. Emmer)	E and AmVox PL 8870
Mozart: Bassoon Concerto in B♭ (K 191) (with Vienna Symphony Orch., cond. Paumgartner)	abe 10167 Phi 369
Mozart: Divertimento No. 8 in F (K. 213) for 2 ob. 2 hn. 2 bn.	Phi. S 06031 R
Mozart: Divertimento No. 9 in B♭ (K. 240) for 2 ob. 2 hn. 2 bn.	Phi. S 06031 R
Mozart: Divertimento No. 12 in E♭ (K. 252) for 2 ob. 2 hn. 2 bn.	Phi. A 00211 L
Mozart: Divertimento No. 13 in F (K. 253) for 2 ob 2 hn. 2 bn.	Phi. A 00211 L
Mozart: Divertimento No. 14 in B♭ (K. 270) for 2 ob 2 hn. 2 bn.	Phi. A 00211 L
Mozart: Divertimento No. 16 in E♭ (K. 289) for 2 ob. 2 hn. 2 bn.	Phi. A 00211 L
Mozart: Serenade No. 10 in B♭ (K. 361) for 2 ob. 2 cl. 2 bst-hn. 2 bn. cbn. 4 hn.	AmVox PL 7470
Mozart: Serenade No. 11 in E♭ (K. 375) for 2 ob. 2 cl. 2 hn. 2 bn.	E and AmVox PL 7490 Phi. A 00291 L
Mozart: Serenade No. 12 in C Moll (K. 388) for 2 ob. 2 cl. 2 hn. 2 bn.	E and AmVox PL 7490 Phi. A 00291 L

J. CHARPENTIER

Boismortier: Concerto à cinque in E Moll (Op. 37) for fl. vn. ob. bn. and cont.	DDP 21-1 HS. HSL 103

DON CHRISTLIEB

Duke: Etude for vn. and bn.	M 6007
Hindemith: Kleine Kammermusik (Op. 24, No. 2) for wind quintet	AmC 17169/70D Set X 149
Hindemith: Hérodiade for chamber orchestra (cond. Craft)	MS 6571
Mozart: Serenade No. 10 in B♭ (K. 361) for 2 ob. 2 cl. 2 bst-hn. 2 bn. cbn. 4 hn.	Cap. CTL 7030 P 8181 CLCX 037
Stockhausen: Zeitmasse (Op. 5) for wind quintet	Col. ML 5275
Strauss, R.: Duo-Concertante for cl. bn. strings and hp. (with Los Angeles Chamber Orch., cond. Byrns)	DCap. CTL 7007 Cap. P 8115 T. LCE 8115
Stravinsky: L'Histoire du Soldat for vn. cl. bn. cnt. tbn. db. and perc. (cond. Stravinsky)	BRG 72007 ML 5672 MS 6272
Villa-Lobos: Nonet—Impressao rapida de todo o Brasil for fl. ob. cl. sax. bn. cel. hp. perc. and chorus	Cap. CTL 7037 P 8191

SAMUEL COHEN (COREYS)

Schuman: Quartettino (1939) for 4 bn.	NMQR 1415

ROBERT COLE
Blackwood: Chamber Symphony for 14 wind (1955)
    (Op. 2)   CRI 144
Cambini: Sinfonia Concertante for ob. and bn. (with
    Accademia dell'Orso)   Per 732
Mozart: Serenade No. 11 in E♭ (K. 375) for 2 ob. 2 cl.   CM 25
    2 bn. 2 hn.   SCM 25
Mozart: Serenade No. 12 in C Moll (K. 388) for 2 ob.   CM 25
    2 cl. 2 bn. 2 hn.   SCM 25

KENNETH COOPER (contrabassoon)
Brahms: Symphony No. 1 in C Moll—finale. Cbn.   CLP 1523
    part.   7eg 8673
Instruments of the Orchestra: Demonstration of   CLP 1523
    contrabassoon range   7eg 8673
Mozart: Serenade No. 10 in B♭ (K. 361) for 2 ob.   LXT 6049
    2 cl. 2 bst-hn. 2 bn. cbn. 4 hn.   SXL 6049

MARCO COSTANTINI
Vivaldi: Bassoon Concerto in E Moll (P. 137) (with   2-Epic Sc 6040
    I Musici)   BSC 111
                                          Phi 2054
                                        Phi 835058

CHARLES CRACKNELL
Dvořák: Serenade in D Moll (Op. 44) for 2 ob. 2 cl.   CCL 30153
    2 bn. cbn. 3 hn. vc. and db.   Mer. 50041
Gounod: Petite Symphonie in B Moll for fl. 2 ob. 2 cl.   CCL 30153
    2 bn. 2 hn.   Mer. 50041

VACLAV CVRČEK
Reicha: Wind Quintet in B♭ (Op. 88, No. 5)   LPM 433
                                        MAB 11

TINA DI DARIO
Beethoven: Three Duos in C, F and B♭ for cl. and bn.   CEd. CE 1013
Villa-Lobos: Trio (1921) for ob. cl. and bn.   Nix WLP 5360
                                        CEd. CE 2002
                                        West. WL 5360
Villa-Lobos: Quartet for fl. ob. cl. and bn.   Nix. WLP 5360
                                          CEd. CE 2002
                                        West WL 5360
Villa-Lobos: Quintet en forme de Chôros for fl. ob. ca.   Nix WLP 5360
    cl. bn.   CEd. CE 2002
                                        West WL 5360

ANDRE DELHEMMES
Beethoven: Sextet in E♭ (Op. 71) for 2 cl. 2 hn. 2 bn.   CF du D. 274
Josquin: La Bernadina for ob. 2 bn. and orch.   RS 29
                                        Non. H 1025
                                        H 71025

SYLIVIA DEUTSCHER
Dufay: 'Musik von Guillaume Dufay'   AVRS 6163

GUSTAVE DHÉRIN
Poulenc: Trio (1925) for pf. ob. and bn.   C. L 2223/4
                                                        D 14213/4
                                                        O 4290/1

ANTON DOOMERNIK
Dvořák: Serenade in D Moll (Op. 44) for 2 ob. 2 cl.
    2 bn. cbn. vc. db.   CHS. H 6
Hindemith: Kleine Kammermusik (Op. 24, No. 2) for
    wind quintet   CHS. H 15
Milhaud: La Cheminée du Roi René for wind quintet   MMS 108
Poulenc: Sextet for piano and wind (with H. Krugt—   CHS H. 15
    pf.)   MMS H. 15

PAUL DRAPER
Casella: Serenata (Op. 50) for cl. bn. tp. vn. and vc.
    (Tarantella only)   C. DB 1788
Mozart: Divertimento No. 16 in E♭ (K. 289) for 2 ob.   HLP 19
    2 bn. and 2 hn.   7er 5096

DROULEZ
Haydn: Sinfonia Concertante in B♭ for ob. bn. vn. vc.
    (with Lamoureux Orch., cond. Mankevitch)   DGG 619169

KARL DVORAK
Dittersdorf: Divertimento in B♭   Mus. G. 28
                                                        Mus. G. S28
Dittersdorf: Partita in D   Mus. G. 28
                                                        Mus. G. S28
Haydn: Divertimento in C (Feldparthie) for 2 ob. 2 cl. Strad STR 622
    2 bn.   Cpt. MC 20104
Haydn: Divertimento in F for 2 ob. 2 cl. 2 bn.   Strad STR 622
                                                        Cpt. MC 20104
Haydn, M.: Divertimento in D   Mus. G. 28
                                                        Mus. G. S28
                                                        AMA AVRS 6182
Mozart: Quintet in E♭ (K. 452) for ob. cl. bn. hn. pf
    (with Bauer-Theussl—pf.)   AMA AVRS 6182
Stamitz, K.: Quartet in E♭ (Op. 8, No. 2) for ob. cl.   Mus. G. 28
    bn. hn.   Mus. G. S28
                                                        AMA AVRS 6182

VERNON ELLIOTT
Britten: The Turn of the Screw   LXT 5038/9
Dohnányi: Variations on a Nursery Song, Var. lV arr.
    cbn. and pf.   C 3621

GÉRARD FAISANDIER
Arnold: Three Shanties for wind quintet   Veg. C 35A 140
Auric: Trio for ob. cl. and bn.   Veg. C 30A 37
Beethoven: Trio in G for fl. bn. and pf.   Veg. C 30S 112
                                                        Non. H. 1025
                                                        H. 71025

Beethoven: Quintet in E♭ (Op. 16) for pf. and wind	Veg. C 30S 112
	CF du D. 308
Beethoven: Sextet in E♭ (Op. 71) for 2 cl. 2 hn. 2 bn.	CF du D. 274
	Non. H. 1025
	H. 71025
Beethoven: Octet in E♭ (Op. 103) for 2 ob. 2 cl. 2 hn. 2 bn.	CF du D. 308
Hindemith: Kleine Kammermusik (Op. 24, No. 2) for wind quint.	Veg. C 37A 72
Ibert: Trois Pièces Brèves for wind quintet	Veg. C 30A 37
Ibert: Cinq Pièces en trio for ob. cl. bn.	Veg. C. 30A 37
Jolivet: Pastorales de Noël for fl. bn. and hp.	Veg. C 37A 73
Josquin: La Bernadina for ob. 2 bn. and orch.	RS 29
Malipiero: Quartet for fl. ob. cl. and bn.	Veg. C 35A 140
Milhaud: La Cheminée du roi René for wind quintet	Veg. C 30A 37
Milhaud: Suite d'après Corette for ob. cl. and bn.	CF du D. 268
Milhaud: Divertissement for wind quintet	CF du D. 268
Mozart: Divertimento No. 3 in B♭ for 2 cl. bn. (arr. ob. cl. bn.)	Veg. C 30S 111
Mozart: Quintet in E♭ (K. 452) for piano and wind	Veg. C 30S 111
Poulenc: Trio for ob. bn. and pf.	⎱ Numbers
Poulenc: Sextet for fl. ob. cl. bn. hn. and pf. (with Jacques Ferrière—pf.)	⎰ not known
Rossini: Quartet No. 2 in G for fl. cl. hn. bn.	Veg. C 37A 71
Schoenberg: Wind Quintet (Op. 25)	Crit. CRD 145
	SCRD 145
Teuscher: Partita for wind quintet	Veg. C 35A 169
Villa-Lobos: Bachianas Brasileiras No. 6 for fl. and bn.	Veg. C 35A 140
Vivaldi: Bassoon Concerto in A Moll (P. 72) (with Paris Chamber Orch., cond. Jouve)	Sel. LP 8702
	T. NLB 6081
	West. WL 5341
Vivaldi: Bassoon Concerto in B♭ (P. 386) (with Chamber Orch., cond. Cartigny)	Sel. LA 1080
Vivaldi: Concerto in G (P. 129) for ob. bn. and orch. (with L'Orchestre de la Société à musique à Chambre de Paris, cond. Cartigny)	LT. MEL 94005
	T. TW 30016
	V. sel LLA 1081

OTTO FLEISCHMANN

Mozart: Divertimento No. 8 in F (K. 213) for 2 ob. 2 hn. 2 bn.	Phi. S 06031R
Mozart: Divertimento No. 9 in B♭ (K. 240) for 2 ob. 2 hn. 2 bn.	Phi. S 06031R
Mozart: Divertimento No. 12 in E♭ (K. 252) for 2 ob. 2 hn. 2 bn.	Phi. A 00211L
Mozart: Divertimento No. 13 in F (K. 253) for 2 ob. 2 hn. 2 bn.	Phi. A 00211L
Mozart: Divertimento No. 14 in B♭ (K. 270) for 2 ob. 2 hn. 2 bn.	Phi. A 00211L
Mozart: Divertimento No. 16 in E♭ (K. 289) for 2 ob. 2 hn. 2 bn.	Phi. A 00211L
Mozart: Serenade No. 10 in B♭ (K. 361) for 2 ob. 2 cl. 2 bst-hn. 2 bn. cbn. 4 hn.	AmVox PL 7470

OTTO FLEISCHMANN—*cont.*
Mozart: Serenade No. 11 in E♭ (K. 375) for 2 ob. 2 cl.   AmVox PL 7490
   2 hn. 2 bn.   E Vox PL 7490
     Phi. A 00291L
Mozart: Serenade No. 12 in C Moll (K. 388) for 2 ob.   AmVox PL 7490
   2 cl. 2 hn. 2 bn.   E Vox PL 7490
     Phi. A 00291L

ALFRED FRANKE
Berwald: Septet (1828) in B♭ minor for cl. bn. hn. vn.
   va. vc. db.   Cyc. 30 CM 017
Mozart: Divertimento in B♭ (K. 196f) for 2 cl. 2 bn.   APM 14141
   2 hn.   SAPM 198023

WILLI FUGMANN
Mozart: Quintet in E♭ (K. 452) for pf. and wind   479003

TIBOR FÜLEMILE
Danzi: Divertimento in G Moll (Op. 56) for wind
   quintet   Qual. LP 1607
Ranki: Pentaerophonia—Tre pezzi per quintetto a fiati   Qual. LP 1607

BERNARD GARFIELD
Bach, C. P. E.: Rondo Andantino (arr. wind quintet)   GC CR 4028
Beethoven: Octet in E♭ (Op. 103) for 2 ob. 2 cl. 2 hn.
   2 bn.   EMS 1
Beethoven: Rondino in E♭ (Op. posth.) for 2 ob. 2 cl.
   2 hn. 2 bn.   EMS 1
Bozza: Variations sur un Thème libre for wind   Eso 505
   quintet   Cpt. MC 20001
Buxtehude: Chorale 'Jesu meine Freude' (arr. wind
   quintet)   GC CR 4028
Carter: Eight Studies and a Fantasy (1950) for wind
   quintet   CRI 118
Danzi: Wind Quintet (Op. 67, No. 2)   Con-Disc 1205
     S 205
Françaix: Wind Quintet   Con-Disc 1222
     S 222
Glanville-Hicks: Concertino da Camera (1943) for pf.
   fl. cl. bn.   AMC.ML 4990
Haydn: Sinfonia Concertante in B♭ (Op. 84) for ob.
   bn. vn. vc.   Number unknown
Hill: Sextet (Op. 39) (1934) for pf. and wind quintet   AMC.ML 4846
Hindemith: Bassoon Sonata (1938)   EMS 4
Hindemith: Kleine Kammermusik (Op. 24, No. 2)   Con-Disc 1205
   wind quintet   S 205
Ibert: Trois Pièces brèves for wind quintet   Eso 505
     Cpt.MC 20001
Milhaud: Deux Esquisses for wind quintet   Eso 505
     Cpt.MC 20001
Milhaud: La Cheminée du Roi René for wind quintet   EMS 6
Milhaud: Pastorale for ob. cl. bn.   EMS 6

BERNARD GARFIELD—*cont.*

Mozart: Bassoon Concerto in B♭ (K. 191) (with Phila-delphia Orch., cond. Ormandy)	BRG 72127
	SBRG 72127
Mozart: Sinfonia Concertante in E♭ (K. 297b) for ob. cl. bn. hn.	Number unknown
Purcell: Pavan (arr. wind quintet)	G CR 4028
Rossini: Quartets No. 1 in F, 4 in B♭, 5 in D and 6 in F for fl. cl. bn. hn.	Per. SLP 737
	5737
Spohr: Nonet in F (Op. 31) for fl. ob. cl. bn. hn. vn. va. vc. db.	Con-Disc 1201
	S 201
	XID 5147
	BAE BM 30 L1804
Taffanel: Wind Quintet in G Moll	Eso 505
	Cpt.MC 20001
	Con-Disc 1222
	S 222
Varèse: Integrales for wind and percussion	EMS 401
Varèse: Octandre for wind	EMS 401
Villa-Lobos: Bachianas Brasileiras No. 6 for fl. and bn.	Phil. PH 110
	Non. H 1030
	H 71030
Villa-Lobos: Quintet en forme de Chôros (1953) for wind quintet	Phil. PH 110
	Non. H 1030
	H 71030
Vivaldi: Bassoon Concerto in B♭ (P. 401) (La Notte) (with Gothic String Ensemble)	CHS. CHC 56
Vivaldi: Concerto for fl. ob. bn. (P. 402)	Wash. 402
Vivaldi: Partita in B♭ for ob. bn. and hpsch.	Wash. 402
Vivaldi: Sonata in A Moll for fl. bn. and hpsch.	Wash. 402
Vivaldi: Trio Sonata in C Moll for fl. ob. bn. and hpsch.	Wash. 402
Weber: Andante e Rondo ongarese in C (Op. 35) (J. 158)	Number unknown
Wilder: Wind Quintet	Phil. PH 110
Wilder: Suite for woodwind	GC CR 4028
Wilder: Buffoonery for bn.	GC CR 4028
Wilder: Wind Quintet No. 2 (1956)	GC CR 4028

HUGO GEHRING

Haydn: Sinfonia Concertante in B♭ (Op. 84) for ob. bn. vn. vc. and orch. (with Stuttgart Pro Musica Orch., cond. Reinhardt)	PL 7390
	CFR 12-312
Mozart: Sinfonia Concertante in E♭ (K. 297b) for ob. cl. bn. hn. and orch. (with Stuttgart Pro Musica Orch., cond. Reinhardt)	PL 7320
	Vox 11830
Mozart: Sinfonia Concertante in E♭ (K. 297b) for ob. cl. bn. hn. and orch. (with Vienna Opera Orch., cond. Swoboda)	WH 20064
Mozart: Harmonie-Musik 'Die Entführung aus dem Serail' for 2 ob. 2 ca. 2 bn. and 2 hn.	APM 14141
	SAPM 198023

LOREN GLICKMAN

Beethoven: Sextet in E♭ (Op. 71) for 2 cl. 2 hn. 2 bn.	CPST 559
	CPT 567

LOREN GLICKMAN—*cont.*

Beethoven: Octet in E♭ (Op. 103) for 2 ob. 2 cl. 2 hn. 2 bn.	CPST 559 CPT 567
Beethoven: Rondino in E♭ (Op. posth.) for 2 ob. 2 cl. 2 hn. 2 bn.	CPST 559 CPT 567
Menotti: The Unicorn, the Gorgon and the Manticore for voices, fl. ob. cl. bn. tp. va. vc. db. perc. (cond. Schippers)	33 CX 1543
Mozart: Serenade No. 11 in E♭ (K. 375) for 2 ob. 2 cl. 2 bn. 2 hn.	CM 25 SCM 25
Mozart: Serenade No. 12 in C Moll (K. 388) for 2 ob. 2 cl. 2 bn. 2 hn.	CM 25 SCM 25
Stravinsky: L'Histoire du Soldat for voices, vn. cl. bn. cnt. tbn. db. perc.	AmC ML 4964 EPHI ABL 3065 Phi A 01193L
Stravinsky: Octet for fl. cl. 2 bn. 2 tp. and 2 tbn.	BRG 72007 ML 4964 ML 5672
Stravinsky: Septet (1953) for cl. bn. hn. vn. va. vc. and pf.	ABL 3391 A 01493L

HEINRICH GÖLDNER

Muthel: Concerto in D Moll for hpsch. 2 bn. and strings (with Schola Cantorum Basiliensis, cond. Wenzinger)	APM 14300 SAPM 198300

HAROLD GOLTZER

Barab: A Child's Garden of Verses for tenor, cl. bn. tp. and pf.	Eso ESJ 5
Wilder: Air for bassoon and strings	AmC.ML 4271

GABRIEL GRANDMAISON

Gervaise: Danceries (arr. wind quintet, Désormière)	D. GAG 15113

WILLIAM GRUNER

Weber: Andante e Rondo ongarese in C (Op. 35) (J. 158)	Vic. 20525 18684

ANNE DE GUICHARD

Berger: Serenade Concertante	Am. Emb. Lib. 574

RUDOLF HÄNZL

Beethoven: Quintet in E♭ (Op. 16) for pf. & wind (with Panhoffer—pf.)	D.LXT 5530 Lon. CS 6063
Beethoven: Sextet in E♭ (Op. 71) for 2 cl. 2 hn. 2 bn.	WL 5003 WP 114
Beethoven: Septet in E♭ (Op. 20) for cl. bn. hn. vn. va. vc. db.	D.LXT 5093 LXT 5529 SXL 2157
Beethoven: Octet E♭ (Op. 103) for 2 ob. 2 cl. 2 hn. 2 bn.	WL 5003 WP 114

Beethoven: Rondino in E♭ (Op. posth.) for 2 ob. 2 cl. 2 hn. 2 bn.	WLP 5262
Haydn: Octet in F for 2 ob. 2 cl. 2 hn. 2 bn.	WL 5002
	WN 18058
Kreutzer: Septet in Eb (Op. 62) for cl. bn. hn. vn. va. vc. db.	D.LXT 2628
	Lon.LLP 420
	D.KK 28538/41
	CM 2129
	CS 6132
Mozart: Divertimento No. 3 in E♭ (K. 166) for 2 ob. 2 ca. 2 cl. 2 hn. 2 bn.	WN 18011
Mozart: Divertimento No. 4 in B♭ (K. 186) for 2 ob. 2 ca. 2 cl. 2 hn. 2 bn.	WN 18011
Mozart: Divertimento No. 8 in F (K. 213) for 2 ob. 2 bn. 2 hn.	West WL 5103
Mozart: Divertimento No. 9 in B♭ (K. 240) for 2 ob. 2 hn. 2 bn.	WN 18011
Mozart: Divertimento No. 12 in E♭ (K. 252) for 2 ob. 2 bn. 2 hn.	West WL 5103
Mozart: Divertimento No. 13 in F (K. 253) for 2 ob. 2 bn. 2 hn.	West WL 5103
Mozart: Divertimento No. 14 in B♭ (K. 270) for 2 ob. 2 bn. 2 hn.	West WL 5103
Mozart: Divertimento No. 16 in E♭ (K. 289) for 2 ob. 2 hn. 2 bn.	WN 18011
Mozart: Divertimento in E♭ (K. 196e) for 2 ob. 2 cl. 2 hn. 2 bn.	WL 5349
Mozart: Divertimento in B♭ (K. 196f) for 2 ob. 2 cl. 2 hn. 2 bn.	WL 5349
Mozart: Serenade No. 10 in B♭ (K. 361) for 2 ob. 2 cl. 2 bst-hn. 2 bn. cbn. 4 hn.	WLP 5229 WL 5229
Mozart: Serenade No. 10 in B♭ (K. 361) for 2 ob. 2 cl. 2 bst-hn. 2 bn. cln. 4 hn. (cond. by Fürtwangler)	G.DB 6707/11 Elec. 91175
Mozart: Serenade No. 11 in E♭ (K. 375) for 2 ob. 2 cl. 2 hn. 2 bn.	WL 5021 West. 18134 Sel.LPG 8345
Mozart: Serenade No. 12 in C Moll (K. 388) for 2 ob. 2 cl. 2 hn. 2 bn.	WL 5021 West 18134 Sel.LPG 8345
Poot: Octet (1948) for cl. bn. hn. 2 vn. va. vc. db.	D.LXT 5294
Schubert: Octet in F (Op. 166) for cl. bn. hn. 2 vn. va. vc. db.	D.LXT 2983 LXT 5455 SXL 2028 Lon. LL 1049 Lon. set LA 124 Am D set EDA 104 D.AK 2060/5
Spohr: Nonet in F (Op. 31) for fl. ob. cl. bn. hn. vn. va. vc. db.	D.LXT 2782 Lon. LL 710
Strauss, R.: Serenade in B♭ (Op. 4) for 2 fl. 2 ob. 2 cl. 2 bn. cbn. 4 hn.	WL 5185
Strauss, R.: Serenade in E♭ (Op. 7) for 2 fl. 2 ob. 2 cl. 2 bn. cbn. 4 hn.	WL 5185

CUTHBERT HARDING
Ashlyn: The Bassoon Song (sung by Jack Cooper)   Or. CB 1109
Trad: Three Blind Mice (narrated by Gilbert Harding
    with Bassoon Trio*)   Or. CB 1109

JOHN HARPER
Handel: Concerto Grosso (Op. 3, No. 1)   RG 400

J. HAULTIER
Haydn: Sinfonia Concertante in B♭ (Op. 84) for vn.
    vc. ob. bn.   MusG. 35
        H. 1024

HENRI HELAERTS
Mozart: Bassoon Concerto in B♭ (K. 191) (Ibert   D.LXT 2990
    Cadenza) (with London Symphony Orch., cond.   Lon. LL 1135
    Collins)   CM 9118
        ACL 240
Mozart: Serenade No. 10 in B♭ (K. 361) for 2 ob. 2 cl.
    2 bst-hn. 2 bn. cbn. 4 hn. (cond. Ansermet)   D.LXT 5121
Stravinsky: L'Historie du Soldat for voices, vn. cl. bn.
    cnt. tbn. db. perc.   D. LXT 5321
Vivaldi: Bassoon Concerto in D Moll (P. 282) (with   D. LX 3100
    Suisse Romande Orch., cond. Ansermet)   Lon. LS 591

FRITZ HENKER
Bach, J. C.: Bassoon Concerto in B♭ (with Saar   KL 61
    Chamber Orch., cond. Ristenpart)   SKL 161
        APM 14199
        SAPM 198199
Boismortier: Concerto in E minor (Op. 37) fl. ob. bn.   APM 14148
    vn. and continuo   SAPM 198031
Haydn: Sinfonia Concerte in B♭ (Op. 84) for ob. bn.   Number not
    vn. vc.   known
Telemann: Concerto in D for 2 ob. tp. and bn.   APM 14114

ALBERT HENNIGE
Beethoven: Duo No. 1 in C. for cl. and bn.   ARC 37174
        epa 37137
Mozart: Divertimento No. 3 in B♭ (K. 439b) for 2 cl.
    and bn.   APM 14117
Mozart: Divertimento No. 5 in B♭ (K. 439b) for 2 cl.
    and bn. (Romance and Polonaise only)   APM 14117
Mozart: Adagio (K. 440d) for 2 bst-hn. and bn.   APM 14117

ERNEST HINCHCLIFF
Beethoven: Septet in E♭ (Op. 20) for cl. bn. hn. vn.   C. LX 109/13
    va. vc. db.   AmC 68096/100D
        set M 180
Godfrey: Lucy Long (arr. bn. and pf.)   G. B 1756
Hinchcliffe: Ri-too-ral-i-tay for bn.   G. B 1756

* Paul Draper recalls playing this with Cuthbert Harding and Ernest Hinch-cliff and believes it was they who also made this recording with Harding.

Schubert: Octet in F (Op. 166) for cl. bn. hn. 2 vn.   C. L 2108/13
va. vc. db.   GQX 10961/6
   AmC 67457/62D
   set M 97

FLORIEN HOLLARD
Mozart: Bassoon Concerto in B♭ (K. Anh. 230a) (with
Winterthur Symphony Orch., cond. Ackermann)   CHS. H 3

PAUL HONGNE
Arrieu: Wind Quintet in C   OL 50122
Bach, J. C.: Quintet in D (Op. 22, No. 1) for fl. ob. vn.   BAM. LD 011
bn. and hpsch.   HS. HSL 117
Bach, J. C.: Quintet No. 1 in E♭ for 2 cl. 2 hn. bn.   OL 50135
Bach, J. C.: Quintet No. 2 in E♭ for 2 cl. 2 hn. bn.   OL 50135
Bach, J. C.: Quintet No. 3 in B♭ for 2 cl. 2 hn. bn.   OL 50135
Bach, J. C.: Quintet No. 4 in E♭ for 2 cl. 2 hn. bn.   OL 50135
Bach, J. S.: Cantata (BWV 8)   ERA LDE 3206
Bach, J. S.: Cantata (BWV 85)   ERA LDE 3134
Bach, J. S.: Cantata (BWV 110)   ERA LDE 3206
Bach, J. S.: Cantata (BWV 140)   ERA LDE 3134
Beethoven: Duo No. 3 in B♭ for cl. and bn.   OL 50033
   OL. LD 62
Beethoven: Trio in G for fl. bn. and pf.   Sel. LPG 8002
   AWT 9430-C
Beethoven: Quintet in E♭ (Op. 16) for pf. and wind   OL 50033
   OL. LC 62
Biscogli: Concerto in D for ob. bn. tp. and orch. (with
orch., cond. Paillard)   ERA 3035
Boismortier: Concerto à cinque in E Moll (Op. 37)   BAM LD 060
Breval: Sinfonia Concertante (Op. 31) fl. bn. and   BAM. LD 081
orch. (with chamber orch., cond. Cartigny)   BAM. LDS 5081
Campra: De Profundis   ERA LDE 3134
Campra: Omnes Gentes   ERA LDE 3182
Couperin, F.: Concert royaux, Les Goûts réunis No. 4
fl. ob. bn. vn. hpsch.   OL 156
Couperin, F.: Sonata: l'Apothéose de Corelli fl. ob.
bn. vn. hpsch.   OL 156
Couperin, F.: Sonata: l'Apothéose de Lully fl. ob. bn.
vn. hpsch.   OL 156
Couperin, F.: Sonata: La Steinkerque fl. ob. bn.   BAM. LD 066
hpsch.   BAM. LDS 5066
Damase: Seventeen Variations for wind quintet   OL 50122
   OL LD 97
Danzi: Wind quintet in B♭ (Op. 56, No. 1)   DL 53005
   OL. LD 43
Danzi: Wind quintet in G Moll (Op. 56, No. 2)   DL 53005
   OL. LD 43
Danzi: Wind quintet in E♭ (Op. 67, No. 2)   PAC. F 230
Dittersdorf: Partita No. 2 in F for 2 ob. 2 hn. bn.
(arr. quintet)   OL 50014
Dittersdorf: Partita No. 4 in A for 2 ob. 2 hn. bn.
(arr. quintet)   OL 50014

PAUL HONGNE—*cont.*

Dittersdorf: Partita No. 20 in D for 2 ob. 2 hn. bn. (arr. quintet)	OL 50014
Fasch: Concerto for 2 ob. 2 bn. 2 hn. and strings.	Cpt. ML 20156
Françaix: Wind Quintet	ERA LDE 3105
Handel: Trio No. 3 in E♭ for ob. vn. and hpsch. and bn.	BAM. LC 011
Hindemith: Kleine Kammermusik (Op. 24, No. 2) for wind quintet	DL 53007 OL. LD 21
Ibert: Trois Pièces Brèves for wind quintet	OL 50122 OL. LD 97
Jolivet: Serenade for wind quintet	ERA LDE 3105
Milhaud: Suite d'après Corette for ob. cl. and bn.	OL. LD 20 DL 53002
Milhaud: La Cheminée du roi René for wind quintet	OL. LD 20 DL 53002
Mondoville: Psaume Cantate Domino	ERA LDE 3245
Mozart: Adagio in F (K. 410) for 2 bst-hns. bn	DF 730051
Mozart: Bassoon Concerto in B♭ (K. 191) (Saar Chamber Orch., cond. Ristenpart)	DF 730039
Mozart: Bassoon Concerto in B♭ (K.Anh. 230a)	ERATO
Mozart: Cassation in E♭ for ob. cl. hn. bn.	OL 50016 OL. LD 51
Mozart: Divertimenti Nos. 1-5 (K. 439b) for 2 cl. & bn.	ERA 3086
Mozart: Quintet in E♭ (K. 452) for pf. and wind (with Veyron-Lacroix—pf.)	OL 50016 OL. LD 51
Mozart: Sinfonia Concertante in E♭ (K. 297b) for ob. cl. hn. bn. (with Oiseau-Lyre Ensemble, cond. Froment)	OL 50006 OL. LD 75
Mozart: Sinfonia Concertante in E♭ (K. 297b) for ob. cl. hn. bn. (with chamber orch., cond. Oubra-dous)	Pat. DXT 192
Mozart: Sinfonia Concertante in E♭ (K. 297b) for ob. cl. hn. bn. (with Saar Chamber Orch., cond. Ristenpart)	DFr EX 25035 DF 730037
Mozart: Serenade No. 10 in B♭ (K. 361) for 2 ob. 2 cl. 2 bst-hn. 2 bn. cbn. 4 hn.	DF 730051
Mozart: Serenade No. 12 in C min. (K. 388) for 2 ob. 2 cl. 2 bn. 2 hn.	DF 730052
Noels Latins du XVIIe Siècle (with Orch., cond. Paillard)	ERA LDE 3208
Onslow: Wind quintet in F (Op. 81)	OL 50049
Onslow: Septet in B♭ (Op. 79) for pf. fl. ob. cl. hn. bn. and db.	OL 50049 OL. LD 107
Platee: Suite des Dances	Orph. 52. 069F
Pleyel: Symphonie Concertante No. 5 in F for fl. ob. hn. bn. (with chamber orch., cond. Froment)	OL 50014
Pleyel: Trio in G min. for fl. cl. bn.	PAC F 230
Rameau: Les Fêtes d'Hébé (with Paris Chamber Orch.)	Orph. 52. 069F
Reicha: Wind quintet in E♭ (Op. 88, No. 2)	OL 50019 OL. LD 65

Reicha: Wind quintet in D (Op. 91, No. 3)	OL 50019
	OL. LD 65
Reicha: Wind quintet in E Moll (Op. 100, No. 4)	OL. LD 23
Rossini: Quartet No. 1 in F for fl. cl. hn. bn.	OL. LD 57
	ERA LDE 3258
Rossini: Quartet No. 4 in B♭ for fl. cl. hn. bn.	OL. LD 57
	ERA LDE 3258
Rossini: Quartet No. 5 in D for fl. cl. hn. bn.	ERA LDE 3258
Rossini: Quartet No. 6 in F for fl. cl. hn. bn.	ERA LDE 3258
Roussel: Divertissement (Op. 6) for pf. fl. ob. cl. hn. bn.	DFr 148
Scarlatti: Quintet in F	BAM. LD 011
Stamitz, K.: Quartet in E♭ (Op. 8, No. 2) for ob. cl. hn. bn.	PAC F 230
Stravinsky: L'Histoire du Soldat for voices, vn. cl. bn. cnt. tbn. db. perc.	Path. DTX 30008
Telemann: Quartet in G for fl. ob. vn. hpsch. bn.	BAM. LD 011
	HS. HSL 117
Telemann: Quartet in E. min. fl. bn. vn. hpsch.	ERA. LDE 3263
	ERA. STE 50163
Tomasi: Variations on a Corsican Theme for wind quintet	OL 50122
	OL. LD 97
Vivaldi: Basoon Concerto in E Moll (P. 137) (with orch., cond. Witold)	LI. TWV 91052
	Cpt. MC 20043
Vivaldi: Basoon Concerto in B♭ (P. 401) (with orch., cond. Paillard)	ERA 42031
Vivaldi: Concerto for ob. bn. and orch. (Op. 8, No. 9) (with ensemble, cond. Witold)	TWV 91052
Vivaldi: Concerto in D (P. 198) for fl. ob. vn. bn. and cont.	BAM. LD 013
Vivaldi: Concerto in D (P. 204) for fl. ob. vn. bn. and cont.	HS. HSL 82
	BAM LD 06
Vivaldi: Concerto in D (P. 207) for fl. ob. vn. bn. and cont.	BAM. LD 013
Vivaldi: Concerto in F (P. 322) for fl. ob. vn. bn. and cont.	HS. HSL 82
	BAM. LD 06
	BAM. LD 013
Vivaldi: Concerto in F (P. 323) for fl. ob. vn. bn. and cont.	BAM. LD 013
Vivaldi: Concerto in G Moll (P. 360) for fl. ob. vn. bn. and cont.	HS. HSL 80
	BAM. LD 01
	BAM. LD 086
Vivaldi: Concerto in G Moll (P. 402) for fl. ob. vn. bn. and cont.	HS. HSL 82
	BAM. LD 06
Vivaldi: Trio Sonata in A Moll (P.p. 7) for fl. bn. and hpsch. (with orchestra, cond. Paillard)	HS HSL 82
	BAM. LD 06
	RG 95
Vivaldi: Trio Sonata E min. ob. bn. vn. hpsch.	BAM 013
Weber: Bassoon Concerto in F (Op. 75) (with Oiseau-Lyre Orch., cond. Froment)	OL 50105
	OL. LD 69

CECIL JAMES

Albinoni: Concerto à cinque in D for 2 obd'am. 2 hn. bn.	CCL 30131

CECIL JAMES—*cont.*

Arnold: Three Shanties for wind quintet — RG 326

Bach, C. P. E.: Six Sonatas (1775) for 2 fl. 2 cl. 2 hn. bn. — PMB 1004

Bach, J. S.: Suite No. 1 in C (BWV. 1066) (with London Baroque Orch., cond. Haas) — XLP 20057

Beethoven: Quintet in E♭ (Op. 16) for pf. and wind (with Gieseking—pf.) — C. CX 1322 / Strad 616 / Ang. 35303 / FCX 543

Beethoven: Sextet in E♭ (Op. 71) for 2 cl. 2 hn. 2 bn. — CCL 30133

Beethoven: Rondino in E♭ (Op. posth.) for 2 ob. 2 cl. 2 hn. 2 bn. — CCL 30133

Beethoven: Octet in E♭ (Op. 103) for 2 ob. 2 cl. 2 hn. 2 bn. — CCL 30133

Beethoven: Marches in F, C and F — CCL 30133 / CEC 32027 / VOG 48008

Boccherini: Sextet in E♭ (Op. 41) for ob. hn. bn. vn. va. db. — West WL 5077 / Nix WLP 5077

Boccherini: Sinfonia Concertante in G (Op. 8) for ob. hn. bn. stgs. — West WL 5077 / Nix WLP 5077 / West WN 18052

Dittersdorf: Partita in D for 2 ob. 2 hn. bn. — PMB 1008

Dvořák: Serenade in D Moll (Op. 44) for 2 ob. 2 cl. 2 bn. cbn. 3 hn. vc. db. — PMB 1001 / AmD DL 7533 / XLP 30011 / R 20604/6

Ferguson: Octet (Op. 4) for cl. hn. bn. 2 vn. va. vc. db. — D K 1095/7

Fricker: Wind quintet — RG 326

Gerhard: Wind quintet — RG 326

Gounod: Petite Symphonie in B Moll for fl. 2 ob. 2 cl. 2 hn. 2 bn. — XLP 30011

Handel: Two Arias for 2 hn. acc. 2 ob. and bn. — P.R. 20617

Handel: Gavotte and March for tp. obs. bns. and s.drm. — P.R. 20617 / AmD DL 4070

Haydn: Divertimento in C (Feldparthie) for 2 ob. 2 hn. 2 bn. — PMA 1013 / XLP 30016

Haydn: Divertimento in F for 2 vn. 2 ca. 2 bn. 2 hn. — P.R. 20578/9 / AmD DL 4076

Haydn: Divertimento No. 3 in B♭ for 2 ob. 2 cl. 2 bn. 2hn. — P. SW 8120/1 / AmD DL 4066

Ibert: Trois Pièces Brèves — C. CX 1687

Jacob: Sextet for piano and wind quintet — C. CX 1687

Kay: Miniature Quartet for fl. cl. hn. bn. — CCL 30120

Lully: Marche pour le régiment du Roi for 4 ob. 2 ca. 2 bn. s.drm. — P.R. 20619

Lully: La Marche pour le Roi de la Chine et Marche du Prince d'Orange — P.R. 20619 / AmD. DL 4081

Mozart: Divertimento No. 3 in E♭ (K. 166) for 2 ob. 2 ca. 2 cl. 2 hn. 2 bn. — D.AK 2225/6 / Lon. Set LA 158

Mozart: Divertimento No. 14 in B♭ (K. 270) (arr. quintet) — C. CX 1687

Mozart: Serenade No. 11 in E♭ (K. 375) for 2 cl. 2 hn. 2 bn. (orig)	CCL 30119
Mozart: Serenade No. 11 in E♭ (K. 375) for 2 ob. 2 cl. 2 hn. 2 bn. (2nd movement only)	D. AK 2225
Mozart: Serenade No. 11 in E♭ (K. 375) for 2 ob. 2 cl. 2 hn. 2 bn.	PMB 1002
	Od. OD 1010
	CCL 30119
	R. 20610/2
Mozart: Serenade No. 12 in C Moll (K. 388) for 2 ob. 2 cl. 2 hn. 2 bn.	PMA 1013
	CCL 30119
	XLP 30016
Mozart: Quintet in E♭ (K. 452) for pf. and wind (with C. Horsley—pf.)	CLP 1029
	XLP 30004
Mozart: Quintet in E♭ (K. 452) for pf. and wind (with W. Gieseking—pf.)	C. CX 1322
	Ang. 35303
	FCX 543
Mozart: Sinfonia Concertante in E♭ (K. 297b) for ob. cl. hn. bn. (with Philharmonia Orch., cond. Karajan)	C. CX 1178
	FCX 308
	QCX 10101
	Ang. 35098
Scarlatti, A.: Concerto in D for fl. tp. bn. and strings (with London Baroque Ensemble, cond. Haas)	CCL 30131
Seiber: Permutatzione à Cinque for wind quintet	RG 326
Strauss, R.: Sonatina (Symphony) No. 2 in E♭ for 2 fl. 2 ob. 3 cl. bst-hn. bcl. 2 bn. 4 hn.	PMA 1006
	XLP 30021
Telemann: Suite in D (1733) for 2 ob. 2 hn. and bn.	PMB 1004

WILFRED JAMES

Barthe: Passacaille for wind quintet	Winner 3476
Haydn: Presto from String Quartet in C (arr. for wind quintet)	Edison Bell 1093
Lefebvre: Suite (Op. 57) for wind quintet (Finale only)	Winner 3476
Onslow: Wind quintet (Scherzo only)	Edison Bell 1093
Pierné: Pastorale (Op. 14, No. 1) for wind quintet	Edison Bell 515
Scarlatti: Andante and Allegro (arr. for wind quintet)	Edison Bell 515

CARL JESCHKE

Mozart: Serenade No. 10 in B♭ (K. 361) for 2 ob. 2 cl. 2 bst-hn. 2 bn. cbn. 4 hn.	Cap. CTL 7030
	P 8181
	CLCX 037

VAL KENNEDY

Beethoven: Marches in F, C and F. (contrabassoon)	CCL 30133
	CEC 32027
Dvořák: Serenade in D Moll (Op. 44) for 2 ob. 2 cl. 2 bn. cbn. 3 hn. vc and db.	P.R. 20604/6
	PMB 1001
	AmD DL 7533
	XLP 30011
Mozart: Serenade No. 11 in E♭ (K. 375) for 2 ob. 2 cl. 2 hn. 2 bn.	CCL 30119
Strauss, R.: Sonatina (Symphony) No. 2 in E♭ for 2 fl. 2 ob. 3 cl. bst-hn. bcl. 2 bn. cbn. 4 hn.	PMA 1006
	XLP 30021

NICHOLAS KILBURN
Lessard: Concerto for flute, clarinet, bassoon and
    strings (with Peninsula Festival Orch., cond.
    Johnson)   CRI 122

FRANZ KILLINGER
Bach: Musical Offering (BWV 1079)   WLP 5070
Mozart: Serenade No. 10 in B♭ (K. 361) for 2 ob. 2 cl.
    2 bst-hn. 2 bn. cbn. 4 hn. (contrabassoon)   AmVox PL 7470

RUDOLF KLEPAC
Mozart: Bassoon Concerto in B♭ (K. 191) (with   DGM 18297
    Salzburg Mozarteum Orch., cond. Maerzendor-   Dec. DL 9834
    fer)   478415
Vivaldi: Bassoon Concerto in E Moll (P. 137) (with   APM 14097
    Lucerne Festival Orch., cond. Baumgartner)   DGG Arch. 3116
Vivaldi: Bassoon concerto in E Moll (P. 137) (with
    Zagreb soloists, cond. Janigro)   AMA AVRS 6051

THOM DE KLERK
de Klerk, A.: Missa Mater Sanctae Laetitiae for female
    chorus, fl. ca. bn.   DAVS 6502
Flothius: Canti e Giuochi for wind quintet and orch.   DAVS 6504
Mozart: Bassoon Concerto in B♭ (K. 191) (with   Phi. AL 2389
    Vienna Symphony Orch., cond. Baumgartner)   Phi. S. AY 835266

JACK KNITZER
Schuman: Quartettino for 4 bassoons (1939)   NMQR 1415

BENJAMIN KOHON
Mozart: Sonata in B♭ (K. 292) for bn. and vc.   G. DB 3442
                                                           Vic. 12149
                                                           JpV. ND 737

KURT KRAMER
Bach, J. S.: Cantata (BWV 160) 'Ich weiss'   D. AWD 8527

YURI KURPEKOV
Janáček: Concertino for 2 vn. va. cl. bn. hn. and pf.   MK DO 6267

ERIKA KUTZING (KUBEY)
Schuman: Quartettino (1939) for 4 bassoons   NMQR 1415

MARTIN VAN LAAR
Otterloo: Sinfonietta for picc. 2 fl. 2 ob. ca. 2 cl. bcl.
    2 bn. cbn. 4 hn.   DAVS 6303

JEAN LANCOUX (Contrabassoon)
Mozart: Serenade No. 10 in B♭ (K. 361) for 2 ob. 2 cl.
    2 bst-hn. 2 bn. cbn. 4 hn. (cond. Ansermet)   D. LXT 5121

KNUD LASSEN
Nielsen: Wind quintet in A (Op. 43)   G. DB 5200/3
Nielsen: Serenata in vano for cl. hn. bn. vc. db.   G. DB 5204

MARTIN LAUG
Bach: Cantata No. 33 Allein zu dir, Herr Jesu Christ   Cant. 641215
    (with Bremen Bach Orch., cond. Heintze)   Cant. 651215
Bach: Cantata No. 95 Christus der ist mein Leben.   Cant. 641215
    (with Bremen Bach Orch., cond. Heintze)   Cant. 651215

NEIL LEVESLEY
Dvořák: Serenade in D Moll (Op. 44) for 2 ob. 2 cl.
    2 bn. cbn. 3 hn. vc. and db.   CCL 30153
Gounod: Petite Symphonie in B Moll for fl. 2 ob.
    2 cl. 2 hn. 2 bn.   CCL 30153

JEAN LOUCHEZ
Mozart: Bassoon Concerto in B♭ (K. 191)   LXT 5332
Vivaldi: Concerto in D (P. 207) for fl. ob. bn. vn.   ERA 3218
    hpsch.   ERA 50118
Vivaldi: Concerto in E Moll (P. 360) for fl. ob. bn. vn. ERA 3218
    hpsch.   ERA 50118
Vivaldi: Concerto in G Moll (P. 402) for fl. ob. bn.   ERA 3218
    hpsch.   ERA 50118
Vivaldi: Trio Sonata in A for fl. bn. hpsch.   ERA 3218
                                                         ERA 50118
Weber: Andante e Rondo ongarese in C (Op. 35)
    (J. 158)   LXT 5332

JOERN MAATZ
Mozart: Divertimento No. 2 in B♭ (K. 439b) for cl.   RSX 25
    and bn.   RSXS 4
                                                         BM 25 R 904
Mozart: Divertimento No. 4 in B♭ (K. 439b) for cl.   RSX 25
    and bn.   RSXS 4
                                                         BM 25 R 904

WERNER MAURUSCHAT
Bach, J. C.: Confiteor tibi omini (with Collegium
    Aureum)   HM 30637

STEVEN MAXYM
Schoenberg: Wind quintet (Op. 26)   Dial 13

JOHN MILLER
Zelenka: Three Sonatas for 2 ob. bn. and cont.   CRM 814
                                                         CRS 1814

HERBERT MITTON (contrabassoon)
Dvořák: Serenade in D Moll (Op. 44) for 2 ob. 2 cl.   CCL 30153
    2 bn. cbn. 3 hn. vc. and db.   Mer. 50041

ALDO MONTANARI
Vivaldi: Bassoon Concerto in C (P. 69) (with Milan
    Angelicum Orch., cond. Gerelli)   Ang. SA 3015
Vivaldi: Bassoon Concerto in B♭ (P. 401) (La Notte)   Dur. SA 106/7
    (with La Scala Orch., cond. Ephrikian)   Csm. CLPS 1029

FREDERICK MORITZ
Recordings by Columbia Symphony Orch., under
    Bruno Walter

R

ENZO MUCCETTI
Vivaldi: Bassoon Concerto in A Moll (P. 72) (with
    La Scala Orch., cond. Valdinoci)   CLPS 1051
Vivaldi: Concerto in G Moll (P. 402) for fl. ob. bn. CLPS 1051
    and orch. (with La Scala Orch., cond. Valdinoci) CLPS 1047

HELMUT MÜLLER
Bozza: Variations for wind quintet   CLP 75-400
Haydn: Divertimento in B♭   CLP 75-400
Hindemith: Kleine Kammermusik (Op. 24, No. 2)
    for wind quintet   CLP 75-400
Stravinsky: Octet (1923) for fl. cl. 2 bn. 2 tp. 2 tbn. CLP 75-400

CHRISTIAN MURATET
Kosma: Divertissement for fl. cl. bn. and pf.   ADE.MA17. LA 543

YURI NEKHLYUDOV
Glinka: Trio Pathétique in D Moll for pf. cl. and bn. M. D 835/6

MORRIS NEWMAN
Handel: Anthem—As pants the hart for cooling   Cant. 655201
    streams (with Collegium Musicum, Rutgers   645201
    Univ., cond. Mann)
Handel: Anthem—O sing unto the Lord a new song Cant. 655201
    (with Collegium Musicum, Rutgers Univ., cond.   645201
    Mann)
Handel: Trio Sonata No. 2 for 2 ob. bn. hpsch.   Wash. 420
Handel: Trio Sonata No. 4 in F for 2 ob. bn. hpsch. Wash. 420
Handel: Trio Sonata No. 6 in D for 2 ob. bn. hpsch. Wash. 420

JOERN NILSSON
Hanff: Four cantatas   Cyc. 30 CM 010

RAY NORVLIN
Mozart: Serenade No. 10 in B♭ (K. 361) for 2 ob. 2 cl. Cap. CTL 7030
    2 bst-hn. 2 bn. cbn. 4 hn.   P 8181
                                    CLCX 037

CAMILLO ÖHLBERGER (contrabassoon)
Mozart: Serenade No. 10 in B♭ (K. 361) for 2 ob. 2 cl. WLP 5229
    2 bst-hn. 2 bn. cbn. 4 hn.   WL 5229

KARL ÖHLBERGER
Beethoven: Quintet in E♭ (Op. 16) for pf. ob. cl. hn. LPM 18638
    bn. (with Gulda—pf.)   SLPM 138638
Beethoven: Sextet in E♭ (Op. 71) for 2 cl. 2 hn. 2 bn. WL 5003
                                    WP 114
                                  West 18189
Beethoven: Septet in E♭ (Op. 20) for cl. hn. bn. vn. WN 18003
    va. vc. db.   WLP 20020
Beethoven: Octet in E♭ (Op. 103) for 2 ob. 2 cl. 2 hn. WL 5003
    2 bn.   WP 114
                                  West 18189

Beethoven: Rondino in E♭ (Op. posth.) for 2 ob. 2 cl. 2 hn. 2 bn.	WLP 5262
Glinka: Trio Pathétique in D Moll for pf. cl. bn.	WL 5019
Haydn: Octet in F for 2 ob. 2 cl. 2 hn. 2 bn.	WL 5002
	WN 18058
Janáček: Concertino for pf. 2 vn. va. cl. hn. bn.	CLP 1749
	WL 5333
	WL 18173
Mozart: Bassoon Concerto in B♭ (K. 191) (with Vienna State Opera Orch., cond. Podsinsky)	WLP 5307
	WL 5307
	WH 20060
	West. 18287
Mozart: Quintet in E♭ (K. 452) for pf. ob. cl. hn. bn. (with Raupenstrauch—pf.)	WL 5007
Mozart: Quintet in E♭ (K. 452) for pf. ob. cl. hn. bn. (with Gulda—pf.)	LPM 18638
	SLPM 138638
Mozart: Divertimento No. 3 in E♭ (K. 166) for 2 ob. 2 ca. 2 cl. 2 hn. 2 bn.	WN 18011
Mozart: Divertimento No. 4 in B♭ (K. 186) for 2 ob. 2 ca. 2 cl. 2 hn. 2 bn.	WN 18011
Mozart: Divertimento No. 8 in F (K. 213) for 2 ob. 2 hn. 2 bn.	WL 5103
Mozart: Divertimento No. 9 in B♭ (K. 240) for 2 ob. 2 hn. 2 bn.	WN 18011
Mozart: Divertimento No. 12 in E♭ (K. 252) for 2 ob. 2 hn. 2 bn.	WL 5103
Mozart: Divertimento No. 13 in F (K. 253) for 2 ob. 2 hn. 2 bn.	WL 5103
Mozart: Divertimento No. 14 in B♭ (K. 270) for 2 ob. 2 hn. 2 bn.	WL 5103
Mozart: Divertimento No. 16 in E♭ (K. 289) for 2 ob. 2 hn. 2 bn.	WN 18011
Mozart: Divertimento in E♭ (K. 196e) for 2 ob. 2 cl. 2 hn. 2 bn.	WL 5349
Mozart: Divertimento in B♭ (K. 196f) for 2 ob. 2 cl. 2 hn. 2 bn.	WL 5349
Mozart: Serenade No. 10 in B♭ (K. 361) for 2 ob. 2 cl. 2 bst-hn. 2 bn. cbn. 4 hn. (cond. Fürtwangler)	G. DB 6707/11
	Elec. 91175
Mozart: Serenade No. 10 in B♭ (K. 361) for 2 ob. 2 cl. 2 bst-hn. 2 bn. cbn. 4 hn.	WLP 5229
	WL 5229
Mozart: Serenade No. 11 in E♭ (K. 375) for 2 ob. 2 cl. 2 hn. 2 bn.	WL 5021
	West 18134
	Sel. LPG 8345
Mozart: Serenade No. 12 in C Moll (K. 388) for 2 ob. 2 cl. 2 hn. 2 bn.	WL 5021
	West 18134
	Sel. LPG 8345
Mozart: Divertimento No. 1 in B♭ (K. 439b) for 2 cl. and bn.	WL 5213
Mozart: Divertimento No. 2 in B♭ (K. 439b) for 2 cl. and bn.	WL 5022
	LPG 8336
Mozart: Divertimento No. 3 in B♭ (K. 439b) for 2 cl. and bn.	WL 5020
	LPG 8317

KARL ÖHLBERGER—*cont.*

Mozart: Divertimento No. 4 in B♭ (K. 439b) for 2 cl. and bn.	WL 5213
Mozart: Divertimento No. 5 in B♭ (K. 439b) for 2 cl. and bn.	WL 5213
Mozart: Sinfonia Concertante in E♭ (K. 297b) for ob. cl. hn. bn. (with Vienna State Opera Orch., cond. Swoboda)	WL 5020 WLP 5020 WN 18041
Rimsky-Korsakov: Quintet in B♭ for pf. fl. cl. hn. bn.	WL 5019 WH 18071
Schubert: Octet in F (Op. 166) for cl. hn. bn. 2 vn. va. vc. db.	C.LWX 364/9 WLP 5094 WL 5094
Strauss, R.: Serenade in B♭ (Op. 4) for 2 fl. 2 ob. 2 cl. 2 bn. cbn. 4 hn.	WL 5185 West 18173
Strauss, R.: Serenade in E♭ (Op. 7) for 2 fl. 2 ob. 2 cl. 2 bn. cbn. 4 hn.	WL 5185 West 18173

RAYMOND OJEDA

Hindemith: Concerto (1948) for tp. bn. and orch. (with San Francisco Little Symphony Orch., cond. Millar)	Fan. 5001

CHRIS OKHUIJSEN (contrabassoon)

Otterloo: Symphonietta for picc. 2 fl. 2 ob. ca. 2 cl. bcl. 2 bn. cbn. 4 hn.	DAVS 6303

FERNAND OUBRADOUS

Auric: Trio (1938) for ob. cl. and bn.	OL 103/4
Bach, J. S.: English Suite No. 3 in G Moll (arr. ob. cl. bn.) (Gavotte only)	OL 120
Bach, J. S.: French No. 3 in B Moll (arr. ob. cl. bn.) (Allemande and Minuet only)	OL 121
Bach, J. S.: Prelude and Fugue No. 48 in B Moll (arr. ob. cl. bn.)	OL 8
Barraud: Trio for ob. cl. bn.	OL 6/7
Beethoven: Duo No. 1 in C for cl. and bn.	OL 79/80
Beethoven: Duo No. 2 in F for cl. and bn.	OL 4
Beethoven: Duo No. 3 in B♭ for cl. and bn.	OL 78
Beethoven: Trio G for fl. bn. and pf.	OL 81/2
Beethoven: Quintet in E♭ (Op. 16) for pf. and wind.	Od. 123902/4
Boismortier: Bassoon Concerto in F (with orch., cond. Désormière)	OL 145
Couperin, F.: Concert Royale No. 4 in E Moll for fl. ob. bn. vn. vc. and cont.	OL 51/2
Couperin, F.: La Crouilli ou la Couperinete (XX) for 2 ob. bn. and cont.	OL 56
Couperin, F.: Les Goûts Réunis No. 9 in E (Il ritratto dell'amore) for ob. bn. vn. vc. and cont.	OL 73/4
Couperin, F.: Les Goûts Réunis No. 13 in G for bn. and vc.	Clc 6020
Couperin, F.: Musette de Choisi (XV) for 2 ob. bn and cont.	OL 56

Couperin, F.: Musette de Taverni (L. 6) (XV) for 2 ob. bn. and cont.	OL 56
Ferroud: Trio in E for ob. cl. and bn.	Pat. PG 84/5
Gallon: Recitative and Allegro for bn. and pf.	OL 9
Glinka: Trio Pathétique in D Moll for pf. cl. and bn.	OL 34/5
Golestan: Chanson du Pays for bn. and pf.	DA 4920
Golestan: Petite Suite Bucolique for ob. cl. and bn.	DA 4919/20
Hahn: Eglogue for ob. cl. and bn.	Pat. PA 929
Haydn: Sinfonia Concertante in B♭ (Op. 84) for ob. bn. vn. vc. (with Paris Conservatoire Orch., cond. Munch)	OL 83/4
Ibert: Andantino and Allegro marziale for ob. cl. and bn.	Pat. PG 90
Ibert: Piéces en Trio for ob. cl. and bn.	OL 5
Milhaud: Pastorale for ob. cl. and bn.	OL 5
Milhaud: Suite d'après Corette for ob. cl. and bn.	OL 17/18
Milhaud: La Cheminée du roi René for wind quintet	Clc 6020
Mozart: Bassoon Concerto in B♭ (K. 191) (cadenza: Oubradous) (with orch., cond. Bigot)	G. L 1026/7 Vic. 13433/4 set M 704
Mozart: Bassoon Concerto in B♭ (K. 230a) (cadenza: Oubradous) (with orch., cond. Fendler)	OL 40/1
Mozart: Sonata in B♭ (K. 292) for bn. and vc.	AS 44 ADE. MS. 30 LA 528
Mozart: Divertimento No. 1 in B♭ (K. 439b) for 2 cl. and bn. (arr. ob. cl. bn.)	OL 64/9
Mozart: Divertimento No. 2 in B♭ (K. 439b) (arr. ob. cl. bn.)	OL 64/9
Mozart: Divertimento No. 3 in B♭ (K. 439b) (arr. ob. cl. bn.)	OL 64/9
Mozart: Divertimento No. 4 in B♭ (K. 439b) (arr. ob. cl. bn.)	OL 15/6
Mozart: Divertimento No. 5 in B♭ (K. 439b) (arr. ob. cl. bn.)	OL 36/7
Mozart: Quintet in E♭ (K. 452) for pf. and wind	C 2017/9 MG 10031 TW 14-002 G. DB 5083
Rivier: Petite Suite for ob. cl. and bn.	
Weber: Bassoon Concerto in F (Op. 75) (J. 187) (Adagio only)	OL 80
Weber: Andante e Rondo ongarese in C (Op. 35) (J. 158)	OL 14

ERNST PAMPERL

Mozart: Quintet in E♭ (K. 452) for pf. and wind	LXT 5293

ERNST PANENKA

Beethoven: Trio in G for fl. bn. and pf.	Number unknown
Dvořák: Serenade in D Moll (Op. 44) for 2 ob. 2 cl. 2 bn. cbn. 3 hn. vc. and db.	Bo. 410 1004
Milhaud: Suite d'après Corette for ob. cl. and bn.	UN LP 1005
Poulenc: Trio (1926) for ob. bn. and pf.	UN 1005
Roland-Manuel: Suite dans le goût espagnole for ob. bn. tp. and cont.	UN 1005

ERNST PANENKA—*cont.*

Strauss, R.: Sonatina No. 1 in F for 2 fl. 2 ob. 3 cl. bst-hn. bcl. 2 bn. cbn. 4 hn.	RG 147 BO 406 1016
Strauss, R.: Suite in Bb (Op. 4) for 2 fl. 2 ob. 2 cl. 2 bn. cbn. 4 hn. (Gavotte only)	RG 147 BO 406 1016
Strauss, R.: Serenade in Eb (Op. 7) for 2 fl. 2 ob. 2 cl. 2 bn. cbn. 4 hn.	RG 147 Bo. 406 1016

KENNETH PASMANIK

Byrd, C.: Bird in the wind for bn.	Washington Records Number unknown
Powell: Program for bn.	CR 6

JÖRG PEISSER

Haydn: Divertimento in C (Feldparthie) for 2 ob. 2 cl. 2 bn.	Strad STR 622 Cpt MC 20104
Haydn: Divertimento in F for 2 ob. 2 cl. 2 bn.	Strad STR 622 Cpt MC 20104

H. PETSCHEK

Beethoven: Trio in G (Op. 11) for fl. bn. and pf.	SPA 28

VINCENT PEZZI

Phillips: American Dance for bassoon and orchestra (with Eastman Rochester Orch., cond. Hanson)	Vic. 18102 set 802
Phillips: Concert Piece for bassoon and strings	Vic. 18102 A.

CORNEILLE PIRNAY

Bayens: Quintet and Divertimento for wind quintet	Alpha DB 33
Quinet: Wind Quintet	Alpha DB 42
Schoemaker: Suite Champêtre for ob. cl. bn.	Alpha DB 42

KAREL PIVONKA

Beethoven: Sextet in Eb (Op. 71) for 2 cl. 2 bn. 2 hn.	SUA 10293
Beethoven: Octet in Eb (Op. 103) for 2 ob. 2 cl. 2 bn. 2 hn.	VVRS 6159
Dvořák: Serenade in D Moll (Op. 44) for 2 ob. 2 cl. 2 bn. cbn. 3 hn. vc. db.	SUA 10326
Kozeluh: Bassoon Concerto in C (with Prague Symphony Orch., cond. Smetaček)	LPV 269 SUA 19033 MAB 5
Mozart: Serenade No. 11 in Eb (K. 375) for 2 ob. 2 cl. 2 bn. 2 hn.	VVRS 6159

RICHARD PLASTER (contrabassoon)

Dvorak: Serenade in D Moll (Op. 44) for 2 ob. 2 cl. 2 bn. cbn. 3 hn. vc. and db.	Bo. 410 1004
Strauss, R.: Sonatina No. 1 in F for 2 fl. 2 ob. 3 cl. bst-hn. bcl. 2 bn. cbn. 4 hn.	RG 147 Bo. 406 1016

Strauss, R.: Suite in B♭ (Op. 4) for 2 fl. 2 ob. 2 cl. 2 bn.   RG 147
   cbn. 4 hn. (Gavotte only)   Bo. 406
   1016

Strauss, R.: Serenade in E♭ (Op. 7) for 2 fl. 2 ob. 2 cl.   RG 147
   2 bn. cbn. 4 hn.   Bo. 406
   1016

RENE PLEISSIER
Caturla: Suite No. 1 for wind octet and pf.   Ang. 35105
Roldan: Ritmico No. 1 for wind quintet and pf.   Ang. 35105
Villa-Lobos: Bachianas Brasileiras No. 6 for fl. and bn.   ALP 1603
   Ang. 35547
   VSM. FALP. 476

BRIAN POLLARD
Danzi: Wind Quintet in B♭ (Op. 56, No. 1)   ART. S 9508
Gebauer: Wind Quintet No. 2 in E♭   ART. S 9508
Ketting: Trio for fl. cl. and bn.   DAVS 6501
Mozart: Andante für eine Orgelwalze (K.V. 616)
   (arr. Vester) for wind quintet   ART. S 9508
Mozart: Fantasie für eine Orgelwalze (K.V. 608)
   (arr. Vester) for wind quintet   ART. S 9508
Ponse: Concerto de camera with solo bassoon (with
   Netherlands Chamber Orch., cond. Goldberg)   DAVS 6402
Ruyneman: Reflexions No. 4 for wind quintet   DAVS 6202
Schat: Improvisations and Symphonies for wind
   quintet   DAVS 6202
Van Baaren: Sovraposizioni II for wind quintet   DAVS 6501

ANDRÉ RABOT
Bach: Brandenburg Concerto No. 1 in F   CDN 1019
Berlioz, G. P.: Trois pièces pour basson   Tep 45. 571 Ld. S
Chabrier: Melodies   Plei. P 3066
Gounod: Petite Symphonie in B Moll for fl. 2 ob. 2 cl.
   2 hn. 2 bn.   LXT 5172
Mozart: Sinfonia Concertante in E♭ (K. 297b) for ob.
   cl. bn. hn. (with orch., cond. Disenhaus)   MFr. 2505
Oubradous: Récit et Variations sur un air populaire for
   bn. and pf.   Pac. 3355
Schubert: Eine Kleine Trauermusik for 2 ob. 2 cl.
   2 hn. 2 bn. cbn.   LXT 5172
Schubert: Minuet and Finale from Octet in F for 2 ob.
   2 cl. 2 hn. 2 bn.   LXT 5172
Stockhausen: Zeitmasse (Op. 5) for wind quintet   Veg. C 30. A 139
Stockhausen: Kontrapunkte   Veg. C 30. A 66
Stravinsky: Octet for fl. cl. 2 bn. 2 tp. 2 tbn.   At. MA 30. LA 541
Varése: Octandre   Veg. C 30. A 271

JOSEPH REINES (contrabassoon)
Yoder: The Cricket and the Bullfrog for piccolo and   U.S. Navy
   contrabassoon   Recording

FRANK RENDELL (contrabassoon)
Beethoven: Marches in F, C and F   CCL 30133
   CEC 32027
   VOG 48008

L. RIOONKA (contrabassoon)*
Krommer-Kramář: Harmonie (Op. 71) for 2 ob. 2 cl.   U. H 13121/3
   2 hn. 2 bn. cbn.   LPM 60
                                U. 5041C

H. ROBERT
Mozart: Serenade No. 10 in B♭ (K. 361) for 2 ob. 2 cl.
   2 bst-hn. 2 bn. cbn. 4 hn. (cond. Ansermet)   D. LXT 5121

KJELL ROIKJER
Bentzon: Racconto No. 3 (Op. 31) for ob. cl. and bn.   G. DB 5285
Mozart: Divertimento No. 14 in B♭ (K. 270) for 2 ob.
   2 hn. 2 bn.   G. DB 5260/1

T. RÖNNEBÄCK
Alfven: Bourrée from Gustav II Adolf (Op. 49) for
   3 bassoons   G. X 7511

OSKAR ROTHENSTEINER
Mozart: Sinfonia Concertante in E♭ (K. 297b) for ob.   C. LX 661/4s
   cl. bn. hn. (with Berlin Philharmonic Orch., cond.   LFX 508/11s
   Konoye)
Mozart: Sonata in B♭ (K. 292) for bn. and vc.   Elec. 60580

IMRE RUDAS
Senallié: Sonata in D Moll for vn. and cont. (arr.
   bn. and pf.) (Allegro spiritoso only)   MR 181

MANFRED SAX
Albicastro: Sonata in B Moll (Op. 1, No. 3) for vn.
   ob. bn. and hpsch.   FGL 25-4316
Anonymous (18 Cent.): Concerto in A for obd'am. bn.
   vn. and hpsch.   FGL 25-4316
Wendel: Quintet for fl. ob. bn. vn. and hpsch.   CT 64-22

OTTO SCHIEDER (contrabassoon)
Mozart: Serenade No. 10 in B♭ (K. 361) for 2 ob.
   2 cl. 2 bst-hn. 2 bn. cbn. 4 hn. (cond. by Fürt-   G. DB 6707/11
   wangler)   Elec. 91175
Strauss, R.: Serenade in B♭ (Op. 4) for 2 fl. 2 ob. 2 cl.
   2 bn. cbn. 4 bn.   WL 5185
Strauss, R.: Serenade in E♭ (Op. 7) for 2 fl. 2 ob. 2 cl.
   2 bn. cbn. 4 bn.   WL 5185

SOL SCHOENBACH
Barber: Summer Music for wind quintet   ML 5441
                                  MS 6114
Beethoven: Quintet in E♭ (Op. 16) for pf. and wind.   ABL 3187
                                  ML 4834
Beethoven: Sextet in E♭ (Op. 71) for 2 cl. 2 hn. 2 bn.   ML 5093
Bozza: Wind Quintet (Scherzo) (Op. 48)   ML 5093

   * Eduard Landa states that this may well be Karel Pivonka, as no bassoon player named Rioonka was known to the Prague players.

Cascarino: Sonata	ML 5821
	MS 6421
Etler: Sonata	ML 5821
	MS 6421
Françaix: Divertissement for ob. cl. and bn.	ML 5613
	MS 6213
Haydn: Divertimento in B♭ (arr. wind quintet)	ML 5093
Hindemith: Kleine Kammermusik (Op. 24, No. 2)	ML 5093
Ibert: Trois Pièces Brèves for wind quintet	ML 5093
Janáček: Mládí for fl. ob. cl. bcl. hn. bn.	ML 4995
	ABR 4057
Janáček: Concertino for pf. 2 vn. 2 cl. hn. bn.	ML 4995
Milhaud: La Cheminée du roi René for wind quintet	ML 5613
	MS 6213
Mozart: Divertimento No. 8 in F (K. 213) for 2 ob. 2 hn. 2 bn.	ML 5715
	MS 6315
Mozart: Divertimento No. 14 in B♭ (K. 270) for 2 ob. 2 hn. 2 bn.	ML 5715
	MS 6315
Mozart: Quintet in E♭ (K. 452) for pf. and wind	ML 4834
	ABL 3187
Mozart: Sinfonia Concertante in E♭ (K. 297b) for ob. cl. hn. bn. (with Philadelphia Orch., cond. Stokowski)	G. DB 10118/21
	Vic. 17732/5
	Set M 760
	CAL 213
	Set CFL 105
Nielsen: Wind quintet in A (Op. 43)	BRG 72133
	SBRG 72133
	ML 5441
	MS 6114
Poulenc: Sextet for piano and wind quintet	BRG 72133
	SBRG 72133
	ML 5613
	MS 6213
Phillips: Concert Piece for bassoon and strings (with Philadelphia Orch., cond. Ormandy)	ML 4629
Reicha: Wind quintet in E♭ (Op. 88, No. 2)	ML 5715
	MS 6315
Schoenberg: Wind quintet (Op. 25)	ML 5217
Stravinsky: Pastorale for vn. ob. ca. cl. and bn.	C. LX 1174
	AmC 72495D
	ML 2122

H. SCHULPZAND

Dvořák: Serenade in D Moll (Op. 44) for 2 ob. 2 cl. 2 bn. cbn. 3 hn. vc. db.	CHS H. 6

GIORGIO SEMPRINI

Vivaldi: Concerto in A Moll for fl. vn. bn. and cont.	Per. 755
	2755
Vivaldi: Concerto in D for fl. vn. bn. and cont.	Per. 755
	2755
Vivaldi: Concerto in D for fl. vn. bn. and cont.	Per. 755
	2755

GIORGIO SEMPRINI—*cont.*
Vivaldi: Concerto in F for fl. vn. bn. and cont.   Per. 755
                                                          2755
Vivaldi: Concerto in G Moll for fl. vn. bn. and cont.   Per. 755
                                                          2755

ANDRÉ SENNEDAT
Gounod: Petite Symphonie in B Moll for fl. 2 ob. 2 cl.
    2 hn. 2 bn.   LXT 5172
Mouret: Symphonies   DGG Arch APM
                                                          14333
                                                          SAPM 198333

Schubert: Eine Kleine Trauermusik for 2 ob. 2 cl.
    2 hn. 2 bn. cbn.   LXT 5172
Schubert: Minuet and Finale from Octet in F for 2 ob.
    2 cl. 2 hn. 2 bn.   LXT 5172

LEONARD SHARROW
Hindemith: Sonata (1938) for bassoon and piano   Ox. OR 103
Mozart: Bassoon Concerto in B♭ (K. 191) (with   G. DB 20182/3
    N.B.C. Symphony Orch., cond. Toscanini)   Vic. 12-0905/6
                                                          Set M 1304
                                                          LM 1030
                                                          DV. L 16063
                                                          FALP 164
                                                          LM 20069
Poulenc: Sonata (1922) for cl. and bn.   REB 7
Poulenc: Trio (1926) for ob. bn. and pf.   REB 7
Schuman: Quartettino (1939) for 4 bassoons   NMQR 1415
Tomasi: Concert champêtre for ob. cl. and bn.   Gal. 5002
Vivaldi: Bassoon Concertos (two in number—details   Library of
    unknown) (with orch., cond. Goberman)   Recorded
                                                             Masterpieces

WILBUR SIMPSON
Danzi: Gipsy Dance (arr. wind quintet)   Aphe 16
Dvořák: Humoresque No. 7 in G♭ (arr. wind quintet)   Aphe 17
Hartley: Divertissement for wind quintet   Aphe AP 16
Haydn: Capriccio in G (Op. 43) (arr. wind quintet)   Aphe 17
Haydn: Sonata No. 13 in E (arr. wind quintet) (Presto
    only)   Aphe AP 16
Hindemith: Kleine Kammermusik (Op. 24, No. 2) for
    wind quintet   Aphe AP 15
Ibert: Trois Pièces Brèves for wind quintet   Aphe AP 15
Klughardt: Wind quintet in C (Op. 79)   Aphe AP 14
Leclair: Sonata in E (Op. 5, No. 9) (arr. wind
    quintet)   Aphe 14
Lefebvre: Suite (Op. 57) for wind quintet   Aphe AP 16
Milhaud: La Cheminée du roi René for wind quintet   Aphe AP 15
Moussorgsky: Ballet of the chickens in their shells
    (arr. wind quintet)   Aphe AP 17
Pierné: Marche des petits faunes (arr. wind quintet)   Aphe AP 17
Pierné: Marche des petits soldats de plombe (Op. 14,
    No. 6) (arr. wind quintet)   Aphe AP 17

Rimsky-Korsakov: Flight of the Bumble Bee (arr.
  wind quintet)   Aphe AP 14
Shostakovitch: Suite—Age of Gold (arr. wind quintet)   Aphe AP 14
Somis: Sonata in D Moll (arr. wind quintet) (Adagio
  and Allegro)   Aphe AP 16
Stravinsky: Pastorale for vn. ob. ca. cl. bn. (arr. wind
  quintet)   Aphe AP 14

J. SLANIČKA
Milhaud: Symphony No. 5 for 2 fl. 2 ob. 2 cl. 2 bn.
  2 hn.   SUA 10475
Mozart: Serenade No. 10 in B♭ (K. 361) for 2 ob. 2 cl.   SUA 10426
  2 bst-hn. 2 bn. cbn. 4 hn.   SUA ST 50426
Stravinsky: Octet for fl. cl. 2 bn. 2 tp. 2 tbn.   SUA 10475

ROLAND SMALL
Beethoven: Octet in E♭ (Op. 103) for 2 ob. 2 cl. 2 bn.   Col. ML 5426
  2 hn.   MS 6116
Dvořák: Serenade in D Moll (Op. 44) for 2 ob. 2 cl.   Col. ML 5426
  2 bn. cbn. 3 hn. vc. db.   MS 6116

OTTO STEINKOPF
Bach, J. S.: Cantata (BWV 36) 'Schwingt freudig
  euch'   Cant. 641208
Bach, J. S.: Cantata (BWV 64) 'Sehet welch' eine
  Liebe   Cant. 641208
Music of Rosemüller, Krieger, Pezel, Theile, Knüpfer,   Elec. C 91111
  Schein, Kuhnau and Schelle   WCX 541
                                                            STC 91111
                                                            SAXW 9521
Muthel: Concerto in D Moll for hpsch. 2 bn. and   APM 14300
  strings (with Schola Cantorum Basiliensis, cond.   SAPM 198300
  Wenzinger)
Telemann: Trio Sonata in D Moll for rec. vad'g. bn.
  and hpsch.   APM 37155
Telemann: Trio Sonata in F for rec. va. bn. and hpsch.   APM 37155

JOSEPH STIDEL
Schubert: Octet in F (Op. 166) for cl. bn. hn. 2 vn. va.
  vc. db.   CX 1423

E. STRÖMBLAD
Alfven: Bourrée from Gustav II Adolf (Op. 49) for 3
  bassoons   G. X 7511

S. SUNDIN
Alfven: Bourrée from Gustav II Adolf (Op. 49) for 3
  bassoons   G. X 7511

AROLD SWILLENS
Haydn: Divertimento in C   Tel. AWT 9410-C
Hindemith: Sonata (1939) for bassoon and piano   CHS. CHS 1250
Stamitz, K.: Quintet in E♭ for ob. bn. hn. 2 va.   Tel. AWT 9410-C
Vivaldi: Concerto in C for bassoon and orch.   CHS. CHS 1254
Vivaldi: Concerto in F for bassoon and orch.   CHS. CHS 1254

CONRAD (HERBERT) TAUSCHER
Telemann: Quartet in D Moll for fl. ob. bn. and cont.
  (T.M. 2)   APM 14515

JANE TAYLOR
Blackwood: Chamber Symphony (Op. 2) (1955) for 14
  wind instruments   CRI 144

C. TIMMERMANS (contrabassoon)
Dvořák: Serenade in D Moll (Op. 44) for 2 ob. 2 cl.
  2 bn. cbn. 3 hn. vc. db.   CHS H 6

KAREL VAČEK
Beethoven: Sextet in E♭ (Op. 71) for 2 cl. 2 hn. 2 bn.   SUP 10293
Foerster: Wind quintet (Op. 95)   LPV 375
                                                        SUP 10314
Janáček: Concertino for pf. 2 vn. va. cl. hn. bn.   SUA 10416
                                                        SUA ST 50416
Krejci: Divertimento for fl. cl. tp. and bn.   U.C. 15117
                                                        SUA 10086
Krommer-Kramář: Harmonie (Op. 71) for 2 ob. 2 cl.   U. H 13121/3
  2 bn. 2 hn. cbn.   LPM 60
  .   U 5041C
Mozart: Quintet in E♭ (K. 452) for piano and wind   SUA 10293
                                                        LPV 332
Trojan: Wind quintet on themes of Czech Folksongs   LPV 375
                                                        SUP 10314

M. VORLÍČEK
Milhaud: Symphony No. 5 for 2 fl. 2 ob. 2 cl. 2 bn.
  2 hn.   SUA 10475
Mozart: Serenade No. 10 in B♭ (K. 361) for 2 ob. 2 cl.
  2 bst-hn. 2 bn. cbn. 4 hn.   SUA 10426
                                                        SUA ST 50426
Stravinsky: Octet for fl. cl. 2 bn. 2 tp. 2 tbn.   SUA 10475

RONALD WALLER
Beethoven: Quintet (unfinished) for ob. 3 hn. bn.   LXT 6170
                                                        SXL 6170
Beethoven: Septet in E♭ (Op. 20) for cl. bn. hn. vn.
  va. vc. db.   CMC 6
Beethoven: Sextet in E♭ (Op. 71) for 2 cl. 2 bn. 2 hn.   LXT 6170
  .   SXL 6170
Beethoven: Octet in E♭ (Op. 103) for 2 ob. 2 cl. 2 bn.   LXT 6170
  2 hn.   SXT 6170
Beethoven: Rondino in E♭ (Op. posth.) for 2 ob. 2 cl.   LXT 6170
  2 bn. 2 hn.   SXL
Compere: Nous sommes de l'ordre de Saint Babouin-
  Chanson (with Dolmetsch Ensemble)   HLPS 7
Mozart: Divertimento No. 3 in E♭ (K. 166) for 2 ob.   LXT 6050
  2 ca. 2 cl. 2 bn. 2 hn.   SXL 6050
Mozart: Divertimento No. 4 B♭ (K. 186) for 2 ob. 2 ca.   LXT 6051
  2 ca. 2 cl. 2 bn. 2 hn.   SXL 6051
Mozart: Divertimento No. 8 in F (K. 213) for 2 ob.   LXT 6050
  2 hn. 2 bn.   SXL 6050

Mozart: Divertimento No. 9 in B♭ (K. 240) for 2 ob. 2 hn. 2 bn.	LXT 6052
	SXL 6052
Mozart: Divertimento No. 12 in E♭ (K. 252) for 2 ob. 2 bn. 2 hn.	LXT 6052
	SXL 6052
Mozart: Divertimento No. 13 in F (K. 253) for 2 ob. 2 bn. 2 hn.	LXT 6051
	SXL 6051
Mozart: Divertimento No. 14 in B♭ (K. 270) for 2 ob. 2 bn. 2 hn.	LXT 6053
	SXL 6053
Mozart: Divertimento No. 16 in E♭ (K. 289) for 2 ob. 2 bn. 2 hn.	LXT 6053
	SXL 6053
Mozart: Divertimento in B♭ (K.A. 227) for 2 cl. 2 bn. 2 hn.	LXT 6053
	SXL 6053
Mozart: Divertimento in E♭ (K.A. 266) for 2 ob. 2 cl. 2 bn. 2 hn.	LXT 6052
	SXL 6052
Mozart: Serenade No. 10 in B♭ (K. 361) for 2 ob. 2 cl. 2 bst-hn. 2 bn. cbn. 4 hn.	LXT 6049
	SXL 6049
Mozart: Serenade No. 11 in E♭ (K. 375) for 2 ob. 2 cl. 2 bn. 2 hn.	LXT 6050
	SXL 6050
Mozart: Serenade No. 12 in C Moll (K. 388) for 2 ob. 2 cl. 2 bn. 2 hn.	LXT 6051
	SXL 6051
Mozart: Adagio in F (K. 410) for 2 bst-hn. and bn.	LXT 6052
	SXL 6052
Rubinus: Der Bauern Schwanz (with Dolmetsch Ensemble)	HLPS 7
de la Torre: Alta (with Dolmetsch Ensemble)	HLPS 7

AMAURY WALLEZ

Bach, J. S.: Cantata (BWV 53)	⎫ Numbers
Bach, J. S.: Cantata (BWV 68)	⎬ not
Bach, J. S.: Cantata (BWV 98)	⎭ known

SHERMAN WALT

Dvořák: Serenade in D Moll (Op. 44) for 2 ob. 2 cl. 2 bn. cbn. 3 hn. vc. and db.	Bo. 410 1004
Guy-Ropartz: Two pieces for wind quintet	Bo. 407
Mozart: Sonata in B♭ (K. 292) for bassoon and cello	Bo. B 210
Piston: Wind quintet	Bo. 407 1005
Reicha: Wind quintet in E♭ (Op. 88, No. 2)	Bo. 407 1005
Strauss, R.: Sonatina No. 1 in F for 2 fl. 2 ob. 3 cl. bst-hn. bcl. 2 bn. cbn. 4 hn.	RG 147 Bo. 406 1016
Strauss, R.: Suite in B♭ (Op. 4) for 2 fl. 2 ob. 2 cl. 2 bn. cbn. 4 hn. (Gavotte only)	RG 147 Bo. 406 1016
Strauss, R.: Serenade in E♭ (Op. 7) for 2 fl. 2 ob. 2 cl. 2 bn. cbn. 4 hn.	RG 147 Bo. 406 1016
Telemann: Suite in D (arr. wind quintet)	Bo. 407 1005
Thuille: Sextet in B♭ (Op. 6) for piano and wind quintet	Bo. 410 1001

SHERMAN WALT—*cont.*

Vivaldi: Bassoon Concerto (P. 45) (with Zimbler Sinfonietta)	LM 2353 LSC 2353
Vivaldi: Bassoon Concerto (P. 46) (with Zimbler Sinfonietta)	LSC 2353 LSC 2353
Vivaldi: Bassoon Concerto (P. 318) (with Zimbler Sinfonietta)	LM 2353 LSC 2353
Vivaldi: Bassoon Concerto (P. 432) (with Zimbler Sinfonietta)	LM 2353 LSC 2353

WILLIAM WATERHOUSE

Beethoven: Quintet in E♭ (Op. 16) for ob. cl. bn. hn. and pf.	HMV
Beethoven: Septet in E♭ (Op. 20) for cl. bn. hn. vn. va. vc. db.	OL 50185 SOL 60015
Britten: Nocturne (Op. 60) for tenor, fl. ca. cl. bn. hn. timp. hp. and orch. (with London Symphony Orch., cond. Britten)	LXT 5564 SXL 2189
Mozart: Quintet in E♭ (K. 452) for ob. cl. bn. hn. and pf.	HMV
Stravinsky: L'Histoire du Soldat for voices, vn. cl. bn. cnt. tbn. db. perc. (cond. Carewe)	LPBR 6017

ARTHUR WEISBERG

Barber: Summer Music for wind quintet	XIP 7009 Disc 1216 216
Beethoven: Quintet in E♭ (Op. 16) for pf. ob. cl. bn. hn. (with F. Glazer—pf.)	Con Disc 1213 S 213
Beethoven: Quintet in E♭ (Op. 16) for pf. and wind	AmSoc. 1004 S 1004
Beethoven: Septet in E♭ (Op. 20) for cl. bn. hn. vn. va. vc. db.	XID 5126 Con. Disc 1214 S 214 BAE BM 30C 1807
Beethoven: Sextet in E♭ (Op. 71) for 2 cl. 2 hn. 2 bn.	CPST 559 ESO 567
Beethoven: Octet in E♭ (Op. 103) for 2 ob. 2 cl. 2 hn. 2 bn.	CPST 559 ESO 567
Beethoven: Rondino in E♭ (Op. posth.) for 2 ob. 2 cl. 2 hn. 2 bn.	CPST 559 ESO 567
Blackwood: Chamber Symphony (Op. 2) (1955) for 14 wind (directed by Arthur Weisberg)	CRI 144
Carter: Eight Etudes and a Fantasy (1950) for wind quintet	CRI 118
Dahl: Allegro and Arioso (1942) for wind quintet	XIP 7009 Con. Disc. 1216 216
Etler: Wind quintet	XIP 7009 Con. Disc. 1216 216
Françaix: Wind quintet	Con. Disc. M 1222

Hindemith: Octet for cl. hn. bn. 2 vn. va. vc. db.	Con. Disc. 1218 S 218 BAE BM L 1808
Laderman: Theme, Variations and Finale (1957) for wind quintet and orch.	CRI 130
Mozart: Quintet in Eb (K. 452) for pf. ob. cl. bn. hn. (with F. Glazer—pf.)	Con. Disc. 1213 S 213
Poulenc: Sextet (Op. 53) (1952) for piano and wind quintet	Con. Disc. 1221 S 221
Riegger: Concerto for piano and wind quintet	XIP 7009 Con. Disc. 1216 216
Riegger: Concerto (Op. 53) (1952) for piano and wind quintet	Con. Disc. 1221 S 221
Schubert: Octet in F (Op. 166) for cl. bn. hn. 2 vn. va. vc. db.	XID 5125 Con. Disc 1220 S 220 BAE Bm 30 L 1814
Stravinsky: Octet for fl. cl. 2 bn. 2 tp. 2 tbn.	BRG 72007 ML 5672
Taffanel: Wind Quintet	Con. Disc. M. 1222
Wilder: Wind Quintet No. 3 (1957)	Con. Disc. 1223 S 223
Wilder: Wind Quintet No. 4 (1958)	Con. Disc. 1223 S 223
Wilder: Wind Quintet No. 6 (1960)	Con. Disc. 1223 S 223

JOOST WESTERVELD

Otterloo: Symphonietta for picc. 2 fl. 2 ob. ca. 2 cl. bcl. 2 bn. cbn. 4 hn.	DAVS 6303

THOMAS WIGHTMAN

Mozart: Divertimento No. 3 in Eb (K. 166) for 2 ob. 2 ca. 2 cl. 2 bn. 2 hn.	D. AK 2225/6
Mozart: Serenade No. 11 in Eb (K. 375) for 2 ob. 2 cl. 2 bn. 2 hn. (2nd movement only)	D. AK 2225

EDWARD WILSON

Beethoven: Sextet in Eb (Op. 71) for 2 cl. 2 bn. 2 hn.	CCL 30133
Beethoven: Octet in Eb (Op. 103) for 2 ob. 2 cl. 2 bn. 2 hn.	CCL 30133
Beethoven: Rondino in Eb (Op. posth.) for 2 ob. 2 cl. 2 bn. 2 hn.	CCL 30133
Beethoven: Marches in F, C and F	CCL 30133 CEC 32027 VOG 48008
Dvořák: Serenade in D Moll (Op. 44) for 2 ob. 2 cl. 2 bn. cbn. 3 hn. vc. and db.	P. R 20604/6 PMB 1001 AMD DL 7533 XLP 30011
Handel: Gavotte and March for tp. obs. bns. and s.drm.	P. R 20617 AMD DL 4070

EDWARD WILSON—*cont.*

Haydn: Divertimento in C (Feldparthie) for 2 ob. 2 hn. 2 bn.	PMA 1013 XLP 30016
Haydn: Divertimento in F for 2 vn. 2 ca. 2 hn. 2 bn.	PR 20578/9 AMD DL 4076
Haydn: Divertimento No. 3 in Bb for 2 ob. 2 cl. 2 hn. 2 bn.	P. SW 8120/1 AMD DL 4066
Lully: Marche pour Le Régiment du Roi for 4 ob. 2 ca. 2 bn. and s.drm.	PR. 20619 AMD DL 4081
Lully: La Marche pour le Roi de la Chine et Marche du Prince d'Orange	P. R 20619 AMD DL 4081
Mozart: Serenade No. 11 in Eb (K. 375) for 2 cl. 2 bn. 2 hn. (Second Minuet and two Trios) (Orig.)	CCL 30119
Mozart: Serenade No. 11 in Eb (K. 375) for 2 ob. 2 cl. 2 hn. 2 bn.	PMB 1002 P. R 20610/2 Od OD 1010
Mozart: Serenade No. 12 in C Moll (K. 388) for 2 ob. 2 cl. 2 bn. 2 hn.	CCL 30119 XLP 30016 PMA 1013
Strauss, R.: Sonatina (Symphony) No. 2 in Eb for 2 fl. 2 ob. 3 cl. bst-hn. bcl. 2 bn. cbn. 4 hn.	PMA 1006 XLP 30021

FRANZ WINTER

Mozart: Bassoon Concerto in Bb (K. 191) (with Frankfurt Chamber Orch., cond. Bamberger)	Har. 7173

JOHANNES WOJCIECHOWSKI

Telemann: Concerto for 3 ob. vn. and cont. with bn.	APM 14109

ZANASI

Vivaldi: Concerto (P. 342) for fl. bn. and orch. (with Milan Chamber Orch., cond. Jenkins)	Wash. 404

German references to 'Basson' between 1696 and 1802 vide Chap. I, s.v. Germany

Dresden 1696.[1]

Chemnitz 1698 and 1728.[2]

Schwerin 1703.[3]

Bohemian Stift Ossegg 1706.[4]

Weissenfels 1707.[5]

Stettin 1714. At the audition for their installation as *Turmbläser* at St. Jacob's, the following were heard at the Rathaus: 'Hermann on Viola, Flöte-douce, Hautbois, Basson and Trompete: and Praetorius on Viola, Hautbois and Basson.'[6]

Danzig 1718. The instrumental inventory of St. Marienkirche specifies: '3 Hautbois nebst einem Basson, preussischer Arbeit.' . . . 'Davon waren gekauft: 1701, 3 Hautbois nebst einem Basson, franz. Arbeit.'[7]

Danzig 1731. Inventory includes 'franz. Basson ohne Namen . . . 1 Basson aus Buchsbaum Holz auf iedwedem Stück stehet "van Heerde" und oden "über dem Nahmen ein Löwe".'[7]

Leipzig 1721:[8] 1730.[9]

Gotha 1729. The Hofkapelle included a 'Fagottist', but in 1731 '3 Hautboisten' and '2 Bassonisten' are mentioned.[10]

Braunschweig/Wolfenbüttel 1735. The 'Capell-Etat' included '5 Hautboisten' and '3 Bassonisten'.[11]

Bayreuth 1748–62. 'Bassonisten' were members of the Hof-Capell und Cammer-musik, whereas from 1738–44, as at Gotha, a 'Fagottist' appears in the lists.[12]

Osnabruck 1750. 'Basson oder Fagott'.[13]

Halle 1751. 'Basson oder Fagott.' In 1766 the Moritzkirche Inventory included 'Ein Basson'.[14]

Greifswald 1752.[15]

Stuttgart 1752–3.[16]

Celle 1757. The Stadtmusikant bought for the church . . . 'Ein Basson'.[17]

Elbing 1757. The Pfarrkirche owned 'Ein Basson'.[18]

Stettin 1763. The effects of a deceased Stadtmusikus included 'Bassons'.[19]

Dresden 1766. The apprentice Stadtpfeifer had to perform on violin and 'Basson'.[20]

Stettin 1766. A box was stolen containing *inter alia* 'Bason [*sic*] und Hautbois Röhren'.[21]

Chemnitz 1775. In a drunken quarrel, one musician struck another with a 'Basson'.[22]

Winterthur 1779. Purchase of 'ein Basson'.

Winterthur 1782. Repair of 'den Basson'.[23]

In the theoretical works of the eighteenth century we find a divergence in practice.

Mattheson (1713)[24] refers to: 'Der stoltze Basson, Basse de Chormorne ([*sic*] *i.e.* Crumhorn) It. Fagotto, *vulgo* Dulcian.'
In this terminology, he was followed by Majer (1732),[25] Stössel (1737 and 1749),[26] Eisel (1738),[27] Quantz (1752 and 1789),[28] Adlung (1758),[29] Petri (1767 and 1782).[30] For the first time we find in Koch (1802)[31] 'Basson, see Fagott' and the French name drops out of the German language thereafter.

<h2 style="text-align:center">FLANDERS</h2>

Grammont 1718. Payment to players 'op den aubois ende basson' . . .[32] The modern Flemish name for the bassoon is *fagot*. It should be noted that bazuin, in both Flemish and Dutch denotes trombone (*Ger.* Posaune).
As an aid to further research, the author has considered it valuable to cite the sources of the foregoing references and gratefully acknowledges the help of Dr. Albert Reimann of Freiburg-im-Breisgau who included most of them in his masterly thesis, *Studien zur Geschichte des Fagotts* (1956) (unpublished), a typescript copy of which he very generously presented to the author.

<h2 style="text-align:center">REFERENCES</h2>

[1] Fürstenau, Moritz: *Zur Geschichte der Musik und des Theaters am Hofe zu Dresden* (Dresden, 1861–2), Vol. II, 59.
[2] Rau, Walter: *Geschichte der Chemnitzer Stadtpfeifer in* Jahrbuch für 1931–2. Jg. XXVIII (Chemnitz, 1932), pp. 52 and 53.
[3] Meyer, Clemens: *Geschichte des Mecklenburg-Schweriner Hof-Kapelle* (Schwerin, 1913), p. 38.
[4] Nettl, Paul: *Inventory included in Beiträge zur böhmischen und mahrischen Musikgeschichte* (Brünn, 1927), pp. 33–39.
[5] Werner, Arno: *Städtische und fürstliche Musikpflege in Weissenfels bis zum Ende des 18 Jahrhunderts* (Leipzig, 1911), p. 124.
[6] Freytag, Werner: *Musikgeschichte der Stadt Stettin im 18 Jahrhundert* (Greifswald, 1936), p. 102.
[7] Rauschning, Hermann: *Geschichte der Musik und Muskpflege in Danzig* (Danzig, 1931), pp. 311 and 312.
[8] Schering, Arnold: *Musikgeschichte Leipzigs* (Leipzig, 1941), Vol. III, p. 135, footnote 5.
[9] *J. S. Bach, Briefe, Gesamtausgabe* edited by Hedwig and E. H. Müller von Asow (Regensburg, 1950), pp. 110–17.
[10] Fett, Armin: *Musikgeschichte der Stadt Gotha* (Thesis, Freiburg i Br., 1951), pp. 145 and 153.
[11] Chrysander, Friedrich: *Geschichte der Braunschweig-Wolfenbüttelschen Capelle und Oper in Jahrbücher für musikalische Wissenschaft* (1863), I, p. 284.
[12] Schiedermair, Ludwig: *Bayreuther Festspiele* . . . (Leipzig, 1908), pp. 111 and 132.
[13] Bosken, Franz: *Musikgeschichte der Stadt Osnabrück* (Regensburg, 1937), p. 143.
[14] Serauky, Walter: *Musikgeschichte der Stadt Halle* (Halle, 1942), p. 61.
[15] Engel, Hans: *Musik und Musikleben in Greifswalds Vergangenheit* (Greifswald, 1929), p. 16b.
[16] Bopp, August: *Beiträge zur Geschichte der Stuttgarter Stiftsmusik* in Wurtt. Jahrbücher . . . Jhg. 1910 (Stuttgart, 1910), p. 234a.
[17] Linnemann, Georg: *Celler Musikgeschichte* . . . (Celle, 1935), p. 152.
[18] Gerigk, Herbert: *Musikgeschichte der Stadt Elbing* in Elbinger Jahrbuch (Elbing, 1929), p. 61.

[19] Freytag: *loc. cit. ante*, p. 98.

[20] Techritz, Hermann: *Sächsische Stadtpfeifer* . . . (Dresden, 1932), p. 20.

[21] Freytag: *loc. cit. ante*, p. 32.

[22] Rau: *loc. cit. ante*, p. 50.

[23] Fehr, Max: *Das Musikkollegium Winterthur, 1629–1837* (Winterthur, 1929), p. 124.

[24] Mattheson, Johann: *Das Neu-Eröffnete Orchestre* (Hamburg, 1713), p. 269.

[25] Majer, J. F. B. C.: *Museum Musicum* (Schwäbisch Hall, 1732), p. 34.

[26] Stössel, J. C. and J. D.: *Kurtzgefasstes Musicalisches Lexikon* (2nd edit.) (Chemnitz, 1749), p. 59.

[27] Eisel, J. P.: *Musicus Autodidaktos* (Erfurt, 1738), p. 100.

[28] Quantz, J. J.: *loc. cit. ante.*

[29] Adlung, Jacob: *Anleitung zu der musikalischen Gelährtheit* (Erfurt, 1758), p. 589.

[30] Petri, J. S.: *Anleitung zur praktischen Musik* (Leipzig, 1782), p. 459.

[31] Koch, H. C.: *Musikalisches Lexikon* (Frankfurt a/M., 1802).

[32] van der Straeten: *loc. cit. ante*, IV, p. 257.

Index

Morris, Claver, 11
Morton, A. and R., 56, 108, 125, 128, 134
Moss, Kate, 2
Mozart, 37, 52, 72, 81, 82, 88–89, 119, 120
Mühlhausen, 82
Müller, Iwan, 40, 41, 51
Muller, L., 125–6
mullerphone (=contrabass clarinet) 125–6
musette, 6
mute, 3
Müthel, J. G., 87

Neri, M., 77
Neukirchner, W., 55
Newton, R., viii, 104, 160, 176–7
nicolo, 17
Niedt, F. E., 35

oboe da caccia, 109
Oehlberger, K., 177
oils for bassoon, 43
Orefice, A., 46
Orff, Carl, 104
Oromszegi, Ott , 165
Oubradous, F., 69, 88
Ozi, E., 45, 48, 49, 52, 158

pads for keys, 51–52
Paisible, James, 13
Parke, W. T., 116, 180
Parr, John, 177–8
Parker, John, 178
Parkinson, J., 178
Parry, Sir H., 136
Pedrell, F., 9
Petzold, J. C., 79
Pezé, 59
phagotum, 7–9
Phillips, Edward, 2
Piccini, 87
Pierné, 103

Pierre, C., 57, 60, 67, 107, 121, 124, 126–7, 132
piffaro, 17
pirouette, 74
Poerschmann, J., 49
Pollux, Julius, 143
pommer, 17–24
Pontecoulant, A. de., 63
Porter, M. M., viii, 161
Porthaux, D., 49, 58
Praetorius, M., 14, 17–24, 28, 73, 106, 109
Profeta, R., 46
Prout, Professor E., 1, 5, 121, 125
Provence, 14, 156–7
Prudent, 57, 58
Puccini, 103
Pulver, J., 13
Purcell, 75

Quantz, J. J., 7, 80
quart-fagott, 20, 107, 112, 114
quint-fagott, 20, 107, 112

rackett, 13
rack-work wing, 56, 59, 60
Ravel, 102, 132, 135, 137
Raviglio, G., 45
reeds, 156–9
Rees, A., 39
Reiner, F., 45
Rendall, F. G., 109
Respighi, 136
Reyer, 122
Reynvaan, J. Verschuere, 37
Riccio, 76
Richter, Hans, 69
Rijkel, C., 28, 36
Rimsky-Korsakov, 98–99, 134
Ritter, G. W., 39, 89, 106
Rosenkron, N., 21, 22
Rosenmüller, J., 78
Rossini, 93–94
Rozet, 13

Printed in Great Britain by
The Camelot Press Limited
London & Southampton

Made in the USA
San Bernardino, CA
17 November 2017